Law and Gender in the An Near East and the Hebrew

This volume examines how gender relations were regulated in ancient Near Eastern and biblical law. The textual corpus examined includes the various pertinent law collections, royal decrees and instructions from Mesopotamia and Hatti and the three biblical legal collections.

Peled explores issues beginning with the wide societal perspective of gender equality and inequality, continues to the institutional perspective of economy, palace and temple, the family and, lastly, sex crimes. All the texts mentioned or referred to in the book are given in an appendix, both in the original languages and in English translation, allowing scholars to access the primary sources for themselves.

Law and Gender in the Ancient Near East and the Hebrew Bible offers an invaluable resource for anyone working on Near Eastern society and culture and gender in the ancient world more broadly.

Ilan Peled is an Assyriologist working at the University of Amsterdam. He is the author of *Masculinities and Third Gender: The Origins and Nature of an Institutionalized Gender Otherness in the Ancient Near East* and editor of *Structures of Power: Law and Gender Across the Ancient Near East and Beyond.*

Law and Gender in the Ancient Near East and the Hebrew Bible

Ilan Peled

Routledge
Taylor & Francis Group
LONDON AND NEW YORK

First published 2020 by Routledge

2 Park Square, Milton Park, Abingdon, Oxon OX14 4RN
605 Third Avenue, New York, NY 10017

Routledge is an imprint of the Taylor & Francis Group, an informa business

First issued in paperback 2022

Publisher's Note

The publisher has gone to great lengths to ensure the quality of this reprint but points out that some imperfections in the original copies may be apparent.

British Library Cataloguing-in-Publication Data
A catalogue record for this book is available from the British Library

Library of Congress Cataloging-in-Publication Data
A catalog record for this book has been requested

ISBN: 978-0-367-37149-4 (hbk)
ISBN: 978-1-03-233779-1 (pbk)
DOI: 10.4324/9780429352867

Typeset in Times New Roman
by Apex CoVantage, LLC

Contents

Acknowledgments

The idea for this book was planted back in March 2015. At the time, I was a postdoctoral fellow at the Oriental Institute of the University of Chicago and had just finished organizing a conference on law and gender in the ancient world, the proceedings of which were eventually published a few years later. The conference was highly successful in forming a platform for discussing the intriguing interface between law and gender in various historical settings, ranging between Mesopotamia, Hatti and Egypt, the Greek and Roman cultures, ancient China, Judaism and Islam. The drawback of such diversity, of course, was the utter incapability of reaching any in-depth discussion focusing on one of these settings. The current book, therefore, owes much to the shortcomings of that conference and its published volume, for these formed the main trigger of this book's inception. In this regard, I wholeheartedly thank everyone at the OI for providing me with the much-needed scholarly environment that facilitated the early stages of working on the current book.

The following years saw a slow progress of consolidating the book manuscript, as life circumstances prevented me at times from dedicating my full time and energy to the book. I was engaged in different enterprises, in different institutions, until finding my academic home in the University of Amsterdam, where I finally could dedicate more of my time to the long-neglected manuscript. The wonderful collegiality I found here means the world to me, and it is with great pleasure that I acknowledge the colleagues who gave me my academic home: Irene Zwiep, Yaniv Hagbi, Resianne Smidt van Gelder-Fontaine and Bart Wallet.

Large portions of this book were written during my endless train trips to/from work in Amsterdam. The beautiful green scenery of rural Netherlands that accompanied these trips certainly was an inspiration!

Several colleagues assisted me with wise advice, especially in the realm of legal thought. I wish to wholeheartedly thank Kristin Kleber and Jan Hallebeek, two experts on ancient law – Mesopotamian and Roman, respectively – who generously shared their knowledge and expertise with me. Martha Roth deserves my special gratitude, for thoughtfully giving me many important comments and corrections and sharing with me her newly- and pre-published articles, to which I would have not had access otherwise.

Special thanks go to everyone at Routledge who were part of the process of production, from peer review to final publication: Amy Davis-Poynter, Ella Halstead and everyone else. It is thanks to them that the process was efficient, professional and even enjoyable – something I do not take for granted!

Finally, and most importantly, my family has always been there with me, in better times and in worse ones. No obstacle is unsurmountable when life grants you with the richest treasure of all, for which I am grateful on a daily basis. Ortal, Dan and Ophir: thank you, I love you.

Abbreviations

AASOR	The Annual of the American Schools of Oriental Research
CAD	I. J. Gelb et al. (eds.), The Assyrian Dictionary of the Oriental Institute of the University of Chicago, Chicago Illinois, 1956 ff.
CC	Covenant Code
CHD	H. G. Güterbock, H. A. Hoffner and Th. P. J. van den Hout (eds.), The Hittite Dictionary of the Oriental Institute of the University of Chicago, Chicago Illinois, 1980 ff.
CTH	E. Laroche, Catalogue des textes Hittites, Paris, 1971
DC	Deuteronomic Code
ESi/Ad/Aṣ	Edicts of Samsu-iluna/Ammi-ditana/Ammi-ṣaduka
HC	Holiness Code
HED	J. Puhvel, Hittite Etymological Dictionary, Berlin and New York, 1984 ff.
HL	Hittite Laws
IM	Tablets in the collections of the Iraq Museum, Baghdad
ITT	Inventaire des tablettes de Tello
KAJ	E. Ebeling, Keilschrifttexte aus Assur juristischen Inhalts, Berlin, 1927
KBo	H. H. Figulla et al., Keilschrifttexte aus Boghazköi, Leipzig and Berlin, 1916 ff.
KUB	H. H. Figulla et al., Keilschrifturkunden aus Boghazköi, Berlin, 1921 ff.
LE	Laws of Ešnunna
LH	Laws of Hammurabi
LLI	Laws of Lipit-Ištar
LUN	Laws of Ur-Namma
MAL	Middle Assyrian Laws
MAPD	Middle Assyrian Palace Decrees
NBL	Neo-Babylonian Laws
NSGU	A. Falkenstein, Die neusumerischen Gerichtsurkunden, München, 1956–57
SMN	Tablets excavated at Nuzi, in the Semitic Museum, Harvard University, Cambridge
SNAT	T. Gomi/S. Sato, Selected Neo-Sumerian Administrative Texts from the British Museum, Chiba, Japan, 1990
VAT	Tablets in the collections of the Staatliche Museen, Berlin

Notes on textual quotations in Part I

This book contains textual quotations from original ancient Near Eastern sources. These sources were written in several different languages – Sumerian, Akkadian, Hittite and Hebrew – and in two different scripts: cuneiform and alphabetic. Therefore, the method of quoting these textual sources requires clarification.

The Akkadian texts are presented in the book in bound script (normalization), even if the original text consisted of logograms; these are normalized into their Akkadian equivalents. A case in point is the sentence "The wages of a hired-worker are [wri]tten on the stele". The transliteration of the original sentence is: á-bi ^{lú}ḫun-gá *ina* $^{\text{na4}}$*na-re-e* [*ša*]-*ṭe*$_4$-*er*; however, it is quoted in the book in its normalized Akkadian form: *idū agrim ina narê* [*ša*]*ṭer*. The phrase *idū agrim*, "wages of a hired-worker", appears in the original text in its logographic form á-bi ^{lú}ḫun-gá, but in the book it is normalized into the phonetic Akkadian *idū agrim*.

Sumerian texts are presented in transliteration. Thus, the sentence "He caught her upon a man" is quoted as follows: ugu lú-ka in-dab$_5$. Non-transliterated isolated Sumerian/logographic terms within the body of the text are given in plain spaced script (e.g., sag), while Hittite terms within the body of the text are given in italicized script (e.g., *wannummiya-*).

Biblical quotations are presented in Hebrew script, not in Latin alphabetic rendering. Hence, the sentence "If your Hebrew brother or sister is sold to you" (Deut. 15:12) is quoted as follows: כִּי יִמָּכֵר לְךָ אָחִיךָ הָעִבְרִי אוֹ הָעִבְרִיָּה, rather than a transcription such as *kî yimmākêr leḵā ʼāḥîḵā hāʻiḇrî ʼōw hāʻiḇrîyāh*. The biblical texts follow the Masoretic version.

Introduction

It is the year 1750 BCE. Not that anyone alive knows it, of course. In the glorious city of Babylon, capital of the Old Babylonian kingdom, the scribes of King Hammurabi are busy preparing a magnificent stele from a dark basalt stone. Carefully they carve into the stone a long and stylized inscription. Millennia later, this inscription will be discovered by archaeologists, and, once its secrets are deciphered, it will become known as "the Laws of Hammurabi", the longest and most elaborate law collection from the ancient Near East. One of the statutes this collection contains orders the following: "If a man's wife is caught lying with another male: they shall bind them and cast them into the water; if the wife's master lets his wife live, then the king shall let his slave live".[1]

This was not the first time, nor the last, that a law collection from the ancient Near East addressed the issues of sex and gender and intervened in people's family life. Identical rulings to the statute quoted previously appear in the Ešnunna, Hittite and Middle Assyrian Laws. Significantly, the Hebrew Bible as well displays a similar statute.

Are we to assume, therefore, that adultery was regarded as a punishable crime in the ancient Near East and the Hebrew Bible? A statute from the Laws of Lipit-Ištar complicates the matter:

> If a young married man has a prostitute from the street, the judges order him not to go back to that prostitute, afterwards he divorces his first-ranking wife (and) gives her the silver of her divorce settlement: he shall not marry that prostitute.[2]

As we see, a married man who had adulterous relations with a prostitute was not punished according to this statute. In case he subsequently divorced his wife, he was not allowed to marry the prostitute, but his adultery remained unpunished. The difference between this statute and the ones mentioned previously is simple: the gender of the supposed perpetrator. Law collections from all over the ancient Near East and the Hebrew Bible decreed harsh punishments for adulterous wives but remained silent when it came to adulterous husbands. This simple example explicates what this book is all about.

The aim of this book is to examine how gender relations were regulated in ancient Near Eastern and biblical law. These two corpora are examined independently from one another and are then assessed vis-à-vis each other.

It is important to note from the start that this book does not confront questions of legal procedure or applicability. It does not aspire to describe how law was enforced in daily life and how – as a result – legal procedure affected gender relations. The book is restricted to the question of how formal law addressed gender-related matters, how it allegedly affected and regulated them, without examining whether and how it actually did. The highly complicated questions of the applicability of law are briefly discussed in the introduction of the book but are not subsequently pursued any further.

Further clarifications concerning the limitations of the present study are due. This book is by and large descriptive and, unlike some of my previous works, maintains a minimal engagement with theory – whether of law or of gender. A significant complication derives from the fact that modern research of law and gender deals with numerous issues that are simply irrelevant to the study of gender and law in the ancient world. We can note, for example, issues such as discrimination in employment opportunities, imprisonment and human rights, health or questions of gender and race. None of these issues have any relevance to ancient Near Eastern or biblical settings, and the methodologies applied for investigating such matters are unproductive for the present study. Even worse: applying irrelevant methodologies is not only unhelpful but, in fact, quite harmful and bound to mar the discussion with anachronisms, improperly applied in the wrong field of research. It is my hope that this book could be used in the future by scholars who are more interested in the theoretical aspects of the field, by using the study I present here as a basis for further elaborating the research of gender and law in the ancient Near East and the Hebrew Bible.

It is beyond the scope of this book to present a thorough discussion of the complicated relationship between the worlds of the ancient Near East and of the Hebrew Bible. The reader may easily consult for these matters the vast and accessible literature on this topic. However, no attempt is made to suggest that direct contact necessarily existed between the two, causing similarities or demanding explanations for discrepancies. It is obvious that the ancient Israelites were influenced by their Mesopotamian counterparts and that the long-lasting legal tradition of Mesopotamia is echoed in the biblical laws as well. In this book I point – where possible – to cases addressed by both corpora, whether similarly or differently.[3]

Needless to say, the topic of ancient Near Eastern law has been investigated at length by many scholars. Gender in the ancient Near East is a vast topic, and though it has been drawing scholarly attention for a few decades now, much in this realm is still left to be discussed. The interface between these two fascinating fields, however, has never been treated exhaustively. In this book, the sphere of legislation is used as a prism to look through at gender dynamics in the ancient Near East and the Hebrew Bible. Thus, some broader questions are examined concerning social, cultural and diachronic variations in the relationship between law and gender.

The cultural frame of this book encompasses the main Mesopotamian cultures – Sumer, Babylonia and Assyria – and at times compares them with the Hittite culture, which in many respects was peripheral to its Mesopotamian counterparts. Thus, the book offers a comparative cross-cultural perspective, considering various cultures of the ancient Near East. The ancient Near Eastern legal traditions are further assessed in this book in comparison with the pertinent evidence from biblical law. Thus, the cross-cultural and diachronic examinations the book offers stretch beyond the boundaries of Mesopotamia and Hatti.[4]

The structure of the book is explained in detail in what follows. It consists of two parts: the first presents thematic discussions, while the second contains the textual sources on which the said discussions are based. The first part is divided into four thematic chapters. Chapter 1 examines issues of equity and inequality between the genders, as evident in various specific topics. Chapter 2 deals with the bureaucratic systems of the palace and the temple, and with economy. Chapter 3 becomes narrower and examines the structure of the family. Chapter 4 explores more specific topics: morality, sex crimes and liminality.

The research framework, both chronologically and geographically, is based by and large on the pertinent sources used. As is explained in what follows in detail, these are official texts that were produced by the ruling elite – most frequently the royal circles – in delineating proper conduct, usually within the frame of a crime-and-punishment rationale: law collections and royal decrees. The earliest relevant records, therefore, derive from the late third millennium BCE (LUN), and the latest ones are roughly dated to the seventh century BCE (NBL).[5] The geographical scope encompasses ancient Mesopotamia (Sumer, Babylonia and Assyria), Hatti and ancient Israel.

Previous research: a concise overview

No academic publication breaks new ground without relying – at least to a certain degree – on previous research. Indeed, the topics of law and of gender, as reflected in the writings of the ancient Near East and the Hebrew Bible, have seen their fair share of academic study. In what follows, I merely mention the most significant relevant publications, and hence this overview of previous research should not be taken as an exhaustive bibliographical survey. All the works mentioned in this section have their own lists of previous literature, and the reader may consult these in case of need.

The academic research of the ancient Near Eastern law collections began with the discovery of the most famous of them all – the black stele of Hammurabi's collection, found in 1901 and published the following year. More discoveries followed, which revealed other collections, some of which predate Hammurabi's. Textual editions of each one of these collections were offered by different scholars, and at times a given collection's *editio princeps* was improved by later editions as philological knowledge was enhanced and new textual copies were found. The authoritative editions commonly used today are found in Roth 1997, which includes previous literature. Updated editions to Roth's are the following: Civil

2011 for LUN, Wilcke 2014 for LUN and LLI and Hoffner 1997 for HL. Each one of these publications also includes previous literature.

Biblical law has drawn scholarly attention for centuries, in fact millennia, as its research went hand in hand with biblical exegesis and interpretation but also had a life of its own. Supplying a list of pertinent studies will do injustice to all the numerous researches that will inevitably remain unmentioned. Many important works combined the two worlds of ancient Near Eastern and of biblical law, such as, to name but a few, Alt 1934, Greenberg 1960, Greengus 2011, Jackson 2000, 2006, Levinson 2011, Otto 1999, Paul 1970, Westbrook 1988b, 2003 (ed.), Wright 2009 and Yaron 1988.

General discussions and volumes of collected essays of law in the ancient Near East and the Hebrew Bible are abundant as well. The most comprehensive of these is still Westbrook's monumental 2003 edited volume, which surveys law along identical parameters in different periods and cultures in the ancient Near East and Egypt. Other volumes or monographs that can be mentioned in this respect usually pursued a concrete aim, surveying specifically defined aspects of the topic, such as Levinson's (ed. 1994) *Theory and Method in Biblical and Cuneiform Law*, Sassoon's (2001) *Ancient Laws and Modern Problems*, Jackson's (2008/2013) *A Comparison of Ancient Near Eastern Law Collections* and Wright's *Inventing God's Law* (2009).

The study of gender relations and dynamics in the ancient Near East and the Hebrew Bible has seen much progress in recent decades. As before, mentioning some of the most notable researches in this respect will do injustice to numerous other important works. I therefore only note the most recent pertinent publications. On sexuality and gender: Parpola and Whiting 2002 (eds.), Bolger 2008 (ed.); specifically on women: Lafont 1999, Asher-Greve and Westenholz 2013, Budin and MacIntish Turfa 2016 (eds., esp. pp. 1–174, 299–341), Lion and Michele 2016 (eds.), Stol 2016; specifically on men: Peled 2016, Zsolnay 2017 (ed.).

The study of ancient Near Eastern and biblical law in conjunction with the topic of gender, in its numerous aspects, is still relatively meager. Some of the works that can be mentioned in this regard are Matthews, Levinson and Frymer-Kensky's (eds. 1998) *Gender and Law in the Hebrew Bible and the Ancient Near East*, Anderson's (2004) *Women, Ideology, and Violence*, Tetlow's (2004) first volume of *Women, Crime, and Punishment in Ancient Law and Society* and Peled's (ed. 2017b) *Structures of Power: Law and Gender Across the Ancient Near East and Beyond*. The noticeable scarcity of such works, and the limited scope of those that were published thus far, merited the composition of the present book.

Was it law?

When assessing ancient Near Eastern and biblical law, the first question one faces is whether the texts we consider "law collections" indeed functioned as such. The debate continues in both Assyriological and biblical circles, with no clear verdict on the matter. In what follows I summarize the main points of consideration and current state of the art.

Mesopotamian law and legal practice: instructive and descriptive texts

Did the inhabitants of the Babylonian kingdom in Hammurabi's time live their lives according to the statutes stipulated by their mighty king on his famous dark basalt stele? Did Hammurabi even intend them to do so? No clear answer can be offered for these questions. The fact remains that numerous discrepancies are found between the stipulations of the different Mesopotamian law collections and the evidence of people's everyday life. The law collections do not cover all aspects of legal reality and could not have possibly functioned as a complete guide for people's behavior. As noted by many scholars, the evidence of legal procedure – in the form of texts such as court decisions and the descriptions of lawsuits – do not mention any law collection as the source on which the legal decisions were based. The high level of illiteracy surely made it even harder for those who lived in more rural or remote areas to be aware of the exact contents of official laws. Some scholars have claimed, therefore, that the law collections were merely the product of royal propaganda or, alternatively, that they were merely the product of the scribal schools, an essential literary genre that had no practical meaning outside the circles of scribes and their trainees.[6]

These doubts concerning the applicability of formal law among ancient Near Eastern societies demand an explanation for my use of the term "statute(s)" when referring to the legal provisions throughout this book. Using this term in ancient Near Eastern contexts may be somewhat controversial. I do not wish to imply that ancient Near Eastern law was statutory in the modern sense of the word, that is, that it stemmed from a systematic and conscious legislative process. However, as I explain in what follows, since at least some correspondence does appear to exist between the instruction of the law collections and texts that attest to daily life, I do not assume that the law collections had no basis in reality whatsoever.

In order to assess the degree of correspondence between the law collections and their possible applicability, I use the terms "instructive texts" and "descriptive texts". To the first group belong texts that were meant to instruct people how to behave: first and foremost, the law collections and, to a lesser degree, royal decrees and instructions and loyalty oaths taken by officials. The second group is harder to delineate, since it includes texts that describe how people actually behaved: court decisions, economic transactions, letters, even literary compositions. All these types of texts could relate to legal matters, and when compared to the first group of the so-called instructive texts, the question of the applicability of the law collections can be tested.

Scholars who have previously addressed these issues usually applied the terms "scholastic" and "functional"/"transactional" to distinguish between these two groups of texts,[7] but I opt instead for "instructive" and "descriptive" because of several reasons. To begin with, this terminology conveys better the essence of the difference between these two groups, in informing us as to their functionality. In addition, I do not assume that the "instructive" texts were in any way less "functional" than the texts I term "descriptive", and I am not at all sure whether the "scholastic" texts were indeed solely scholastic in nature. Deeming the law collections or the royal edicts "scholastic" implies that their functionality was limited to the realm of the scribal circles, utterly denying any legal functionality they might had; as is explained in what follows, I doubt this view.

Indeed, examples of correspondence between formal law and actual occurrences in daily life are rare. It does not mean, however, that they are utterly nonexistent. Here a few examples should be considered, beginning with the Ur III period, during which the earliest law collection – the so-called Laws of Ur-Namma – was produced. LUN §9 declares that a man who divorces his wife is required to give her the sum of one mina (=60 shekels) of silver. This "instructive" text has exact parallels in at least two "descriptive texts" from the same period: court decisions known as di til-la ("case complete") texts. These two court decisions detail cases of divorce, and in both instances the husband was required to pay his divorced wife the sum of one mina of silver – exactly as LUN §9 demands.[8] One of these texts (NSGU 4) is dated to Šulgi's 39th reigning year, while the other (SNAT 372) is dated to the sixth year of Amar-Sîn – Šulgi's successor to the throne. Even though King Šulgi is commonly regarded by modern scholars as the true commissioner of the LUN, we have no knowledge as to when exactly this collection was composed during Šulgi's long reign of 48 years. Hence, it cannot be ruled out that text NSGU 4 describes a case that was decided prior to the composition of LUN. However, SNAT 372 is undoubtedly later, and the court decision it documents was definitely made at a time when the LUN was already composed. Though none of these two di til-las mentions the LUN as its source of judgment, the fact remains that these "instructive" and "descriptive" texts are in perfect agreement.

We shall move on to the Old Babylonian period. As mentioned previously, one of the claims frequently made by scholars who assume that the law collections had no practical meaning whatsoever is that these alleged sources of law are never referred to in documented daily cases that dealt with legal situations. This, however, may not be entirely accurate. Several scholars already drew attention to the Old Babylonian letter A 3529,[9] which refers to a stele where wages were documented: "The wages of a hired-worker are [wri]tten on the stele".[10] This passage from the letter was compared to the almost contemporaneous[11] LH §§273–274, where daily wages for hired workers are fixed.[12] In this example as well, therefore, we see a plausible correlation between an "instructive" law collection and a "descriptive" letter. Moreover, the letter might refer to an official law collection for establishing legal daily practice.[13]

The correspondence between official law and daily life can be tested through yet another example. Returning to the example with which the book opens, we have several statutes from ancient Near Eastern and biblical law collections of punishments decreed for adulterous wives. These can be compared with an Old Babylonian legal case of divorce, documented in IM 28051.[14] The lawsuit was filed by a man named Erra-malik against his wife, Ištar-ummī. The husband demanded to divorce his wife on account of several charges: he claimed that she was stealing his property from him but, more significantly, that he caught her cheating on him. The circumstances are described as follows: "He caught her upon a man. He tied her to the body of the man on the bed, (and) carried her to the assembly".[15]

According to the text, therefore, the betrayed husband, upon catching his wife with her lover in the act, apprehended them and brought them to trial before the local assembly. The lover's fate remains unknown, but Ištar-ummī suffered a harsh punishment: her nose was pierced, and she was paraded naked along the town, publicly humiliated. The question needs to be asked, therefore: how similar is this case, and its aftermath, to the pertinent statutes found in the different ancient Near Eastern law collections? The answer is clear: though most law collections prescribed execution for an adulterous wife, the punishment of mutilating her nose is explicitly attested in MAL A §15. The correlation between official law and the evidence of daily practice cannot be ignored here.[16]

A clear correspondence between official law and actual legal practice is found in an example from the Middle Assyrian period. According to MAL B §6, if someone intends to purchase a field or a house, the sale should be publicly announced three times during one month, in the presence of noblemen, so that other offers or contestations to the transfer can be made. Then, the transfer can proceed, and it should be documented on tablets. The procedure stipulated in the law is attested in the Middle Assyrian text VAT 8919,[17] which lists objects deposited in storage, among which the following: "one container of the herald's proclamations concerning the (purchases of) houses of the Inner City[18]".[19] VAT 8919 not only confirms that the procedure as described in the MAL was indeed put into effect but also confirms that the documentation of the procedure was performed in accordance with what the statute decreed. Even the wording of the "instructive" statute and the comparable "descriptive" administrative text is parallel: both texts use the terms "proclamation" (*sasû*), "herald" (*nāgiru*) and "Inner City" (*libbi āli*).

Records from the Hittite kingdom supply us with further evidence for parallels between "instructive" and "descriptive" texts, for example in the sphere of homicide. The Hittite Laws address the topic of homicide several times, and in all pertinent statutes the sanction determined for the crime was the payment of a fine, whether in the form of silver, slaves or land; in contrast with all other law collections that addressed homicide (LUN, LE, LH, MAL), talionic execution is never attested in these contexts.[20] Outside the Laws, a letter sent by the Hittite monarch Hattušili III to his Kassite counterpart Kadašman-Enlil II of Babylonia demonstrates that, indeed, homicide was not punished in Hatti by execution but rather by financial compensation. Hattušili states it explicitly several times, while trying to persuade the Babylonian king that his messengers can safely travel to Hatti.[21]

The last example to consider derives from the Neo-Babylonian period and involves the beneficiaries of inheritance in case the deceased had children from multiple wives. Here again we see clear correspondence between an "instructive" law collection and a "descriptive" marriage agreement. NBL §15 determines that if a man becomes widowed and then remarries, once he dies the sons of his first wife will receive two-thirds of the inheritance, and the sons of the second wife will inherit the remaining one-third. In VAT 5049 – a marriage agreement from the second reigning year of Nabopolassar, founder of the Neo-Babylonian

Empire – we read of a married man named Nabû-zēr-kitti-līšir, who had no sons. He therefore wished to marry a second wife, hoping she would bear him a son. An agreement was then drawn up between Nabû-zēr-kitti-līšir and the father of the woman he wished to marry. According to the agreement, if in the future both wives would bear sons, those of the first wife will be entitled to two-thirds of their father's inheritance, and those of the second wife will inherit the remaining one-third.[22] This Neo-Babylonian agreement, therefore, is identical to the instruction of NBL §15.[23]

These are merely a few scattered and isolated examples, and additional ones could have been noted. They do cover, however, all the major periods and cultures discussed in this book, and they suffice to demonstrate one significant point: any assumption that the Mesopotamian law collections had no basis in reality, that they were never applied in daily life and reflected no legal reality of any sort is, in all likelihood, unwarranted. It seems too dismissive and reductionist. Even if most of the statutes we encounter in these collections were not always enforced or enacted, they probably did reflect the main legal notions of the social elites, and in one way or another were known in wider social circles and practiced by them. Even the elites, eventually, stemmed from and existed within the same sociocultural environment shared by the whole of the population. Some of the law collections, like Lipit-Ištar's or Hammurabi's, were copied numerous times, and their copies are found in numerous places. It is not hard to imagine, therefore, that people knew about their existence, and even illiterate populations had real knowledge of their contents, by way of oral transmission and thanks to the presence of scribes and other literate persons all over the ancient Near East.

Biblical law and legal practice: the nature of the legal texts in the Pentateuch

What we refer to as "biblical law" has been studied and discussed by scholars exhaustively. The laws found in the Hebrew Bible are religious in nature and were believed to have been given to the people of Israel by God himself, through the mediation of Moses. As such, they mostly pertain to religious or cultic obligations and regulations. Around 60 of them, however, do pertain to civil or criminal matters.[24] The priestly laws are by and large irrelevant to most of the discussions in this book, as they concern cultic matters rather than civil ones.[25]

Most of the provisions in the Pentateuch that we regard as "laws", "provisions" or "statutes" appear in three main clusters, known by scholars as the "Book of the Covenant", the "Holiness Code" and the "Deuteronomic Code". The first cluster deals with civil law (Exod. 21:1–22:16), moral-social law (Exod. 22:20–23:9) and laws of cult (Exod. 23:10–19 // 34:17–26). The main part of this cluster – Exod. 21:1–22:16[26] – is regarded as the law collection known as the "Covenant Code".[27] The second cluster (Lev. 17–26) mostly concerns cultic regulations, and it is sometimes considered to be related to other parts of the so-called Priestly Code(s) of Leviticus and Numbers 1–9. The third cluster (Deut. 12–26, with some repetition in Deut. 27) repeats some of the earlier rules but also supplies new ones, such as directives concerning the appointment of judges, rules of war, levirate marriage, divorce and regulations concerning the status of the king and the prophets.

What concerns us, however, are the Pentateuchal civil statutes. These are included in two of the previously mentioned clusters, the "Covenant Code" and the "Deuteronomic Code", while some issues relating to civil law are also referred to in the "Holiness Code". These three "codes" formed three distinct law collections, but it should be noted that the very term "code" is quite inappropriate for designating these groups of legal provisions, since the process of codification of these provisions is quite vague and the very functionality of these textual clusters as obligating legal directives is questionable. The modern term "code", therefore, is probably anachronistic and misleading in this case.[28] Additional statutes of civil character are scattered randomly throughout the Pentateuch, such as the regulations for treating a woman suspected of adultery (Num. 5:12–31) or the rules of inheritance in the absence of male heirs (Num. 27:8–11).

Scholarly discourse concerning the applicability of biblical law depends heavily on the previously discussed debate over Mesopotamian law. Biblical scholars resort to Mesopotamian sources as a model for comparison, mainly because of the complexities involved in the scarcity of pertinent biblical texts. This can be seen clearly in the following statements made by Westbrook:[29]

> since the law codes were theoretical documents, it is difficult to know how far they represent the law in practice. The ideological agenda of the biblical codes is obvious, but the cuneiform codes, some of which served the purposes of royal propaganda, may have been no less colored by ideology, idealization, or hyperbole. There is also the suspicion, especially strong in the case of the Middle Assyrian Laws, that some of the punishments reflect the scribal compilers' concern for perfect symmetry and delicious irony rather than the pragmatic experience of the law courts. Certainly, the few documents of practice, including those contemporary with the codes, show striking discrepancies in matters of detail, especially as regards punishments, which tend to be milder than in the codes. But they do conform to the general principles, structures, and procedures found in the law codes.

Wells (2008) offered a thorough treatment of the legal validity of biblical law, including a survey of past and current scholarly views. He divided the matter into several levels of perceived legal authority: from "Authoritative Law",[30] through "Competing sets of Authoritative Law",[31] to "Theoretical Treatises".[32]

The "Authoritative" approach regards the legal contents of the Pentateuch as having indeed formed obligating statutes that reflected actual legal procedure among the Israelites and Judeans. This approach, however, has very few advocates nowadays. One reason is that it fails to account for the fact that many provisions seem to contradict one another. The second approach is more minimalist in this regard. According to it, the legal provisions found in the Pentateuch indeed had a certain authoritative essence, but they did not form a coherent legal system, and – despite their authors' intention – they never became the official legal system according to which people lived in Israel or Judah. The third approach goes further in detaching scholarly views from notions of the authoritative nature of biblical legal provisions. According to this approach, the Mesopotamian law collections were merely the product of members of the scribal circles who organized and documented knowledge in the form of lists. As such, therefore, these collections of legal provisions did not differ from astronomical, mathematical, omen and other types of lists and had nothing to do with people's daily lives. The biblical laws are regarded by the advocates of this perspective in a similar light, as reflecting religious ideology rather than real legal purposes.

Some of these approaches were integrated by certain scholars. For example, Westbrook (1985, 1989) and Greengus (1994) accepted the possibility that the Mesopotamian law collections stemmed from scribal traditions but claimed that they nonetheless reflected true legal customs and habits.

We can see, therefore, that scholarly views on the questions of the applicability and legal authority of Mesopotamian law collections and biblical legal provisions differ and range between minimalist, maximalist and intermediate perspectives. As noted by Wells, the most feasible way to decide how authoritative the Pentateuchal laws actually were is to compare them with texts that describe actual legal practice. Since no such texts exist in the Hebrew Bible, Wells suggested to resort to relevant Mesopotamian texts and compare them to the contents of the biblical law provisions, assuming "a process of reasoning from the known to the unknown", and concluding that "the evidence below counters any hasty or wholesale rejection of potential connections between biblical law and legal practice".[33] Wells has demonstrated that some Pentateuchal provisions were either concerned with similar legal topics, shared similar legal reasoning or exhibited similar legal penalties to several texts of legal practice – such as contracts and trial records – from the ancient Near East.[34]

Questions and aims

This book mainly addresses the following questions: How were gender dynamics regulated in the Mesopotamian (and Hittite) legal tradition, as attested in official legal sources? How were they regulated in the parallel biblical legal sources? What can be deduced from the comparison between the ancient Near East and the Hebrew Bible in this respect?

In attempting to answer these main questions, the book engages with several subordinate topics, whether directly and explicitly, or indirectly and implicitly. Was gender inequality perpetuated through various legal and social mechanisms? If so: How? Did the public and the private arenas have different arrays of norms and customs concerning gender relations? How was the division of labor, roles and tasks between the genders manifested in official legal texts? What sources of authority were exclusive for women in bureaucratic and organizational systems? How was the management of the family governed by official law? Can we trace social attitudes to gender-based marginal groups? Which acts were defined as sex crimes, and how were they sanctioned? All these questions might seem random at first glance, but they are far from that. These questions are treated throughout the different chapters of the book, as it progresses from discussions of social inequality (Chapter 1), economy, palatial and cultic systems (Chapter 2), familial circles (Chapter 3) to marginal groups and sex crimes (Chapter 4).

Ultimately, the book aims to enhance our understanding of the use of legal institutions for the enforcement of social and cultural norms of gender roles, gender relations and sexual behavior in various social settings in the ancient Near East and in ancient Israel during the biblical era. In a sense, it aims to understand social stratification: how social elites monitored large populations and dictated their gender and sexual customs, using legal institutions. Additionally, though to a lesser degree, this book offers a humble outlook on ethnic diversity. Considering the varied ethnic groups that inhabited the ancient Near East and produced law collections – the Sumerians, Babylonians, Assyrians and Hittites – the question should be asked whether we can observe clear differences between them and between them and the ancient Israelites.

To be sure, I do not claim that a clear and direct connection necessarily existed between the ancient Near Eastern law collections and the biblical legal provisions found in the Pentateuch. The scholarly literature on this topic is vast, and I refrain from taking sides in the debate. The similarities, however, are noteworthy and presented in this book regardless of their possible origins. The geographical, cultural and relative chronological[35] proximity of the Mesopotamian, Hittite and biblical texts in question seem strong enough to merit the joint inclusion of all these texts in the present book.[36]

Structure of the book

This book is divided into two parts. The first part includes the analyses and discussions that form the examination of the interrelations between law and gender. The examination is divided into four main themes, each of which is discussed in a separate chapter. The themes are divided based on their scope, advancing from a macro perspective to a micro perspective. We therefore begin in Chapter 1 ("The societal perspective: social status and gender (in)equality") by looking at society at large; continue in Chapter 2 ("The institutional perspective: bureaucracy and economy: the palace, temple and beyond") by assessing social institutions; proceed in Chapter 3 ("The familial perspective: regulation of family life") to the smaller societal unit of the family; and conclude in Chapter 4 ("The individual perspective: morality and sex crimes") by examining the lives of individuals. Understandably, all human behavior is social, and hence even the final chapter – which reflects the individual perspective – examines topics that are essentially societal. In this regard, even though the book advances along a rationale of narrowing the perspective and enlarging its resolution, it keeps looking at society all the time – just replacing the lenses, so to speak. Within each section the evidence is usually presented chronologically, from the earliest Mesopotamian law collections to the latest ones, followed by the evidence from Hittite sources. The biblical evidence is brought in a separate subsection. Each law collection is discussed separately, usually according to the order of statutes within the collection. This rationale is meant to point to possible chronological developments and cultural similarities.

Since this book is heavily dependent on textual sources and their interpretation, I deemed it necessary to supply the readers with complete access to all the pertinent texts I use in my analysis of law and gender in the ancient Near East and the Hebrew Bible. The second part of the book, therefore, contains all the relevant sources – statutes and legal provisions – mentioned in the first part. These are given in their original languages (cuneiform texts either in transliteration or normalization/bound script, biblical texts in Hebrew) as well as in English translation. The rationales behind the method of presentation of the texts in the second part are explained in the introduction of that part.

Sources of information

The textual corpus used in this book consists mostly of law collections from the ancient Near East and the Hebrew Bible. To a lesser extent, royal decrees, instructions and loyalty oaths of palace officials are used. These texts are similar to the law collections in the sense that they were stipulated by the royal elite, bore legal implications and were meant to formalize and standardize people's behavior. However, their scope was much narrower, and they were usually meant to regulate the conduct of specific individuals, such as palace personnel, cult attendants or other officials. All these texts reflect the manner in which social morals were embedded in legal thought and perpetuated through formal mechanisms.

Statute numbers from Mesopotamian law collections (§x) are specified in this book in accordance with Roth's 1997 edition. The only exceptions are the Laws of Ur-Namma, which are numbered according to Civil's 2011 new edition of this collection. The Hittite Laws are numbered according to Hoffner's 1997 authoritative edition. Passage and line numbers (§x xx–xx) in excerpts from Hittite royal edicts and instruction texts follow Miller 2013. References to biblical texts (Book x:xx–xx) are based on the Masoretic version.

Ancient Near Eastern law collections

Laws of Ur-Namma (LUN)

This collection was probably composed by the second ruler of the Ur III dynasty, King Šulgi, in the first half of the twenty-first century BCE. Written in the Sumerian language, six copies of LUN are known. None of these copies contains the complete collection, and together they contain 88 statutes. The number of missing statutes is unknown but probably does not exceed around ten percent of the whole collection.

Laws of Lipit-Ištar (LLI)

This collection was composed by Lipit-Ištar, an early second-millennium ruler of Isin, around 1930 BCE. Similarly to LUN, it was written in Sumerian, but, unlike its predecessor, many copies of it are known: no fewer than 17, though some of them probably belonged to the same source. These copies, however, are all fragmentary, and only some 44 statutes of this collection are preserved.

Laws of Ešnunna (LE)

This collection was likely composed by Daduša, ruler of the kingdom of Ešnunna, around 1770 BCE. This is the earliest law collection we know of to have been written in Akkadian, and though only three copies of it have been found – one of which is a scribal exercise – together they contain the 66 statutes that make up the whole collection.

Laws of Hammurabi (LH)

The most famous of all ancient Near Eastern law collections was composed by Hammurabi, King of Babylon, around 1750 BCE. It probably contained close to 300 statutes, of which 282 are preserved. The importance of LH is evident by the fact that over 50 copies of it have been found to date, from all over the ancient Near East.

Hittite Laws (HL)

The only ancient Near Eastern law collection to have been composed outside of Mesopotamia was the Hittite one. Written in the Indo-European Hittite language, its date of composition is disputed, and most scholars are divided between two options: either ca. 1650 BCE (under King Hattušili I) or ca. 1500 BCE (under King Telipinu). The collection was originally inscribed on two large tablets, each containing 100 statutes. Most of the 200 statutes that HL contained are known today from about 40 different copies.

Middle Assyrian Laws (MAL)

This is the only collection known from Assyria. It was originally composed around 1350 BCE, but we only have later copies of it, dating to around 1075 BCE. The MAL contained at least 14 different tablets, but only one of them (so-called Tablet A) preserves most of its original statutes, while the others are fragmentary, and most of their content is lost. Around 125 statutes are known from this collection, 60 of which from "Tablet A".

Neo-Babylonian Laws (NBL)

The only first-millennium law collection derives from the Neo-Babylonian period. Only one copy of it has survived, and it contains merely 15 statutes. The original extent of this collection is unknown. Its date of composition is likewise unknown and is tentatively ascribed by scholars to around 700 BCE.

Ancient Near Eastern royal decrees and instructions

Edicts of Samsu-iluna/Ammi-ditana/Ammi-ṣaduka (ESi/Ad/Aṣ)

Three of King Hammurabi's successors – beginning with his son and heir Samsu-iluna –issued nearly identical edicts. These centered on social and economic equity and covered such topics as debt absolution, slave redemption and tax exemption. Some scholars suggest that the purpose of these edicts was to offer reforms of Hammurabi's famous law collection, but without actually changing or contesting the original collection.[37] Since these three edicts are almost identical, they are referred to in this book jointly.

AASOR 16.51 (=SMN 553)

This royal edict was stipulated in the court of the Hurrian kingdom of Nuzi during the fourteenth century BCE. It issues an order banning members of the palace personnel from forcing their daughters into poverty or prostitution without the king's consent. These women were regarded as belonging to the palace like their fathers, and the purpose of the edict was hence to make sure that they were not lost for the palace.

Middle Assyrian Palace Decrees (MAPD)

A series of 23 decrees issued by nine consecutive kings of the Middle Assyrian kingdom in the course of 300 years. The compilation was found in the royal capital Aššur. All the decrees were assembled in the reign of King Tiglath-pileser I (ca. 1114–1076 BCE), who issued the last four of them. The decrees stipulate instructions for the women who lived in the royal quarters and for several male palace officials, some of whom may have been eunuchs.

Hittite instructions

The Hittites produced a large corpus of royal instruction texts. These were meant to regulate the tasks and behavior of wide-ranging types of officials, most of whom were engaged in the palace administration. This was eventually developed into a long-lasting tradition of over four centuries, from the earliest phases of Hittite documented history in the late seventeenth century BCE to the collapse of the empire in the early twelfth century. The Hittite instruction texts mentioned in this book – CTH 252, 258.1, 261.I, 264 and 265 – differ in date, function and authorship. They all, nonetheless, belong to a wider group of documents stipulated by the palace to its subordinates in an obligating legal manner.

Biblical law collections

The "Covenant Code"

The first cluster of civil or criminal legal provisions in the Hebrew Bible is included in Exod. 21–23, a segment known as the "Book of the Covenant". Some of the topics it covers are civil law (Exod. 21:1–22:16), moral-social law (Exod. 22:20–23:9) and laws of cult (Exod. 23:10–19 // 34:17–26). The main part of this cluster – Exod. 21:1–22:16[38] – is regarded as the law collection known as the "Covenant Code".[39] Scholars who follow the "documentary hypothesis" assume that this part of the Bible belongs to "source E", which originated in the northern kingdom of Israel. According to the theory, the Israelite authors of this collection took a separate earlier legal text – or utilized oral knowledge of these legal rules – and integrated it into their version of what will eventually become the Pentateuch. After the Assyrian exile, sources "E" and "J" were merged in Judah into one.

The "Holiness Code"

The second legal collection of the Hebrew Bible mostly contains cultic and religious regulations, but a few civil statutes are also found in it. This collection, known by scholars as the "Holiness Code", appears in Lev. 17–25. Some associate it further with other legal provisions that appear in the so-called Priestly Code(s) of Leviticus and Numbers 1–9. Opinions differ as to the circumstances of composition of this collection. According to the majority of scholars who follow the "documentary hypothesis", it was the latest collection to have been composed, and it was authored by the priestly circles that produced "source P" after the Babylonian exile, at a time when the priesthood prevailed as the authoritative element in society and not the monarchy anymore. Since this legal collection is distinguishable from the rest of "source P", some dub it "(source) H" (for "Holiness"), an independent subsection within "source P".

The "Deuteronomic Code"

The third biblical law collection is named after the book (and probable source, following the terminology of the "documentary hypothesis") in which it appears: Deuteronomy. The collection encompasses Deut. 12–26, while some provisions are repeated in Deut. 27, in the form of vows taken collectively by the people. This collection draws many elements from the earlier "Covenant Code" and repeats, at times exactly verbatim, many of the earlier statutes. However, it also introduces many new statutes.

Technical terms

Some of the terms mentioned in this book were left untranslated, in order to simplify the discussions; these are listed and briefly explained in what follows:[40]

- *biblu(m)*, "ceremonial marriage gifts": payment given from the household of the groom to the household of the bride;
- *ilku*: a civil/tax obligation, associated with *urāšu* and *qāštu* obligations;
- *kušata* (Hittite), "brideprice": payment given from the household of the groom to the household of the bride;
- *nudunnû(m)*, "marriage settlement"/"dowry": payment given from the household of the groom to the household of the bride or from the household of the bride to her or her husband upon their marriage;
- *šeriktum* (OB)/*širku* (MA)/*širiktu* (NB), "dowry": payment given from the household of the bride to her or her husband upon their marriage;
- *terḫatum* (OB), *terḫetu* (MA), "bridewealth"/"dowry": payment given from the household of the groom to the household of the bride or at times vice versa;
- *zubullû(m)*, "bridal gift": payment given from the household of the groom to the household of the bride or at times vice versa.

Weight and measurement units

- *biltu(m)*, Sumerian gú(-un), "talent": weight unit, equal to 3,600 shekels, 30 kilograms;
- *kurru(m)*, Sumerian gur, "kor": capacity unit, equal to 300 liters;
- *manû*, Sumerian mana/ma-na, "mina": weight unit, equal to 60 shekels, 500 grams;
- *šiqlu(m)*, Sumerian gín, "shekel": weight unit, equal to 8.3 grams;
- *qû(m)*, Sumerian sila/sìla, "liter": capacity unit, equal to 1 liter;
- *uṭṭa/etu*, Sumerian še (and derivatives), "grain": weight unit, equal to .05 grams.

Notes

1 *šumma aššat awīlim itti zikarim šanîm ina itūlim ittaṣbat ikassûšunūtima ana mê inaddûšunūti šumma bēl aššatim aššassu uballaṭ u šarrum warassu uballaṭ* (LH §129).

2 tukum-bi guruš dam-tuku kar-kid-dè tílla-a in-tuku-àm kar-kid-bi-ir nu-un-ši-gur-ru-da di-kud-e-ne in-na-an-eš egir-bi-ta dam-nitadam dam-a-ni ba-an-tag$_4$ kù dam-tag$_4$-a-ni ù-na-an-sum kar-kid-bi nu-un-tuku-tuku (LLI §30).

3 See, for example, Levinson's (2000: 121) comment concerning Roth's edition of the Mesopotamian law collections: "ancient Israel participates in the intellectual and literary tradition represented by the legal collections translated here". This comment is representative of the common opinion held by most scholars concerning the relationship between ancient Near Eastern and biblical law. Some, however, do claim a direct relationship: Wright (2009) argued that CC was composed as a direct borrowing from LH, and Otto (1995: 241–242, 1999: 2–3) suggested that MAL A is the origin of DC. I do not endorse, nor reject, any of these views.

4 For discussions on the relationship between Mesopotamia and Hatti in the sphere of law, see recently Peled 2017a. Comparisons between ancient Near Eastern and biblical law are abundant; the reader may consult, to name but a few, Paul 1970, Westbrook 1985, 1988b, Otto 1994, Greengus 1994, 2011, Wells 2008 and Peled 2018.

5 This only refers to the dating of the ancient Near Eastern sources; the highly complicated – and debated – chronology of biblical law is not discussed in this book. Scholars who follow the "documentary hypothesis" assume that the order of composition of the biblical law collections was: CC, DC, HC.

6 For the law collections as royal propaganda, see Finkelstein 1961, 1965. For these texts as the product of the scribal curriculum, see Kraus 1960 and Bottéro 1992: 156–184. General discussions of these matters are abundant; see, *inter alia*, Roth 1997: 4–7 and Peled 2017b, both with previous literature. See also, recently, Roth 2019: 75–77, who characterized the association between these two types of sources using the term "complementarity".

7 See most recently Roth 2019: 74, 75–77.

8 The two di til-la's in question are NSGU 4 (=L 6579 // ITT 3/2 6579) and SNAT 372; see general discussion in Culbertson 2009: 153–154 and details on p. 200.

9 See edition and discussion in Sweet 1958: 104–111.

10 *idū agrim ina narê* [*ša*]*ṭer* (A 3529:12–13).

11 It is commonly accepted that A 3529 was written in the times of Samsu-iluna, Hammurabi's immediate successor; see for example Roth 1997: 10 n. 1.

12 Kuhrt 1995: 112 and Roth 1997: 5–6.

13 For further discussion of this letter, see, among others, Kuhrt 1995: 112 and Roth 1997: 5–7.

14 See editions in van Dijk 1963: 70, 72 and Greengus 1969: 34.

15 ugu lú-ka in-dab$_5$ / su lú-ka ^{giš}nú-a / in-kéš / pu-úh-ru-um-šè in-íl (IM 28051 obv. 12–15).

16 For further discussion of IM 28051 in this context, see Peled 2017a: 29–30.

17 See edition in Postgate 1988: 106–111 (text no. 50).

18 A designation of the city of Aššur.

19 *ištēn quppu ša sasû nāgiri ša bītāti ša libbi āli* (VAT 8919=KAJ 310: 19–20).

20 The statutes in question are HL §§1–6, 43–44a, 174; for the homicide cases described in HL §§37–38 there was no penalty. The other ancient Near Eastern law collections that addressed homicide (LUN, LE, LH, MAL) exhibit both financial compensation and talionic execution, depending on the nature of the case. For homicide in these collections, as well as in biblical law, see most recently Peled 2018: 5, 7–11, 2019c: 10–11.

21 The passage in question – CTH 172 = KBo 1.10 + KUB 3.72 rev: 14–25 – is too long to be quoted here. The reader may find its English translation in Beckman 1996: 136. See also in Greengus 1994: 66.

22 For an edition and translation of VAT 5049, see Roth 1989: 41–42.

23 See also in Wunsch 2012: 20.

24 For a survey of each one of the law collections of the Pentateuch, see Patrick 1985 (CC: pp. 63–96; HC and the "Priestly Code(s)": 145–188; DC: 97–144).

25 See Westbrook 1985: 248 n. 3.

26 Westbrook (1994: 15) suggested to extend the definition of this collection, so that it also includes Exod. 22:17–19. Levinson (1994: 53) claimed that the "more conventional demarcation" of this collection covers Exod. 20:22–23:33.

27 This collection is occasionally designated by scholars by the Hebrew word *mišpāṭîm*, "judgments" or "laws".

28 This view is held by most researchers of biblical law; see already Paul 1970: 3 n. 5, with previous literature; see also the discussion of ancient Near Eastern and biblical law collections in Westbrook 1985.

29 Westbrook 2003: 70–71.

30 Advocated, for example, by Gregory Chirichigno, Ze'ev Falk and Moshe Greenberg.

31 Advocated, for example, by Eckart Otto and Bernard Levinson.

32 Advocated by Jean Bottéro and applied in his writings to the Mesopotamian law collections, followed and applied to biblical law by scholars such as Lisbeth Fried, Dale Patrick and Anne Fitzpatrick-McKinley.

33 Wells 2008: 231–232.

34 Wells 2008: 241–243.

35 The Hebrew Bible, as we know it today, is, of course, the result of a complex centuries-long process of compilation, edition and canonization; its origins, however, go back to eras contemporaneous with at least the latest Mesopotamian law collection of the Neo-Babylonian period.

36 Some scholars indeed claim that certain parts of biblical law derived directly from some of the ancient Near Eastern law collections. For example, Wright (2009) relates CC to LH, and Otto (1995: 241–242, 1999: 2–3) relates parts of DC to MAL A.

37 Hallo 2003: 362.

38 Westbrook (1994: 15) suggested to extend the definition of this collection, so that it also includes Exod: 22:17–19. Levinson (1994: 53) claimed that the "more conventional demarcation" of this collection covers Exod. 20:22–23:33.

39 This collection is occasionally designated by scholars by the Hebrew word *mišpāṭîm*, "judgments" or "laws".

40 The exact meaning of a given term could change over time. Translations and explanations are based on the pertinent dictionaries (CAD for Akkadian, HED for Hittite) and previous discussions and translations found in Roth 1997: xvi, 270–271, 2014: 145–147, Richardson 2000: 340 and Huehnergard 2011: 579–585.

Bibliography

Alt, Albrecht. 1934. *Die Ursprünge des israelitischen Rechts*. Leipzig: Hirzel. [reprinted: 1953. *Kleine Schriften zur Geschichte des Volkes Israel*. Munich: Beck. Pp. 278–332.]

Anderson, Cheryl B. 2004. *Women, Ideology, and Violence: Critical Theory and the Construction of Gender in the Book of the Covenant and the Deuteronomic Law*. London: Clark.

Asher-Greve, Julia M. and Westenholz, Joan G. 2013. *Goddesses in Context: On Divine Powers, Roles, Relationships and Gender in Mesopotamian Textual and Visual Sources*. Fribourg: Academic Press Fribourg.

Beckman, Gary. 1996. *Hittite Diplomatic Texts*. Atlanta, GA: Scholars Press.

Bolger, Diane R. (ed.) 2008. *Gender Through Time in the Ancient Near East*. Lanham, MD: AltaMira Press.

Bottéro, Jean. 1992. *Mesopotamia: Writing, Reasoning, and the Gods* (trans. Zainab Bahrani and Marc Van de Mieroop). Chicago, IL: University of Chicago Press.

Budin, Stephanie L. and MacIntish Turfa, Jean (eds.) 2016. *Women in Antiquity: Real Women Across the Ancient World*. London; New York: Routledge, Taylor & Francis Group.

Civil, Miguel. 2011. "The Law Collection of Ur-Namma". In *Cuneiform Royal Inscriptions and Related Texts in the Schøyen Collection*, edited by Andrew R. George. Bethesda, MD: CDL Press. Pp. 221–286.

Culbertson, Laura. 2009. *Dispute Resolution in the Provincial Courts of the Third Dynasty of Ur* (PhD dissertation, University of Michigan). Ann Arbor, MI.

Finkelstein, Jacob J. 1961. "Ammiṣaduqa's Edict and the Babylonian 'Law Codes'". *Journal of Cuneiform Studies* 15/3: 91–104.

Finkelstein, Jacob J. 1965. "Some New *Misharum* Material and Its Implications". In *Studies in Honor of Benno Landsberger on His Seventy-Fifth Birthday, April 21, 1965*, edited by Hans Gustav Güterbock and Thorkild Jacobsen. Chicago, IL: University of Chicago Press. Pp. 233–246.

Greenberg, Moshe. 1960. "Some Postulates of Biblical Criminal Law". In *Yehezkel Kaufmann Jubilee Volume*, edited by Menahem Haran. Jerusalem: Magnes Press, The Hebrew University. Pp. 5–28. [reprinted: 1995. *Studies in the Bible and Jewish Thought*. Philadelphia, PA: Jewish Publication Society. Pp. 25–41].

Greengus, Samuel. 1969. "A Textbook Case of Adultery in Ancient Mesopotamia". *Hebrew Union College Annual* 40: 33–44.

Greengus, Samuel. 1994. "Some Issues Relating to the Comparability of Laws and the Coherence of the Legal Tradition". In *Theory and Method in Biblical and Cuneiform Law: Revision, Interpretation, and Development*, edited by Bernard M. Levinson. Sheffield: Sheffield Academic Press. Pp. 60–87.

Greengus, Samuel. 2011. *Laws in the Bible and in Early Rabbinic Collections: The Legal Legacy of the Ancient Near East*. Eugene, OR: Cascade Books.

Hallo, William W. 2003. "The Edicts of Samsu-iluna and His Successors". In *The Context of Scripture. Volume II: Monumental Inscriptions from the Biblical World*, edited by William W. Hallo and K. Lawson Younger, Jr. Leiden: Brill. Pp. 362–364.

Hoffner, Harry A. Jr. 1997. *The Laws of the Hittites: A Critical Edition*. Leiden: Brill.

Huehnergard, John. 2011. *A Grammar of Akkadian* (third edition). Winona Lake, IN: Eisenbrauns.

Jackson, Bernard S. 2000. *Studies in the Semiotics of Biblical Law*. Sheffield: Sheffield Academic Press.

Jackson, Bernard S. 2006. *Wisdom-Laws: A Study of the Mishpatim of Exodus 21:1–22:16*. Oxford: Oxford University Press.

Jackson, Samuel A. 2013 [2008]. *A Comparison of Ancient Near Eastern Law Collections Prior to the First Millennium BC*. Piscataway, NJ: Gorgias Press.

Kraus, Fritz R. 1960. "Ein zentrales Problem des altmesopotamischen Rechts: Was ist der Codex Hammu-rabi?" *Genava* 8: 283–296.

Kuhrt, Amélie. 1995. *The Ancient Near East c. 3000–330 BC* (vol. 1). London; New York: Routledge, Taylor & Francis Group.

Lafont, Sophie. 1999. *Femmes, Droit et Justice dans l'Antiquité orientale. Contribution à l'étude du droit pénal au Proche-Orient ancien*. Fribourg: Editions Universitaires.

Levinson, Bernard M. 1994. "The Case of Revision and Interpolation Within the Biblical Legal Corpora". In *Theory and Method in Biblical and Cuneiform Law: Revision, Interpretation, and Development*, edited by Bernard M. Levinson. Sheffield: Sheffield Academic Press. Pp. 37–59.

Levinson, Bernard M. 2000. "*Law Collections from Mesopotamia and Asia Minor*. Martha T. Roth, Piotr Michalowski". *Journal of Near Eastern Studies* 59/2: 119–121.

Levinson, Bernard M. 2011. *"The Right Chorale": Studies in Biblical Law and Interpretation*. Tübingen: Mohr Siebek.

Lion, Brigitte and Michele, Cécile (eds.) 2016. *The Role of Women in Work and Society in the Ancient Near East*. Berlin: De Gruyter.

Matthews, Victor H., Levinson, Bernard M. and Frymer-Kensky, Tikva S. (eds.) 1998. *Gender and Law in the Hebrew Bible and the Ancient Near East*. Sheffield: Sheffield Academic Press.

Miller, Jared L. 2013. *Royal Hittite Instructions and Related Administrative Texts*. Atlanta, GA: Society of Biblical Literature.

Otto, Eckart. 1994. "Aspects of Legal and Reformulations in Ancient Cuneiform and Israelite Law". In *Theory and Method in Biblical and Cuneiform Law: Revision, Interpretation, and Development*, edited by Bernard M. Levinson. Sheffield: Sheffield Academic Press. Pp. 160–196.

Otto, Eckart. 1995. "Rechtsreformen in Deuteronomium XII—XXVI und im Mittelassyrischen Kodex der Tafel A (KAV 1)". In *Congress Volume Paris 1992*, edited by John A. Emerton. Leiden: Brill. Pp. 239–273.

Otto, Eckart. 1999. *Das Deuteronomium: Politische Theologie und Rechtsreform in Juda und Assyrien*. Berlin: De Gruyter.

Parpola, Simo and Whiting, Robert M. (eds.) 2002. *Sex and Gender in the Ancient Near East: Proceedings of the 47th Rencontre Assyriologique Internationale, Helsinki, July 2–6, 2001*. Helsinki: Neo-Assyrian Text Corpus Project.

Patrick, Dale. 1985. *Old Testament Law*. Atlanta, GA: John Knox Press.

Paul, Shalom M. 1970. *Studies in the Book of the Covenant in the Light of Cuneiform and Biblical Law*. Leiden: Brill.

Peled, Ilan. 2016. *Masculinities and Third Gender: The Origins and Nature of an Institutionalized Gender Otherness in the Ancient Near East*. Münster: Ugarit-Verlag.

Peled, Ilan. 2017a. "Gender and Sex Crimes in the Ancient Near East: Law and Custom". In *Structures of Power: Law and Gender Across the Ancient Near East and Beyond*, edited by Ilan Peled. Chicago, IL: The Oriental Institute of the University of Chicago. Pp. 27–40.

Peled, Ilan. 2017b. "Introduction: Structures of Power: Law and Gender Across the Ancient Near East and Beyond". In *Structures of Power: Law and Gender Across the Ancient Near East and Beyond*, edited by Ilan Peled. Chicago, IL: The Oriental Institute of the University of Chicago. Pp. 1–12.

Peled, Ilan. 2018. "The Laws of Delict in the Hebrew Bible and Their Ancient Near Eastern Forerunners: Analyzing and Comparing Social Attitude to Crime". *Journal for Semitics* 27/2: 1–22.

Peled, Ilan. 2019. "Delict in the Law Compendia of Mesopotamia and Hatti: Qualitative and Quantitative Analyses". *Journal for Semitics* 28/1: 1–21.

Postgate, John N. 1988. *The Archive of Urad-Šerūa and His Family. A Middle Assyrian Household in Government Service*. Rome: Denicola.

Richardson, Mervyn E. J. 2000. *Hammurabi's Laws: Text, Translation and Glossary*. Sheffield: Sheffield Academic Press.

Roth, Martha T. 1989. *Babylonian Marriage Agreements: 7th—3rd Centuries B.C.* Kevelaer: Butzon & Bercker; Neukirchen-Vlyun: Neukirchener Verlag.

Roth, Martha T. 1997. *Law Collections from Mesopotamia and Asia Minor* (second edition). Atlanta, GA: Scholars Press.

Roth, Martha T. 2014. "Women and Law". In *Women in the Ancient Near East: A Sourcebook*, edited by Mark W. Chavalas. London; New York: Routledge. Pp. 144–174.

Roth, Martha T. 2019. "Justice, Crime, and Punishment". In *Ancient Mesopotamia Speaks: Highlights of the Yale Babylonian Collection*, edited by Agnete W. Lassen, Eckart Frahm and Klaus Wagensonner. New Haven, CT: Yale University Press. Pp. 73–81.

Sassoon, John. 2001. *Ancient Laws and Modern Problems: The Balance Between Justice and a Legal System*. Lingfield, Surrey: Third Millennium Publishing.

Stol, Marten. 2016. *Women in the Ancient Near East*. Berlin: De Gruyter.

Sweet, Ronald F. G. 1958. *On Prices, Moneys, and Money Uses in the Old Babylonian Period* (PhD dissertation, University of Chicago). Chicago, IL.

Tetlow, Elisabeth M. 2004. *Women, Crime, and Punishment in Ancient Law and Society. Volume 1: The Ancient Near East*. New York: Continuum.

van Dijk, Jacobus. 1963. "Neusumerische Gerichtsurkunden in Bagdad". *Zeitschrift für Assyriologie und Vorderasiatische Archäologie* 55: 70–90.

Wells, Bruce. 2008. "What Is Biblical Law? A Look at Pentateuchal Rules and Near Eastern Practice". *The Catholic Biblical Quarterly* 70: 223–243.
Westbrook, Raymond. 1985. "Biblical and Cuneiform Law Codes". *Revue Biblique* 92: 247–264.
Westbrook, Raymond. 1988. *Studies in Biblical and Cuneiform Law*. Paris: Gabalda.
Westbrook, Raymond. 1989. "Cuneiform Law Codes and the Origins of Legislation". *Zeitschrift für Assyriologie und Vorderasiatische Archäologie* 79: 201–222.
Westbrook, Raymond. 1994. "What Is the Covenant Code?" In *Theory and Method in Biblical and Cuneiform Law: Revision, Interpretation, and Development*, edited by Bernard M. Levinson. Sheffield: Sheffield Academic Press. Pp. 15–36.
Westbrook, Raymond. 2003. "Introduction: The Character of Ancient Near Eastern Law". In *A History of Ancient Near Eastern Law*, edited by Raymond Westbrook. Leiden: Brill. Pp. 1–90.
Wilcke, Claus. 2014. "Gesetze in sumerischer Sprache". In *Studies in Sumerian Language and Literature: Festschrift Joachim Krecher*, edited by Natalia V. Koslova, Ekaterina Vizirova and Gábor Zólyomi. Winona Lake, IN: Eisenbrauns. Pp. 455–616.
Wright, David P. 2009. *Inventing God's Law*. Oxford: Oxford University Press.
Wunsch, Cornelia. 2012. "Legal Narrative in the Neo-Babylonian Trial Documents: Text Reconstruction, Interpretation, and Assyriological Method". In *Law and Narrative in the Bible and in Neighbouring Ancient Cultures*, edited by Klaus-Peter Adam, Friedrich Avemarie and Nili Wazana. Tübingen: Mohr Siebeck. Pp. 3–33.
Yaron, Reuven. 1988. *The Laws of Eshnunna* (second edition). Jerusalem: Magnes Press, The Hebrew University.
Zsolnay, Ilona (ed.) 2017. *Being a Man: Negotiating Ancient Constructs of Masculinity*. London; New York: Routledge, Taylor & Francis Group.

Part I

1 The societal perspective

Social status and gender (in)equality

Introduction

We begin the survey of law and gender in the ancient Near East and the Hebrew Bible by examining the broad – and, admittedly, at times hardly definable – topic of status and equality between the genders. This chapter surveys the question of social differentiation between the genders as based on various statutes and other texts. Unlike the following chapters, the current one is not thematically oriented and is more generally defined.

Social status was established in the ancient world according to numerous factors of classification: economic (whether one was rich or poor), civil (whether one was free or a slave), nativity (whether one was local or foreign), age (whether one was young or old), organizational (whether one belonged to the palace or temple systems), marital (whether one was married or single) and the like. According to some of these classification factors the individual could be labeled as belonging to a specific social group, frequently one of two opposing options, such as either local or foreigner. Others formed a spectrum somewhere along which the individual was located, such as how rich a person was. At times both types of social classification were combined: someone's age, for example, reflected his location along a chronological spectrum, but at the same time related him to a specific age group, thus defining him as either a boy, adolescent, adult or elderly. Each one of these age groups had its own rules of conduct and attached tasks, privileges and obligations.

Another factor that strongly influenced the individual's social status was his or her gender. A person's array of social statuses combined all the previously mentioned classifications, and frequently additional others, supplementing his or her gender status as a man or a woman. This, of course, was hardly unique to Mesopotamia, Hatti or ancient Israel, but we must bear these basic considerations in mind when assessing the sociological aspects of these ancient cultures.

Social differentiation was apparent in the Old Babylonian world through the division between the *awīlum* and *muškēnum* classes, a division that was probably kept in the Neo Babylonian period as well, even though the evidence from the later period is less concrete. In the Assyrian world we do not find the *muškēnum*, but the *a'īlu* possibly did exist as a designation of a distinct social class. For example, the statute MAL A §21 begins as follows: "If a man strikes a man's daughter, and causes her to abort her fetus".[1] The labeling of the victim as "a man's daughter" is peculiar, because we would have expected her to be designated by the standard legal definition for married women, "a man's wife". As a pregnant woman she had to be married, since extramarital sexual relations of any kind were strictly forbidden. The term *mārat a'īle* can therefore be understood in this case as "a daughter (=female member) of the *a'īlu* (class)". An alternative possibility is that the said woman had recently become widowed, but was impregnated by her husband shortly prior to his death. She could then return to live in her father's household and remain under his auspices, while being pregnant with her deceased husband's child. Such a scenario might seem improbable but certainly not impossible. Ancient Near Eastern law frequently presents rare or unique cases, even more peculiar than this hypothetical scenario. With no additional information supplied by the text, we remain ignorant as to the wider context of this statute.

One of the major social categorizations in the ancient world was the division between free persons and slaves. In the current chapter, therefore, these two categories are discussed separately. This separation serves to evaluate gender equality – or the lack of it – between men and women who belonged to the same social group and shared the same social status, because statutes issued for free persons cannot be assessed similarly to those assigned for enslaved ones. One of the interesting questions we thus aspire to answer is whether gender differentiation was materialized differently among free persons comparing to the way it existed among slaves. The conclusions we reach are bound to shed new light on the broader issues of social differentiation and slavery in ancient times, adding new information to the extensive research that has already been carried out on these topics.

The two opening sections of this chapter, hence, present the evidence concerning gender inequality and equality among free persons, while the two subsequent ones examine the same topics among slaves. The final section of the chapter assesses the topic of women's protection in society. This topic involves both equality and inequality but is distinguished from the previous discussions of the chapter, since it highlights statutes and rules that were issued especially for women, allegedly protecting them but in effect possibly discriminating them.

Gender inequality among free persons

Our opening section focuses on the legal means by which gender inequality was meant to be perpetuated among free persons. The vast majority of statutes were obviously issued for free persons, who formed the majority in society. Some statutes denied women certain rights, while others referred to professions or activities that belonged exclusively to the feminine domain. Another aspect of gender inequality is found in women's legal obligations to observe certain rules of conduct and standards of chastity, while no parallel statutes were formally stipulated for men.

ANE law

Many statutes in the different ancient Near Eastern law collections were stipulated solely for women, reflecting either discrimination or exclusivity. For example, in LE §24 a *muškēnum*'s wife or son is lawlessly detained and killed by the detainer, a crime for which the perpetrator was to face execution. This statute reveals a norm known from other sources, according to which creditors could detain their debtors' family members in order to pressure them to pay off the debt. Though LE §24 deems the act illicit, the punishment it entails applies to the killing of the detainee, and not to the act of detaining itself. This statute thus portrays a free woman – albeit a member of the lower *muškēnum* class – as an object used for pressuring her husband.[2]

Certain professions were conducted exclusively or mostly by women, and at times the performance of these professions was regulated by official law.[3] For example, only women were documented in the law collections as holding the occupation of *sābītu*(*m*), woman-innkeeper.[4] LUN §D9 is fragmentary, but appears to detail the payments and taxes involved in a credit-sale of beer by a woman-innkeeper; LE §15 forbade a woman-innkeeper (and also a male merchant) to receive any payment from a slave; LE §41 determined that a woman-innkeeper will sell the beer of a foreigner for him at the regular rate; LH §108 prescribed death by drowning to a woman-innkeeper who accepted silver but not grain as payment for her beer; LH §109 prescribed execution for a woman-innkeeper who sheltered criminals;[5] LH §111 determined the interest to be charged by a woman-innkeeper when loaning beer, similarly to LUN §D9; ESi/Ad/Aṣ §16 exempted women-innkeepers from their debts, while ESi/Ad/Aṣ §17 exempted their customers from paying them any outstanding fee; ESi/Ad/Aṣ §18 prescribed execution for a woman-innkeeper for a fraud which nature remains unclear because of a break in the text.

The importance of all these statutes lies in the fact that they illustrate the independence of the women-innkeepers. In societies where women were by and large subordinate to men, such institutionalized independence was rare. Even when these statutes specify obligations or sanctions, they still portray the woman-innkeeper as a female who handles her own business as an entrepreneur. Significantly, as we can see, the pertinent statutes derive from Ur III and Old Babylonian sources. Whether the phenomenon was characteristic of other places and times is unknown.[6]

Understandably, the profession of wet-nurse (LUN §E2, LH §194) was also exclusive to women, as well as intentional self-abortion (MAL A §53). These two issues highlight the involvement of women in matters of childbirth and childrearing, social niches with which they were associated more intensively than men. LUN §E2 determined the fees paid to a wet-nurse for her services, while LH §194 specified a talionic punishment – cutting off her breast – for a negligent wet-nurse who concealed the death of a child put under her care by his parents. According to MAL A §53, a woman who aborted her own fetus was to be talionically impaled. These three statutes are found in three different law collections, deriving from different periods and cultures (Sumerian Ur III, Old Babylonian and Middle Assyrian), and hence generalizations will be of little value in this case. Nonetheless, it can be suggested that these three statutes demonstrate that the positive involvement of women in the beginning of one's life would award them their due payment (LUN §E2), while their negative involvement in this crucial phase would lead to harsh sanctions (LH §194, MAL A §53). Both the positive and the negative aspects of this case were not applicable to men.[7]

An attitude favorable towards women is reflected in LH §29, according to which in case a man was taken captive by an enemy and was hence unable to perform his service obligation (*ilku*), and his son was too young to perform the task, his wife was to receive the ownership over one-third of their assets, with which she was to raise their son. In a sense, then, this statute shifts the economic authority and responsibility within the family, for better or worse, from the absent father to the mother.[8]

A different situation of economic hardship that reflected gender inequality within the family relates to people who were sold for slavery, as attested both in LH and in ESi/Ad/Aṣ.[9] According to LH §117, a man who ran into debt could sell his wife and children to clear his debt. According to ESi/Ad/Aṣ §20, such a person could sell his wife, children or himself.[10] As the head of the family, the man was in charge of all economic matters, and therefore it was his actions that led to the dire situation of accumulating debts. He was also the one who held the responsibility to solve the situation, but as we can see, according to the solution offered by LH §117 and ESi/Ad/Aṣ §20, it was not the man himself who paid the price but rather his wife and children, who were enslaved.

LH §153 treated an unfaithful wife who plotted the murder of her husband. No statute addressed a case of a husband plotting the murder of his wife in a similar context. This should be assessed in relation to the fact that no ancient Near Eastern statute ever bans a married man from fornicating; men were only regarded as perpetrators if they fornicated with married women, thus offending the betrayed husbands.[11]

The MAPD stipulate various directives which limited women.[12] In a broken context, MAPD §1 prohibits midwives and *qadiltu* women from leaving the palace, probably unaccompanied. MAPD §3 probably stipulated similar directives to women who worked in the palace but resided with their husbands outside of it. The broken context prevents a definite establishment of the contents of this clause. Further restrictions were the prohibitions on a palace woman from dispensing precious (MAPD §5) and ordinary (MAPD §6) items which belonged to the palace. MAPD §7 considered a menstruating woman to be ritually unclean and forbade her to approach the king close to the time of making sacrifices. Punishments were decreed for palace women uttering blasphemy (MAPD §10, and probably also §14), improperly swearing by the name of the god (MAPD §11) or cursing any member of the royal household, palace official or another woman of the palace (MAPD §17). MAPD §18 obliged a royal concubine or a palace woman to punish her slave-woman in case the said slave committed an offense. They were required, however, to avoid killing the slave, otherwise they would be held accountable for the misdeed. MAPD §19 prohibited a palace woman from standing without witnesses with a man "in a flirtatious manner" (*namutta*) and decreed execution for an eyewitness – whether male or female – of such an occurrence, who did not report it. MAPD §21 required palace women to be dressed and covered properly when court attendants arrived at these women's request and, further, that a certain distance was kept between them when they met.

What stood at the basis of the requirement of women to remain sexually and morally chaste was the patriarchal nature of ancient Near Eastern societies. This can be seen, to give but one example, in the various statutes that obliged women to remain under the auspices of their husbands, and the various complications involved in their husbands' absence. Thus, LH §133b explicitly uses the phrase "I[f] that woman does not keep her [b]ody (chaste), and enters another's house".[13] Another expression of this attitude is found in MAL A §40, which obliged all females but prostitutes and slave-women – whether unmarried, married or widows – to be veiled when in public.[14] No statutes ever required men to remain chaste, veil themselves while in public, stay confined to their homes or – generally speaking – be put in a constant state of subordination to a governing figure of the opposite gender. Gender inequality was widespread in the ancient Near East, and, as we see, it was deeply embedded in formal law.

DISCRIMINATION OF WOMEN

Gender inequality did not necessarily reflect a negative attitude towards women as much as the will to maintain androcentric superiority. At times, however, women were discriminated against for no obvious reason other than their gender. Such negative notions lie at the core of the following discussion.

Women's inferior status as compared to men's was occasionally perpetuated in official statutes. This is especially apparent in tablet A of the MAL, which was almost entirely dedicated to rules that governed women's lives. Thus, we find in the MAL statutes variously referring to women caught stealing from a temple (MAL A §1), uttering blasphemy (MAL A §2) or stealing from someone's house (MAL A §5).[15] There should be no reason why men would not be involved in similar felonies, but the fact remains that no similar statutes were issued against possible male perpetrators.

As is discussed previously, according to the MAL, Assyrian women were obliged to be veiled when seen in public. This was true whether they were married, widows, concubines or still unmarried women who lived in their father's household; unmarried *qadiltu* women, however, were not to be veiled in public, nor were prostitutes and slave-women (MAL A §40). If a man wished to veil his concubine, he was required to publicly marry her (MAL A §41). No similar chastity requirements are attested for men.

Generally speaking, the MAL seems to have been rather harsh towards women. On top of various specific statutes, a general ruling concluded tablet A of the MAL, which allowed a husband to physically hurt his wife in various ways (MAL

A §59). This ruling explicitly served as an extra means of punishment, "Additionally to the punishments of [a man's wife] that are [written] in the document".[16]

NBL §7 relates to a woman engaged in magic. No parallel statutes in this collection relate in a similar manner to men, even though we know from numerous non-legal sources that both men and women could practice magic in Mesopotamia. Indeed, MAL A §47 considers members of both sexes to be potential practitioners of magic. However, the fragmentary state of NBL prevents any sweeping conclusions in this regard.[17]

Biblical law

Biblical law as well exhibits attitudes that clearly differentiated between men and women. At times these seem to have discriminated against women, serving to perpetuate men's superiority. For example, even though a husband was not allowed to sell his wife, he could nonetheless sell his daughter as a slave to be married by her purchaser (Exod. 21:7). No equivalent practice existed for selling sons into slavery for similar purposes.

The HC included a prohibition on having sexual intercourse with a menstruating woman, labeling her state as "defilement" (טומאה) (Lev. 18:19).[18] In its second attestation, the prohibition applies punishment – banishment from the community – for both the man and the woman involved (Lev. 20:18).[19]

A passage in Numbers refers to vows to God made by women and the fulfillment of these vows (Num. 30:3–17). It begins with the statement that a man who has made a vow to God must keep it (Num. 30:3) but continues by specifying several cases of women who make such vows without having the liberty of having a final decision as to fulfilling their vows. A vow made by a young woman that still resided in her father's house could be annulled, and she was forgiven by God if her father heard her making the vow and persuaded her against it on the spot; but if her father said nothing she was obliged by her vows (Num. 30:4–6). The same rules applied to a married woman who was under the auspices of her husband: her vows could be annulled only if her husband heard her and persuaded her immediately after making the vows; but if he wished to annul her vows after a while, he was to bear responsibility for her misconduct (Num. 30:7–9, 11–16). A widow and a divorcée were required to fulfill their vows with no exception (Num. 30:10), since they had no governing male who could annul their vows.[20]

The rules of handling a conquered city in DC show further characteristics of gender differentiation. These rules specify different treatment to members of the enemy population based on their gender: men were to be killed (Deut. 20:13) while women and children were to be taken as booty (Deut. 20:14).[21] It can be debated, of course, which one of the genders had a better fate.

The next example of gender asymmetry involves a specific legal situation. If two men were fighting, and the wife of one of them came to his rescue and grabbed his opponent's genitals, her hand was to be cut off (Deut. 25:11–12).[22] This severe punishment likely reflects the view that the woman has breached fundamental rules of modesty, making physical contact bearing sexual connotation with a man other than her husband; this in spite of the fact that the woman was doing so while attempting to assist her husband. This ruling is somewhat reminiscent of MAL A §8, according to which a woman who has crushed a man's testicle during a quarrel was to have her finger cut off. The two statutes naturally differ: the biblical provision has a moral essence, while the Assyrian one relates to causing injury and bodily damage and hence belongs in the legal sphere of delict.[23]

The Hebrew Bible expresses several times an objection to the practice of magic. In Exod. 22:17 only female practitioners are mentioned, and as such they were to be put to death. In Lev. 20:27, however, both men and women appear as potential practitioners of magic, and as such they were to be executed. This can be assessed in comparison to MAL A §47 and NBL §7 discussed previously. In both cases it appears that different law compendia regarded the issue of gender differentiation and magic differently, and the discrimination against women in this regard did not form a consistent or definite phenomenon.[24]

Even though numerous commentaries exist on the Book of Exodus, they do not necessarily comment on gender and the practice of magic. In one of the commentaries that did address these issues, Houtman claimed that the prohibition on the practice of magic in Exod. 22:17, albeit referring explicitly to women alone, was a general prohibition referring to both sexes. The reason why the text was explicit in referring to women, according to him, was that women were the ones who practiced it more than men.[25] This conjecture seems unwarranted, as it contradicts and distorts the explicit contents of the biblical text. In addition, Houtman claimed that the term מכשפה did not denote a sorceress but a woman who tried to seduce men. In this sense, her actions did not necessarily involve the practice of magic per se, but were nonetheless condemned because they contradicted the chaste behavior expected from women.[26] This claim as well has no support whatsoever in the biblical text and remains implausible. The gender-based discrepancies between Exod. 22:17 and Lev. 20:27 result from the simple fact that these two rulings stem from two different biblical sources – like many other discrepancies between the different law collections of the Hebrew Bible, some of which are mentioned in the present book.

Gender equality among free persons

Despite the abundant evidence presented in the previous section concerning gender inequality in official law, much additional evidence exists for the opposite. Frequently enough statutes were formulated specifically in order to emphasize that the law was to be applied to men and women in the same way.

ANE law

A similar attitude to persons of either gender appears in many statutes. We may consider the following examples:

LLI §18 relates to estate owners, either male or female, who fail to pay their taxes. Similarly, MAL A §44 relates to an Assyrian, whether a man or a woman, who is held by another as a pledge for a debt. MAL A §47 relates to a person, either a man or a woman, engaged in the forbidden practice of magic. MAL C §§2, 3[27] relate to free people, either male or female, who are illegally sold for a debt or as a pledge.

Two groups of statutes in LE (§§26–28) and in HL (§§28a+b+c, 29) specified regulations of betrothal. All these statutes demonstrate explicitly that both parents of the bride were involved in the process, and both were required to give their consent to it. Both parents were legally liable in case the betrothal was canceled, and both were responsible for making the financial compensation involved. In these cases, therefore, the mother enjoyed a similar status of authority as the father.[28]

According to LH §§151–152, a married couple could grant each other an official document that protected one spouse against being held responsible for a debt incurred on the other spouse prior to the marriage (LH §151). However, if a debt was incurred during their marriage, both spouses were equally responsible for it (LH §152).

LH §§192–193 were meant to prevent adopted sons of childless palace attendants from repudiating their adoptive parents. Both statutes explicitly mention both father and mother as the adoptive parents whom the said child must not repudiate.[29]

LH §194 refers to a child given by his parents to a wet-nurse. Though the beginning of the statute only mentions the father as giving his son to the wet-nurse, two later references in the statute mention both parents as responsible for the child: "the wet-nurse contracts for another child without (asking) his father and his mother . . . because she contracted for another child without (asking) his father and his mother".[30] According to the statute, the wet-nurse should have consulted both parents of the child that was under her care. This statute, therefore, can be considered together with the rules of betrothal and their implications concerning mutual parental authority as discussed previously.

Three consecutive clauses in the MAL treat a person harming another person of the opposite gender: a woman hitting a man (MAL A §7) or crushing his testicles (MAL A §8), and a man sexually harassing[31] a woman (MAL A §9). For hitting a man, a woman would be fined and whipped; for crushing his testicles, she would be mutilated: one finger cut off in case one testicle was damaged, unknown organs mutilated in case both testicles were harmed. Similarly, a man sexually harassing a woman would be mutilated: the finger that harassed the woman was to be cut off, and the lip that kissed her was to be cut off. Both seem to have formed a talionic punishment. We can therefore see that in these examples from the MAL an offense bearing some sort of sexual nature would lead to a talionic punishment in the form of severe bodily mutilation, regardless of the gender of the perpetrator. Similar indifference as to a person's gender appears in the following statute – MAL A §10 – which describes a case of homicide, in which both perpetrators and victims are explicitly said to be either male or female.

Occasionally, statutes, which at first glance seem to have been meant to protect women, were actually related to sexual and moral chastity and thus reflected broader issues of social norms of morality. In this regard, it might be somewhat naïve to assume that the purpose of these statutes was to defend women.[32] Thus, MAL A §§17 and 18 deal with someone's accusations that another man's wife has been adulterous, and the accuser's punishment in case he cannot prove his claims. Were these statutes meant to protect Assyrian women from false accusations, or were they meant to signify and emphasize social morals of chastity? We should consider in this regard MAL A §19, in which a similar accusation – of being sexually penetrated – was directed at a man. The punishment for making such an accusation without being able to prove it was identical to the one specified in MAL A §18. The subsequent MAL A §20 banned homosexual intercourse and decreed a punishment for one of the men involved, but it is not clear whether the penetrating or penetrated one. Whether this statute proscribed homosexual intercourse per se, or rape, which in this case was homosexual,[33] it should be considered in the current discussion together with its three predecessors. It seems, therefore, that the MAL regarded both genders similarly in the case of (false) accusations of sexual misconduct. The one difference is that only men were regarded as possibly making such accusations, whether against men or women.

Finally, a few statutes of the HL explicitly treated men and women equally. For example, several statutes that specified the punishment for killing a free person (HL §§1, 3, 6) stated explicitly that the victim was either a man or a woman,[34] and the sentence was the same, whatever the victim's sex was. Furthermore, HL §19a, a statute dealing with the abduction of a Hittite person by a Luwian, referred to the victim as "whether man or woman".[35]

Biblical law

The Hebrew Bible required that each one of the genders would maintain its basic typical characteristics and not assume the typical characteristics that were perceived as defining the opposite gender. One of the famous examples in this regard is the prohibition of men and women from wearing each other's attire (Deut. 22:5).[36] One of the widely accepted explanations for this prohibition was offered by Mary Douglas, in her famous research of taboos and restrictions in the Hebrew Bible. She analyzed this restriction as part of her overall discussion of biblical rules of purity and pollution, arguing that the essence of such prohibitions in biblical law stemmed from an omnipresent social aspiration to maintain boundaries, whether symbolic or actual, between different categories. Mixture of categories, according to Douglas, was perceived by the Israelites as contrasting God's holiness and completeness and hence hybrids of all sorts were abominable.[37] The will to maintain proper social order was firmly based on categories of social status. Gender separation and segregation was but one aspect of this categorization. Other examples will now be considered.

A son who beat (Exod. 21:15) or cursed (Exod. 21:17, Lev. 20:9) his father or mother was to be executed. Similarly, a son who was disobedient and disrespectful to his father and mother was to be stoned to death by his entire community (Deut. 21:18–21), and the list of curses in Deuteronomy included the condemnation of anyone who disparages his father and mother (Deut. 27:16). These rules of respect towards parental authority gave someone's mother the same status of importance as his father.[38] This accords with the attitude reflected in several ancient Near Eastern statutes as discussed previously, especially LH §§192–193.

An ox that gored to death either a man or a woman was to be killed. In case the animal owner did not take due precautions, he could be executed or pay a fine (Exod. 21:28–31). As has already been noted,[39] the text makes it explicit that the victim may be male or female.

Biblical law banned several types of deviations from the customary worship of God, mentioning both males and females as possible perpetrators. Thus, in expressing utter objection to the practice of magic, HC prescribed execution for either a man or a woman who engages in it (Lev. 20:27).[40] In rejecting idolatry, DC demanded that any person – either man or woman – found worshiping any godly being other than YHWH is to be stoned to death (Deut. 17:2–5).[41] The phrase "either man or woman", or its close variants,[42] is repeated three times in this short passage. It seems safe to assume that the specific detailing of both genders in these rulings was meant to convey the notion of totality, viewing society as comprised of both genders. The mutual liability of both genders before the law here, therefore, forms another aspect of equality between them.

Gender inequality among slaves

Slaves formed a specific and clearly defined social group in the ancient world.[43] People could lose their freedom and thus become enslaved or be born into this status. The former case could be due to several reasons: clearing a debt, becoming a war captive or being sanctioned this way following the committing of a crime. The latter case was simpler: a person born to slave parents usually assumed their slave status. Either way, slavery – whether acquired or hereditary – formed a legal status in itself, and as such constituted a legal matter, involving an elaborate system of rules and regulations. Some of these highlighted the inequality between male and female slaves.

ANE law

Many of the statutes regarding slaves found in ancient Near Eastern law collections exhibit different stipulations for male and female slaves. One basic example involves the group of statutes relating to a man who causes a pregnant slave-woman to miscarry. Understandably, no such statutes could be stipulated for male slaves in a similar situation. According to various law collections, a man hitting a woman, thus causing her to miscarry, was required to pay compensation. In case the woman was a free one (LUN §33, LH §§209, 211, HL §17), the compensation was significantly higher than in case she was a slave (LUN §35, LH §213, HL §18). The fact remains that penalties existed even if the victim was a slave.[44] The law, therefore, provided a certain protection in these cases, even if the woman was of a low social status as a slave was. In case of miscarriage, the punishment should be viewed as financial compensation made to the male owner of the woman. In the case of death, the options vary: in case she was a free woman, the punishment was moral rather than financial: the killer (LUN §34,[45] MAL A §50) or his daughter (LH §210) would be executed.[46] If, however, she was a slave, another slave (LUN §36) or payment (LH §214) was to be given in her place, which seems to be a financial rather than a moral punishment. In all cases, the punishment cannot be viewed as a means of protecting women,[47] as much as a means to make amends for the man who lost his asset – her husband (in the case a of a free woman – though the husband is not actually attested in the texts) or owner (in the case of a slave-woman).[48]

Pregnancy differentiates between male and female slaves on another occasion: LH §§118 and 119 both relate to slaves being sold by their owner who ran into debt; the former treats both genders equally, but the latter details a specific case of a slave-woman who bore her master children. In this case, her owner was required to pay his debt and redeem her, a demand absent from LH §118.

A different issue in which gender inequality involved slaves can be seen in the matter of slaves insulting free persons. LUN §§30 and 31 specify the punishments for a slave-woman who insults or hits her superiors. We know of no identical statutes to have been stipulated for a male slave.[49]

LE §§22 and 23 mention a slave-woman being detained by a person because of claims the said person has against the slave's owner. No male slave is mentioned in similar circumstances (LE §24 mentions a free woman in a similar context, discussed previously).

LE §§33–35 refer to cases of a child of a slave-woman given to a free person for rearing or in adoption. In all cases, the child is regarded as his mother's rather than as his father's. The social status of the mother dictates her child's social status, regardless of the identity of the unmentioned father, whether the father was a slave himself or whether he was unknown. Adoption by a free person, however, alters the child's social status.[50]

An interesting case appears in LH §175, a statute that discusses the social status of children born to a slave father and a free mother ("of the *awīlum* class"). The statute declares that the children will be free and not slaves. It is thus demonstrated that in this case social status was determined on the basis of social, rather than gender, considerations. The superior social status of the free female parent prevailed over the superior gender status of the slave male parent. LH §176a ensured that the dowry of the said woman remain hers after her husband dies, as well as half of the financial assets they have accumulated during their marriage. The other half belongs to the slave owner. This division of the assets is documented in LH §176b as well.[51]

Finally, HL §24 specifies the penalties imposed on a person who harbors runaway slaves. In case the escaped slave was male, the penalty was double than in case it was a female slave.

Biblical law

According to the CC and the DC, a male slave was to be released after six years of servitude (Exod. 21:2, Deut. 15:12). However, in the former collection a female slave had no such privilege (Exod. 21:7),[52] unless she was mistreated by her master, in which case she was to be released free of charge (Exod. 21:11). Paul interpreted this statute as describing a situation in which a man sells his daughter in order to get married, in which case the privilege of redemption was avoided because "she is provided with the protection of marriage for life".[53] This does not explain why in the parallel statute of Deut. 15:17 the practice is different, and female slaves are explicitly granted their manumission.[54]

The different practices should be explained as the result of the different traditions reflected in the two sources of the law, E (CC) and D (DC). Indeed, Brin suggested that the explicit inclusion of female slaves in Deut. 15:17 was "intended to add another unit to a law that originally spoke about a male slave, now interpreted as applying by extension to females".[55] Jackson interpreted these different regulations as based on factors of "breeding" and sexual services. In his view, male slaves could be used for sexual services – that is, for producing offspring that will be permanently enslaved to the master – without having their status changed. Female slaves, conversely, could not be used for sexual services without having their status changed.[56] Jackson claimed that "[s]exual activity alters the status of the woman debt-slave, but not that of the male", and suggested that the background for the different statutes lay, at least in part, in the perception that the bond between a mother and her child was stronger than that of a father and his child.[57] According to Jackson, all this portrays the female slave as powerless and passive, because the male slave has a choice to be set free or remain with his master after six years, while the female slave is subject to her master's decision and will.[58]

Jackson claimed that the different rules for male and female slaves in Exodus reflect the original legislation, while the identical rule for both genders in Deuteronomy was stipulated later. The author of the later statute, according to Jackson,

> reconciled the apparent contradiction that he had created, by viewing the case of the *amah* as one where the permanency of slavery was the result of the *voluntary* act of the slave herself, as (for the *eved*) in Exod. 21.5–6.[59]

In Jackson's view, therefore, the authors of the DC were aware of the earlier tradition of the CC and provided their own exegesis, interpretation and harmonization of it.[60]

Numerous other commentators have addressed these differences between the statutes of Exodus and Deuteronomy in this respect. To mention but a few, Weinfeld assumed that these differences reflect the humane view of women in Deuteronomy,[61] while Rüterswörden claimed that they highlight the fact that in the minds of the authors of Deuteronomy, marriage could not be forced upon women – it had to be voluntary rather than compulsory.[62] Pressler, on the other hand, claimed that the statutes of Exodus dealt with a young woman purchased for concubinage, in contrast with those of Deuteronomy, and this is the source of the divergence.[63] According to Frymer-Kensky, the difference implies that at the time when the Deuteronomic rules were stipulated "there were no more *'amah* arrangements for acquiring wives".[64]

Gender equality among slaves

Similarly to free persons, slaves as well are attested in a relatively large number of statutes that convey a clear notion of gender equality. This equality did not necessarily result from positive attitudes: rather than reflecting any sense of parity or fairness, it usually stemmed from the simple indifference of law concerning these people. It did not matter whether the particular person was a man or a woman. The status of slave was the only lens through which the law considered some of the people discussed in the present section, and hence their gender association was immaterial. On other occasions, the wording of a given statute was explicit in stating that the law was applicable to both male and female slave.

ANE law

Some of the statutes seem to relate to male and female slaves identically. In such cases, it is specified explicitly that the statute refers to both a male and a female. A probable case in point is LUN §16, which determined a two silver-shekel prize for a person who brings a runaway slave back to his/her owner. A male slave is not actually attested in the pertinent text, due to a break at the beginning of the protasis, where only an escaped slave-woman is attested. However, the apodosis refers to the slave as sag, "person", a gender-neutral term that strongly implies that both male and female slaves were meant.

LLI §12 and LH §16 specify the punishment for a person who harbors a runaway slave, whether the slave was male or female, while LH §17 specifies the reward a person is to receive in case he seizes and returns a runaway slave, whether male or female, to their rightful owner. Similarly, LE §15 forbids a merchant or a woman-innkeeper to accept any commodity from a slave, either male or female. Various statutes (LE §§40, 49, 50, LH §§7, 118, 278–281, ESi/Ad/Aṣ §21, MAL C §1) mention in passing male and female slaves equally as commodities that can be purchased, sold for a debt or stolen, while several other statutes (LE §§51, 52, LH §15, MAL A §4) mention male and female slaves equally in relation to their slave status.

In the HL we encounter several statutes that explicitly treat male and female slaves equally. For example, a group of statutes dealing with the killing (HL §§2, 4) or injury (HL §§8, 12, 14, 16) of a slave made it explicit that the victim was either male or female (ARAD-*an na-aš-ma* GÉME-*an*, "(male) slave (acc.) or slave-girl (acc.)"), and the sentence was identical regardless of the slave's sex.

HL §196 states that if slaves – a man and a woman – committed an unspecified abominable act (*ḫurkel*),[65] they were to be separated, settled in different locations and a sheep is to be sacrificed as a ritual substitute for each one of them. Whatever the crime they committed was, the male and the female slaves were to be treated identically.

The instructions for the provincial post commanders (*auriaš išḫaš*, Akkadian *bēl madgalti*, "lord of the watchtower") make it clear that the duties of these officials included judging the local population under their responsibility, together with other officials and the elders. The post commanders were to make sure as soon as they returned to their hometown that no pending legal case remained unresolved. They were specifically instructed to deal with legal matters pertaining to slaves, whether male or female (CTH 261.I §40' 29–32).

Biblical law

As noted previously, Hebrew slaves were to be released after six years of servitude (Exod. 21:2, Deut. 15:12). Though in CC this privilege was exclusive to male slaves (Exod. 21:7), DC ordered the same for female slaves (Deut. 15:12, 17).

The punishment for a slave owner who caused significant damage to his slave was identical whether the slave was a man or a woman; the text explicitly mentioned both genders. A master who beat his slave – whether male or female – to death was to be punished (Exod. 21:20), while an eye or tooth injury – whether caused to a male or a female slave – was to be sanctioned by the release of the slave (Exod. 21:26–27).[66]

An ox that gored to death either a male or a female slave was to be killed, and his owner was to pay the slave owner a fine of 30 shekels of silver (Exod. 21:32).[67] Since the sanction was identical regardless of the slave's gender, it is clear that the law was meant to reflect a certain moral sense and not just an economic one. In other legal contexts that shed light on people's financial worth we do see a distinction between the genders.[68]

Protection of women

The closing section of this chapter differs from the previous sections that discuss gender inequality. It regards issues where women were favored and socially protected, for no obvious reason other than their sex. Gender inequality did not usually reflect a positive attitude towards women, but this is exactly what lies at the core of the current section. The structural division between discussions of free persons and of slaves is not maintained here, in contrast with the previous sections of this chapter.

ANE law

Since women were by far socially inferior to men, in certain circumstances statutes were set in order to protect them. This is apparent, for example, in the sphere of family law. On certain occasions husbands were obliged by law to protect their wives or provide for them even against these husbands' will, for example when taking a second wife (LH §148), having children from a woman other than their wife (LLI §27) or if their wife lost her favor with them (LLI §28).[69]

Another type of statute from the realm of family law that usually aims at offering certain legal protection or special support for women are statutes that pertain to widows. These are discussed in Chapter 3, and therefore will not be treated here. It should only be noted that the basic aim of such statutes was to secure the well-being of a married woman whose male provider – her husband – has perished. A similar type of statute to those protecting widows are statutes that were meant to protect women whose husbands were absent – either because they had voluntarily left the country or because they had involuntarily fallen into captivity. These statutes as well are discussed in Chapter 3. The essence of all these statutes was economic, and they were chiefly meant to regulate the economic affairs that ensued following the irregular situation in which the male financial provider of the family was absent, and a female – his wife – was to assume this position, without actually being able to do so.

We can note two examples from the MAL that clarify these matters. MAL A §45 secured the welfare of a woman whose husband was taken captive by an enemy and thus could not support her. The statute secured her provision for two years, during which her community was to support her, and released her from her marital duties after that period had ended, so that she could remarry as if she were a widow. Similarly, MAL A §46 secured the welfare of a widow by determining the identity of the male persons who were to be responsible for her provision after the death of her husband.

LH §127 stipulated a punishment for a man who falsely accused an *ugbabtu* priestess or the wife of another man. Since the statute also involved a priestess, and the punishment (shaving off half of the man's hair)[70] was not financial, it cannot be claimed that this statute was meant to protect the economic asset of the male authoritative figure of the offended woman, as was the case on certain other occasions. This statute was clearly concerned with the woman's reputation and was meant to protect it.

Another type of statute that aimed at protecting women in a specific situation referred to a case in which a man beat a pregnant woman, and thus caused her to miscarry her fetus. This group of statutes is discussed in pp. 34–35.

The Hittite instructions given to the provincial post commanders were discussed in pp. 37–38. As was mentioned, these officials were responsible – among other duties, and in cooperation with other officials and the local elders – to decide in legal issues in provincial towns. The post commanders were explicitly instructed to resolve any pending cases of slaves and of lone women[71] (CTH 261.I §40' 29–32), a clear indication that this part of the instructions was concerned with protecting otherwise defenseless women.

Biblical law

The first example we consider of the protection of women in biblical law belongs to the rules of slaves. A man who purchased a slave-woman in order to marry her, but then changed his mind, was to let her be redeemed; he was forbidden to sell her to foreigners (Exod. 21:8). Had he married another woman in her stead, he was still required to supply her with the three basic obligations of a husband to his wife: food, attire and sexual intercourse (Exod. 21:10). Failing to fulfill these three obligations would require him to release her free of charge (Exod. 21:11).[72]

This kind of legal protection granted to female slaves is unique to biblical law, and no parallels are known to it from any ancient Near Eastern collection.[73]

The next example belongs to the sphere of injury and homicide. If two men fight and one of them accidentally harms a pregnant woman, he is to be punished in accordance with the harm he causes: for miscarriage he shall pay a fine according to her husband's claims and the court decision; otherwise the punishment will be talionic: execution in case life is lost, bodily mutilation in case of injury (Exod. 21:22–25).[74]

The final example belongs to family law. A man who recently got married was exempt for one year from military service or other civil obligations, so that he could stay at home and make his newly wedded wife happy (Deut. 24:5).[75] It seems safe to assume that the purpose of this statute was to protect the patrilineal lineage by securing the man's right to establish an heir.[76]

Notes

1 *šumma a'īlu mārat a'īle imḫaṣma ša libbiša ultaṣlēš.*
2 For a discussion of this norm in the ancient Near East, see recently Stol 2016: 320–322.
3 For discussions of female professions in the ancient Near East and women's engagement in the ancient Near Eastern economy, see recently the pertinent contributions in Lion and Michele (eds.) 2016, especially the following: for the Ur III period: Garcia-Ventura 2016, Lafont 2016; for the Old Assyrian period: Michele 2016; for the Old Babylonian period: Démare-Lafont 2016 (this article also discusses evidence from other periods, from Ur III to the Neo-Babylonian); for the Middle Assyrian period (Nuzi): Lion 2016; for the Neo-Assyrian and Neo-Babylonian periods: Quillien 2016. Additionally, see recently the comprehensive discussion in Stol 2016: 339–390.
4 LUN §D9, LE §§15, 41, LH §§108, 109, 111, ESi/Ad/Aṣ §§16–18.
5 See Roth's (1998, esp: 178–181) important discussion of this statute, in relation to the so-called Nippur Homicide Trial and the trial case IM 28051 discussed previously (pp. 6–7). Roth concluded – based on her analysis of LH §109, the "Nippur Homicide Trial" and IM 28051 – that women were assumed to be potentially intimidated by men, and hence potentially ignored criminal acts, thereby causing legal obstruction. Such inferiority and intimidation, however, could not have been accepted as alleviating reasons for the obstruction of legal procedure, and the sanction such women might face was execution. Roth further suggested that the underlying social assumption as reflected in these texts was that women – especially wives – were obliged to maintain their chastity and loyalty to men – especially husbands – and that those who behaved in an "unwifely" manner – especially adulteresses – breached the most fundamental rules of society.
6 For a discussion of the woman-innkeeper, especially – but not exclusively – as evident in LH §110, see Roth 1999; see further discussions of this profession recently in Démare-Lafont 2016: 313–319 and Langlois 2016.
7 For discussions of the wet-nurse in Mesopotamia, see recently Démare-Lafont 2016: 319–323 and Stol 2016: 375–381.
8 For the implications of this statute for the regulation of family life, see p. 67.
9 For further discussion of the selling of family members / oneself into debt-slavery, see p. 49.
10 "himself" restored.
11 See further discussion in pp. 94–97.
12 Generally on the MAPD, see recently Stol 2016: 514–516, with previous literature.
13 *šu[mma] sinništum šî [pa]garša la iṣṣurma ana bīt šanîm īterub.*

14 For a discussion of veiling in Mesopotamia, Hatti and the Hebrew Bible, see recently Stol 2016: 22–28.
15 Statutes such as MAL A §§3, 4, 6 should probably be evaluated differently, because they describe a woman stealing from her own husband, thus the offense is domestic rather than public and different in its essence than the ones presently discussed.
16 *uššer ḫīṭāni ša* [*aššat a'īle*] *ša ina ṭuppe* [*šaṭruni*].
17 For further discussion of this issue, see p. 31.
18 Compare MAPD §7 discussed in pp. 28, 56.
19 For discussions on menstruation and the biblical prohibitions on sexual intercourse with a menstruating woman, see Wasserfall 1999 (ed.) and esp. Meacham 1999.
20 For discussions of these statutes, see Falk 1964: 113 and Fleishman 2002.
21 For a commentary on these statutes, see Tigay 2003: 189.
22 For discussions of this statute, see Paul 1990: 335–339, Pressler 1993: 74–77, 99 and Greengus 2011: 140–141.
23 For delict in biblical law, see Peled 2018.
24 For discussions on gender differentiation in the legal attitude to magic in the ancient Near East and the Hebrew Bible, see Westbrook 2006: 51–52 and Peled Forthcoming. Houtman (2000: 211) rejected the view that such gender differentiation actually existed; see what follows.
25 Houtman 2000: 211.
26 Houtman 2000: 212.
27 The section that mentions the male figure in MAL C §2 and the beginning of MAL C §3 is restored.
28 See further discussion in p. 64.
29 See further discussion of these statutes in p. 50.
30 *mušēniqtum balum abišu u ummišu ṣiḫram šaniamma irtakas . . . aššum balum abišu u ummišu ṣiḫram šaniam irkusu.*
31 Two felonies are performed: "laying a hand" and kissing. The former is said to be *kî būre ēpussi*, understood by Roth (1997: 157) as "attacking her like a rutting bull(?)". I assume that the bull metaphor expresses a sexual innuendo, and hence the laying of the hand was probably a forced fondling.
32 For the legal protection of women, see pp. 38–39.
33 See discussion in p. 101.
34 LÚ-*an našma* MUNUS-*an* (acc.) / LÚ-*aš našma* MUNUS-*za* (nom.).
35 LÚ-*an=aku* MUNUS-*an=aku*.
36 For discussions of this statute, see Römer 1974 and Harland 1998.
37 Douglas 1966.
38 See also in Paul 1970: 64–65, and, specifically on Exod. 21:17, in Levinson 2011: 211 n. 33. Pressler (1993: 108 n. 42) claimed that the rules of Deut. 21:18–21 (and also of Deut. 22:20–24, not discussed here) were an interpretation of the fifth and seventh commandments and as such formed sins against the community and God no less than crimes against individuals. For a discussion of Exod. 21:15, 17, see Fleishman 1992.
39 See, *inter alia*, Paul 1970: 80 n. 1 and Brin 1994: 91, 92 and n. 5.
40 But see differently in Exod. 22:17, where only women appear as possible practitioners of magic. See further discussion in p. 31.
41 For a commentary of this passage, see Tigay 2003: 162–163.
42 אִ֫ישׁ אוֹ-אִשָּׁה, "man or woman (nom.)" (Deut. 17:2), אֶת-הָאִישׁ הַהוּא אוֹ אֶת-הָאִשָּׁה הַהִוא, "that man or that woman (acc.)" (Deut. 17:5), אֶת-הָאִישׁ, אוֹ אֶת-הָאִשָּׁה, "the man, or the woman (acc.)" (Deut. 17:5).
43 The pertinent literature on slavery is vast; for discussions focusing on slavery and gender differentiation, see, *inter alia*, Pressler 1998 (esp. 168–169) and Westbrook 1998.
44 Exceptional in this regard is the MAL, which only considered free women in such cases (MAL A §§21, 50, 51; §52 was concerned with a prostitute, who, though socially inferior to a free married woman, was still superior to a slave).

45 In LUN §34 this is restored.
46 In LH §212 the sanction is financial, because the slain woman belonged to an inferior social status (*muškēnum* rather than *awīlum*), but the high fine (30 shekels of silver) was still larger than in the case of a slain slave-woman (20 shekels of silver; see LH §214).
47 For the protection of women, see pp. 38–39.
48 For causing miscarriage as a legal theme in ancient Near Eastern and biblical law, see Fuller 1994.
49 It is not impossible that such statutes originally appeared consecutively to the current ones, since at this point in the collection there is an estimated gap of some eight lines (see Civil 2011: 248). The lack of evidence, however, prevents the substantiation of any speculation in this regard.
50 See discussion in pp. 80–81.
51 See also in p. 61.
52 But see differently in Deut. 15:12, 17: "If your Hebrew brother or sister is sold to you . . . And you shall also do the same to your slave-woman", כִּי-יִמָּכֵר לְךָ אָחִיךָ הָעִבְרִי, אוֹ הָעִבְרִיָּה . . . וְאַף לַאֲמָתְךָ, תַּעֲשֶׂה-כֵּן.
53 Paul 1970: 53.
54 For these different rules stipulated for male and for female slaves, see also Schenker 1988, Pressler 1998 and Westbrook 1998. For a recent discussion of Deut. 15:12–18, see Rossi and Guillaume 2018.
55 Brin 1994: 38.
56 Jackson 2000: 193–197, 205.
57 Jackson 2000: 196.
58 Jackson 2000: 197.
59 Jackson 2000: 194.
60 Jackson 2000: 195.
61 Weinfeld 1972: 282.
62 Rüterswörden 2012: 64.
63 Pressler 1993: 2 n. 9, 1998. Westbrook (1998: 218–220) as well assumed that the Exodus statutes refer to concubinage rather than to marriage.
64 Frymer-Kensky 2003: 2008–2009.
65 For *ḫurkel*, see p. 104 n. 29.
66 For a commentary on these statutes, see Sarna 2003: 124 (on Exod. 21:20) and 127 (on Exod. 21:26–27); for discussions of these statutes, see Greengus 2011: 122–130, 169, 288.
67 For discussions of this statute, see Jackson 2006: 168 n. 254, 240–241 n. 4, 450, with previous literature, and Greengus 2011: 135, 173–174.
68 Lev. 27:3–7, see p. 48.
69 These statutes are discussed in what follows under family law, see pp. 72, 78, 82, 83.
70 *muttassu ugallabu*, "they shall shave half his (hair?)".
71 *wannummiya-*; see Kloekhorst 2008: 956–957, s.v. "*u̯annum(m)ii̯a-*" and Miller 2013: 385 n. 440.
72 For discussions of these statutes, see, *inter alia*, Paul 1969, Fleishman 2000 and Wright 2009: 144–145, 148.
73 See Paul 1970: 54. Partially similar statutes from different ancient Near Eastern law collections (see, e.g., LLI §§27, 28, LH §148) offer certain legal protection for free women but not for slaves.
74 For discussions of these statutes, see, *inter alia*, Paul 1970: 70–77, Westbrook 1986 and Lafont 1994: 108–118.
75 "So he shall make his wife which he took happy", וְשִׂמַּח, אֶת-אִשְׁתּוֹ אֲשֶׁר-לָקָח.
76 See, in this regard, Pressler 1993: 101.

Bibliography

Brin, Gershon. 1994. *Studies in Biblical Law: From the Hebrew Bible to the Dead Sea Scrolls*. Sheffield: JSOT.

Civil, Miguel. 2011. "The Law Collection of Ur-Namma". In *Cuneiform Royal Inscriptions and Related Texts in the Schøyen Collection*, edited by Andrew R. George. Bethesda, MD: CDL Press. Pp. 221–286.

Démare-Lafont, Sophie. 2016. "Women at Work in Mesopotamia: An Attempt at a Legal Perspective". In *The Role of Women in Work and Society in the Ancient Near East*, edited by Brigitte Lion and Cécile Michele. Berlin: De Gruyter. Pp. 310–327.

Douglas, Mary. 1966. *Purity and Danger: An Analysis of Concepts of Pollution and Taboo*. London; New York: Routledge.

Falk, Ze'ev W. 1964. *Hebrew Law in Biblical Times: An Introduction*. Jerusalem: Wahrmann Books.

Fleishman, Joseph. 1992. "Offences Against Parents Punishable by Death: Towards a Socio-Legal Interpretation of Ex. xxi 15, 17". *Jewish Law Annual* 10: 7–37.

Fleishman, Joseph. 2000. "Does the Law of Exodus 21:7–11 Permit a Father to Sell His Daughter to Be a Slave?" *Jewish Law Annual* 13: 47–64.

Fleishman, Joseph. 2002. "A Father's Versus a Husband's Authority to Annul a Vow (Numbers 30:4–17)". In *Jewish Law Association Studies 12, The Zutphen Conference Volume*, edited by Hillel Gamoran. Binghamton, NY: Global Publications, State University of New York at Binghamton. Pp. 71–78.

Frymer-Kensky, Tikva. 2003. "Israel". In *A History of Ancient Near Eastern Law*, edited by Raymond Westbrook. Leiden: Brill. Pp. 975–1046.

Fuller, Russell. 1994. "Exodus 21:22–23: The Miscarriage Interpretation and the Personhood of the Fetus". *Journal of the Evangelical Theological Society* 37/2: 169–184.

Garcia-Ventura, Agnès. 2016. "The Sex-Based Division of Work *Versus* Intersectionality: Some Strategies for Engendering the Ur III Textile Work Force". In *The Role of Women in Work and Society in the Ancient Near East*, edited by Brigitte Lion and Cécile Michele. Berlin: De Gruyter. Pp. 174–192.

Greengus, Samuel. 2011. *Laws in the Bible and in Early Rabbinic Collections: The Legal Legacy of the Ancient Near East*. Eugene, OR: Cascade Books.

Harland, Peter J. 1998. "Menswear and Womenswear: A Study of Deuteronomy 22:5". *Expository Times* 110: 73–76.

Houtman, Cornelis. 2000. *Exodus/Vol. 3, Chapters 20–40. Historical Commentary on the Old Testament*. Leuven: Peeters.

Jackson, Bernard S. 2000. *Studies in the Semiotics of Biblical Law*. Sheffield: Sheffield Academic Press.

Jackson, Bernard S. 2006. *Wisdom-Laws: A Study of the Mishpatim of Exodus 21:1–22:16*. Oxford: Oxford University Press.

Kloekhorst, Alwin. 2008. *Etymological Dictionary of the Hittite Inherited Lexicon*. Leiden: Brill.

Lafont, Bertrand. 2016. "Women at Work and Women in Economy and Society During the Neo-Sumerian Period". In *The Role of Women in Work and Society in the Ancient Near East*, edited by Brigitte Lion and Cécile Michele. Berlin: De Gruyter. Pp. 149–173.

Lafont, Sophie. 1994. "Ancient Near Eastern Laws: Continuity and Pluralism". In *Theory and Method in Biblical and Cuneiform Law: Revision, Interpretation, and Development*, edited by Bernard M. Levinson. Sheffield: Sheffield Academic Press. Pp. 91–118.

Langlois, Anne-Isabelle. 2016. "The Female Tavern-Keeper in Mesopotamia: Some Aspects of Daily Life". In *Women in Antiquity: Real Women Across the Ancient World*, edited by Stephanie L. Budin and Jean MacIntosh Turfa. London; New York: Routledge, Taylor & Francis Group. Pp. 113–125.

Levinson, Bernard M. 2011. *"The Right Chorale": Studies in Biblical Law and Interpretation*. Tübingen: Mohr Siebek.

Lion, Brigitte. 2016. "Work and Gender in Nuzi Society". In *The Role of Women in Work and Society in the Ancient Near East*, edited by Brigitte Lion and Cécile Michele. Berlin: De Gruyter. Pp. 354–370.

Lion, Brigitte and Michele, Cécile (eds.) 2016. *The Role of Women in Work and Society in the Ancient Near East*. Berlin: De Gruyter.

Meacham, Tirẓah. 1999. "An Abbreviated History of the Development of the Jewish Menstrual Laws". In *Women and Water: Menstruation in Jewish Life and Law*, edited by Rahel R. Wasserfall. Hanover, MA: Brandeis University Press. Pp. 23–39.

Michele, Cécile. 2016. "Women Work, Men Are Professionals in the Old Assyrian Archives". In *The Role of Women in Work and Society in the Ancient Near East*, edited by Brigitte Lion and Cécile Michele. Berlin: De Gruyter. Pp. 193–208.

Miller, Jared L. 2013. *Royal Hittite Instructions and Related Administrative Texts*. Atlanta, GA: Society of Biblical Literature.

Paul, Shalom M. 1969. "Exodus 21:10, A Threefold Maintenance Clause". *Journal of Near Eastern Studies* 28/1: 48–53.

Paul, Shalom M. 1970. *Studies in the Book of the Covenant in the Light of Cuneiform and Biblical Law*. Leiden: Brill.

Paul, Shalom M. 1990. "Biblical Analogues to Middle Assyrian Law". In *Religion and Law: Biblical-Judaic and Islamic Perspectives*, edited by Edwin B. Firmage, Bernard G. Weiss and John W. Welch. Winona Lake, IN: Eisenbrauns. Pp. 333–350.

Peled, Ilan. 2018. "The Laws of Delict in the Hebrew Bible and Their Ancient Near Eastern Forerunners: Analyzing and Comparing Social Attitude to Crime". *Journal for Semitics* 27/2: 1–22.

Peled, Ilan. Forthcoming. "Magic in the Hebrew Bible: The Legal Perspective". In *A Handbook of Ancient and Medieval Jewish Magic*, edited by Siam Bhayro and Ortal-Paz Saar. Leiden; Boston: Brill.

Pressler, Carolyn. 1993. *The View of Women Found in the Deuteronomic Family Laws*. Berlin: De Gruyter.

Pressler, Carolyn. 1998. "Wives and Daughters, Bond and Free: Views of Women in the Slave Laws of Exodus 21.2–11". In *Gender and Law in the Hebrew Bible and the Ancient Near East*, edited by Victor H. Matthews, Bernard M. Levinson and Tikva S. Frymer-Kensky. Sheffield: Sheffield Academic Press. Pp. 147–172.

Quillien, Louise. 2016. "Invisible Workers: The Role of Women in Textile Production During the 1st Millennium BC". In *The Role of Women in Work and Society in the Ancient Near East*, edited by Brigitte Lion and Cécile Michele. Berlin: De Gruyter. Pp. 473–493.

Römer, Willem H. P. 1974. "Randbemerkungen zur Travestie von Deuteronomy 22:5". In *Travels in the World of the Old Testament: Studies Presented to Professor M. A. Beek on the Occasion of His Sixty-Fifth Birthday*, edited by Mattieu S. H. G. H. van Voss, Philo H. J. Houwink ten Cate and Nico A. van Uchelen. Assen: Van Gorcum. Pp. 217–222.

Rossi, Benedetta and Guillaume, Philippe. 2018. "An Alternative Reading the Law of the Hebrew 'Slave' (Deuteronomy 15:12–18)". *Res Antiquae* 15: 3–30.

Roth, Martha T. 1997. *Law Collections from Mesopotamia and Asia Minor* (second edition). Atlanta, GA: Scholars Press.

Roth, Martha T. 1998. "Gender and Law: A Case Study from Ancient Mesopotamia". In *Gender and Law in the Hebrew Bible and the Ancient Near East*, edited by Victor H. Matthews, Bernard M. Levinson and Tikva S. Frymer-Kensky. Sheffield: Sheffield Academic Press. Pp. 173–184.

Roth, Martha T. 1999. "The Priestess and the Tavern: LH §110". In *Munuscula Mesopotamica: Festschrift für Johannes Renger*, edited by Barbara Böck, Eva Cancik-Kirschbaum and Thomas Richter. Kevelaer: Butzon and Bercker. Pp. 445–464.

Rüterswörden, Udo. 2012. "Gesetz und Erzählung anhand der Josephsgeschichte". In *Law and Narrative in the Bible and in Neighbouring Ancient Cultures*, edited by Klaus-Peter Adam, Friedrich Avemarie and Nili Wazana. Tübingen: Mohr Siebeck. Pp. 53–68.

Sarna, Nahum M. 2003. *The JPS Torah Commentary: Exodus*. Philadelphia, PA: Jewish Publication Society.

Schenker, Adrian. 1988. "Affranchissement d'une esclave selon Ex 21,7–11". *Biblica* 69: 547–556.

Stol, Marten. 2016. *Women in the Ancient Near East*. Berlin: De Gruyter.

Tigay, Jeffery H. 2003. *The JPS Torah Commentary: Deuteronomy*. Philadelphia, PA: Jewish Publication Society.

Wasserfall, Rahel R. (ed.) 1999. *Women and Water: Menstruation in Jewish Life and Law*. Hanover, MA: Brandeis University Press.

Weinfeld, Moshe. 1972. *Deuteronomy and the Deuteronomic School*. Oxford: Clarendon Press.

Westbrook, Raymond. 1986. "Lex Talionis and Exodus 21:22–25". *Revue Biblique* 93: 52–69.

Westbrook, Raymond. 1998. "The Female Slave". In *Gender and Law in the Hebrew Bible and the Ancient Near East*, edited by Victor H. Matthews, Bernard M. Levinson and Tikva S. Frymer-Kensky. Sheffield: Sheffield Academic Press. Pp. 214–238.

Westbrook, Raymond. 2006. "Witchcraft and the Law in the Ancient Near East". In *Recht gestern und heute: Festschrift zum 85. Geburtstag von Richard Haase*, edited by Joachim Hengstl and Ulrich Sick. Wiesbaden: Harrassowitz. Pp. 45–52.

Wright, David P. 2009. *Inventing God's Law*. Oxford: Oxford University Press.

2 The institutional perspective

Bureaucracy and economy: the palace, temple and beyond

Introduction

The impact of administrative and economic factors on social behavior is significant in assessing the nature of gender relations within a given society. Texts deriving from administrative and economic contexts supply us with valuable insights concerning the division of labor, tasks and functions, while various statutes and juridical texts addressing parallel issues complement the picture. These sources tell, frequently rather laconically, the stories of faceless and often unnamed people. We can thus learn whether gender played a role in determining values, wages and rates, and in assigning specific people to specific tasks.

In this chapter we distinguish between two different arenas: the bureaucratic – a sphere that encompassed the organizational systems of the palace and the temple – and the economic – a sphere that covered social occurrences that took place outside of the institutions of the palace and the temple but were at times still related to them.

The chapter begins with an assessment of the economic sphere: salaries and wages earned and paid by different people, and the differences between the genders in this realm. We continue with an overview of gender-related factors involved in debt-slavery.

The next topic involves the palace and certain adoption practices of its personnel. Moving on to the sphere of the temple, religion and cult provide a unique niche for examining the formality of gender relations. Similar to juridical and legal systems, they were organized in structured hierarchical models of control and power relations. A special place was reserved for women in various religious and cultic institutions, allowing them a role of importance in society. Statutes and regulations were sometimes stipulated in order to embed these roles within formal social reality. One notable example involves the *nadītu* priestesses of Old Babylonian Sippar, whose religious role was accompanied by a system of legal regulations.[1]

Another aspect of the relation between gender and administration is the issue of gender identity in palace bureaucracy. This issue is manifested in the employment of eunuchs as high officials in royal courts across the ancient world. Men's prowess in the ancient world was frequently associated with sexual virility. Castration, however, altered the male person's biology to the extent that it did not match his original sex anymore, thus causing a conflict between his gender and sexual images. Since eunuchs were prominent figures in the Neo-Assyrian court, the question must be asked: how did these men, presumably considered physically flawed, gain social acceptance? These high officials are known to have occasionally led the army in battle. How did their soldiers accept their authority, given their allegedly flawed manliness? This case demonstrates the complexity of conflicting social conventions, as manifested in the function of ancient bureaucracies. The pertinent legal evidence in this case is limited to several sources, all predating the first millennium.[2]

Salaries, wages and people's value

The first topic in this chapter involves certain aspects of the economy that belong to an administrative system that existed outside the palace and the temple, two institutions that lie at the core of the sections to follow. Here we survey the evidence concerning salaries, wages and the value of people according to their gender.

ANE law

One of the ways for the modern researcher to assess gender differentiation in ancient times is to examine people's value. Put simply, men and women had a different economic value in society. This can be seen in the different wages men and women earned when performing similar tasks and the different prices paid for male or female slaves. Since the evidence from the law collections at our disposal is meager, and only derives from the Ur III and Hittite periods, it must be taken with caution and not as necessarily representative of Mesopotamian and ancient Near Eastern social and economic history at large.

LUN §D8 specified the wages of certain female and male workers. Its fragmentary state, however, allows for different reconstructions and understandings of it. According to Civil's edition, the daily wages of two different types of female weavers were 20 silas of grain, while the daily wages of male doormen[?][3] were 6 silas and the daily wages of their (female[?])[4] helpers were 1 sila.[5] According to Wilcke, however, the said wages were monthly rather than daily.[6] As important as the differences between Civil's and Wilcke's interpretations are, they are of little significance for the present study. Be the case as it may, this statute clearly indicates that, at least in this case, women who performed valued tasks earned higher wages than men who performed lesser ones; whether their wages were monthly or daily is immaterial as long as the duration was identical for all tasks performed by both genders. In this case we can see that the essence of the task determined its performer's salary and not the performer's gender.

LUN §D9 detailed the payments and taxes involved in a credit-sale of beer by a woman-innkeeper. This statute demonstrates how these women were integrated into the economic system, hardly a trivial matter, given the usual relatively low socioeconomic status of women. An innkeeper had to operate as an independent entrepreneur, and such independence was very rare for women. Even though both men and women could be innkeepers, only female ones are referred to in the law collections. This fact emphasizes the unique situation of these women, uniqueness that required special statutes to be issued in order to regulate their activities. Whether banning or authorizing the affairs of these women, the legislators saw no need to issue parallel statutes for male innkeepers. The women-innkeepers' uniqueness, no doubt, stemmed from their relative independence, which was otherwise usually reserved for men alone.[7]

The last statute of this collection to be considered in the present discussion is LUN §E2, which detailed the payments received by a woman for nursing a man's child for three years. The same statute also determined the yearly payment for a wet-nurse. As discussed in Chapter 1, this profession was obviously exclusive to women and sheds light on a specific socioeconomic niche they filled.

We now turn to the Hittite culture. In the HL, women were paid lower salaries than men for performing the same task for the same duration. For example, a person who harbored a runaway slave was required to pay a fine equivalent to one month's working wage: 12 shekels of silver in case of a man, but only 6 shekels of silver in case of a woman (HL §24). Other statutes specify different wages, but all maintain the same rule, according to which men earned significantly higher salaries than women. For one month's work a man was paid one shekel of silver, but a woman was only paid half a shekel of silver (HL §150). For agricultural work a man was paid 1,500 liters of barley for three months (HL §158a), while a woman was paid 600 liters for the same work and time span (HL §158b). Arguably, men could work harder because their physical strength was supposedly superior to women's, but the statutes only refer to the type of the task and its duration, and hence there is no reason to assume that the eventual outcome of women's work was significantly less than that of men's. The wages, however, were markedly different, which could not have resulted from significant differences between the work men and women could perform. In contrast, a man who has bought an unskilled person was to pay the same price – 20 shekels of silver – whether the person he purchased was a man or a woman (HL §177).

Biblical law

The concluding chapter of Leviticus includes a section that sets the rates of donations given to the temple, based on the value of people of various ages (Lev. 27:3–7). According to these specifications, a man aged 20 to 60 years was worth 50 shekels of silver (Lev. 27:3), while a woman of the same age group was worth 30 shekels (Lev. 27:4); a boy aged 5 to 20 years was worth 20 shekels, and a girl was worth 10 shekels (Lev. 27:5); a male child aged one month to 5 years was worth 5 shekels while a female child of the same age was worth 3 shekels (Lev. 27:6); a man older than 60 was worth 15 shekels, and a woman was worth 10 (Lev. 27:7).[8]

According to these stipulations, females earned significantly less – usually around half – than males in each age group. This is paralleled by the evidence from the HL, according to which women were to earn salaries half as high as men did.

Selling into debt-slavery[9]

The themes of law, gender and the status of slaves are discussed elsewhere in this book. The current section focuses specifically on the economic aspects of slavery, as evident from the Old Babylonian and Middle Assyrian periods and the biblical CC.

ANE law[10]

Several statutes in LH addressed the issue of debt-slavery. These statutes detail various possible cases. In the first of these cases, in order to cope with his debts, a man could sell his wife, son or daughter for a period of three years, after which they were to be released (LH §117). In a different case, a man could sell his slave, whether male or female, for the same purpose, but in this case the buyer was entitled to extend the slavery period beyond three years and even sell the said slave (LH §118). A third case related to the sale of a slave-woman who bore children to her original owner. In this case, he was required to pay off his debt and redeem her (LH §119). According to ESi/Ad/Aṣ §20, a man who ran into debt could sell his wife, children or himself.[11] From a different angle of the debt-slavery topic, LH §151 secured that creditors did not seize a husband or a wife for a debt of their spouse that was created prior to the marriage. LH §152 related to a debt that was created after the marriage took place; in this case, both husband and wife were responsible for clearing the debt; see further discussion of these statutes in pp. 32, 67–68.

MAL A §32, however, determined that a married woman who resided in her father's household was responsible for the debts of her husband. The statute did not mention whether the debts were created before or after the marriage took place. Be that as it may, this situation is different than described in the LH – and not in the woman's favor. MAL C §2 forbade a man to sell another man's son or daughter who resided in his household. Similarly, MAL C §3 forbade such a sale into a foreign land.

Biblical law

Debt-slavery is mentioned several times in the Hebrew Bible. Exod. 21:2–11 specified the rules of conduct for male and female Hebrew persons who were sold into slavery. These rules are repeated in Deut. 15:12–18. As in LH §117, a person in debt could sell his family members – CC specifically mentions his daughter – to clear his debts, but they were to be released after a period. In LH §117 the period was three years, while in Exod. 21:2 the period ended after six years. The biblical law of Exodus only allowed male slaves to be released, while according to Exod. 21:7 females were to remain enslaved. Had the slave refused to leave his master, his enslavement was to be perpetuated (Exod. 21:5–6). The statement in Deuteronomy that redemption was applicable for male and female slaves alike (Deut. 15:17) contradicts the parallel statute in Exodus, according to which the option of redemption was not open to female slaves at all. The discrepancy derives from the different sources of CC and DC; see discussion in pp. 35–36.

Adoption by unique palace personnel

This section involves a phenomenon attested in the Mesopotamian laws but not in the biblical ones: male and female palace attendants who did not produce descendants and hence were supplied by the law with an institutionalized solution, in the form of adoption regulations. The evidence is restricted to three statutes from the Old Babylonian collection of LH and should therefore not be taken as representative of Mesopotamian history at large. The matter of adoption is discussed in Chapter 3, as part of the assessment of familial regulations. However, when the adopter or adoptee mentioned in the law bears a specific professional title, he or she ceases to be regarded – from the legislative point of view – as an individual person, and becomes part of the institutional system. The three statutes presented in what follows should be evaluated within this context.

ANE law

A group of three statutes in LH – §§187, 192 and 193 – deals with the adopted children of male or female palace personnel: the male *girseqû* and the female *sekretu*. LH §187 states that an adopted child reared by a *girseqû* or a *sekretu* cannot be reclaimed by his biological parents. The two other statutes elaborate on the consequences of the breaching of this ruling. LH §192 prescribes the cutting off of the child's tongue in case he denounces his adoptive parent, while LH §193 prescribes the plucking of his eye in case he does not only denounce his adoptive parent, but further, returns to the house of his biological parents. The harsh measures specified in these statutes were clearly meant to secure the existence of heirs for the *girseqû* and the *sekretu*, who served in the palace and, in all likelihood, could not have biological children of their own.[12]

The emphasis on the importance of adoption by both the *girseqû* and the *sekretu* is very suggestive as to the gender roles they could – or could not – perform. We have ample evidence that the *girseqû* was typically childless, but whether this childlessness derived from castration or social circumstances is unclear. Since the *sekretu* was a female, it is clear that no physical condition could be imposed upon her in order prevent her from bearing children. Having offspring was a highly significant issue in Mesopotamia and formed one of the most important aspects of fulfilling someone's gender expectations, whether male or female. The inability to perform this capacity was considered to contrast with the normative gender image, and when it was institutionalized it labeled the individual as belonging to a distinct gender class. This is echoed in LH – §§187, 192 and 193, which supply a legal framework for this institutionalized gender otherness.[13]

Biblical law

The statutes discussed previously have no comparable evidence in the Hebrew Bible. Offices such as those of the *girseqû* and the *sekretu* are unattested, and adoption at large did not constitute a legal issue to be found in the biblical legal corpus.

Female cult personnel

The Mesopotamian cultic system included a vast number of professional titles, designating both men and women. Several statutes regulated the activities and expected conduct of many of the female cult attendants. Most ancient Near Eastern law collections included references to female cult personnel,[14] though only in LH are these regulations found abundantly. Most of these statutes pertain to economic matters such as property ownership and inheritance rights and were thus meant to decide the socioeconomic conditions of these women. No parallel statutes were stipulated for male cult attendants because, as men, their socioeconomic conditions did not differ from those of other men. Only female cult attendants differed from other women in this respect, and hence required official rules to determine their special status in society as women who were engaged in the cultic system. Biblical law, on the other hand, mostly ignored this issue, including only one statute that referred to the cult attendant known as *qadēš* (masc.)/ *qĕdēšā* (fem.).

ANE law

Female cult personnel are already attested in the earliest Mesopotamian law collection, and even in Middle Assyrian and Hittite royal instruction texts.[15] The earliest relevant reference is LUN §12, which related to a man who has sexual intercourse with a high priestess (ereš-diĝir). Civil was hesitant in restoring the unclear portions on the text, and hence offered two possible interpretations for this statute: either punishment for the man who had intercourse with the high priestess or a regulation, such as succession or inheritance rights, regarding their children.[16] Wilcke, however, in the most recent treatment of this statute, was more decisive and offered a plausible restoration and interpretation, according to which this statute prescribed execution by burning for both man and priestess.[17]

The next mention of female cult attendants in a law collection is LLI §22, which determined the division of inheritance between brothers and their sister who became a priestess, either an *ugbabtu, nadītu* or *qadištu*. She was regarded as an equal heir and was thus to receive an equal share of the inheritance to her brothers.

In the LH we encounter on various occasions references to several titles of female cult personnel: *kulmašītu, nadītu, qadištu* and *ugbabtu*, and in similar contexts the *sekretu* – a female palace attendant, the *šugītu* – a female designation of an unclear nature,[18] and the male *girseqû*, who was typically a childless palace attendant.

Some of these statutes supply valuable information concerning the socioeconomic status of the *nadītu* in Old Babylonian times. For example, in LH §40 she was portrayed as the owner of a field, similar to a male merchant. Less positively, LH §110 banned a *nadītu* or an *ugbabtu* who did not reside in the cloister from entering a tavern and drinking beer therein. The punishment prescribed for a perpetrator was harsh: she was to be burned.[19] As mentioned in Chapter 1, a more favorable statute – LH §127 – was meant to protect an *ugbabtu* (and similarly, a married woman) from unsubstantiated accusations.

LH §137 refers to a man who divorces either a *šugītu* who bore him children (*ša mārī uldušum*) or a *nadītu* who provided him with them (*ša mārī ušaršûšu*). The distinction between the *šugītu* and the *nadītu* in this case is clear and highlights the fact that *nadītu*s typically did not produce children of their own. The statute orders that the man returns his divorced wife her dowry and also gives her half of the property, as well as their children. When the children grow up and become the rightful owners of the property, they are to grant their mother a share equal to that of an heir, and she is then entitled to marry again as she pleases. Giving a divorced wife back her dowry was not exceptional,[20] but giving the divorced *šugītu*/*nadītu* half of the property was.

The group of statutes LH §§144–147 relates to the status of a married *nadītu* in comparison with other, secondary, wives of her husband. The first two of these statutes regulate the relationship of a *nadītu* and a *šugītu* in this respect. LH §144 addresses a situation in which a *nadītu* gives her husband a slave-woman who bears him children. If the husband then wishes to marry a *šugītu*, the statute forbids him to do so. In contrast, LH §145 addresses a situation in which the *nadītu* did not provide her husband with children, in which case he was indeed allowed to marry a *šugītu* if he wanted. Even then, however, the *šugītu* could only have the status of a secondary wife, and not equal to that of the *nadītu*. LH §146 details yet a third situation: the *nadītu* gives her husband a slave-woman who bears him children and subsequently aspires to have an equal status to her *nadītu* mistress. The statute forbids the *nadītu* to sell the slave-woman, because she bore the children. On the other hand, the statute overrules the slave-woman's aspirations and perpetuates her slave status. In the fourth situation, described in LH §147, the said slave-woman did not bear children, and hence her *nadītu* mistress is allowed to sell her.

What is common to all the statutes discussed previously is that they permitted polygamy because a *nadītu* did bear her husband children. As is discussed in what follows, polygamy is addressed elsewhere in the LH. When it did not involve female cult personnel like the *nadītu*, it was allowed when someone's first wife was immoral and disrespectful to him (LH §141), or if she was struck by a skin disease (LH §148–149).

Another group of statutes in this collection, LH §§178–184, relates to the subsistence and inheritance rights of several female cult personnel. Interestingly, apart from one exception (LH §182), this group was structured in pairs, in which the first statute introduces a case, to which the following statute presents a certain complementary part.

LH §178 refers to a woman that could either be an *ugbabtu*, *nadītu* or *sekretu*. According to this statute, if her father awarded her a dowry, but did not grant her permission to lease her assets to whomever she pleases, her brothers may take possession of these assets and provide her with her subsistence. If her brothers fail to do so, she was entitled to award these assets to a tenant, who in return would provide her with her subsistence, and after her death these assets would return to the possession of her brothers. The point of this statute is that the woman could enjoy the assets her father gave her, but she could not sell these assets outside of the family. The following statute (LH §179) is identical, but with the exception that her father did grant her permission to lease the assets, in which case her brothers were not allowed to interfere.

LH §180 omits the *ugbabtu*, but probably was meant to relate to her as well, since it continues the previous two statutes. It presents a case in which the father awarded no dowry to the said daughter, and she was hence entitled to a share similar to that of any of the other heirs, but she could not sell it outside of the family. Thus, her status was similar to that of her male brothers, with the exception that she could not sell her share. LH §181 is similar to LH §180, but it refers to a slightly different group of titles: *nadītu*, *qadištu* and *kulmašītu*, whom their father dedicated to a deity without granting them a dowry. They were entitled to a share of one-third of the inheritance, but were not allowed to sell it. Both statutes declare that the share belongs to the priestesses' brothers, that is, after her death her brothers (or, presumably, their rightful heirs) will get it. In this sense, this inheritance should be viewed as a deposit.

LH §182 deals with a specific case that differs from the previous ones: that of a *nadītu* dedicated to Marduk in Babylon, who did not receive any dowry. She was entitled to a share identical to that of any of her brothers and was allowed to give it in lease as she pleases. We can thus see that these specific women enjoyed a unique socioeconomic legal status, even within the group of female cult attendants.

LH §183 relates to a different title – *šugītu* – who was awarded a dowry by her father and was given to a man in marriage. In this case, she was deprived of any right of inheritance from her family assets. According to the following statute, LH §184, in case the *šugītu* was not awarded a dowry and given in marriage, her brothers were to grant her a dowry and give her in marriage. So in principle these statutes are identical and present the same situation. In case the procedure detailed in the former statute was not materialized, the latter statute was meant to secure it.

From the Middle Assyrian period we have references to female cult attendants in the MAL as well as in the MAPD. MAL A §40 presents an elaborate set of regulations concerning the requirement for various classes of women to be veiled or unveiled when in public. One of these classes is the *qadiltu*. In case she was married, she had to be veiled, similarly to any other woman. An unmarried *qadiltu*, however, was to remain unveiled, in contrast with other unmarried women, who were designated in this statute as the daughters of a man. The difference probably lies in the fact that an unmarried *qadiltu* did not belong to a governing male figure (father), since she was dedicated to the temple.

The *qadiltu* was further mentioned in MAPD §1, together with the midwife. However, the broken context prevents a clear understanding of the nature of this order. It was related to her entrance and departure to/from the palace, probably in some prohibiting context.

Turning to Hittite sources, Queen Ašmunikkal's edict to the personnel serving in the institution of the royal mausoleum included a stipulation that young women could be sent as brides to the men serving as the mausoleum personnel, but no men or women serving there were allowed to be married outside of the institution (CTH 252 13–15).

Biblical law

The myriad Mesopotamian terms for female cult attendants have no parallels in the Hebrew Bible. A rare exception is the much-discussed *qĕdēšā*, who had a masculine counterpart, the *qadĕš*, literally "holy one". The *qadĕš*/*qĕdēšā* as allegedly cult prostitutes are attested in Deuteronomy 23:18, 1 Kings 14:24, 15:12 and 22:47, 2 Kings 23:7, Hosea 4:14 and Job 36:14. Other than one occurrence, however, none of these references is of a legal nature, and thus the legal status of these cult attendants – whether engaged in sexual activity or not – is hard to determine. The sole exception is the legal provision in Deut. 23:18, which laconically proscribes any Israelite woman or man from becoming a *qĕdēšā* (fem.) or *qadĕš* (masc.). Though this verse establishes the legal status of these professions as illicit, it still does not clarify their exact nature or detail any roles or tasks that might have been attached to them. These terms, however, are obvious cognates of the Akkadian feminine *qadištu*/*qadiltu* and should be interpreted as somehow related to it.

The discussion of the alleged "sacred prostitution" in the ancient Near East and the Hebrew Bible falls beyond the scope of this book.[21] It should be noted, however, that the biblical terms *qadĕš*/*qĕdēšā* were interpreted by certain scholars as referring to male and female cult attendants who were engaged in sexual activity as part of their cultic performance.[22]

Eunuchs and castration

Castration, as a measure altering the basic sexual physiques of the individual, inevitably causes significant change to someone's gender image, as a consequence of the physical alteration. It thus generates unique social circumstances that, at times, call for the stipulation of official regulations. In this section we examine the evidence for such regulations.

ANE law

The topic of eunuchs and castration in the ancient Near East has been discussed by scholars extensively. Most scholars agree that certain palace officials were indeed castrated, especially those designated as lú-sag (Sumerian/logogram in non-Sumerian texts)/*ša rēši* (Akkadian) in Middle and Neo-Assyrian times. Whether the same titles designated eunuchs or non-castrated palace officials in other periods or cultures (especially Old and Middle Babylonian Mesopotamia and Hatti; in texts from the latter only the logographic term lú-sag is attested) is harder to answer with any certainty, nor is it entirely clear whether other titles of Mesopotamian palace officials (most notably *girseqû* and tiru/*tīru*) designated eunuchs.[23] In what follows we examine the pertinent evidence in this respect from several ancient Near Eastern sources: Old Babylonian, Middle Assyrian and Hittite Law collections and royal edicts.

We begin with the references to the *girseqû* in the LH. As is discussed previously, three statutes in this collection – LH §§187, 192 and 193 – highlight the importance of adoption by these palace officials, which suggests that they did not have biological children. While this does not prove that they were castrated,[24] it leaves the possibility open.

More concrete evidence for castration – albeit in a different context altogether – appears in MAL A. Castration as a corporal punishment was an extremely rare sanction in the ancient Near East and is only known from two statutes in this collection. In both cases castration was imposed as a talionic punishment for sexual misbehavior: a man who fornicated with the wife of another man could face execution or facial mutilation and castration (MAL A §15), while a man engaged in homosexual intercourse[25] was to be sodomized and castrated (MAL A §20).

Roughly contemporaneous with the MAL, or slightly later, the collection of royal edicts known as "Middle Assyrian Palace Decrees" (MAPD) contains several references to officials who in all likelihood were eunuchs serving in the palace.[26] In MAPD §8 a passage relates to some of the court attendants (*mazziz panūte*, "those who stand in front (of the king)"), who are being checked, probably to make sure that their castration procedure was adequate. In case it was not, they were required to undergo the procedure again.[27] MAPD §20 reiterates these rules by stating that palace attendants (*mazziz panūte ša šarre*, "royal court attendants",[28] and *širkū ša ṣābē ekalle*, "dedicatees of the palace personnel") were to undergo an inspection before entering the palace, and, if required, they were to undergo the procedure of castration again. MAPD §9 orders that a royal eunuch (*ša rēš šarre*) may not enter the women's quarters in the palace without the supervision of high officials. In MAPD §21 royal eunuchs (*ša rēš šarrānu*) are jointly referred to together with court attendants (*mazziz panūte*) and dedicatees (*širkū*) as persons forbidden to eavesdrop on the palace women, a felony punishable by 100 blows and the cutting off of one ear. Royal eunuchs (*ša rēš šarrānu*) are further mentioned in MAPD §22, however, in a broken context, which does not supply further information on them.

A somewhat similar text is the Hittite compilation of instructions given for palace servants designated by the logographic term lú-sag, a text that is seen by some as a royal oath rather than purely an instructions compilation. Either way, it is debated whether these officials were castrated or not. There is no clear evidence against this assumption, other than the fact that no clear attestation of their actual castration exists. The evidence in favor of viewing them as eunuchs is meager and circumstantial and can be summarized as follows: in contemporaneous Assyria the title they bore in all likelihood designated eunuchs, their attestations in the Hittite instructions are similar in many respects to the attestations of their Mesopotamian counterparts in the MAPD and elsewhere, they probably served as guardians of the Hittite royal women's quarters and had access to the king's inner chambers, capacities that in other periods and cultures were at times fulfilled by eunuchs.[29]

Biblical law

Bodily blemish was considered negatively in the Hebrew Bible, as contradicting purity and holiness. Accordingly, in DC men whose genitals – whether testicles or penis – were damaged were excluded from the congregation (Deut. 23:2).[30] Tigay suggested that this statute may have reflected the Israelite notions that associated emasculation with paganism, "or because of revulsion against mutilation".[31] Castration in itself, however, was not banned by law.

We should further mention in this context the biblical terms *sārîs/sārīsŷm* (sg./pl.) (סריס/סריסים), understood by many scholars to designate eunuchs. These terms are obviously related to the Akkadian *ša rēši*, and there are certain hints that they indeed referred in the Hebrew Bible to castrated palace officials.[32] However, unlike in Mesopotamia, they never appear in legal contexts and no regulations were stipulated for them, and they are hence not discussed here any further.

Purity of palace and temple personnel

The importance of maintaining the clean and pure state of palace and temple officials in the ancient world resulted from the belief that defilement had both physical and spiritual aspects, and therefore dirt and pollution were unholy, contaminating and hazardous. It was thus essential to establish rules of conduct for such officials and embed these rules within the legal system.

ANE law

No statute in any ancient Near Eastern law collection refers to purity requirements of officials, whether of the palace or the temple, but some evidence relevant to this topic appears in several royal decrees from the Middle Assyrian and Hittite kingdoms.

MAPD §7 excluded menstruating women from the proximity to the king at times when sacrificial procedures were about to be performed. This ruling pertains to cultic purity and reflects the perception of menstruating women as impure.[33]

The Hittite instructions to the temple personnel required these cult attendants who had sexual intercourse in their home to bathe afterwards before returning to sleep in the temple (CTH 264 §10' ii 73"–iii 2). Failing to bathe after having sex, and thus performing the temple work in an impure condition, would lead to the execution of the perpetrator and of any person who knew of the offense without reporting it (CTH 264 §14' iii 68–83). These regulations reflect the perception that sexual intercourse – or probably more accurately, the bodily fluids involved – were perceived as impure.

According to the Hittite instructions given to palace servants concerning maintaining the king's purity, some officials were not punished alone for offenses they committed. Rather, their wives and children were punished with them, even though they had nothing to do with the offense. For example, a member of the palace kitchen personnel who was found to be guilty of causing impurity to the king

(CTH 265 §7" 17'–19'), a maker of the royal step-coach who used hide of inferior quality than required without reporting it (CTH 265 §10" 9'–13', §12" 18'–20'), and a palace chef whose offense is unknown because of breaks in the text (CTH 265 §§16"–17" 1'–7'). The sanction these persons suffered together with their wives and children was said to have been an ominous fate to be inflicted by the gods, but it presumably had an earthly form no less than a divine one.

Both men and women were required to remain in a pure bodily state when engaged in cultic performance. Failure to do so would result in harsh sanctions and on one occasion was not limited to the male perpetrator alone but also included his wife and family. Possible causes of such defilement were bodily fluids that were perceived as impure, such as menstruation blood, semen and sexual secretions. All these stipulations appeared in royal edicts, but none was included in any of the law collections.

Biblical law

Because of their holiness,[34] priests were required to marry only virgin girls (Lev. 21:13, 14). Hence, they were forbidden to marry prostitutes, divorcées and widows (Lev. 21:7, 14), who could not have been virgins. Further, the daughter of a priest was forbidden to engage in prostitution; the penalty she would face was execution, because in such acts she has defiled her father (Lev. 21:9). We see in all these commandments a strong link between sexual intercourse – and probably more accurately, semen and bodily secretions – and defilement, from which the priestly personnel were required to keep away.[35]

The daughter of a priest who has married a man who was not a priest himself was excluded from eating of the sacred donations the priests received (Lev. 22:12). Had she divorced or become a widow without having offspring and returned to her father's house, she was to eat of his food but no stranger was to do the same (Lev. 22:13). These rules are probably also reminiscent of the topics discussed previously, of purity among the priestly circles.[36]

Notes

1 The pertinent literature on the *nadītu* is vast; the classic research is still Harris 1963.
2 For eunuchs and castration in the ancient Near East and the Hebrew Bible, see Peled 2013, 2016: 203–237 and 2017: 128–134.
3 The term is reconstructed; see explanation in Civil 2011: 280.
4 Civil 2011: 280.
5 Civil 2011: 244, 251; commentary on p. 280.
6 Wilcke 2014: 565–566.
7 For a discussion of the woman-innkeeper in this and other statutes, see pp. 27, 40 n. 6.
8 For a discussion of these rules, see Wenham 1978.
9 For a general discussion of debt-slavery in the ancient Near East and the Hebrew Bible, see Westbrook 1995, esp. pp. 1643–1645, 1651–1653 and 1656–1660.
10 For a discussion of women given for debt-slavery in the ancient Near East, see recently Stol 2016: 311–320.
11 "himself" restored.

12 See discussion in Peled 2016: 244–246. For the mention of the *sekretu* in other statutes of LH, alongside *ugbabtu* and *nadītu*, see pp. 51–52.
13 For the *girseqû* and his gender identity, see Peled 2016: 239–252.
14 Only LE and NBL contained no such statutes.
15 The pertinent Mesopotamian terms have been discussed extensively; for the most recent comprehensive discussions, see Stol 2016: 584–604 (on the *nadītu*), 567–568, 579–580 (on the *ugbabtu*), 608–614 (on the *qadištu*/*qadiltu*), 615–616 (on the *kulmašītu*) and 566–574 (on the ereš-diĝir).
16 Civil 2011: 258.
17 Wilcke 2014: 539.
18 See discussion most recently in Stol 2016: 178–182.
19 For a discussion of this statute, see Roth 1999, who surmised that it was meant to prevent these women from establishing a tavern as their business or from operating as creditors attached to a tavern.
20 The same rule is attested in LH §§138, 142 and 149; only in LH §141 did a wife that decides to leave her husband not receive her dowry back, but this was due to the fact that she "appropriates properties, disperses her household, mistreats her husband" (*sikiltam isakkil bīssa usappaḫ mussa ušamṭa*).
21 The literature is vast; see, to name but a few, Westenholz 1989, Henshaw 1994: 228–236, Silver 2006 and Budin 2008. See further literature in Peled 2016: 158 n. 647.
22 The pertinent literature is vast; the reader may consult, to name but a few, Gruber 1986, Westenholz 1989 and Henshaw 1994: 218–221, 243–247 (Hebrew Bible), 222–225 (Ugarit).
23 For a recent comprehensive treatment of the topic, see Peled 2016: 203–237, 239–257.
24 These same statutes mention alongside the *girseqû* the female *sekretu*, and nothing suggests that she was physically incapable of pregnancy and birth.
25 It is unclear whether the penetrating or the penetrated one; see discussion in p. 101.
26 For a discussion of these texts, with a comparison to similar Hittite ones, see Peled 2013: 785–789.
27 *lu ša rēš šarre lu mazziz pane ša la marruruni iqabbiu ša šanuttešu ana mazziz panutte iddunuš*, "they shall report whether a royal eunuch or a courtier who is not *checked*. For a second time, they shall give him for becoming a courtier".
28 Literally: "those who stand in front of the king".
29 See Peled 2013: 785–789.
30 For a commentary on this statute, see Tigay 2003: 209–211.
31 Tigay 2003: 210.
32 See recent discussions in Peled 2016: 232–234 and 2017: 133–134, both with previous literature.
33 Compare the biblical prohibitions in Lev. 18:19 and Lev. 20:18; see p. 30.
34 "Because holy he is to his god", כִּי-קָדֹשׁ הוּא, לֵאלֹהָיו (Lev. 21:7); "Because I, YHWH, consecrate him", כִּי אֲנִי יְהוָה, מְקַדְּשׁוֹ (Lev. 21:15).
35 For a discussion of Lev. 21:7, 13, 14, see Zipor 1987; for a discussion of Lev. 21:9, see Carmichael 2006: 88–90.
36 See Carmichael 2006: 88.

Bibliography

Budin, Stephanie L. 2008. *The Myth of Sacred Prostitution in Antiquity*. New York: Cambridge University Press.

Carmichael, Calum. 2006. *Illuminating Leviticus: A Study of Its Laws and Institutions in the Light of Biblical Narratives*. Baltimore, MD: The Johns Hopkins University Press.

Civil, Miguel. 2011. "The Law Collection of Ur-Namma". In *Cuneiform Royal Inscriptions and Related Texts in the Schøyen Collection*, edited by Andrew R. George. Bethesda, MD: CDL Press. Pp. 221–286.

Gruber, Mayer. 1986. "Hebrew qêdēšāh and Her Canaanite and Akkadian Cognates". *Ugarit-Forschungen* 18: 133–148.

Harris, Rivkah. 1963. "The Organization and Administration of the Cloister in Ancient Babylonia". *Journal of the Economic and Social History of the Orient* 6/2: 121–157.

Henshaw, Richard A. 1994. *Female and Male: The Cultic Personnel. The Bible and the Rest of the Ancient Near East*. Allison Park, PA: Pickwick Publications.

Peled, Ilan. 2013. "Eunuchs in Hatti and Assyria: A Reassessment". In *Time and History in the Ancient Near East: Proceedings of the 56th Rencontre Assyriologique Internationale at Barcelona 26–30 July 2010*, edited by Lluís Feliu, Jaume Llop, Adelina Millet Albà and Joaquín Sanmartín. Winona Lake, IN: Eisenbrauns. Pp. 785–797.

Peled, Ilan. 2016. *Masculinities and Third Gender: The Origins and Nature of an Institutionalized Gender Otherness in the Ancient Near East*. Münster: Ugarit-Verlag.

Peled, Ilan. 2017. "Men in Question: Parallel Aspects of Ambiguous Masculinities in Mesopotamian and Biblical Sources". In *"And Inscribe the Name of Aaron": Studies in Bible, Epigraphy, Literacy and History Presented to Aaron Demsky* (*MAARAV, A Journal for the Study of the Northwest Semitic Languages and Literatures*, vol. 21/1–2), edited by Yigal Levin and Ber Kotlerman. Rolling Hills Estates, CA: Western Academic Press. Pp. 127–148.

Roth, Martha T. 1999. "The Priestess and the Tavern: LH §110". In *Munuscula Mesopotamica: Festschrift für Johannes Renger*, edited by Barbara Böck, Eva Cancik-Kirschbaum and Thomas Richter. Kevelaer: Butzon and Bercker. Pp. 445–464.

Silver, Morris. 2006. "Temple/Sacred Prostitution in Ancient Mesopotamia Revisited. Religion in the Economy". *Ugarit-Forschungen* 38: 631–663.

Stol, Marten. 2016. *Women in the Ancient Near East*. Berlin: De Gruyter.

Tigay, Jeffery H. 2003. *The JPS Torah Commentary: Deuteronomy*. Philadelphia, PA: Jewish Publication Society.

Wenham, Gordon J. 1978. "Leviticus 27:2–8 and the Price of Slaves". *Zeitschrift für die Alttestamentliche Wissenschaft* 90/2: 264–265.

Westbrook, Raymond. 1995. "Slave and Master in Ancient Near Eastern Law". *Chicago-Kent Law Review* 70/4: 1631–1676.

Westenholz, Joan G. 1989. "Tamar, *qĕdēšā*, *qadištu*, and Sacred Prostitution in Mesopotamia". *Harvard Theological Review* 82/3: 245–265.

Wilcke, Claus. 2014. "Gesetze in Sumerischer Sprache". In *Studies in Sumerian Language and Literature: Festschrift Joachim Krecher*, edited by Natalia V. Koslova, Ekaterina Vizirova and Gábor Zólyomi. Winona Lake, IN: Eisenbrauns. Pp. 455–616.

Zipor, Moshe A. 1987. "Restrictions on Marriage for Priests, Leviticus 21:7, 13–14". *Biblica* 68: 259–267.

3 The familial perspective

Regulation of family life

Introduction[1]

The familial circle was one of the most notable social structures regulated by formal legal systems. The law monitored relations within the nuclear and extended family, and provided rules by which a new family was created by marriage, split by divorce and reorganized through inheritance. All these regulations were influenced by the relations between males and females, and in turn influenced these relations and shaped them. Extensive research in recent years has brought to light rich evidence of the ancient Near Eastern socioeconomic world, which illuminates numerous aspects of gender division and relations. These heavily influenced family life in the ancient Near East and the biblical world.

The first topic discussed in this chapter pertains to the way slaves were integrated into family life, from which we continue to discuss several aspects of the family life of free people. The first of these involves parental authority: how did parents exert their authority within the legal frame? We then move on to several different aspects of the institution of marriage, which lay at the core of family life. We discuss betrothal, the formation of marriage and the economic dynamics that accompanied it. Marriage could terminate through divorce or widowing, and both issues are treated in the next couple of sections, followed by the topic of inheritance.

Adoption is treated next. An elaborate system of adoption existed in various societies of the ancient Near East, and gender played a crucial role in it. To give but one example, we have evidence from Nuzi of fathers who adopted their own daughters as "sons" for the sake of securing their inheritance.[2] Several different aspects of adoption are attested in the law collections as well.

The final two sections in this chapter address phenomena that formed alternatives to the standard model of the family in the ancient world: polygamy and prostitution. These not only offered alternatives to the standard familial model but also undermined and even threatened it, and hence drew the attention of legislators.

Slaves and family life

The topic of gender equality and inequality among slaves was studied in Chapter 1, while the economic aspects of debt-slavery were treated in Chapter 2. We now turn to discuss another aspect of the class of slaves: their family life.[3]

ANE law

The legal evidence concerning slaves and their family life is abundant and derives from most ancient Near Eastern law collections. The pertinent statutes mostly deal with mixed marriage between slaves and free persons, but occasionally address other issues, such as extra and premarital sexual intercourse involving slave-women and adoption.

All the family laws relating to slaves in LUN specify rules of marriage. LUN §4 orders that in case slaves get married, and then the male is freed, the female is to remain a slave. According to the following statute – LUN §5 – if a slave marries a free woman, and gives his son (as slave) to his master, that son will be entitled to one half of the inheritance; the master's consent is required for the son's enslavement. According to LUN §8, a man who seduced an unmarried slave-woman was to pay a compensation of five shekels of silver. In comparison, had she been a betrothed free woman, her seducer was to be executed (LUN §6). Lastly, a slave who married his mistress was to be executed (LUN §E6).

Only one statute in LLI is relevant to the current discussion. According to LLI §25, if a slave-woman became someone's secondary wife and bore him children, in addition to those he had from his primary wife, that slave-woman and her children were to be released from their slave status, but the children were not to have any right of inheritance.

The cluster of three consecutive statutes LE §§33–35 was dedicated to the status of slavery and adoption.[4] According to LE §33, if a slave-woman has deceived her master by giving her child to be reared by a free woman, and that child was later on identified by the master, the latter was allowed to seize and take hold of the child. According to LE §34, if a palace slave-woman gave her child to be reared by a *muškēnum*, the child was to be returned to the palace, but according to LE §35 if the adopter belonged to the higher *awīlum* class, he was to keep the child and give the palace (a slave of) an equal value. In all these cases the slave parent who was responsible for the child was the mother, and her status as slave was hereditary, thus dictating her child's status as belonging to a master or to the palace. However, if the unlawful adopter was an *awīlum*, he could keep the child and pay compensations of equal value to the palace, which functioned as the legal entity that originally owned the child.

Interestingly, social status appears to have prevailed over gender factors in LH §175. This statute ruled that if a slave – whether belonging to the palace or to a *muškēnum* – married a woman of the *awīlum* class, their children were to remain free like their mother rather than become slaves like their father. According to LH §176a, if that woman has brought her dowry into their joint household, and they later accumulated additional assets, when the slave dies the woman will take her dowry, while whatever they accumulated together was to be divided evenly between her – for keeping for her children – and her deceased husband's owner. However, according to LH §176b, if she had no dowry, whatever was accumulated by her and her husband was to be divided evenly between her and the owner.

The HL specified concrete rules for marriage between free persons and slaves. Three consecutive statutes – HL §§31–33 – dealt with divorce between such mixed couples who had children. In all cases the property was to be divided equally between the divorcées, but the number of children each one of them kept varied. If the husband was free and his wife was a slave, he was to take all the children but one, who was to remain with the mother (HL §31). In case the husband was a slave while his wife was free (HL §32), or if both were slaves (HL §33), the mother was to take all the children but one, who was to remain with the father.

The next three statutes – HL §§34–36 – referred to the possible change of social status. The social status of a free woman married to a slave was not to be changed (HL §34), while a free woman who married a shepherd was to be enslaved for three years (HL §35).[5] In the former case, it is not clear whether the status that was not to be changed was the woman's newly acquired slavery – as she became the wife of a slave – or her original status as a free woman. According to yet another statute, if a slave has paid a *kušata* to a free young man, who, in return, became his son-in-law, the young man's social status was not to be changed (HL §36). Hoffner explained that this procedure enabled the slave to secure for his grandchildren the status of free persons.[6] HL §175 reiterates the rule of HL §35 by stating that a free woman married to a shepherd or foreman was to be enslaved for either two or four years.

Biblical law

The CC opens with a passage that stipulates certain conditions of slavery. A male slave was to be released from his servitude after six years. Had he been married at the time of his purchase, his wife was to be released with him. But had his master given him a wife, and she bore him children, the woman and her children were to remain the property of the master after the slave was released. Had the slave chosen to remain with his master or family, the servitude was to be perpetuated and signified by piercing the slave's ear, as a token of his willful life-slavery (Exod. 21:2–6).[7] Commentating on this passage, Westbrook noted that it was "emblematic of the conflict between the principles of family law and property law that resulted from recognition of slave marriage".[8] Slaves were regarded as their masters' property, but even their owners were obliged by certain rules that resulted from the fact that slaves could marry and establish their own family. As mentioned, if a master gave one of his slave-women to one of his slaves in marriage, that slave-woman and her children remained the possession of the master when the male slave was to be freed (Exod. 21:4). Westbrook commented that in this rule "[t]he master's property rights take precedence over the husband's marital rights".[9]

A man who purchased a slave-woman in order to marry her, but has then changed his mind, was to let her be redeemed; he was forbidden to sell her to foreigners (Exod. 21:8). Had he married another woman in her stead, he was still required to supply her with the three basic obligations of a husband to his wife: food, attire and sexual intercourse (Exod. 21:10). Failing to fulfill these three obligations would require him to release her free of charge (Exod. 21:11). A man who purchased a slave-woman in order to give her in marriage to his son was required to grant her legal rights as if she were his daughter (Exod. 21:9).[10]

If a man has sex with a slave-woman who was promised to another man but had not yet been ransomed or freed, an inquiry was to be conducted, and the couple was not to be executed. A sacrifice was to be made by a priest in order to absolve the man from his sin (Lev. 19:20–22). Frymer-Kensky claimed that this statute was meant "to protect and control the body of a female slave but not as much as betrothed or free women", because having sex with the latter would have been regarded as adultery.[11] This view is questionable, however, and Frymer-Kensky herself mentions different interpretations.[12]

A woman caught as a spoil of war was allowed to be taken in marriage. She was to mourn her parents for one month and then become her captor's wife. Had he changed his mind about marrying her, he was required to release her free of charge and prohibited to sell her to another (Deut. 21:10–14).[13]

Parental legal authority

Though legal authority was mostly exercised within various social circles, by local courts, assemblies of nobility and elders, and at times by the king himself, on rare occasions parents had the lawful right to intervene in legal matters that involved their daughters. When it comes to gender differentiation, the main question to be asked is: was there a difference between the father's authority and the mother's? Did authority stem exclusively from parental status – in which case gender differentiation was immaterial – or did gender play a role in it as well? And what about changes in parental legal authority? When, and under which circumstances, did it change or terminate?

ANE law

In assessing gender and parental legal authority, we examine several Old Babylonian statutes, from LE and LH, and a couple of statutes from HL. The earliest evidence of these is the most telling one. LE §27 overrules the validity of marriage taken place without the consent of the woman's parents, and with no nuptial contract and ceremonies being performed by the man for her parents, even if the woman resides in his house for a whole year. Though the woman is designated as the daughter of her father, the statute states explicitly that the consent of both her father and mother is absent, and the unperformed contract and ceremonies as meant for both father and mother. According to this statute, therefore, the daughter seems to legally belong to her father, but both her parents should express their approval of the marriage, and both are to be included in the legal process the marriage entails. The following statute (LE §28), however, states that if the contract and ceremonies for both parents were performed, the marriage is valid, and future adultery by the woman will be punishable by death.

The last comment betrays another gender-related matter: the validation of the marriage is supplemented and highlighted by the prohibition on adultery by the wife, a matter that concerns her husband rather than her father. This is a testimony to the fact that by getting married the legal governing male figure in women's lives was changed from their father to their husband. Another piece of evidence for the legal authority husbands had concerning the procedure of their marriage is found in LH §128. According to this statute, a husband-to-be was required to issue a formal contract to the woman he married, otherwise the marriage was invalidated.

As is discussed previously,[14] another statute in which both father and mother are mentioned jointly is LH §194. Here mutual parental legal authority is reflected by the fact that a wet-nurse commits a crime by trying to conceal the death of a baby that was under her care from both parents, "without (asking) his father and his mother" (*balum abišu u ummišu*).

Yaron addressed the issue of mothers' legal authority in his discussion of the status of the mother in LE §§26–28. He focused on the Akkadian connective *u*, which can either be understood as expressing cumulation/conjunction ("and"; in this case: "the father and the mother") or alternation ("or"; in this case: "the father or the mother").[15] Yaron concluded that maternal consent was not compulsory, because "[i]t is difficult to assume that patriarchal societies . . . would endow a mother with the power of vetoing arrangements for the marriage of her daughter, arrangements made in accordance with the wishes of the father".[16] He suggested that the phrase "her father and her mother" in these contexts should be understood as an ellipsis for "her father, or (after his death) her mother".[17] In effect, therefore, Yaron rejected the possibility that maternal consent was as significant as paternal consent in the cases previously discussed. His argumentations, however, were tentative rather than textually substantiated.

Evidence from the HL suggests as well that parental consent included both parents when it involved their daughter's marriage. As is discussed in greater detail in what follows, both father and mother are attested in HL §§28a+b+c and 29 as involved in the legal procedure of giving their daughter in marriage.

As we see, parents, especially fathers, could – and more often than not, did – intervene in the betrothal of their daughters. This issue is discussed in the following section.

Biblical law

According to the rules of CC, a father could refuse his daughter's forced marriage. Thus, though a man who seduced a virgin girl was required to marry her (Exod. 22:15), her father could object to the marriage and prevent it (Exod. 22:16). As Paul explained, the damage in this pair of statutes is economic and was caused to the girl's father. Hence, the perpetrator was to cover the financial losses he caused to the father.[18] This is the background of the parental – in this case, paternal – authority, and the reason why the father was entitled to cancel the marriage.

A woman who has made vows to God was obliged to fulfill them. However, in case she was not married, her father could annul her vows (Num. 30:6). In case she was married, the right to annul a woman's vows to God was given to her husband (Num. 30:9, 13).[19] As with the case of LE §28, we see here evidence for the transference of legal authority over women from their fathers to their husbands, when their social status changes from unmarried daughters to wives.

Additionally, joint paternal and maternal parental authority is apparent in Deut. 21:18–21, according to which a son who is consistently disobedient and disrespectful (בן סורר ומורה) to both his father and his mother was to be punished.[20] Fewell and Gunn, however, assumed that even in such cases, the parental legal authority was by and large paternal, and the mother's shared authority merely represented an extension of her husband's authority within the family.[21]

Betrothal and its infringement

In the ancient Near East, the infringement of promised marriage was regarded with great severity because of the grave financial aspects of marriage. The damage was perceived as economic, equal to the infringement of an important financial transaction. However, a rare reference in biblical law to such infringement conveys an objection that was moral in nature, rather than economic.

ANE law[22]

Several statutes were meant to secure the betrothing of women. In principle, the head of the household was responsible for making sure that his daughters are married. However, in case he failed to do so, the responsibility shifted to his sons, as in LLI §23 and LH §184.

LUN §6 determined that a betrothed woman was not to be taken into his house by a man who was not her prospective husband. A man who committed such a felony was to be executed. According to LUN §14, false accusations that someone has had sexual intercourse with a betrothed woman required the compensation of 20 shekels of silver.

LUN §15 and LE §25 ruled that a father who has canceled a planned marriage was to compensate his would-be son-in-law with double the amount of the wedding gifts.[23] LLI §29 ruled the same, but added that the man's comrade, to whom the woman was given instead, was forbidden to marry her. This statute considers the woman to be the wife of the first man. These three statutes resemble LH §161, for which see what follows. LE §26 presents a case in which the betrothed girl was abducted and deflowered without the consent of her parents, in which case the perpetrator was to be executed.

According to LH §156, a man who chose a bride for his son but had sexual relations with her before the marriage took place was required to pay her a compensation of 30 shekels of silver and give her back her dowry;[24] the betrothal was to be canceled, and she was free to marry any other man.

Three consecutive statutes in LH deal with marriage that has been canceled after the *biblum* and *terḫatum* were already given to the prospective father-in-law. If the future husband is the one who initiated the cancellation, he was to lose whatever he gave (LH §159); if the future father-in-law is the one who initiated the cancellation, he was to return twice the sum he was given (LH §160); if the latter situation occurred because a comrade of the prospective husband has slandered him, the father-in-law was to return twice the sum he was given, and the comrade was forbidden to marry the bride-to-be (LH §161). This latter statute resembles LUN §15, LE §25 and §LLI 29 mentioned previously.

The MAL addressed these issues as well. MAL A §30 dealt with a complicated case of canceled engagement. According to the statute, marriage has been settled between two households, and the prospective groom's father has delivered to the prospective bride's father the *biblu* and *zubullû*.[25] But before the ceremony itself has taken place, another son of the groom's father has died, leaving making his wife who resided in her own father's household a widow. In such a case, the deceased's father was to bring the widow under the auspices[26] of the prospective groom's household, which in effect formed a marriage-like situation. Under these circumstances, the prospective bride's father was entitled to cancel the marriage, and hence the prospective groom's father could give the widow in marriage to his son whose engagement has been canceled. The father could take back the *biblu* and *zubullû* he previously gave, besides any consumable commodity, which was not to be returned. As noted by Saporetti, the procedure of bringing the widow under the auspices of her deceased husband's brother was very similar in its functionality to levirate marriage.[27]

The MAL considered several other scenarios of betrothal cancellation and offered legal solutions to each of them. If a future husband has given the *zubullû* but his prospective bride then died, he could either marry another daughter of his future father-in-law or take back the *zubullû*, besides any animal or consumable commodities, which were not to be returned (MAL A §31). If a man had performed gestures of betrothal for a woman, such as anointing her or giving her dishes at the banquet, they were not to be returned (MAL A §42). If these betrothal gestures were performed, but the prospective groom has died or fled, his father was to give her in marriage to one of his other sons who was at least ten years old; if both father and son have died, a grandson who was at least ten years old was to marry her; if all sons were too young, the prospective bride's father was allowed to give her to one of them, or alternatively cancel the engagement and return the gifts that were given; if there were no sons, her father was to return the gifts besides any consumable commodity (MAL A §43).[28]

Turning to the first millennium, NBL §8 ruled that once the marriage conditions have been settled and documented by the fathers of the prospective bride and groom, they were not to be altered. These conditions included the exchange of the bride's dowry and groom's property. According to NBL §9, a father who promised his daughter a dowry but then lost some of his assets could reduce her dowry accordingly.

The HL included several statutes that regulated the conditions of betrothal and its cancellation. A man who abducted a girl betrothed to another was required to compensate her prospective groom for whatever the groom has given her parents (HL §28a).[29] If the parents of a betrothed girl gave her to another man, they were to compensate the original groom (HL §28b) or cancel the betrothal to the second man (HL §28c). If a prospective groom has delivered the *kušata* to his betrothed wife's parents, but her parents wish to cancel the engagement, they were to pay him back double the amount of the *kušata* he gave them (HL §29). If the prospective groom is the one who has canceled the engagement, he was to lose the *kušata* he has given (HL §30).

Biblical law

If a man had sexual intercourse with a slave-woman who was promised to another man, but had not yet been ransomed or freed, an inquiry was to be conducted, and the couple would not be executed. A sacrifice was to be made by a priest in order to absolve the man from his sin (Lev. 19:20–22). Thus, we see that the act was perceived as a moral misbehavior rather than a financial felony. According to Frymer-Kensky, this results from the fact that the slave-woman was not freed yet, which means that, in effect, she was not legally betrothed. Had she been betrothed, the paramour would have faced execution for committing adultery.[30]

Economic dynamics in marriage life

Family relations, and the familial structure as a whole, were heavily based on economic factors, as evidenced in both ancient Near Eastern and in biblical sources. The role of affection and emotion, though they should definitely not be dismissed, is far less attested in juridical sources. This can be explained as the result of the utilitarian nature of legal documentation, where love and hate were far less significant than signed contracts and legal obligations.

ANE law[31]

The evidence for the preoccupation of ancient Near Eastern law collections with the financial aspects of marriage and family derives almost exclusively from the two largest Mesopotamian collections: LH and MAL.

Several statutes in LH were concerned with a case in which the head of the household was taken captive.[32] If a man was taken captive and his son was too young to perform his father's *ilku* obligation, one third of the family estate was to be given to the mother, with which she was to raise her son (LH §29); she thus became legally the family head *de facto*, in the absence of an appropriate male figure: the father was absent and the son was too young. If there were sufficient means of subsistence, the captive's wife was to remain in the house and not to move to another man's house (LH §133a).[33] However, in case there were no sufficient means of subsistence, the wife was allowed to move to another man's house and bear him children. If her former husband eventually returned, the woman was to return and live with him, but her children were to remain with their father (LH §135). The identity of the father had greater gravity in this case than that of the mother. According to the following statute, however, if the original husband was not taken captive but fled his city, and if he eventually returned, his former wife was not to return and live with him (LH §136).

LH §§38, 39 demonstrate that the male head of the household could assign family assets to female members of the family – his wife or his daughter – as long as the said assets were not attached to his *ilku* obligation.

Two other statutes dealt with the issue of marriage and debts. According to the first, a husband or a wife could grant his/her spouse a contract that guarantees that a creditor cannot seize[34] the spouse on account of a debt incurred prior to the wedding (LH §151). This statute was probably meant to defend people from being used for clearing debts through enslavement after marriage. If, however, the debt was created after the marriage took place, both husband and wife were equally responsible for settling it (LH §152). These two statutes, it appears, treated men and women equally.

The MAL supplies a detailed account of financial aspects of marriage life, the evidence deriving exclusively from tablet A of the collection. MAL A §3 describes the penalties for a wife caught stealing from her husband, whether he is healthy (unspecified punishment), ill or dead (execution). Those who receive the stolen goods from her were to face the same punishment as her. MAL A §4 elaborates on this issue, stating that if the receivers of the stolen property were slaves – whether male or female – their nose and ears were to be cut off, the husband was to cut off his wife's ears, and the stolen property was to be returned to him. But if he did not wish to harm his wife, the slaves were not to be harmed as well, and the stolen property was not to be returned to him. MAL A §5 describes a case of someone's wife caught stealing from another person. Her husband was to return the stolen property and cut off her ears, or else the owner of the stolen property was to cut off her nose. According to MAL A §6, he who received the stolen property from her bore liability for the crime as well.

Adultery and fornication are among the sex crimes discussed in detail in Chapter 4. Since these misdemeanors had financial implications for marriage life, they are treated here as well. The MAL dedicated several highly detailed statutes to varying possible situations where adultery could occur. Not surprisingly, the emphasis was put on married women as perpetrators, or men who seduced them, thus becoming perpetrators themselves. Either way, the offended party from the point of view of the law was the betrayed husband. And since marriage formed an economic institution, the implications of adultery were economic no less than moral. MAL A §22 discusses a married woman who travels with a man other than her husband, father, brother or son. If that man was to swear that he did not know of her marriage, he was to pay her husband a compensation of two talents (=7,200 shekels) of lead. If he knew of her marriage, he was to pay compensations and swear that he did not fornicate with her. Had she claimed that he did fornicate with her, he was to undergo the divine-River-Ordeal. Had he refused, he was to be treated as the husband treated his wife. The following statute – MAL A §23 – presents a different case of adultery, in which a married woman was lured by another woman into her house for a man to have sexual intercourse with her there. The sanction in this case was corporal rather than financial – execution – and hence bears no economic implications to be discussed here. MAL A §24 describes a case of a woman who has left her husband and joined for several days the household of another man, who was unaware that she was married. Her husband was to mutilate her and not take her back into his house. The woman who hosted her was to have her ears cut off, but her husband could redeem her by paying the sum of 3 talents and 30 minas (=12,600 shekels) of lead. We therefore see here the economic dynamics of marriage life in action. The statute continues by declaring that if the man in whose household the escaped woman resided did know that she was married, he was to pay a triple fine, unless he denied such knowledge and successfully passed the divine-River-Ordeal to prove it. The betrayed husband was required to undergo the ordeal as well; refusing to do so would clear the other man. Had the betrayed husband not mutilated his wife, he was required to take her back without imposing any sanction on her.

According to MAL A §27, if a married woman resides in her father's household, but her husband only visits her without living there, the husband was to take back any assets he gave her as part of the marriage arrangements, but he had no rights to any of her father's property. According to MAL A §32, a wife was responsible for her husband's debts and crimes, whether she resided in the household of her father or her father-in-law. This is to be compared with LH §§151–152, where the law differentiated between a debt created before or after the marriage took place.

An interesting statute determines that the property of a widow who moved into her new husband's house became his property, while the property of a man who moved into a woman's house became hers (MAL A §35). This statute evidently treats men and women identically in this respect.

A pair of statutes addresses the issue of marriage and debt-slavery. If a man gives in marriage a woman who was given to him by her father as a pledge in order to clear a debt, and then a creditor claims her from that man, the creditor will receive her value but not her. If her owner cannot pay, the creditor will take hold of him (in slavery?) instead (MAL A §39). The rest of the statute is fragmentary, and hence obscure. Interestingly, this topic reoccurs almost ten statutes later, rather than in the consecutive statute. Thus, according to MAL A §48, a man who possessed his debtor's daughter as a pledge and wanted to give her in marriage was required to obtain her father's permission. Had her father died, her brothers were the ones whose permission was required. Had one of them wished to redeem her, he was allowed one month to do so, but had he failed, the creditor was allowed to give her in marriage as he pleased.

MAL A §45 describes a situation in which a married man was caught by the enemy and did not return to his wife for two years, while she had no father-in-law or sons to support her. That woman was to work for persons whose identity is lost in a break,[35] and in return they were to support her. Alternatively, she could declare her situation publicly, and then her local community – represented by judges – was to award her a field and a house that she could then sell for obtaining her sustenance for two years. After this period she was to receive the official legal status of a widow and be allowed to remarry. If later on her first husband returned, she was to return to live with him, but the children she bore to her second husband were to remain with their father. The first husband was required to pay the price his wife previously received for the field and the house she sold, and to take these assets back. If the first husband died in the foreign country where he was caught, the field and the house were to be awarded by the king to whomever he wished. As discussed elsewhere in this book, this topic of a married man caught by the enemy is also addressed by several statutes of LE and LH; note especially LH §135, which shares many similarities with MAL A §45.

Concluding with evidence from Hittite texts, an edict of King Tudḫaliya I concerning administrative and penal reform included a ruling that a killer could redeem himself by paying compensation to his victim's family, either using property or his family members: wives and children (CTH 258.1 §5' 3–9). This situation reminds us the opposite ruling of LH §151, which prevented people from selling their spouses for slavery in clearing premarital debts.

Biblical law

In Num. 36:6–9 we encounter legal rules of marriage and inheritance that follow the affair of the daughters of Zelophehad and its subsequent decisions concerning the inheritance rights of daughters (Num. 27:1–11). This passage was meant to make sure that each Israelite tribe kept its ancestral plots and assets, none of which were to be moved from one tribe to another. It hence determined that daughters who inherited from their fathers could marry any man they wanted as long as that man belonged to their tribe (Num. 36:8). This ruling was interpreted by Hiers as a "clear implication" that the assets of daughters who inherited from their fathers became the property of their husbands upon their marriage.[36] Understanding the biblical law in this light portrays it as conveying a different attitude than that expressed in the somewhat thematically parallel ruling of MAL A §35, according to which upon entering the house of his/her newly wedded spouse, a person's property belonged to the hosting spouse, whether male or female.[37]

A man who disliked his newly wedded wife and falsely accused her of not being a virgin upon their marriage was to pay her father a compensation of 100 (shekels of) silver, and live with her without possibility of divorcing her in the future (Deut. 22:13–19).[38] As noted by Pressler, "[t]he fine of one hundred shekels suggests that financial concerns may well underlie the law".[39] If the essence of the crime was merely moral, and the perceived victim was the defamed girl, we would have expected to see a different punishment for the slanderous husband. The fact that the perpetrator is required to pay a heavy fine to the girl's father shows that the actual victim in this case was the girl's original governing male figure – her father – and that the crime had financial implications. These, in all likelihood, involve the father's loss in case the false accusations were accepted and the marriage been canceled. In such a case, it would have been highly difficult for the father to marry off his daughter again and receive the expected financial gains involved.[40] Noteworthy is that the sum of 100 shekels of silver was likely double the amount of a standard brideprice.[41] Rofé followed the Sages (חז“ל) in claiming that the fine paid by the slandering husband was double the amount of a brideprice because of the principle of a double fine set for any crime, as attested in Exod. 22:8.[42]

Another ruling that was strongly related to the economic dynamics of marriage life was the levirate marriage (Deut. 25:5–10). This issue is discussed in what follows,[43] but in its essence, it was meant to keep the financial assets within the familial unit and not disperse them outside of the family.

Termination of marriage: divorce

As we have seen, the formation and upholding of the institution of marriage entailed numerous economic and financial aspects. It is no surprise, therefore, to see that the termination of this institution was no less characterized by such features. The importance of divorce is evident by the fact that almost all law collections addressed it. Ancient Near Eastern law collections were predominantly concerned with the financial aspects of the separation between the married couple, while the pertinent biblical evidence suggests that the focal point of the Hebrew Bible was moral, restricting certain types of men from marrying divorced women.

ANE law[44]

The law distinguished between various cases of divorce, according to several factors: the gender of the initiator, the reason for the divorce, the moral behavior of both husband and wife prior to the divorce, whether it was the first or second marriage and whether the couple had children. All these factors could be taken into account when settling the divorce conditions; in the end, it was – yet again – mostly about money.

In LUN, four statutes – three of which consecutive – refer to divorce. The first of these determines that a man who has divorced his wife was required to pay her 60 shekels of silver (LUN §9). Had she previously been a widow, however, he was only to pay her half the amount: 30 shekels of silver (LUN §10). And if their relationship was not settled officially, the man was not obliged not pay the woman anything upon their separation (LUN §11), as he was not legally her husband, and she has not become now his legal divorcée. According to a fourth statute, a woman who divorced her husband was obliged to wait six months before she was allowed to marry another man (LUN §B7).

The next collections – LLI and LE – each dedicated one statute to divorce. LLI §30 declares that a man who has divorced his wife in order to live with a prostitute was not allowed to marry the said prostitute. According to LE §59, a man who had children and decided to divorce his wife and marry another woman was to be expelled from his house and lose his property.[45] Both these statutes seem to have limited men's possibility to arbitrarily leave their wives and, generally speaking, were meant to protect and stabilize the familial structure in early Old Babylonian times. In both cases the law did not utterly prohibit men from leaving their wives and families, but it did pose restrictions and sanctions that would have encouraged these men to seriously consider their decisions before acting too hastily.[46]

A sequence of no fewer than seven statutes in LH – §§137–143 – was dedicated to varying issues leading to divorce. The first four statutes settled the financial circumstances of cases in which the husband was the initiator. LH §137 referred to a man divorcing his wife – either a *šugītu* or a *nadītu* – with whom he had children, whether biological or adopted. The woman was to have her dowry back and, in addition, to receive one half of her husband's properties. She was to raise their children, and once they have grown up they were to give her a share of the family assets equal to their own. She was also allowed to remarry as she wished. The following statute (LH §138) was concerned with a man divorcing his first-ranking wife with whom he did not have children. He was to give her silver equal to her *terḫatum* as well as give her back her dowry. In the absence of *terḫatum* the husband was to give his divorcée 60 shekels of silver (LH §139) or 20 if he was a *muškēnum* (LH §140).

The next three statutes address cases in which the wife was the one who initiated the divorce. In all cases the main concern of the law involved the woman's moral behavior. Had she been squandering the family assets or behaving disrespectfully towards her husband, she was to leave empty-handed, or alternatively her husband was allowed to marry another woman without divorcing her, demoting her to a slave status (LH §141). She could also face execution by drowning (LH §143). However, if the woman was prudent, while her husband was adulterous and disrespectful of her, she was to receive back her dowry and return to her father's household (LH §142).

A different case involving divorce is detailed in LH §§148–149: if someone's wife became ill with a skin disease (*la'bum*) he was allowed to marry another woman (for polygyny see what follows) but not to divorce his ill wife (LH §148). If, as a consequence, she chose to leave her husband, they were to divorce, and he was to give her back her dowry (LH §149).

The basic rule in the MAL for divorce is found in MAL A §37: had the husband been the initiating party of the divorce, he was to decide whether to give his wife anything or let her leave his house empty-handed. If the wife resided in her father's household and her husband initiated a divorce, he was to take with him any property he previously gave her but not the *terḫatu*, which was to remain hers (MAL A §38). MAL A §36 determined a five-year period during which a husband could go abroad, leaving his wife without providing her with means of sustenance. If she had sons, they could ha be hired out to provide their needs. But if the situation remained unchanged, and her husband did not return, after five years the marriage could be canceled and she was allowed to remarry as she pleased. Such one-sided divorce was not to occur if the husband's absence did not result from his own initiative: whether because he was unlawfully seized, arrested or sent on a mission by the king. In such case the husband was required to prove the circumstances of his absence, give his wife's second husband a replacement wife and take back his own wife. In case the said woman married another man before five years had passed and bore him children, when her first husband returned he was allowed to take her and the children as his own.

The HL as well dedicated several statutes to the handling of divorce, mostly covering economic issues. If the divorce was initiated by the wife, her husband was probably[47] to give her financial compensation in accordance with the children she had borne, but the properties and the children were to remain in his possession (HL §26a). Had the husband been the one who initiated the divorce, he was probably[48] to sell his wife for 12 shekels of silver (HL §26b+c). These statutes are all fragmentary and based on restorations, some of which are far from certain.[49]

Biblical law

In the rules of conduct stipulated for priests, they were limited to marrying only virgin girls. Hence, divorced women – similarly to widows and prostitutes – were forbidden for priests to marry (Lev. 21:7, 14). The daughter of a priest who became a widow or divorced without having children and returned to her father's house was allowed to eat his food (Lev. 22:13).

A man who initiates a divorce and his divorcée remarries and then remains without her second husband – whether following another divorce or because he has died – was not allowed to take back his previous wife (Deut. 24:1–4). The meaning and purpose of this statute are vague, and it has no direct parallel anywhere else in the Hebrew Bible nor in the ancient Near Eastern law collections.[50] Westbrook maintained that the essence of this statute was economic and that it was meant to prevent the first husband from obtaining the financial assets his divorcée has acquired during her second marriage.[51] This interpretation, though reiterated by others,[52] is speculative and cannot be substantiated. Otto suggested that the purpose of this statute was to protect women and curtail men's power and capability to divorce their wives too hastily. In Otto's view, this was another example for the tendency seen in the laws of Deuteronomy of treating women with more dignity than earlier biblical legal corpora.[53] This subjective view cannot be substantiated any more than other ones, leaving the actual reasons behind the statute of Deut. 24:1–4 still poorly understood.

Termination of marriage: widowing

The alternative manner for marriage to end is when one of the couple dies. In such cases, similarly to what we have seen in the previous section, many financial matters were to be resolved. Here, however, instead of determining how should property be divided between a man and a woman who were previously legally bound, the law had to decide how the remaining spouse was to be affected by the death of his wife/her husband. The laws referred much more frequently to widows than to widowers, which emphasizes the legislators' will to regulate and determine women's social and economic status once their status as subject to their husbands has changed. When the law did refer to a widower it was in relation to his rights to take hold of his deceased wife's dowry or the marriage gifts he has given her family. Biblical law only referred to widows but not in relation to their socioeconomic status as much as in stipulating rules for protecting them and the continuation of their family. Almost all legal references are made to free persons, the sole exceptions being two references in LH to interclass marriage between a male slave and a woman of the *awīlum* class.

ANE law[54]

As with divorce, widowing was also addressed by almost all of the ancient Near Eastern law collections.[55] The pertinent statutes detailed various rulings that usually determined financial matters resulting from the new familial circumstances created by the death of one of the spouses, usually the husband. Less frequently, they specified restrictions on the remarrying of the living spouse.

The basic rule in LUN that pertained to the financial situation of a widow established her as the sole heir of her deceased husband (LUN §E4). A somewhat parallel statute referred to the financial status of a husband who outlived his wife: he was legally permitted to keep the family assets but upon remarrying had to return his deceased wife's dowry to her paternal household (LUN §B8).

Three consecutive statutes in LUN addressed the issue of a widow who has moved into her father-in-law's household. These statutes presented three different alternatives, depending on the widow's financial situation. She was permitted to keep her slaves and marriage gifts (LUN §27), or pay her father-in-law ten shekels of silver if she did not have slave-women (LUN §28). According to the third option – if she had no slaves or silver – she was exempt from the obligation of paying anything to her father-in-law (LUN §29).

Several other statutes in this collection related to the remarrying of widows and widowers. According to LUN §10, a widow who remarried and then divorced was to receive from her divorcé half the amount a regular divorcée would receive: 30 shekels of silver instead of 60. As was mentioned, according to LUN §B8 a widower could keep his deceased wife's dowry as long as he remained unmarried, but as soon as he remarried he was to return it to his deceased wife's household. Remarrying also entailed certain restrictions. For example, LUN §E5 prescribed the death penalty to a man who married his deceased older brother's widowed wife. Since the sanction seems to have been imposed on the man alone, it is inferred that the widow herself was not punished, meaning that the law did not hold her responsible in this situation, and the man alone, as the one who possessed the authority, was regarded as legally liable.

A pair of statutes in LE referred to widowing and clarified what was to be done with the silver of the *terḫatum* given by the husband to his wife's family as part of the marriage arrangements. LE §17 states that if the husband originally brought the *terḫatum* to the household of his father-in-law, and either one of the spouses has died, the silver was to be given to its "original owner", namely the widower (in case his wife died) or his heir (in case he died). According to LE §18, if the wife has entered her husband's house as part of their marriage, and either one of the spouses has died, the widow/er was only allowed to take the assets that were accumulated since the marriage took place, and the *terḫatum* was to remain in the possession of the father who originally received it.[56]

No fewer than 11 statutes in LH settled the rights for the marriage gifts and the dowry following the death of one of the spouses. LH §150 determined that if a man issued his wife with an official document granting her the family assets after his death, the matter was not to be challenged by their children. The wife was to divide the inheritance as she pleased but not to sell the assets outside of the family. LH §171 added that a widow was to take her dowry and *nudunnûm* and remain in her husband's house, but she was not allowed to sell this property, since her children were to inherit it after her death. LH §172 stated that if the deceased husband has left his widow no financial document she was to take her dowry and in addition was entitled to a share of the estate equal to that of one heir; had her children tried to force her to leave the house, they were to pay a penalty; had she decided to leave the house, she was to take her dowry but give her children the *nudunnûm* her husband formerly granted her; she was then allowed to remarry. According to LH §173, had she borne children to her second husband, after her death all her children from both husbands were to inherit equal shares of her dowry. However, LH §174 stressed that had she not borne her second husband children, her dowry was only to be inherited by the children she bore to her first husband. LH §177 reiterated some of the previous rules by allowing a widow who had young children to remarry, pending official approval of the judges; the assets she had from her deceased husband were not to be sold but to be kept by her and her new husband for her children to inherit.

Three additional statutes regulated the rights for the *terḫatum* and the dowry in case the husband outlived his wife. Had she borne children, they were to inherit the value of her dowry (LH §162, see what follows). However, if she had no children, and her father has returned to her husband the *terḫatum* he initially received from him, the dowry was to be returned to the father-in-law (LH §163). Alternatively, if the father-in-law did not return the *terḫatum*, its value was to be deducted from the dowry, and the widower was only required to give his father-in-law the remaining sum (LH §164).

LH is the only collection to address widowing within interclass marriages. LH §176a dealt with a case of a slave who married a woman of the *awīlum* class who brought her dowry to their joint household, and they later on accumulated assets together. When the slave died his wife was to take her dowry, but whatever they had accumulated together was to be divided evenly between her – for keeping for her children – and her deceased husband's master. According to LH §176b, had she had no dowry, whatever was accumulated by her and her husband was to be divided evenly between her and his former master.

The MAL as well dedicated much attention to widowing. These statutes were concerned with the inheritance of the deceased man and mostly with the welfare of his widow. A widow without children who resided in her father's house had no rights to her deceased husband's property; her husband's brothers who had not inherited yet were to divide his property between them (MAL A §25). However, had she had sons, they were to inherit their deceased father, and in case there were no sons – that is, presumably, if she only had daughters – the widow was to receive her deceased husband's property (MAL A §26). A widow with no sons who resided in her father's household could be given by her father to reside under the auspices[57] of her father-in-law's household (MAL A §30); in case her father-in-law had also died she was legally a widow and hence free to go anywhere she pleased (MAL A §33).[58]

A widow who remarried without a formal marriage agreement and resided in her new husband's house for two years became legally his wife and hence was not to be banished (MAL A §34), and any property she brought with her became her husband's (MAL A §35).

If a married man became imprisoned by an enemy and did not return for two years, his wife was allowed to remarry by obtaining the legal status of a widow. If her first husband then returned, she had to return to him, but any children she bore to her second husband were to remain with their father (MAL A §45).

If a husband did not issue his wife with a written document of financial ownership, and she then became a widow, her sons were to provide for her sustenance, and she was to live in the house of one of them. Had she been a second wife without her own sons, her husband's sons were to take care of her. If she had sons, but one of her husband's sons born to another woman was to marry her, he was to provide for her sustenance rather than her own sons (MAL A §46).

Even in the fragmentary, mostly lost NBL, we encounter four consecutive statutes that treated widowing. NBL §10 determined that when a married woman with no children has died, her dowry was to be returned to her father's household. However, it is probable[59] that, according to NBL §11, she could award prior to her death her dowry to her husband or to anyone she wanted. NBL §12 stated that if her husband who has received her dowry died, and she had no children, she was to receive her dowry back from her husband's property. In case her husband gave her a marriage gift, she was to receive it in addition to the dowry. If she had no dowry, she was to receive a part of her husband's property as decided by a judge. NBL §13 ruled that if a widow who had sons remarried, she was to take her dowry from her deceased husband's property and anything that he has given her, and both her and her second husband were to use these assets. If she bore sons to her second husband, all her children from both husbands were to inherit her dowry equally after her death.

The HL ignored most of the issues discussed by the various Mesopotamian law collections regarding widowing. It only ruled that if someone's wife has died, he was to take her dowry, but if she has died in her father's house and had children, her husband was forbidden to take her dowry (HL §27). The only other reference to widowing in this collection involves levirate marriage. In order to keep the family assets within the patrilineal milieu, efforts were made to remarry a widow within the family. The HL offered several alternative solutions in this respect, clustered in two statutes. According to the first, one of the following: the business partner of the deceased, his son or the deceased's brother was to marry the widow (HL §192).[60] According to the second, the deceased's brother was to marry the widow, or alternatively his father, or – if both were dead – the brother's son was to do it (HL §193).

Biblical law

The Hebrew Bible orders on numerous occasions that female widows are to be protected and not to be taken advantage of. In Exod. 22:21–23 those who infringe this rule are threatened to be killed by God, so that their wives will become widows themselves. In a sense, therefore, this ruling can be seen as a vicarious talion.[61]

The levirate marriage was a special institution that was put into effect in case a married man has died without an heir. Thus, the brother of the deceased was to marry the widow, so that she did not remarry outside of the family. The first son she then bore to her new husband was to keep the name of the deceased (Deut. 25:5–6). If the deceased's brother refused to perform the levirate marriage, a ceremony was to be performed in which he was publicly condemned by the widow, as a man who refused to preserve his brother's house (Deut. 25:7–10). The exact purpose of the levirate marriage has been a source of some dispute among scholars. Some suggest that it was meant to keep the assets of the nuclear family within the extended family, others claim that it was meant to maintain the deceased man's name by securing him an offspring, while others suggest that it aimed at protecting the widow and securing her welfare.[62] Be the case as it may, the biblical rules of levirate are interestingly comparable with MAL A §30, and especially HL §§192–193, as discussed previously.

Inheritance

The law did not only regulate how the familial structure was established, handled and terminated but also how it was prolonged. Inheritance rules were concerned with the financial benefits of certain individuals, and more often than not reflected the differences in status between males and females. Strict rules regulated the financial flow from one generation to another, but inheritance did not necessarily shift straight down along the genealogical line, since parents, spouses and other relatives could also inherit.

ANE law[63]

Inheritance was naturally a key issue in the ancient Near East – as it is in any given society. Not surprisingly, therefore, an elaborate legislative system surrounded this topic, and, as with the cases of divorce and widowing, almost all ancient Near Eastern law collections addressed it.[64]

As we have already seen, LUN §E4 established a widow as her deceased husband's heir. This collection, however, was not unanimous in this regard. According to other statutes, had a man died with no male heirs, his unmarried daughter was to inherit from him (LUN §B2), and if his elder daughter was married[?], her younger – unmarried – sister was to be his heir (LUN §B3).[65]

LLI §21 dealt with the marriage gift and the rights to its inheritance. Since the text is broken, we cannot know whether the said marriage gift was the husband's or the wife's. What we can gather from the preserved parts of this statute is that the marriage gift belonged to the heir of its original owner, whether the husband or the wife, and thus that the owner's brothers had no right to inherit it. The following statute (LLI §22) established a daughter who became an *ugbabtu*, *nadītu* or *qadištu* as an equal heir to any of her male brothers.

The cluster of statutes LLI §§24–27 dealt with several cases of inheritance rights of children born to different wives of the same man. According to LLI §24, a secondary wife's dowry was only to be inherited by her children, while all other assets were to be divided between all children of the primary and the secondary wives alike. LLI §25 presents a case in which someone marries his slave-woman as a secondary wife and has children born from both wives. Though the slave-woman and her children were to be released from their slavery, her children had no inheritance rights, in contrast with those of the primary wife. According to LLI §26, if someone married his slave-woman after his primary wife has died, the deceased wife's son was to be the primary heir, while the son of the former slave-woman was also to have inheritance rights. The last statute in the cluster – LLI §27 – differs from the previous ones; it did not refer to children of different wives, but to a case in which someone's wife had no children and he had a child born from a prostitute. That man was thus required to provide the prostitute with her needs, and their son was to be his heir.

LH §135 was discussed previously. It treated a case in which a man was taken captive, and since his wife had no sufficient means of subsistence, she has gone to live with another man and borne him children. In case her original husband eventually returned, she was to return and live with him, but her children remained with their father, and hence were to be his heirs.

Disinheritance due to committing a sexual felony was dealt with by LH §158: if following someone's death his son was found having sexual intercourse with his stepmother[66] who was a principal wife and bore children, that son was to be disinherited.

Several non-consecutive statutes in LH specified the rules of inheritance among brothers, beginning with the basic ruling, according to which when a woman has died her dowry was to be inherited by her children and not to be claimed by her father (LH §162). If all brothers but the youngest had wives when their father died, they were to assist the youngest to marry by giving him an additional share beyond what they have all divided between themselves; this addition was to form his *terḫatum* (LH §166). If a man has remarried after the death of his first wife and had children from both wives, after his death the estate was to be divided equally between the children, but the mothers' dowries were only to be divided between their respective children (LH §167). If a man had children both from his wife and from a slave-woman, and he recognized all of them to be legally his children, then after his death they were all to inherit from him equally, but a son of the wife was the first to choose his preferred share of the estate (LH §170). If, however, the man did not recognize the children born to the slave-woman as his legal children, they were not to inherit from him. They and their mother were to be released from their slavery. The wife was to take her dowry and *nudunnûm* and remain in her husband's house but was not allowed to sell it, since it was to become her children's inheritance (LH §171).

The group of statutes LH §§178–184 was treated and discussed previously.[67] These were meant to secure subsistence and inheritance privileges of certain female cult personnel and stemmed from the unique position and socioeconomic status of these women. We will now discuss their implications regarding inheritance procedures. If a father awarded his daughter who is an *ugbabtu*, *nadītu* or *sekretu* a dowry without permitting her to lease it, her brothers will take possession of it and provide her with her subsistence. But if they did not take care of her, the daughter could lease the dowry in return for support, and after her death the dowry is to be returned to her brothers (LH §178). If the father granted his daughter permission to lease her dowry, her brothers cannot overrule the decision (LH §179). If her father awarded her no dowry, the daughter had inheritance rights identical to any of her brothers, but she was not allowed to sell it outside the family (LH §§180, 181). The only exception was a *nadītu* dedicated to Marduk in Babylon, who was entitled to lease her inheritance (LH §182). A *šugītu* whose father or brothers awarded her a dowry and arranged her marriage had no inheritance rights (LH §§183, 184). In effect, therefore, the dowry functioned as the daughter's inheritance, in case she was an *ugbabtu*, *nadītu*, *qadištu*, *kulmašītu*, *sekretu* or *šugītu*. However, the exact manner in which the inheritance was to be materialized could vary. In the absence of a dowry, her inheritance status was equal to that of any of her male brothers, with the exception that she was prohibited from selling her inheritance outside of the family.

The MAL dedicated several statutes to the question of inheritance rights of a widow and her children, some of which were discussed previously. The first of these ruled that a widow without children who resided in her father's household was not to inherit from her deceased husband; rather, his brothers who have not inherited yet were to divide the dead man's property between them (MAL A §25). The reason for this ruling was that her father took care of her needs, and there were no heirs for whom inheritance was to be kept. However, if the widow who resided in her father's household had sons, they were to inherit their deceased father (MAL A §26). This statute then declared that if there were no sons, the woman was to take hold of her deceased husband's property. Since this last ruling seems to contradict the one of MAL A §25, it possibly referred to a situation in which the widow had daughters. Had a widow remarried while being pregnant from her deceased husband, and her new husband did not legally adopt the child, the latter was not to inherit from her second husband or bear responsibility for his debts; rather, he was to inherit from the property of his deceased father (MAL A §28).

Three additional statutes in this collection pertained to inheritance rights, but were scattered rather randomly and had no connecting thread between them. A woman's property upon her marriage – her dowry, any property she brought in from her father's house and received from her father-in-law – only belonged to her sons to inherit, and her father-in-law's sons had no rights to inherit it. However, if her husband "intends to take control of her",[68] he was to decide to which of his sons this inheritance was to be given (MAL A §29). A man could marry his concubine by veiling her in front of witnesses, and when he died, if he had no sons from his legal wife, his sons from the concubine were to inherit from him (MAL A §41). Lastly, MAL A §49 is fragmentary and hence mostly incomprehensible; its preserved portions seem to deal with the inheritance of a dead prostitute's brothers, but nothing more substantial can be inferred.

In the latest of the collections, NBL, we encounter several regulations of inheritance rights. A father who documented the property he promised to his son for his marriage could not reduce that sum after it has been agreed upon with the bride's father; if his wife died, he remarried and his second wife bore him sons, they were to take one third of what remained of his property (NBL §8).[69] As discussed previously, the dowry of a widow who remarried and had children from both husbands was to be inherited by all children equally (NBL §13). However, the property of a man who died after remarrying following the death of his first wife, and who had children from both wives, was to be divided unequally between his children. The sons of his first wife were to inherit two-thirds of the property, while the sons of the second wife were to inherit the remaining one-third, similarly to NBL §8. The statute then mentions the daughters who still resided in the family household, but unfortunately the text breaks off at this point, leaving us ignorant of what was to be done with them. It is clear, however, that they were not to inherit similarly to their brothers (NBL §15).

Considering how much attention was paid to rules of inheritance in almost all other collections, it is somewhat surprising that the HL only dedicate one statute to this topic. According to it, a mother could disinherit her son, or later on re-establish him as heir (HL §171).

Biblical law

Following a petition made by the orphaned daughters of Zelophehad (Num. 27:1–7), God stipulates to Moses the following rules of inheritance: in case a man dies without having a male child, his daughter is to inherit from him (Num. 27:8); in the absence of daughters the order of alternative heirs was to be as follows: the deceased's brothers (Num. 27:9), the brothers of his father (Num. 27:10) or his closest relative (Num. 27:11). As we can see, even though all the heirs mentioned in the list are males, daughters were still preferred over all other heirs besides sons. These rules still leave open the question of inheritance rights of widows.[70]

If a man had male children from two women, he was required to make his elder son his primary legal heir – thus granting him an inheritance twice as large as other heirs – even if he was the son of a wife hated by the father. The father was forbidden to make a younger son his primary legal heir, even if he was the son of a wife preferred by the father (Deut. 21:15–17).[71] This statute, therefore, favors the right of the firstborn (primogeniture) over any personal preference a husband might have towards any of his wives.

Adoption

Adoption formed another aspect of family formation that pertained to several other aspects of family life, such as duties, tasks and inheritance rights. In the ancient Near East, the institution of adoption usually served financial needs and for that reason was integrated in formal law. Biblical law, on the other hand, has no reference to adoption.

ANE law[72]

The evidence concerning ancient Near Eastern adoption rules in law collections derives almost exclusively from LH, with two additional statutes from LLI and one from LE. It therefore seems to reflect a legal tradition that was related to the Old Babylonian socioeconomic system. As such, the evidence is hardly informative as to other regions and periods of the ancient Near East.

Beginning with the evidence from the earlier collections, LLI §20b determined that if a man neglected an adopted son who was given to him for apprenticeship, that child was to be returned to his mother. Interestingly, this statute specifically identified the child as belonging to his mother. The following statute (LLI §20c) presented a similar case, but one in which the child was female rather than male. Since it is broken, however, we are ignorant of the verdict, and thus unable to establish whether gender played any role in distinguishing between the two cases. LE §32, in contrast with LLI §20b, identified the father – rather than the mother – as the child's biological parent. This statute stated that if the father failed to supply the provisions for his child's rearing for three years, he was to pay the caregiver ten shekels of silver and take back his child.

All other references to adoption in the laws derive from LH. LH §185 generally stated that a newborn adopted by a man was not to be reclaimed by his biological parents. LH §186, however, declared that if the adoptee was a child who was looking for his parents at the time of the adoption, he was to return to them.

The three statutes LH §§187, 192 and 193 – dealing with adoption by the palace attendants *girseqû* and *sekretu* – were discussed in Chapter 2.

A child adopted by a craftsman who has taught him the craft could not be reclaimed by his biological parents (LH §188), but in case the craft was not taught, the child was to return to his father's house (LH §189). If the adopter did not regard the adoptee as equal to his other children, the adoptee was to return to his original father's house (LH §190). If a man disinherited an adopted child because he had biological children born to him, he was to give the adoptee an inheritance of a one-third share of his property, but not from a field, orchard or house, and the adoptee was then to leave (LH §191). This division is similar to LH §181 discussed previously, where a daughter who became a priestess without receiving a dowry from her father was entitled to one-third of his inheritance.

All these statutes identify the adopter as a man; that is, the adopting mother – if she existed – had no role in the legal procedure. The only exception is the case of the *sekretu*, who was a woman without children of her own and hence formed a unique legal case. The biological parents are not identified as such, that is, as a father and a mother, but as a father's household. This stresses the socioeconomic aspects of the adoption procedure. These aspects are what lay at the core of the need for the lengthy and detailed jurisdiction we encounter in LH concerning adoption.

Biblical law

We have no evidence for legal rules of adoption in the Hebrew Bible. As we have seen, even the ancient Near Eastern evidence is limited to the Old Babylonian period and, within it, mostly to the LH. It is therefore not surprising to see that biblical law also ignored this topic.

Polygamy

Polygamy is not frequently legally allowed in most human societies. When it is, it usually involves special legal regulations. The same was true of the ancient Near East and the Hebrew Bible: though monogamy was the general rule, polygamy was allowed under certain circumstances. However, other than one statute in LLI, and possibly another in MAL, polygamy is only attested in one ancient Near Eastern law collection – LH – which emphasizes its rarity. Similarly, biblical law only rarely referred to it. Polyandry, however, is unattested, as it is indeed an even rarer phenomenon throughout human history. We can therefore be more accurate in saying that the only polygamous form we encounter in the sources here discussed is polygyny.

ANE law[73]

The earliest legal provision to address polygamy is LLI §28. This statute allowed a man whose first wife has lost her sight/attractiveness[74] or became paralyzed to marry a second wife, but not to banish his first wife. The second wife was then to support the first one.

The rest of the pertinent evidence mostly derives from LH. This collection includes several statutes that allowed for polygyny under various circumstances: in case someone's wife exhibited immoral behavior (LH §141), if she did not provide her husband with children (LH §144–147) or if a skin disease had struck her (LH §148–149).

The first of these cases – LH §141 – allowed a husband to demote his squandering and disrespectful wife to slavery in his house and marry another woman without officially divorcing his first wife.

As is discussed previously,[75] we then encounter a group of statutes that center on polygyny triggered by the lack of descendants. A man married to a *nadītu* who provided him with children (by giving him a slave-woman who bore them) was forbidden to marry a *šugītu* (LH §144). The slave-woman was to retain her slave status even though she bore children to the *nadītu*'s husband, but her mistress was forbidden to sell her (LH §146). If, however, the slave-woman did not bear children, her mistress was allowed to sell her (LH §147). In case a married *nadītu* did not provide her husband with children, he was allowed to marry a *šugītu*, but the latter was to remain secondary in rank to the *nadītu*, who remained the primary wife (LH §145).

In case someone's wife was struck with a skin disease (*la'bum*), he was allowed to marry another woman without divorcing his wife but was required to continue to take care of her (LH §148). This statute is a clear parallel to LLI §28 discussed previously. If the sick wife preferred to divorce him when he took a second wife, her husband was to give her back her dowry (LH §149).

Finally, a statute in MAL describes a situation that could potentially lead to polygyny. MAL A §30, which was already discussed,[76] presents a case quite similar to a levirate marriage: a widow was to be taken in marriage by her deceased husband's brother. That man, however, was already engaged, and hence could marry two women, unless the father of his fiancée exercised his right to cancel his daughter's marriage under these circumstances.

Biblical law

Biblical law is not explicit as regards polygamy, whether in permitting or prohibiting it. The only legal provision that expresses objection to such practice is Lev. 18:18, which proscribed simultaneous marriage to two sisters. This, however, is a specific case that seems to belong in the realm of incestuous prohibitions, similarly to its preceding verses, rather than an utter ban on polygamous marriage. Evidence hinting at the opposite is found in Deut. 21:15–17, a statute that determined the right of the firstborn son to be established as first heir, thus receiving an inheritance share twice as large as that of the other heirs. The statute declares that if a man had two wives, one loved and the other loathed, he was obliged to rank his elder son as first heir even if that son was born to the wife loathed by the father. This statute thus indirectly proves that polygyny was not utterly prohibited in biblical law.

A more complicated issue was introduced by the levirate marriage.[77] This could lead to polygamy, since the deceased's brother was compelled to marry the childless widow even if he was already married. This obligation was only overruled if his wife and the widow were kin relatives, in which case the incest prohibitions of Lev. 18[78] prevailed over the necessity to perform the levirate marriage.

Prostitution

Prostitution formed an institution that existed outside the familial structure, and in a sense threatened it. Sexual intercourse was morally – and usually, legally – limited to the married couple, and hence any other frame within which sex could occur was prohibited. In this sense, prostitution always existed within a twilight zone parallel to the family. The law was sometimes required to regulate these complex relations in a formal manner.

ANE law[79]

References to prostitution in ancient Near Eastern law collections derive mostly from MAL, with a few attestations in several other sources.

Two statutes in LLI refer to married men and their association with prostitutes. A married man who had no children from his wife, but did have a child from a prostitute, was obliged to support the prostitute but not to let her live in his house with his wife, and the child was to be his heir (LLI §27). As mentioned previously, a married man who had sexual relations with a prostitute, and later on divorced his wife, was forbidden to marry the prostitute after his divorce (LLI §30). It seems plausible that these statutes were meant to prevent men from leaving their wives for prostitutes and thus reduce the predicament prostitution formed for the institution of marriage.

Turning to MAL, the issue of veiling as stipulated in MAL A §40 was discussed in Chapters 1 and 2. This statute specified which classes of Assyrian women were required to be veiled in public and which were forbidden to do so. In contrast with married women, widows, concubines and unmarried daughters who resided in their father's house, prostitutes were forbidden to veil themselves in public. The same applied to unmarried *qadiltu*-women and slave-women. The sanction of a prostitute who did veil herself in public was harsh: she was to be given 50 rod blows and have hot pitch poured over her head. This statute was meant to signify prostitutes as socially distinct from married women. In the wider sense, it marked prostitution as a contrasting concept to marriage. In MAL A §49 a prostitute is mentioned in a broken context that probably discussed inheritance rights. MAL A §52 referred to prostitutes in a more positive manner than MAL A §40: a man who beat a pregnant prostitute and caused her to miscarry was to pay a full financial compensation for the life that was lost. The sanction was identical if the woman was not a prostitute (MAL A §50), so in this case no differentiation or discrimination appears to have existed against prostitutes.

HL §194 deemed continual sexual relations of a father and his son with a slave or a prostitute to be a non-illegal act. This contrasted with HL §191, in which free women in a similar situation were forbidden. We can hence see that these statutes regarded prostitutes as belonging to a lesser social class than regular women, being grouped together with slave-women.[80]

Finally, a royal edict from fourteenth-century Nuzi, AASOR 16.51 (=SMN 553), includes a prohibition on the palace personnel to allow any of their daughters to become destitute or a prostitute without having the king's permission.[81]

Biblical law

Prostitution was perceived negatively in biblical legal contexts, especially when related to sanctity. Thus, priests were forbidden to marry prostitutes (Lev. 21:7, 14), and their daughters were forbidden to practice prostitution (Lev. 21:9). Also, temple prostitution – if the terms *qĕdēšā* (fem.) or *qadēš* (masc.) indeed designated such a profession – was strictly forbidden (Deut. 23:18), and their earnings would not be accepted as donations to the temple (Deut. 23:19).[82] Outside the cultic and priestly circles, however, no laws seem to have banned prostitution or denounced it.

Notes

1 For discussions of numerous legal aspects of family life in the ancient Near East and the Hebrew Bible, see the various pertinent articles in Westbrook 2003a (ed.). The discussions most relevant to this book are those that pertain to periods and cultures from which we have law collections, i.e., Ur III (Lafont and Westbrook 2003: 200–205), Old Babylonian (Westbrook 2003: 385–393), Middle Assyrian (Lafont 2003: 535–540), Neo-Babylonian (Oelsner, Wells and Wunsch 2003: 933–938), Hittite (Haase 2003: 634–637) and biblical (Frymer-Kensky 2003: 1007–1015). For women in the family according to biblical sources, see Marsman 2003: 47–324.

2 See Huehnergard 1983, Grosz 1987 and Ben-Barak 1988.
3 For a discussion of marriage among slaves in the ancient Near East and the Hebrew Bible, see Westbrook 1998: 223–237.
4 For a discussion of this group of statutes, see Yaron 1988: 88–89, 165–171.
5 One of the two surviving manuscripts of this statute (KBo 6.3 ii 25–26) adds that her husband eloped with her without paying a brideprice, which might explain her three-year enslavement.
6 Hoffner 1997: 186.
7 This symbolic piercing of the slave's ear is mentioned again in Deut. 15:16–17, though only his will to remain with his master is mentioned, not his wish to remain with his family.
8 Westbrook 1998: 223.
9 Westbrook 1998: 224.
10 For discussions of these statutes, see, *inter alia*, Paul 1969, Fleishman 2000 and Wright 2009: 144–145, 148.
11 Frymer-Kensky 2003: 1005. See also p. 67.
12 Frymer-Kensky 2003: 1005 n. 38. For further discussion of this statute, see Westbrook 1988b: 101–109.
13 For a discussion of this statute, especially in relation to the rules of Deut. 15:15–17 and Deut. 15:18–21, see Pressler 1993: 9–15, 20; see further Washington 1998: 204–207 and Reeder 2017.
14 Pp. 27, 32.
15 Yaron 1988: 156–158. On these two functions of the connective *u* in Akkadian, see most recently Roth 2017: 213–214. For the connective *waw* (ו) in biblical legal texts, see Brin 1994: 101–103.
16 Yaron 1988: 157.
17 Yaron 1988: 157–158.
18 Paul 1970: 96.
19 See discussion of these rules in p. 30.
20 For a discussion of this statute, especially in relation to the rules of Deut. 15:10–14 and Deut. 15:15–17, see Pressler 1993: 17–20. For a discussion of joint parental authority as seen in these and other biblical statutes, see Anderson 2004: 56–58.
21 Fewell and Gunn 1993: 100.
22 For a discussion of betrothal in the ancient Near East, see recently Stol 2016: 72–92.
23 For a detailed discussion of LE §25, see Yaron 1988: 190–200.
24 Text: *mimma ša ištu bīt abiša ublam ušallamšimma*, "he shall pay her back everything that she has brought from her father's house".
25 Restored, erroneously omitted from text; see Roth 1997: 164.
26 Roth 1997: 193 n. 22, referring to CAD A/1: 217, s.v. "*aḫuzātu*".
27 See Saporetti 1979: 5. See also Westbrook 1991: 88–89.
28 For a discussion of MAL A §43 (together with MAL A 30 and 33) and its interpretation as reflecting forms of levirate marriage, see Westbrook 1991: 88–89.
29 A different manuscript of this statute required the girl's parents to compensate her prospective groom. In practice, they were supposed to give him back whatever he originally gave them for the betrothal.
30 Frymer-Kensky 2003: 1005. See also p. 63 previously.
31 For a discussion of the institution of marriage in the Old Babylonian period, with its financial, legal and economic implications, see Westbrook 1988a.
32 For discussions of the topic of a husband taken captive and the consequences for his wife, see Jackson 2013: 166–168 and Clancier 2014: 19–23.
33 This statute is partially reconstructed but with high degree of plausibility.
34 Presumably for slavery.
35 One of which could have been her father.
36 Hiers 1993: 129–130.

37 See discussion of these rules in p. 80.
38 For discussions of this statute, see, *inter alia*, Pressler 1993: 22–31, Matthews 1998: 108–112 and Edenburg 2009. For a discussion of Deut. 22:13–21, see Wells 2005, Greengus 2011: 55–59, and a thorough treatment in Locher 1986.
39 Pressler 1993: 28.
40 See in this regard also Mayes 1981: 309.
41 In Deut. 22:28–29 the brideprice is set at 50 shekels of silver.
42 "For any illegal case . . . he shall pay his colleague double". (עַל-כָּל-דְּבַר-פֶּשַׁע . . . יְשַׁלֵּם שְׁנַיִם לְרֵעֵהוּ) (Exod. 22:8); Rofé 1976: 23 and n. 13.
43 See pp. 76–77.
44 For a discussion of divorce in the ancient Near East, see recently Stol 2016: 209–233; see also Jackson 2013: 115–118.
45 For discussions of LE §59, see Yaron 1988: 211–222 and Roth 1997: 70 n. 32.
46 For a discussion of LLI §30 and LE §59, see Westbrook 1984.
47 The text is partially broken and the context not entirely clear.
48 The text is partially broken, and its understanding relies on restoring HL §26b+c vis-à-vis each other, which is not at all certain.
49 See in this regard Hoffner 1997: 181.
50 The first to discuss this statute from a purely legal perspective was Yaron 1966. For comprehensive discussions of it, see Carmichael 1979: 10–21, Westbrook 1986 and Pressler 1993: 45–62, 105.
51 Westbrook 1986, 1991: 156.
52 See, *inter alia*, Frymer-Kensky 2003: 1010–1011.
53 Otto 1998: 137–138.
54 For a discussion of widows in the ancient Near East, see recently Stol 2016: 275–299.
55 LLI is the sole collection in which no such statutes are to be found. However, since it has not been preserved in its entirety – like most other ancient Near Eastern law collections – and widowing seems to be such a popular topic that all other collections did address it, it can hypothetically be suggested that LLI did contain statutes pertaining to widowing, but these are now lost in one of the gaps we have of this text. Such suggestions will remain conjectural until further manuscripts of LLI are found and the extant gaps are finally closed.
56 For a discussion of this statute and its complexities, see Yaron 1988: 179–190 and Roth 1997: 69 n. 6. For a discussion of LE §§17, 18, see Westbrook 1995.
57 *aḫuzātu*; see p. 85 n. 26.
58 For discussions of MAL A §30, 33 and 43, and their interpretation as reflecting forms of levirate marriage, see Westbrook 1991: 88–89 and Greengus 2011: 21–22, 42.
59 The text is fragmentary at this point.
60 These options are offered and explained in Peled 2015: 290–291.
61 See Phillips 2002: 129. The biblical obligations to protect widows and orphans have been discussed by numerous scholars; see, to name but a few, Patterson 1973, Gowan 1987, van der Toorn 1994: 134–140, Sneed 1999 and Bennett 2002.
62 For discussions of this statute, see, *inter alia*, Westbrook 1977, 1991: 69–89, Pressler 1993: 63–74, 88 n. 30 and Otto 1998: 138–140. Frymer-Kensky (2003: 1012) claimed that levirate was not an institution of marriage, but rather of sexual intercourse meant for producing offspring: "levirate is copulation until conception, not marriage".
63 For discussions of women as heirs in the ancient Near East, see recently Justel 2016: 88–91 and Stol 2016: 300–303; for inheritance in the law collections, see Jackson 2013: 119–122.
64 LE conspicuously lacks any statute pertaining to inheritance. Since this collection is known to us in its entirety, it cannot be suggested that it originally included certain rules of inheritance that are now lost.
65 LUN §B3 is fragmentary, and hence these interpretations are uncertain.

66 Though the text is not explicit in this regard, that the woman was not his biological mother is inferred from the fact that mother-son relations are dealt with – and are punishable with death – in the previous statute, LH §157. The mention that she was a principal wife (*rabītum*) shows that there was at least one more wife – a secondary one – who in all likelihood was the perpetrator's biological mother.
67 Pp. 52–53.
68 *ipūagši*; as noted by Roth (1997: 193 n. 21), "The full legal implications of this action are unclear".
69 Roth (1997: 149 n. 10) commented: "I.e., not the preferential or double share" as in LH §181.
70 For discussions of these statutes, see Ilan 2000 and Seebass 2000.
71 For a discussion of this statute, especially in relation to the rules of Deut. 15:10–14 and Deut. 15:18–21, see Pressler 1993: 15–17, 20; see further Carmichael 1979: 31–32 and Greengus 2011: 70, 72.
72 For a comprehensive discussion of adoption in the Old Babylonian period, see Obermark 1992; see also, more generally, Couto-Ferreira 2016: 30–32; for adoption in the law collections, see Jackson 2013: 122–124.
73 For discussions of polygamy in the ancient Near East, see Friedl 2000, Westbrook 2004 and, recently, Stol 2016: 165–192.
74 The Sumerian term/logogram igi – literally, "eye" – has numerous possible meanings and can thus be interpreted in more than one way. Civil (1985: 2) translated it as "sight", while Roth (1997: 31) opted for "attractiveness".
75 See p. 52.
76 See p. 66.
77 See discussion in pp. 76–77.
78 See pp. 100, 104 n. 32.
79 For discussions of prostitution in the ancient Near East, see Cooper 2006 and, recently, Stol 2016: 399–418.
80 See discussion in Peled 2015: 289.
81 Pfeiffer and Speiser 1936: 37 (transliteration), 103 (translation); for a new translation and discussion, see Roth 1997: 195–196.
82 See discussion and literature in p. 54.

Bibliography

Anderson, Cheryl B. 2004. *Women, Ideology, and Violence: Critical Theory and the Construction of Gender in the Book of the Covenant and the Deuteronomic Law*. London: Clark.

Ben-Barak, Zafrira. 1988. "The Legal Status of the Daughter as Heir in Nuzi and Emar". In *Society and Economy in the Eastern Mediterranean (c. 1500–1000 B.C.): Proceedings of the International Symposium Held at the University of Haifa from the 28th of April to 2nd of May 1985*, edited by Michael Heltzer and Eward and Lipiński. Leuven: Peeters. Pp. 87–97.

Bennett, Harold V. 2002. *Injustice Made Legal: Deuteronomic Law and the Plight of Widows, Strangers, and Orphans in Ancient Israel*. Grand Rapids, MI: Eerdmans.

Brin, Gershon. 1994. *Studies in Biblical Law: From the Hebrew Bible to the Dead Sea Scrolls*. Sheffield: JSOT.

Carmichael, Calum M. 1979. *Women, Law, and the Genesis Traditions*. Edinburgh: Edinburgh University Press.

Civil, Miguel. 1985. "New Sumerian Law Fragments". In *Studies in Honor of Benno Landsberger on His Seventy-Fifth Birthday, April 21, 1965*, edited by Hans

Gustav Güterbock and Thorkild Jacobsen. Chicago, IL: University of Chicago Press. Pp. 1–12.

Clancier, Philippe. 2014. "Hommes guerriers et femmes invisibles. Le choix des scribes dans le Proche-Orient Ancient". *Clio. Women, Gender, History* 39/1: 19–36.

Cooper, Jerold S. 2006. "Prostitution". *Reallexikon der Assyriologie und Vorderasiatischen Archäologie* 11: 12–22.

Couto-Ferreira, Erica M. 2016. "Being Mothers or Acting (Like) Mothers? Constructing Motherhood in Ancient Mesopotamia". In *Women in Antiquity: Real Women Across the Ancient World*, edited by Stephanie L. Budin and Jean MacIntosh Turfa. London; New York: Routledge, Taylor & Francis Group. Pp. 25–37.

Edenburg, Cynthia. 2009. "Ideology and Social Context of the Deuteronomic Women's Sex Laws (Deuteronomy 22:13–29)". *Journal of Biblical Literature* 128/1: 43–60.

Fewell, Dana N. and Gunn, David M. 1993. *Gender, Power, and Promise: The Subject of the Bible's First Story*. Nashville, TN: Abingdon Press.

Fleishman, Joseph. 2000. "Does the Law of Exodus 21:7–11 Permit a Father to Sell His Daughter to Be a Slave?" *Jewish Law Annual* 13: 47–64.

Friedl, Corinna. 2000. *Polygynie in Mesopotamien und Israel. Sozialgeschichtliche Analyse Polygamer Beziehungen Anhand Rechtlicher Texte aus dem 2. und 1. Jahrtausend v. Chr*. Münster: Ugarit-Verlag.

Frymer-Kensky, Tikva. 2003. "Israel". In *A History of Ancient Near Eastern Law*, edited by Raymond Westbrook. Leiden: Brill. Pp. 975–1046.

Gowan, Donald E. 1987. "Wealth and Poverty in the Old Testament: The Case of the Widow, the Orphan, and the Sojourner". *Interpretation* 41/4: 341–353.

Greengus, Samuel. 2011. *Laws in the Bible and in Early Rabbinic Collections: The Legal Legacy of the Ancient Near East*. Eugene, OR: Cascade Books.

Grosz, Katarzyna. 1987. "Daughters Adopted as Sons at Nuzi and Emar". In *La Femme Dans Le Proche-Orient Antique: Compte Rendu de la XXXIIIe Rencontre Assyriologique Internationale (Paris, 7–10 Juillet 1986)*, edited by Jean-Marie Durand. Paris: Éditions Recherche sur les Civilisations. Pp. 81–86.

Haase, Richard. 2003. "The Hittite Kingdom". In *A History of Ancient Near Eastern Law*, edited by Raymond Westbrook. Leiden: Brill. Pp. 619–656.

Hiers, Richard H. 1993. "Transfer of Property by Inheritance and Bequest in Biblical Law and Tradition". *Journal of Law & Religion* 10: 121–151.

Hoffner, Harry A. Jr. 1997. *The Laws of the Hittites: A Critical Edition*. Leiden: Brill.

Huehnergard, John. 1983. "Five Tablets from the Vicinity of Emar". *Revue d'assyriologie et d'archéologie orientale* 77: 11–43.

Ilan, Tal. 2000. "The Daughters of Zelophehad and Women's Inheritance: The Biblical Injunction and Its Outcome [Num. 27:1–11; 36:1–12]". In *Exodus to Deuteronomy. A Feminist Companion to the Bible*, edited by Athalya Brenner. Sheffield: Sheffield Academic Press. Pp. 176–186.

Jackson, Samuel A. 2013 [2008]. *A Comparison of Ancient Near Eastern Law Collections Prior to the First Millennium BC*. Piscataway, NJ: Gorgias Press.

Justel, Josué J. 2016. "Women, Gender and Law at the Dawn of History: The Evidence of the Cuneiform Sources". In *Women in Antiquity: Real Women Across the Ancient World*, edited by Stephanie L. Budin and Jean MacIntosh Turfa. London; New York: Routledge, Taylor & Francis Group. Pp. 77–100.

Lafont, Bertrand and Westbrook, Raymond. 2003. "Neo-Sumerian Period (Ur III)". In *A History of Ancient Near Eastern Law*, edited by Raymond Westbrook. Leiden: Brill. Pp. 183–226.

Lafont, Sophie. 2003. "Middle Assyrian Period". In *A History of Ancient Near Eastern Law*, edited by Raymond Westbrook. Leiden: Brill. Pp. 521–563.

Locher, Clemens. 1986. *Die Ehre einer Frau in Israel: Exegetische und rechtsvergleichende Studien zu Deuteronomium* (vol. 22). Göttingen: Vandenhoeck & Ruprecht; Freiburg: Universitätverslag. Pp. 13–21.

Marsman, Hennie J. 2003. *Women in Ugarit and Israel: Their Social and Religious Position in the Context of the Ancient Near East*. Leiden: Brill.

Matthews, Victor H. 1998. "Honor and Shame in Gender-Related Legal Situations in the Hebrew Bible". In *Gender and Law in the Hebrew Bible and the Ancient Near East*, edited by Victor H. Matthews, Bernard M. Levinson and Tikva S. Frymer-Kensky. Sheffield: Sheffield Academic Press. Pp. 97–112.

Mayes, Andrew D. H. 1981. *Deuteronomy, New Century Bible*. Grand Rapids, MI: Eerdmans.

Obermark, Peter R. 1992. *Adoption in the Old Babylonian Period* (PhD dissertation, Hebrew Union College-Jewish Institute of Religion). Cincinnati, OH.

Oelsner, Joachim, Wells, Bruce and Wunsch, Cornelia. 2003. "Neo-Babylonian Period". In *A History of Ancient Near Eastern Law*, edited by Raymond Westbrook. Leiden: Brill. Pp. 911–974.

Otto, Eckart. 1998. "False Weights in the Scales of Biblical Justice? Different Views of Women from Patriarchal Hierarchy to Religious Equality in the Book of Deuteronomy". In *Gender and Law in the Hebrew Bible and the Ancient Near East*, edited by Victor H. Matthews, Bernard M. Levinson and Tikva S. Frymer-Kensky. Sheffield: Sheffield Academic Press. Pp. 128–146.

Patterson, Richard D. 1973. "The Widow, the Orphan, and the Poor in the Old Testament and the Extra-Biblical Literature". *Bibliotheca Sacra* 130: 223–234.

Paul, Shalom M. 1969. "Exodus 21:10, A Threefold Maintenance Clause". *Journal of Near Eastern Studies* 28/1: 48–53.

Paul, Shalom M. 1970. *Studies in the Book of the Covenant in the Light of Cuneiform and Biblical Law*. Leiden: Brill.

Peled, Ilan. 2015. "Crime and Sexual Offense in Hatti". *Near Eastern Archaeology* 78/4: 286–293.

Pfeiffer, Robert H. and Speiser, Ephraim A. 1936. *One Hundred New Selected Nuzi Texts*. New Haven, CT: American Schools of Oriental Research.

Phillips, Anthony. 2002. *Essays on Biblical Law*. Sheffield: Sheffield Academic Press.

Pressler, Carolyn. 1993. *The View of Women Found in the Deuteronomic Family Laws*. Berlin: De Gruyter.

Reeder, Caryn A. 2017. "Deuteronomy 21.10–14 and/as Wartime Rape". *Journal for the Study of the Old Testament* 41/3: 313–336.

Rofé, Alexander. 1976. "Family and Sex Laws in Deuteronomy and the Book of the Covenant". *Beit Mikra: Journal for the Study of the Bible and Its World* 22/1: 19–36. [Hebrew].

Roth, Martha T. 1997. *Law Collections from Mesopotamia and Asia Minor* (second edition). Atlanta, GA: Scholars Press.

Roth, Martha T. and Johnson, Janet H. 2017. "Response: Law and Gender Across the Ancient Near East and Beyond". In *Structures of Power: Law and Gender Across the Ancient Near East and Beyond*, edited by Ilan Peled. Chicago, IL: The Oriental Institute of the University of Chicago. Pp. 213–220.

Saporetti, Claudio. 1979. *The Status of Women in the Middle Assyrian Period*. Malibu, CA: Undena Publications.

Seebass, Horst. 2000. "Zur juristischen und sozialgeschichtlichen Bedeutung des Töchtererbrechts nach Numbers 27:1–11 und 36:1–12". *Biblische Notizen* 102: 22–27.

Sneed, Mark R. 1999. "Israelite Concern for the Alien, Orphan, and Widow: Altruism or Ideology?" *Zeitschrift für die Alttestamentliche Wissenschaft* 111: 498–507.

Stol, Marten. 2016. *Women in the Ancient Near East*. Berlin: De Gruyter.

van der Toorn, Karel. 1994. *From Her Cradle to Her Grave: The Role of Religion in the Life of the Israelite and the Babylonian Woman*. Sheffield: JSOT.

Washington, Harold C. 1998. " 'Lest He Die in the Battle and Another Man Take Her': Violence and the Construction of Gender in the Laws of Deuteronomy 20–22". In *Gender and Law in the Hebrew Bible and the Ancient Near East*, edited by Victor H. Matthews, Bernard M. Levinson and Tikva S. Frymer-Kensky. Sheffield: Sheffield Academic Press. Pp. 185–213.

Wells, Bruce. 2005. "Sex, Lies, and Virginal Rape: The Slandered Bride and False Accusation in Deuteronomy". *Journal of Biblical Literature* 124/1: 41–72.

Westbrook, Raymond. 1977. "The Law of the Biblical Levirate". *Revue Internationale des Droits de l'Antiquité* 24: 65–87.

Westbrook, Raymond. 1984. "The Enforcement of Morals in Mesopotamian Law". *Journal of the American Oriental Society* 104/4: 753–775.

Westbrook, Raymond. 1986. "The Prohibition on Restoration of Marriage in Deuteronomy 24:1–4". In *Studies in Bible*, edited by Sara Japhet. Jerusalem: Magnes Press. Pp. 387–405.

Westbrook, Raymond. 1988a. *Old Babylonian Marriage Law*. Horn: Berger.

Westbrook, Raymond. 1988b. *Studies in Biblical and Cuneiform Law*. Paris: Gabalda.

Westbrook, Raymond. 1991. *Property and the Family in Biblical Law*. Sheffield: JSOT.

Westbrook, Raymond. 1995. "A Death in the Family: Codex Eshnunna 17–18 Revisited". In *Studies in Honour of Reuven Yaron*, edited by Alfredo M. Rabello (Israel Law Review 29). New York: Cambridge University Press. Pp. 32–42.

Westbrook, Raymond. 1998. "The Female Slave". In *Gender and Law in the Hebrew Bible and the Ancient Near East*, edited by Victor H. Matthews, Bernard M. Levinson and Tikva S. Frymer-Kensky. Sheffield: Sheffield Academic Press. Pp. 214–238.

Westbrook, Raymond. 2003. "Old Babylonian Period". In *A History of Ancient Near Eastern Law*, edited by Raymond Westbrook. Leiden: Brill. Pp. 361–430.

Westbrook, Raymond. 2004. "Polygamie". *Reallexikon der Assyriologie und Vorderasiatischen Archäologie* 10: 600–602.

Wright, David P. 2009. *Inventing God's Law*. Oxford: Oxford University Press.

Yaron, Reuven. 1966. "The Restoration of Marriage". *Journal of Jewish Studies* 17: 1–11.

Yaron, Reuven. 1988. *The Laws of Eshnunna* (second edition). Jerusalem: Magnes Press, The Hebrew University.

4 The individual perspective

Morality and sex crimes

Introduction

The legal framework of sexual intercourse in the ancient Near East only permitted such relations to occur between a man and a woman who were married to one another. Any deviation from this basic rule was deemed illicit. We therefore encounter in the ancient Near Eastern and biblical law collections several felonies grouped under the category of sex crimes: premarital sex, adultery and rape, incest and forbidden kin relations. It can immediately be observed that all these felonies are related in one way or another to the institution of marriage. As such, they can be assessed against the background of the regulation of family life, as discussed in the previous chapter. In the current chapter, however, we focus on the individuals involved rather than on the familial structure. These issues occupy the first three sections of this chapter.

Two other types of acts that were sometimes considered sexual felonies were homosexual intercourse and bestiality. These, however, are poorly represented in the ancient Near Eastern law collections: homosexual intercourse is only referred to once in the MAL, and bestiality is attested in four statutes of the HL. Both types of misdemeanors are forbidden in biblical law as well. These issues occupy the final two sections in this chapter.

Virginity and premarital sex

Female virginity is considered to be a significant virtue in many ancient – and at times also modern – societies and is frequently related to the financial aspects of the marriage institution. In the ancient world, therefore, premarital sex endangered the potential financial profit of the household from the future marriage of its daughters and was therefore perceived highly negatively. For this reason, among the patriarchal societies of the ancient Near East and the biblical era only women's virginity was important, while men's virginity was practically immaterial. Both the Mesopotamian and biblical legal corpora clearly reflect this perspective.

ANE law[1]

The significance ascribed to female virginity and avoidance of premarital sexual intercourse in Mesopotamia[2] is made clear by the fact that – other than the mostly lost NBL – all Mesopotamian law collections relate to this topic. Interestingly, however, each collection contains no more than one or two relevant statutes, while LUN contains four of them.

Four statutes in LUN referred to different aspects of premarital sexual intercourse. A man who seduced a girl betrothed to another and took her into his household was to face execution (LUN §6). If, however, that girl was the one who initiated the sexual intercourse, and her prospective husband killed her, the killer was not to face any penalty; no punishment was specified for the man who had sex with her (LUN §7).[3] A man who had sexual intercourse with an unmarried slave-woman and took her into his household was to pay five shekels of silver (LUN §8), presumably – though the text is not explicit in this regard – to her owner.[4] A man who falsely accused another man of having sex with a betrothed woman was to pay a fine of 20 shekels of silver (LUN §14).

LLI §33 reiterates the issue of false accusations as we have seen in LUN §14, but from the point of view of the accused daughter: it states that a man who made the unfounded accusation that another man's unmarried daughter had sexual intercourse was to pay a fine of ten shekels of silver. Since this fine is half as much as that stated in LUN §14, we can speculate whether the differences resulted from the possible outcome of the accusations. In LUN §14 they could lead to the seducer's execution (as in LUN §6, in case the girl was betrothed to another man), while in LLI we do not encounter a statute that prescribes similar punishment for the girl. The fine in LLI §33 could derive from the potential financial loss the accusations would cause to the girl's family, in case her future marriage was now in jeopardy.

Two further relevant statutes are found in LE. According to the first, a man who abducted and deflowered a girl betrothed to another without the consent of both her parents was to be executed (LE §26). The essence of the crime of deflowering a betrothed girl was not involuntary sex, even though she was abducted, but the infringement of another man's exclusive rights over the woman who was supposed to become his wife. A man who deflowered a slave-girl that did not belong to him was to pay her owner 20 shekels of silver, and she was to remain in the possession of her owner (LE §31). This should be compared to LUN §8, in which the compensation to be paid was only five shekels of silver, and the law did not force the seducer to return the slave-woman to her owner.

Yaron has discussed the differences between the two situations described in LE §26 and in LE §31.[5] The former involves the defloration of a free man's daughter, while the latter entails the defloration of a slave-woman. The crime treated by LE §26 was much harsher – as evident from its penalty – because it infringed on her future marriage, which caused considerable financial losses to both her father and future husband. In the broader sense, such a crime undermines the whole institution of marriage and therefore cannot be tolerated. In LE §31, however, the victim is a virgin slave-woman, and the institution of marriage is therefore irrelevant. The slave-woman's owner is the only one who suffers any kind of loss, because she was considered his property. But this loss probably was not financial, and had more to do with illicit use of another person's property. Given the nature of slavery in the ancient Near East, the female victim never constituted a relevant issue from the point of view of law. As noted by Yaron, the statute concludes with the command that the slave-woman will remain the property of her owner, in order to clarify that her deflowerer cannot obtain any rights to her by paying the fine determined by the law.[6]

One statute in LH declared that a man who forcibly[7] deflowered a girl betrothed to another was to be executed, while the girl had no liability (LH §130). This statute is parallel to LUN §6 and LE §26, though the economic factors apparent in LE §26 are absent in LH §130. It might be suggested, therefore, that the immoral aspect of rape was also part of the crime against which LH §130 was stipulated, and not just the infringement of the rights of the groom-to-be, or the financial damage caused to both families involved in the future wedding.

If we turn to Assyria, a man who has raped a virgin girl was liable to financially compensate her father three times her value and – unless her father objected – he was then to marry her. The father was also entitled to hand the rapist's wife over to be raped, and then to keep her. If the father objected to the marriage of his daughter with her rapist, he could give her in marriage to anyone he wished (MAL A §55). If it was not a case of rape, and the sexual relations were consensual, the man was compelled to pay her father the triple compensation but not to marry her, and the father was free to decide how to treat his daughter (MAL A §56).

The common denominator of all these legal references to virginity was the social and legal status of the girl involved. As an unmarried girl she resided in her father's household and formed a valuable economic asset for him, as the head of the family. Upon her marriage her family was to earn considerable income in the form of the gifts delivered by the groom.

Biblical law[8]

Biblical legal references to virginity and premarital intercourse are not rare, and some resemble equivalent provisions from the ancient Near Eastern collections discussed previously. A man who seduced an unbetrothed virgin girl was required to pay a brideprice and marry her. Had her father refused the marriage, the seducer was nonetheless required to pay the brideprice (Exod. 22:15–16). This ruling is repeated in Deuteronomy, where it is stated that the man was required to pay the girl's father 50 shekels of silver and marry her without possibility of divorcing her in the future (Deut. 22:28–29).[9] These provisions are partially parallel to MAL A §55.[10]

The felony in these cases was not merely moral but mostly financial. A man who seduced a virgin girl deprived the head of her household – her father – of the potential financial gain involved in the brideprice he would have received upon her marriage. The victim, therefore, was the father, and the perpetrator was required to compensate him for his losses. The compensation would have had the form of the brideprice the seducer paid her father when marrying her (Exod. 22:15). If, however, the father did not allow the marriage to take place, the seducer was required to pay him the brideprice nonetheless (Exod. 22:16), and thus the father was still compensated for his loss.[11]

If a man has sex with a slave-woman who was promised to another man but has not yet been ransomed or freed, an inquiry will be conducted, and the couple will not be executed. A sacrifice was to be made by a priest in order to absolve the man from his sin (Lev. 19:20–22). Since the slave-woman has not been redeemed yet, her status was not that of a betrothed woman, and hence the sexual intercourse was not considered adultery.[12]

A man who made false accusations that his newly wedded wife was not a virgin was to pay a fine of 100 shekels of silver to her father and marry the woman without possibility of ever divorcing her. The girl's father and mother were to protect her in front of the town elders, who judged the case (Deut. 22:13–19). If, however, the husband's claims were found to be justified, the girl was to be stoned to death by her community members (Deut. 22:20–21).[13] The former of these two statutes was already discussed.[14] While the offense it regulates involved slander, and formed by and large a financial crime, the latter statute emphasizes the importance of virginity by establishing premarital sexual intercourse performed by a girl as a serious crime against her father, household and entire community. Pressler noted that the girl's crime had several aspects: against her husband, against her father and household and against her entire community. By entering into marriage while not being virgin she has infringed on her husband's exclusive right to her sexuality; the cancellation of the marriage entailed a heavy financial loss for her father and household, intensified by the complication of marrying her off in the future; and since the crime undermined her father's authority, it threatened the social order at large.[15]

We can therefore see that biblical law expressed a financially oriented attitude to female virginity and premarital sexual intercourse, similar to the one we encounter in the various Mesopotamian law collections.

Adultery and rape[16]

The topic of adultery and rape in the ancient Near East and the Hebrew Bible has been researched extensively. The pertinent secondary literature is accordingly immense, and for the most part easily accessible. The two felonies resulted from essentially the same case: a man who had sexual intercourse with a woman to whom he was not married. Had the sexual relations been under compulsion, the act was defined as rape, while had the woman been compliant while married to another man, it was an act of adultery. Other legal alternatives involved a complicit girl who was betrothed to another man, or an unbetrothed complicit girl who resided in her father's household. The sanctions that ensued depended on these varying definitions and, accordingly, could include both paramours or only one of them.

ANE law[17]

The gravity of the felonies under discussion is evident, yet again, from the fact that most ancient Near Eastern law collections addressed them. The boundaries between the definitions of these felonies, however, could be blurred on certain occasions. For example, as was already mentioned, LLI §30 presents a case of a married man who had sexual relations with a prostitute. Though he was ordered by the judges not to return to the prostitute, his acts were not regarded as constituting a punishable legal felony. On the other hand, as we see in what follows, a married woman who had sexual relations with any man other than her husband would have been severely punished. This emphasizes the aspects of gender differentiation in the attitude to sex crimes.

In LE, a married woman who was caught having adulterous sexual relations was to be executed (LE §28). However, there were exceptions: if a married man was caught by the enemy and detained for a long time, and if his wife married another and bore him children, when her first husband came back, she was required to return to him, but no sanction of any kind was to be imposed upon her (LE §29). This statute clearly implies that the woman performed no adultery, since there was no objection to her marrying another man while her husband was in captivity. Somewhat similarly, if a married man fled his city, his wife was entitled to marry another man, and even if her first husband eventually came back, she was not to return to him (LE §30). This statute allowed yet again what otherwise could be regarded as adultery, or even polyandry, implying that the first husband's malevolent acts led to the legal cancellation of his marriage.

A different case involved a man who has deflowered a slave-woman who did not belong to him. He was to pay a fine of 20 shekels of silver, and the slave-woman remained in the possession of her owner (LE §31). The motivation behind this statute was to prevent the infringement of a man's right of ownership, rather than a matter of prohibiting extramarital sex or rape.

The LH dealt at length with the matter of adultery, dedicating to it a cluster of consecutive statutes, LH §§129–136.[18] The opening statute in the cluster ordered that an adulterous wife and her lover were to be executed, but if the husband spared his wife, her lover was to be spared as well (LH §129). False accusation of adultery was dealt with by a couple of statutes. According to the first, if a husband accused his wife of adultery she was required to swear by the god to her innocence (LH §131); according to the second, if such an accusation was made without specifying who was the accuser, the woman was to undergo the divine-River-Ordeal to prove her innocence (LH §132). The following statutes described cases that were – or were not – considered adultery. If a married man was captured (by the enemy), and during his absence his wife had sufficient means of sustenance, she was not allowed to go and live with another man (LH §133a). Failing to follow this rule was considered adultery, and thus resulted in her execution (LH §133b). If, however, the wife had no sufficient means of sustenance, she was allowed to go and live with another man (LH §134). If she bore her second husband children, and then her first husband returned, she was to return to him, but the children were to remain with their father (LH §135). If the first husband's absence resulted from intentional escape from the city, and he later on returned, his wife was to remain with her second husband (LH §136). These rulings are identical to those found in LE §§29–30.

The MAL related extensively to the matters of adultery and rape, dedicating to them no fewer than a dozen statutes. A married woman was expected to resist any attempt of seduction by a man who was not her husband. A man who raped her was to face execution (MAL A §12). Consensual sex between a married woman and a man who knew that she was married to another would lead to the execution of both paramours (MAL A §13). The following statute elaborates and states that the male lover was to be punished identically to the way the betrayed husband punished his adulterous wife. If the lover had no knowledge that the woman was married, he bore no guilt, and the husband was only to punish his wife after having proved his charges (MAL A §14). If the husband caught the paramours and proved their misdemeanor in court, they were to be executed. The husband could choose to kill them both, have their faces mutilated (and additionally castrate the lover) or have them both released. Either way, their punishment – or lack of it – was to be identical (MAL A §15).[19] If the woman initiated the adulterous relations, her husband was only to punish her, but in case she was raped, and her rapist was found guilty in court, he was to suffer the punishment that otherwise she would have faced (MAL A §16). In case a man accused another man's wife of adultery, without any witnesses to prove the accusation, both the accuser and the husband were to undergo the divine-River-Ordeal (MAL A §17). If the accuser could not prove his claims, he was to suffer 40 rod blows, perform one month of the "king's service", have something of his[20] cut off and pay a fine of one talent (=3,600 shekels) of lead (MAL A §18).

The economic implications of MAL A §§22–24 are discussed in Chapter 3. We will now address these statutes in relation to the moral implications of the perception of adultery and rape. In the first situation, a married woman traveled with a man who was not her husband or immediate kin relative (father, brother or son). If her male companion was unaware that she was married he was to pay her husband two talents (=7,200 shekels) of lead. In case he was aware of her marital status he was to pay the compensations and swear that they did not have sex. If the woman claimed that they did have sex, her companion was to undergo the divine-River-Ordeal. Refusing to do so would imply his guilt and he was hence to be punished by the woman's husband similarly to the way the husband punished his wife (MAL A §22). In the second situation a woman lured into her house a married woman, with the intention that a man would have sex with that married woman. The man was to be punished as a person who fornicated with a married woman, while his female accomplice was to be punished as an adulterous woman: they were both to be executed. However, if the betrayed husband did not punish his wife, no one else was to be punished. Had the wife been lured unknowingly and revealed what happened immediately afterwards, she was considered an innocent victim and only the two perpetrators were to be killed (MAL A §23). In the third situation a married woman has left her husband's household and was hosted for several days by another woman in the house of another man, without the latter's knowledge that she was married. She was to be mutilated by her husband and not to return to him. Her hostess was to have her ears cut off, but her husband could redeem her by paying 3 talents and 30 minas (=12,600 shekels) of lead. If he knew that the woman who was brought into his house was married, he was required to pay a triple fine. Otherwise, he had to undergo the divine-River-Ordeal in order to prove his ignorance of her marital status. Her husband had to undergo the same test; refusal would clear the hostess's husband of guilt. If the betrayed husband refused to mutilate his wife, he was prohibited from punishing her in any other way, and she was to return to him (MAL A §24).

A different case discussed in the MAL relates to the rape of an unmarried girl, as was already mentioned.[21] If a man raped a virgin girl, her father was to take the rapist's wife, hand her over to be raped and keep her. The rapist was to pay the father silver three times his daughter's value and marry her. If her father objected to the marriage, the rapist was nonetheless required to pay the triple fine, and her father was to give her in marriage to whomever he wished (MAL A §55). If, however, the sexual relations were consensual, the man's wife was not to be involved, and he was to pay the triple fine. The girl's father had the liberty to treat his daughter as he pleased (MAL A §56).

The HL related to adultery and rape in a strikingly similar manner as the Hebrew Bible did (see the following). A man who has raped a woman married to another in an uninhabited area[22] was to be executed. However, if their relations took place in an inhabited area,[23] the woman's consent was assumed, and she was hence to be executed for adultery. If her husband found and killed them on the spot, he was not to face charges (HL §197). If the husband brought the paramours to be judged at the palace and wished his wife to be released, so was to be done with her lover. But if the husband wished their execution, the king was to have the final decision whether to have them killed or not (HL §198).

Biblical law

The prohibition on fornication appears already in HC: "And you shall not *have sex* with your colleague's wife, to defile in her" (Lev. 18:20).[24] Here men were required to refrain from having sexual intercourse with women married to other men. The prohibition is repeated two chapters later, this time with a specification of the punishment: execution of both perpetrators (Lev. 20:10). Like many other statutes of Leviticus, this issue is addressed in a similar fashion in Deuteronomy, where the fornication of a man with a married woman resulted in their execution (Deut. 22:22).

If a man had sex in an inhabited place ("in the city") with a virgin girl who was betrothed to another man, both of them were to be put to death: the girl because she did not object and the man for violating a woman that belonged to another (Deut. 22:23–24). This ruling is identical to the previous one (Deut. 22:22), which demonstrates that in this respect betrothal was considered as legally obligating as marriage. If, however, the said sexual relations occurred in an isolated place ("in the field"), the girl's consent was not assumed and the act was regarded as a case of rape rather than adultery, and only the man was to be executed (Deut. 22:25–27).[25] As was noted by numerous commentators in the past, these provisions are strikingly similar to HL §197.

Other than statutes that proscribed adultery, the Hebrew Bible includes a famous section that specified a practical procedure that was meant to be put into effect in case a married woman was suspected by her husband of adultery without any witness or proof ("*sotah* ordeal/judgment", מבחן/דין סוטה, Num. 5:12–31). The suspected woman was to undergo a procedure called "the ordeal of the bitter water", performed by the priest at the temple. The ordeal was supposed to prove her guilt or clarify and proclaim her innocence.[26]

Incest and forbidden kin relations

Norms of permitted and prohibited sexual relations within the familial circles vary between social groups. Rules concerning immediate relations – within the nuclear family – are relatively universal and homogeneous and usually involve clear bans in the form of incestuous prohibitions. Regulations concerning relations between different members of the extended family, however, are far less universal and may vary greatly. Either way, the formal rules of behavior in such matters were meant to monitor and regulate the sexual interaction between the individual and his immediate social environment. We will now view how the ancient Near Eastern and biblical legal corpora related to these issues.

ANE law[27]

Somewhat surprisingly, most ancient Near Eastern law collections did not stipulate any regulation banning or explicitly permitting specific types of sexual unions within the family – whether nuclear or extended. Other than one statute in LUN, the pertinent evidence is only found in LH and HL. It is therefore problematic to generalize and ascribe similar notions to other parts and times of the ancient Near East. Since it does not seem conceivable that incest – at any possible level of kin proximity – was permitted when the law was silent about it, we can only speculate why statutes similar to the ones we find in LH are absent from other Mesopotamian law collections. This is especially true of those collections that were composed in chronological and geographical proximity to LH, such as LE, a complete collection known to us in its full extant.

We begin with the only Mesopotamian statute outside LH to refer to forbidden kin relations. LUN §E5 states that a man who married his deceased older brother's widow was to be executed. Since no penalty is specified for the woman, it is clear that the law put all the legal liability on the male, viewing him as the sole person responsible for the sexual interaction.

The LH dedicated five statutes to the regulation of sexual behavior. A man who had sex with his daughter was to be banished from the city (LH §154), while a man who had sex with his daughter-in-law was to be executed (LH §155). If she was promised to his son, but not yet married to him, and his father had sex with her, the father was to pay a compensation of 30 shekels of silver, return any property that she brought and the planned marriage was canceled (LH §156). A man and his mother who had sex after the father has died were both to be executed (LH §157). If she was his stepmother and had children, her stepson who had sex with her was to be disinherited (LH §158).

A few notes should be made on this group of statutes. First, they were all intergenerational, and thus reflect vertical relations: father-daughter/mother-son. In such relations one party was older and – in theory – on a higher level of hierarchy. However, when we view the penalties specified, we see that gender was the dominant factor rather than age. In forbidden father-daughter relations, the male was the sole person to be punished (LH §§154–156), while in forbidden mother-son relations it was either the male (LH §158) or both of them (LH §157). We can therefore conclude that these rules highlight, yet again, that men were the ones who had authority and control in matters pertaining to sexual relations. As such, they were regarded by the law as the liable party in case misdemeanors occurred. In contrast, women mostly lacked the required authority and power to take the initiative in these matters and were hence exempt from legal liability.

The most elaborate set of regulations of incest and kin relations in the ancient Near East is found in the HL.[28] The prohibitions specified in this collection were stipulated, as always, from the perspective of the man as initiator of the act. As such, the following sexual partners were prohibited for him: his biological mother, daughter and son (HL §189), stepmother while his father is alive (it was not an offense after his father has died; HL §190), free sisters and their mother simultaneously (HL §191), brother's wife while the brother is alive, stepdaughter, mother-in-law and sister-in-law (HL §195). All these pairings were termed *ḫurkel*, "abomination", and hence were probably implicitly punishable by death.[29]

Biblical law

In most of the discussions up until now, the evidence that stemmed from the ancient Near Eastern law collections was more abundant than that gathered from biblical law. When it comes to legal provisions pertaining to incest, however, the opposite is true.[30] The cluster of provisions in Lev. 18:6–18 provides the most detailed account of forbidden incestuous and kin relations in any legal collection from the ancient Near East, paralleled in this respect only by the pertinent sections in the Hittite collection. It begins with the general stipulation: "No man is to *sexually approach*[31] any of his relatives" (Lev. 18:6). The subsequent specifications of the forbidden relations are divided into two groups, each of which has a different reasoning for the prohibitions it contains. The first – and larger – group (Lev. 18:7–16) includes a man's female kin relatives with whom he was not allowed to have sexual intercourse. The second group (Lev. 18:17–18) includes multiple female partners with whom a man was forbidden to have contemporaneous sexual relationships. These women were not necessarily the man's relatives but were related to one another, and their proximity led to the prohibitions. Some of these restrictions are repeated in Lev. 20:11–12, 14, 17, 19–21, where the punishments of both male and female perpetrators are also specified. These are the restrictions in question:

- someone's biological mother (Lev. 18:7, repeated in Deut. 23:1);
- stepmother, wife of his father (Lev. 18:8 // Lev. 20:11; execution);
- sister, whether from the same father or mother (Lev. 18:9 // Lev. 20:17; banishment from community);

- granddaughter, whether from his son or his daughter (Lev. 18:10);
- stepsister, daughter of his stepmother (Lev. 18:11);
- aunt, whether the sister of his father (Lev. 18:12 // Lev. 20:19) or his mother (Lev. 18:13 // Lev. 20:19), or the wife of his uncle, brother of his father (Lev. 18:14 // Lev. 20:20; die childless);
- daughter-in-law, wife of his son (Lev. 18:15 // Lev. 20:12; execution);
- sister-in-law, wife of his brother (Lev. 18:16 // Lev. 20:21; die childless);[32]
- woman and her daughter (Lev. 18:17 // Lev. 20:14; execution);
- woman and her granddaughter, daughter of her son or her daughter (Lev. 18:17);
- woman and her sister, as long as she is alive (Lev. 18:18).

The significant point for the current research is the fact that only men were regarded as possible perpetrators, and only women[33] were regarded as their possible targets. The main difference between the LH, HL and the biblical prohibitions involves their justification: the biblical prohibitions are included in HC and are explained as resulting from God's demand of the Israelites to remain holy and pure. The ancient Near Eastern law collections, on the other hand, supply no reasoning whatsoever, and there was certainly no religious background to the statutes they included. If any reasoning is ever supplied (for example, in Hammurabi's prologue, or scattered across the HL), it is social rather than religious.

If my understanding of the punishment specified in Lev. 20:17 as banishment is correct, and the punishment specified in Lev. 20:20 was intended for the similar crimes of Lev. 20:19 as well, then we may speculate that "vertical" (inter-generational) crimes were perceived more severely than "horizontal" (intra-generational) ones, maybe because they broke the parent-descendant connection. Similarly, as we have seen, the incest prohibitions in LH were all "vertical".

Several incest prohibitions are repeated in the list of curses in Deuteronomy: a man's relations with his father's wife (Deut. 27:20), sister – whether from the same father or mother (Deut. 27:22) – and mother-in-law (Deut. 27:23).

Same-sex intercourse[34]

The attitude to same-sex intercourse in the ancient world is another topic that has drawn much scholarly interest in recent decades. As we have seen, the acceptable formal legal frame in the ancient Near East and the Hebrew Bible for sexual intercourse was limited to two individuals of the opposing sex who were married to each other. Deviations from this model were deemed illicit and were legally sanctioned. Same-sex intercourse definitely deviated from this pattern, because two men or two women could not be married to one another. This, however, was not necessarily the reason behind social objections to same-sex relations, which – if they existed – probably had more to do with gender-role divisions and social classifications, none of which was necessarily reflected in formal law. Be that as it may, this topic hardly seems to have preoccupied the ancient Near Eastern law collections, and in biblical law it is only mentioned twice, rather laconically. These few attestations only refer to male same-sex intercourse, never to females.

ANE law

The ancient Near Eastern law collections hardly ever relate to same-sex relations. The sole exception is found in MAL A §§19–20. A man who has spread unfounded rumors that another man was regularly being sexually penetrated was to suffer 50 rod blows, perform one month of the "king's service", have something of his cut off[35] and pay a fine of 1 talent (=3,600 shekels) of lead (MAL A §19). This statute clearly depicts receptive homosexual intercourse in a bad light, since it entails heavy sanctions against spreading unfounded rumors concerning a man being sexually penetrated, thus implying that the act was perceived negatively.

The following statute has been the source of much debate, since its interpretation is undetermined. It was either meant to proscribe homosexual intercourse or homosexual rape. According to it, a man who had engaged in homosexual intercourse was to be sodomized and castrated (MAL A §20). It is not clear which one of the two men involved in the act was the accused: the penetrating or the penetrated one. If homosexual intercourse itself was prohibited, then both men would have been perceived as perpetrators, and hence it is possible that only the receptive role was condemned. Since the penalty included sodomizing the guilty man, it seems unlikely that the very same behavior that was forbidden was to be repeated as part of its own sanction – unless, of course, a talionic punishment was meant. An alternative possibility is that this statute was directed against rape, which in this case was homosexual. In this case, the penetrating man was the perpetrator and not the penetrated one.

Biblical law[36]

Male same-sex relations were banned in the Levitical HC: "Do not lie with a man as the lying of a woman; that is abomination" (Lev. 18:22).[37] The prohibition is repeated two chapters later, where the sanction – execution of both men – is specified as well (Lev. 20:13). These provisions clearly express a moral judgment against male same-sex intercourse, defining it "an abomination" and sentencing both men involved to death. In this sense the biblical law appears to be very different than the MAL.

Bestiality[38]

The final topic to be discussed is bestiality. This act forms a unique deviation from the normative frame of sexual intercourse in almost every society throughout human history. Many social and cultural factors stand behind the universal objection to bestiality. This act involves non-productive sexuality and blurs the hierarchical boundaries between the categories of human and non-human. In certain cases, the social objection to bestiality was eventually embedded in formal law.

ANE law

The HL is the sole ancient Near Eastern law collection to refer to bestiality. Rather than settling with a general prohibition of it, the HL specified the forbidden animals in several statutes: cow (HL §187), sheep (HL §188), pig and dog (HL §199). In the first two statutes the act was defined as an "abomination", and all three prescribed the death penalty for the perpetrator and sometimes also for the animal. The perpetrator was also forbidden to approach the king during his trial, since the sinful act of bestiality was perceived as polluting and contaminating. In an additional statute, intercourse with a horse or a mule was defined as "not an offense", but the act still defiled the individual, who was forbidden to approach the king or become a priest (HL §200a). Since this book deals with the ways gender was perceived and regulated through formal law, no further analysis of these intriguing statutes is offered.[39] What is relevant to the current discussion is that only men were regarded in the Hittite Law collection as possible perpetrators in performing bestiality. In this sense, bestiality formed another deviation from the legally acceptable frame of sexual intercourse: the marriage institution. Within this frame, only men possessed the authority and power to initiate sexuality, which in the case of bestiality took a forbidden form.

Biblical law

Biblical law considered bestiality a severe sin, mentioning it four times, in all three biblical law collections. In Exod. 22:18 bestiality is generally prohibited, punishable by death. In Lev. 18:23 it is specified that both men and women were prohibited from conducting sexual intercourse with animals, but no punishment is explicitly detailed. Lev. 20:15–16 supplies the most detailed reference to the act, by stating that both human – whether man or woman – and animal are to be killed. Additionally, the list of curses in Deuteronomy includes the condemnation of bestiality (Deut. 27:21). Sarna suggested that these prohibitions were "aimed at idolatrous practices, otherwise unrecorded, of the official pagan religious or popular cults",[40] while Carmichael assumed that they were meant to reinforce the distinction between humans and animals,[41] a suggestion which is reminiscent of Mary Douglas's view of biblical taboos as reflecting the will to maintain the separation between categories.[42]

Houtman discussed the prohibition in Exod. 22:18 in conjunction with the ban on the practice of magic in Exod. 22:17. He rejected the opinion that these two prohibitions were related to forbidden idolatry, suggesting instead that Exod. 22:17 did not in fact address magic and that the reason behind Exod. 22:18 was that the "animal is not a suitable partner for man (cf. Gen. 2:18–24). Sodomy [=bestiality] implies dehumanization, violation of the holiness of human beings (cf. 22:30)".[43] This view is close to the one expressed by Carmichael and contrasts with that expressed by Sarna.

In contrast with HL, the Hebrew Bible did not detail the types of forbidden animals but rather categorically forbade the act, deeming it once *teḇel* (תבל),

"perversion".[44] Similarly to HL, both human and animal who had engaged in the act were to be put to death. The most notable difference from HL is that the Hebrew Bible specifically mentioned both men and women as possible perpetrators.

Notes

1 For discussions of female virginity and defloration (forced and consensual), see Cooper 2002 and, recently, Stol 2016: 13–17.
2 We have no reference to these matters in the HL.
3 This is according to Civil's (2011: 246, 257) understanding of the statute. Roth (1997, 1997: 18, 2014: 148) assumed that the woman was to be executed and her lover was to be spared. In essence, both interpretations convey a similar rationale: the seducing woman was killed, and her lover was left unpunished.
4 The di til-la text NSGU 45 (=L 3532 // ITT 2/1 3532) from the fourth reigning year of Šū-Sîn indeed demonstrates that this was the price paid for purchasing a slave-woman; see edition and translation in Culbertson 2009: 94, and details in p. 170.
5 Yaron 1988: 278–282.
6 Yaron 1988: 282.
7 *ukabbilšima*, "pins her down".
8 For a discussion of virginity in the Hebrew Bible, see Frymer-Kensky 1998.
9 For discussions of these statutes, see Pressler 1993: 35–41 and Greengus 2011: 63–64, 67, 69.
10 For discussions of this parallelism, see Wright 2009: 130–132, 182–183 and Greengus 2011: 64, 67.
11 Paul 1970: 96.
12 See pp. 63, 67.
13 For discussions of these two statutes, see Locher 1986, Pressler 1993: 22–31 and Wells 2005.
14 See p. 70.
15 Pressler 1993: 30–31.
16 For discussions of adultery and fornication in ancient Near Eastern and biblical law, see, to name but a few, Phillips 1981, Westbrook 1990, Lafont 1999: 29–92, Greengus 2011: 48–59 and, recently, Peled 2017a: 28–30.
17 For discussions of adultery, fornication and rape in the ancient Near East, see recently Stol 2016: 234–253 (on adultery and fornication), 254–267 (on rape). For one of the earliest treatments of these issues, still not entirely outdated, see Finkelstein 1966.
18 LH §130, however, is exceptional in this cluster, as it refers to the deflowering of a betrothed girl rather than to a married woman.
19 Westbrook (1990: 551, 555) speculated that the linkage set by the law between the punishments of the two paramours, as seen both in MAL and HL, was meant to prevent married men from prostituting their wives and blackmailing other men.
20 Scholars usually assume that the statute referred to the man's hair or beard, but this is nowhere explicit; see brief discussion in Part II commentary of MAL A §18.
21 See p. 93.
22 ḪUR.SAG-*i ēpzi*, "he seizes (her) in the mountain".
23 É-*ri=ma ēpzi*, "he seizes (her) in the house".
24 וְאֶל-אֵשֶׁת, עֲמִיתְךָ--לֹא-תִתֵּן שְׁכָבְתְּךָ, לְזָרַע: לְטָמְאָה-בָהּ.
25 For discussions of the statutes of Deut. 22:22–27, see Pressler 1993: 31–35 and Greengus 2011: 18, 48, 51, 60–63, 81.
26 The literature on this peculiar procedure is vast; the reader may consult, to name but a few, Fishbane 1974, Frymer-Kensky 1984, Matthews 1998: 102–108 and Rosen-Zvi 2012.

27 For discussions of incest in the ancient Near East, see Lafont 1999: 173–237 and, recently, Stol 2016: 268–274.
28 For a recent discussion of this topic, see Peled 2015.
29 Scholars usually assume that the term *ḫurkel*, "abomination", denoted the most severe sexual taboos and necessitated the death penalty even in cases where execution was not implicit; see Hoffner 1997: 224 and Peled 2010b: 254–255, both with previous literature.
30 Scholarly discussions of sexual offenses – especially concerning incest—in biblical law are abundant; the reader may consult, to name but a few, Elliger 1955, Epstein 1967, Horton 1973, Halbe 1980, Tosato 1984, Carmichael 1995, 1997, Ziskind 1996, Frymer-Kensky 2003: 1036, 1037 and McClenney-Sadler 2007.
31 This translation is not literal but clearly implied by the context. The original Hebrew phrase is לגלות ערווה, *legallōwṯ 'erwāh*, literally "reveal the genitals".
32 This prohibition contradicts the law of levirate marriage and overruled it.
33 The prohibition on homosexuality appears separately (see later on). The Hebrew Bible conspicuously does not proscribe homosexual kin relations, probably because the ban on homosexuality inherently includes it.
34 For discussions of same-sex relations in the ancient Near East and the Hebrew Bible, see, to name but a few, Nissinen 1998, Wold 1998, Peled 2010a and, recently, 2017b: 137–147.
35 Presumably his hair or beard (see Roth 1997: 159 and 192 n. 14, implicitly following CAD G: 8, s.v. "gadāmu"), but this is not explicit in the text. CAD (G: 8, s.v. "gadāmu") relies on the supposed parallel statute LH §127 (sic; erroneously "172" in CAD), but the verb there is different (*gullubu*, "to shave"), and even there no object is specified ("they shall shave half his (hair?)").
36 For discussions of homosexuality in biblical law, see, to name but a few, Wenham 1991, Olyan 1994, Otto 1996, Stone 1997 and Greengus 2011: 80–83.
37 וְאֶת-זָכָר--לֹא תִשְׁכַּב, מִשְׁכְּבֵי אִשָּׁה: תּוֹעֵבָה, הִוא.
38 For general discussions of bestiality in the ancient Near East, especially in the legal sphere, see Hoffner 1973, esp: 82–83, 85, 90, Greengus 2011: 83–85 and Peled 2019a, 2019b: 80–83.
39 The topic is extensively discussed in Peled 2019a.
40 Sarna 2003: 136–137.
41 Carmichael 2006: 184 n. 19.
42 See p. 33.
43 Houtman 2000: 213.
44 Lev. 18:23; probably from the root בלל, "to mix", "confuse (categories)".

Bibliography

Carmichael, Calum M. 1995. "Incest in the Bible". *Chicago-Kent Law Review* 71: 123–147.

Carmichael, Calum M. 1997. *Law, Legend, and Incest in the Bible: Leviticus 18–20*. Ithaca, NY: Cornell University Press.

Carmichael, Calum M. 2006. *Illuminating Leviticus: A Study of Its Laws and Institutions in the Light of Biblical Narratives*. Baltimore, MD: The Johns Hopkins University Press.

Civil, Miguel. 2011. "The Law Collection of Ur-Namma". In *Cuneiform Royal Inscriptions and Related Texts in the Schøyen Collection*, edited by Andrew R. George. Bethesda, MD: CDL Press. Pp. 221–286.

Cooper, Jerold S. 2002. "Virginity in Ancient Mesopotamia". In *Sex and Gender in the Ancient Near East: Proceedings of the 47th Rencontre Assyriologique Internationale,*

Helsinki, July 2–6, 2001, edited by Simo Parpola and Robert M. Whiting. Helsinki: Neo-Assyrian Text Corpus Project. Pp. 91–112.

Culbertson, Laura. 2009. *Dispute Resolution in the Provincial Courts of the Third Dynasty of Ur* (PhD dissertation, University of Michigan). Ann Arbor, MI.

Elliger, Karl. 1955. "Das Gesetz Leviticus 18". *Zeitschrift für die Alttestamentliche Wissenschaft* 67/1: 1–25.

Epstein, Louis M. 1967. *Sex Laws and Customs in Judaism*. New York: KTAV.

Finkelstein, Jacob J. 1966. "Sex Offenses in Sumerian Laws". *Journal of the American Oriental Society* 86/4: 355–372.

Fishbane, Michael. 1974. "Accusations of Adultery: A Study of Law and Scribal Practice in Numbers 5:11–31". *Hebrew Union College Annual* 45: 25–45.

Frymer-Kensky, Tikva. 1984. "The Strange Case of the Suspected Sotah (Numbers 5: 11–31)". *Vetus Testamentum* 34/1: 11–26.

Frymer-Kensky, Tikva. 1998. "Virginity in the Bible". In *Gender and Law in the Hebrew Bible and the Ancient Near East*, edited by Victor H. Matthews, Bernard M. Levinson and Tikva S. Frymer-Kensky. Sheffield: Sheffield Academic Press. Pp. 79–96.

Frymer-Kensky, Tikva. 2003. "Israel". In *A History of Ancient Near Eastern Law*, edited by Raymond Westbrook. Leiden: Brill. Pp. 975–1046.

Greengus, Samuel. 2011. *Laws in the Bible and in Early Rabbinic Collections: The Legal Legacy of the Ancient Near East*. Eugene, OR: Cascade Books.

Halbe, Jörn. 1980. "Die Reihe der Inzestverbote Lev 18:7–18. Entstehung und Gestaltungsstufen". *Zeitschrift für die Alttestamentliche Wissenschaft* 92: 60–88.

Hoffner, Harry A. Jr. 1973. "Incest, Sodomy, and Bestiality in the Ancient Near East". In *Orient and Occident: Essays for Cyrus H. Gordon on the Occasion of His Sixty-Fifth Birthday*, edited by Harry A. Hoffner Jr. Neukirchen-Vluyn: Neukirchener. Pp. 81–90.

Hoffner, Harry A. Jr. 1997. *The Laws of the Hittites: A Critical Edition*. Leiden: Brill.

Horton, Fred Jr. 1973. "Form and Structure in Laws Relating to Women: Leviticus 18:6–18". *Society of Biblical Literature Seminar Papers* 1: 20–33.

Houtman, Cornelis. 2000. *Exodus/Vol. 3, Chapters 20–40. Historical Commentary on the Old Testament*. Leuven: Peeters.

Lafont, Sophie. 1999. *Femmes, Droit et Justice dans l'Antiquité orientale. Contribution à l'étude du droit pénal au Proche-Orient ancien*. Fribourg: Editions Universitaires.

Locher, Clemens. 1986. *Die Ehre einer Frau in Israel: Exegetische und rechtsvergleichende Studien zu Deuteronomium* (vol. 22). Göttingen: Vandenhoeck & Ruprecht; Freiburg: Universitätverslag. Pp. 13–21.

Matthews, Victor H. 1998. "Honor and Shame in Gender-Related Legal Situations in the Hebrew Bible". In *Gender and Law in the Hebrew Bible and the Ancient Near East*, edited by Victor H. Matthews, Bernard M. Levinson and Tikva S. Frymer-Kensky. Sheffield: Sheffield Academic Press. Pp. 97–112.

McClenney-Sadler, Madeline G. 2007. *Re-covering the Daughter's Nakedness: A Formal Analysis of Israelite Kinship Terminology and the Internal Logic of Leviticus 18*. London; New York: T & T Clark International.

Nissinen, Martti. 1998. *Homoeroticism in the Biblical World: A Historical Perspective* Minneapolis, MN: Fortress.

Olyan, Saul. 1994. " 'And with a Male You Shall Not Lie the Lying Down of a Woman': On the Meaning and Significance of Leviticus 18:22 and 20:13". *Journal of the History of Sexuality* 5: 179–206.

Otto, Eckart. 1996. "Homosexualität im Alten Orient und im Alten Testament". In *Kontinuum und Proprium. Studien zur Sozial- und Rechtsgeschichte des Alten Orients und des Alten Testaments*, edited by Eckart Otto. Wiesbaden: Harrassowitz. Pp. 322–330.

Paul, Shalom M. 1970. *Studies in the Book of the Covenant in the Light of Cuneiform and Biblical Law*. Leiden: Brill.

Peled, Ilan. 2010a. "Expelling the Demon of Effeminacy: Anniwiyani's Ritual and the Question of Homosexuality in Hittite Thought". *Journal of Ancient Near Eastern Religions* 10/1: 69–81.

Peled, Ilan. 2010b. " '*Amore, more, ore, re . . .*': Sexual Terminology and the Hittite Law". In *Pax Hethitica: Studies on the Hittites and Their Neighbours in Honour of Itamar Singer*, edited by Yoram Cohen, Amir Gilan and Jared L. Miller. Wiesbaden: Harrassowitz. Pp. 247–260.

Peled, Ilan. 2015. "Crime and Sexual Offense in Hatti". *Near Eastern Archaeology* 78/4: 286–293.

Peled, Ilan. 2017a. "Gender and Sex Crimes in the Ancient Near East: Law and Custom". In *Structures of Power: Law and Gender Across the Ancient Near East and Beyond*, edited by Ilan Peled. Chicago, IL: The Oriental Institute of the University of Chicago. Pp. 27–40.

Peled, Ilan. 2017b. "Men in Question: Parallel Aspects of Ambiguous Masculinities in Mesopotamian and Biblical Sources". In *"And Inscribe the Name of Aaron": Studies in Bible, Epigraphy, Literacy and History Presented to Aaron Demsky* (*MAARAV, A Journal for the Study of the Northwest Semitic Languages and Literatures*, vol. 21/1–2), edited by Yigal Levin and Ber Kotlerman. Rolling Hills Estates, CA: Western Academic Press. Pp. 127–148.

Peled, Ilan. 2019a. "Bestiality in Hittite Thought". *Journal of the Ancient Near Eastern Society* 34.

Peled, Ilan. 2019b "Categorization and Hierarchy: Animals and Their Relations to Gods, Humans and Things in the Hittite World". In *Animals and Their Relations to Gods, Humans and Things in the Ancient World*, edited by Raija Mattila, Sebastian Fink and Sanae Ito. Wiesbaden: Springer Verlag. Pp. 79–93.

Phillips, Anthony. 1981. "Another Look at Adultery". *Journal for the Study of the Old Testament* 20: 3–25.

Pressler, Carolyn. 1993. *The View of Women Found in the Deuteronomic Family Laws*. Berlin: De Gruyter.

Rosen-Zvi, Ishay. 2012. *The Mishnaic Sotah Ritual: Temple, Gender and Midrash*. Leiden: Brill.

Roth, Martha T. 1997. *Law Collections from Mesopotamia and Asia Minor* (second edition). Atlanta, GA: Scholars Press.

Roth, Martha T. 2014. "Women and Law". In *Women in the Ancient Near East: A Sourcebook*, edited by Mark W. Chavalas. London; New York: Routledge. Pp. 144–174.

Sarna, Nahum M. 2003. *The JPS Torah Commentary: Exodus*. Philadelphia, PA: Jewish Publication Society.

Stol, Marten. 2016. *Women in the Ancient Near East*. Berlin: De Gruyter.

Stone, Ken. 1997. "The Hermeneutics of Abomination: On Gay Men, Canaanites, and Biblical Interpretation". *Biblical Theology Bulletin* 27/2: 36–41.

Tosato, Angelo. 1984. "The Law of Leviticus 18:18: A Re-examination". *Catholic Biblical Quarterly* 46: 199–214.

Wells, Bruce. 2005. "Sex, Lies, and Virginal Rape: The Slandered Bride and False Accusation in Deuteronomy". *Journal of Biblical Literature* 124/1: 41–72.

Wenham, Gordon J. 1991. "The Old Testament Attitude to Homosexuality". *Expository Times* 102: 359–363.

Westbrook, Raymond. 1990. "Adultery in Ancient Near Eastern Law". *Revue Biblique* 97: 542–580.

Wold, Donald J. 1998. *Out of Order: Homosexuality in the Bible and the Ancient Near East*. Grand Rapids, MI: Baker Books.

Wright, David P. 2009. *Inventing God's Law*. Oxford: Oxford University Press.

Yaron, Reuven. 1988. *The Laws of Eshnunna* (second edition). Jerusalem: Magnes Press, The Hebrew University.

Ziskind, Jonathan R. 1996. "The Missing Daughter in Leviticus 18". *Vetus Testamentum* 46: 125–130.

Summary, analysis and conclusions

In conclusion of the discussions this book offers, I will first summarize the main outcomes of the different chapters, subsequently analyze and compare the different legal corpora and finally offer my main insights and conclusions concerning law and gender in the ancient Near East and the Hebrew Bible.

1 Analysis: summary and conclusions of individual chapters

The four chapters of the book reveal a multifaceted picture of mixed sources, cultures, periods and themes. In what follows, the main contents of these chapters are summarized, as well as some insights gained from the information they detail.

Chapter 1: The societal perspective: social status and gender (in)equality

In the opening chapter the question of gender differentiation was discussed separately for free persons and for slaves. Within each group, legal evidence for gender inequality was discussed first, followed by the legal evidence for equality between the genders.

Gender inequality among free persons

ANE law

The laws documented several situations that highlight women's discrimination or exclusivity. To begin with, the patriarchal nature of ancient Near Eastern societies demanded that women always remained under a male figure's authority, either father or husband. Complications therefore arose when the husband was absent, whether because he was captured by an enemy or had fled the city. In such cases, the law supplied the wife with legal defense, because she was subordinate and vulnerable.

The law further imposed requirements on women to remain publicly chaste. The Middle Assyrian rules of veiling symbolized women's subordination, but at the same time functioned as markers of gender otherness, of the "different" types of women. Since the law ordered that certain priestesses, prostitutes and slaves were forbidden to veil themselves, veiling was portrayed as a desirable feminine quality, which functioned as a visual means of demarcating socially and morally appropriate femininity.

Two further examples belong to the world of debt and gender inequality. Creditors could detain their debtors' family members – wives and children – in order to pressure them to pay off the debt, while, partially similarly, a debtor could sell these same family members into slavery to clear his debt. In all these cases the active agents – both creditor and debtor – were males, while the passive agents who suffered the consequences of the economic situation were females and children.

One final legal situation that should be mentioned in this context is intentional self-abortion, which resulted in execution. This situation was obviously an exclusively feminine domain; the perceived perpetrator was the woman, who had no legal control over her body and fetus.

Certain professions were conducted exclusively or mostly by women. The two most notable ones attested in the laws were the woman-innkeeper (^{munus}lú-geštin/^{munus}lú-kurun/*sābītu*(*m*)) and the wet-nurse (um-me-da/*mušēniqtum*). In the laws only female innkeepers are attested, even though it is clear from other sources that both men and women could perform this profession. The laws portray the woman-innkeeper as a self-sufficient woman, who was not dependent on another person for her sustenance. While this is an important rare example for institutionalized female independence in the ancient Near East, the evidence only derives from Ur III and Old Babylonian sources. The wet-nurse was obviously a profession that was exclusive to women. The law documented the payments involved in the practice of the trade but also the harsh sanctions for malpractice.

Certain legal situations were attested in the MAPD, where both genders were limited because of gender-related issues. Though these instructions regulated and limited palace attendants of both genders, they were mainly concerned with women. Most of the regulations pertained to women's chastity, but both men and women were required to take measures in order to keep it. In this sense, women's behavior and actions were limited by these regulations, and men were limited in their contact with the said women.

Biblical law

Biblical law as well included statutes in which women's discrimination or exclusivity was apparent. Even though – in contrast with ancient Near Eastern law – wives could not be sold for debt-slavery, daughters could be. A different situation that highlights women's exclusivity was the prohibition against having sexual intercourse with a menstruating woman. Finally, women's vows to God could be annulled by their governing male figures, whether fathers or husbands. Women who had no such governing male figure – widows and divorcées – were obliged to fulfill their vows with no exception.

Gender equality among free persons

ANE law

Many ancient Near Eastern statutes expressed a similar attitude to persons of either gender. The fact that the law applied to both genders was made explicit, in order not to leave any doubt concerning legal liability, that is, that a person was not exempt from punishment based on his/her gender. We can mention in this regard sanctions for failure to pay taxes; people held as a pledge for debt; engagement in forbidden aggressive magic; joint parental authority in approving their daughter's betrothal or in paying the consequences if it was breached; joint parental authority as adopting parents and as parents involved in a wet-nurse's malpractice; mutual financial responsibility of a married couple towards one another; victims in several cases of homicide; victims in one case of abduction.

The MAL regarded both genders similarly in the case of false accusations of sexual misconduct. However, only men are attested as possibly spreading slander, whether against women or against other men. We can therefore see here that gender symmetry existed for the victims of unfounded false accusations of sexual misconduct, while for perpetrators there was gender asymmetry. The reason was probably that such perpetrators were the active agents in these cases, while the victims were the passive ones. Activism, even if a negative one, was by and large a masculine domain, rather than a feminine one.

Biblical law

A similar attitude to both genders can be observed at times in biblical law as well. For example, sons were required to keep the honor of both their parents. Ignoring this rule was regarded as a grave sin, bearing social implications and sanctioned publicly.

Several statutes were specifically applied to both genders, whether expressing equal status as victims or equal legal liability as perpetrators. Thus, members of both genders were explicitly attested as possible victims of a goring ox, as engaged in the forbidden practice of magic and as possible performers of idolatry or apostasy.

Gender inequality among slaves

ANE law

Ancient Near Eastern laws mention occasionally specific legal situations in which female slaves figure prominently, and certain rules were stipulated exclusively for them. We can mention cases such as causing a pregnant slave-woman to miscarry (and paying a compensation to her owner); the obligation of the master to redeem his slave-woman who bore him children and was sold to another person; the punishment of a slave-woman for insulting or hitting her superiors; the detaining of a slave-woman on account of her owner's debt; rules concerning a slave-woman who gave her child to be reared by a free person; the right of children of a slave-father and free mother to remain free; and the order that if someone harbored a runaway slave, his fine was double in case the slave was male.

Biblical law

The most notable gender differentiation between slaves in biblical law appears in the CC, where the rule of releasing slaves after six years only applied to males. In the DC, however, this rule applied to both genders. Different commentators offered different interpretations for this difference, but, for whatever reason, a clear inequality existed in this respect in the CC.

Gender equality among slaves

ANE law

Several statutes in the ancient Near Eastern law collections referred to slaves of both genders identically, mentioning explicitly both male and female slaves: stating the prize for returning runaway slaves; decreeing punishment for harboring runaway slaves; stipulating a prohibition on purchasing commodities from slaves; and occasional mentions of slaves, at times referring to them as commodities being bought, sold or stolen. In Hittite Law, an identical attitude was expressed regarding male and female slaves who were victims of homicide or injury, or perpetrators of performing unspecified abominable acts.

Biblical law

Though the CC only allowed male slaves to be released after six years of servitude, the DC changed this rule and explicitly granted both male and female slaves their manumission after the said period. Slaves of both genders were protected against abuse or killing by their master: in case of the former, they were to be released; in case of the latter, their master was to be punished. Finally, the rulings concerning an ox that gored a slave to death were identical for both male and female slave victims.

Protection of women

ANE law

Ancient Near Eastern family law occasionally protected women. If a husband married a second wife, he was still required to take care of his first wife; married women whose husband was absent – whether because he has died, became imprisoned by an enemy or fled the city – were given certain special legal rights that were meant to mitigate the fact that their male provider was absent; false accusations of women's misconduct were harshly punished and so was hitting a pregnant woman and causing her to miscarry.

Biblical law

Biblical law also included certain statutes that were meant to protect women: female slaves who were purchased for marriage were protected by law against mistreatment, and they were not to be resold; hitting a pregnant woman and causing her to miscarry resulted in the payment of a fine, execution if she dies and mutilation if she was injured; lastly, a newly wedded man was exempt for one year from military and civil obligations, in order to remain with his new wife.

Chapter 1: Conclusions

We have seen that some statutes denied women certain rights, while others referred to professions or activities that belonged exclusively to the feminine domain. Additionally, we have seen that certain legal obligations were put into effect in order to keep certain rules of conduct and standards of chastity; these applied only to women. A more gender-balanced picture emerges from the examination of other statutes, which were explicitly applied equally to both genders, whether by sanctioning perpetrators or by protecting victims.

When it comes to slaves, certain legal situations and stipulations were aimed explicitly – and at times exclusively – at females. These were not abundant and mainly preserved the right of property of slave-women's owners, including their sexuality and reproductivity, and perpetuated the subordinate status of these women. As was noted by Westbrook,[1] since slave-women were the property of their owner, the involvement of outsiders in their sexuality and offspring was governed by property law, as the perceived victim in such matters was their owner. At the same time, slave-women's sexuality and productivity were governed by family law. When these two sets of law came into conflict, the exact circumstances dictated which one was to prevail, and at times these conflicts resulted in compromise between the two. Gender equality among slaves is also occasionally apparent. This, however, did not necessarily reflect a positive attitude towards women as much as legal indifference to gender differentiation, since slaves constituted property and were not regarded as persons who had similar rights to free persons.

We have further seen that at times specific rules were stipulated in order to protect women, who were otherwise legally inferior to men and hence needed formal law to come to their aid.

Chapter 2: The institutional perspective: bureaucracy and economy: the palace, temple and beyond

The second chapter examined two interrelated spheres: the economy at large and the two main socioeconomic institutions in the ancient world, the palace and the temple. In examining economy and gender, the topics treated were salaries and wages and gender dynamics in the phenomenon of debt-slavery. In assessing the palace and the temple, the issues examined were adoption by palace personnel, women in the religious and cultic systems and the function of eunuchs in palace bureaucracy.

Salaries, wages and people's value

ANE law

The legal sources suggest that men and women had different economic value in society; the pertinent evidence, however, is limited to the Ur III and Hittite periods. According to one statute in LUN, women who performed valued tasks earned higher wages than men who performed lesser ones for the same duration; so, in this case, the essence of the task prevailed over considerations of gender differentiation. Further evidence from LUN sheds light on the involvement of women-innkeepers and wet-nurses in the Ur III economy. In Hatti, women were paid significantly lower salaries than men for performing the same task for the same duration; however, unskilled workers cost the same, whether they were men or women.

Biblical law

According to the amounts of donations specified in HC, which reflected people's worth, females earned significantly less – usually around half – than males, in several different age groups. This seems to be similar to the evidence of HL, but different from LUN, as noted previously.

Selling into debt-slavery

ANE law

Several statutes in LH dealt with debt-slavery. The main regulations they stipulated were the following: a debtor could sell his wife and children in order to clear his debt, but after three years they were to be released; a debtor could also sell his male or female slave, in which case the buyer could extend the slavery period beyond three years, or sell the slave to another person; a slave-woman who bore children to her master could be sold, but her master was obliged to redeem her; married couples were not legally responsible for each other's debts that were incurred prior to the marriage.

The MAL addressed several issues that pertain to debt and debt-slavery: a wife who resided in her father's household was legally responsible for her husband's debts; a man was forbidden to sell into slavery a person – whether man or woman – who did not belong to his family, but resided in his house.

Biblical law

Both CC and DC detail rules of conduct of debt-slaves. Similarly to LH, a debtor could sell his family members (DC mentions daughters in this respect) to clear his debt, but they were to be released after six years. The main difference between the two biblical collections lies in the fact that CC only grants male slaves their manumission, explicitly denying it to females, while in DC both men and women are explicitly granted manumission after six years of servitude.

Adoption by unique palace personnel

ANE law

The practice of adoption by specific palace personnel, as embedded in official law, is only attested in Old Babylonian sources. Three statutes in LH regulate adoption procedures by specific types of male (*girseqû*) and female (*sekretu*) palace officials who could not – or were not allowed to – produce descendants of their own. Lack of procreativity went against one of the main social expectations of persons of both genders in the ancient world. Since the lack of procreativity of these officials was somehow institutionalized, official law intervened and supplied them with the necessary compensation, in the form of official rules of adoption. No parallel legislation existed in biblical law.

Female cult personnel

ANE law

Most Mesopotamian law collections, as well as Middle Assyrian and Hittite instruction texts, stipulated regulations concerning female cult attendants, most frequently the *nadītu* of the Old Babylonian period. The LH mainly referred to the economic implications of these women's activities, their possibilities of accumulating wealth and their marriage, divorce and inheritance rights. In contrast, the few Middle Assyrian and Hittite references to female cult attendants pertained to their moral behavior rather than to any economic implications attached to their role.

Summarizing the statutes discussed in this section reveals an interesting picture. Though several law collections refer to female cult attendants, most of the evidence derives from LH and pertains to the *nadītu*. Each one of the other collections only contains one relevant statute – if at all – and the female titles other than that of the *nadītu* (13 mentions) are more scarcely attested: *ugbabtu*: 5, *qadištu/qadiltu*: 4, *kulmašītu*: 1, ereš-diĝir: 1. The terms *šugītu* (5 mentions) and *sekretu* (3 mentions) – attested only in the LH – did not designate cult attendants. We can see, therefore, that when formal law was concerned with women engaged in cult, it was mostly preoccupied with regulating and controlling the economic framework of their rank and place in society. Only rarely was the law concerned with matters of morality and the behavior of these women, as we see in LUN §12, LH §§110 and 127 and MAL A §40.

Biblical law

The only female cult attendant attested in biblical law is the *qĕdēšā*, referred to laconically in Deut. 23:18, which proscribed Israelite women or men from becoming a *qĕdēšā* (fem.) or *qadēš* (masc.). Even if the biblical term is a cognate of the Akkadian *qadištu*/*qadiltu*, it still supplies no additional information concerning the *qĕdēšā*, other than the fact that the occupation was illicit for the Israelites.

Eunuchs and castration

ANE law

The evidence from the ancient Near Eastern law collections concerning palace eunuchs can be summarized as follows: the *girseqû* was probably a typically childless male palace attendant, attested in LH; the laws supplied regulations of adoption that secured heirs for these persons; castration appears to have formed a corporal punishment in the MAL, by "turning" a perpetrator of sexual misbehavior "into a *ša rēšī*", a designation of an official who, in all likelihood, was a palace eunuch; the MAPD contain several references to officials who in all likelihood were palace eunuchs; the Hittite instructions/oaths of the lú-sag-officials hint at the possibility that these palace attendants were eunuchs.

We can therefore see that in the MAL castration formed a rare talionic punishment, but in other second-millennium law collections and royal instructions, castration was an institutionalized means of producing specific palace attendants, such as the *girseqû* (about whom the evidence is still vague) and the *ša rēši*/lú-sag attested in Assyrian and Hittite sources.

Biblical law

The DC ordered that men whose genitals were damaged were to be excluded from the congregation. Castration, however, was not banned by law, and no biblical law collection ever mentions eunuchs.

Purity of palace and temple personnel

ANE law

Middle Assyrian and Hittite royal instructions obliged both men and women to remain in a pure bodily state when performing their cultic tasks. The sanctions for disobeying these orders were harsh. One such sanction even included the male perpetrator's wife and family. Perceived defilement was caused by bodily fluids such as menstruation blood, semen and sexual secretions.

Biblical law

Priests were required in the HC to remain pure, for example by not marrying non-virgin women such as prostitutes, divorcées or widows. Priests' daughters were forbidden to become prostitutes, and if they married a man who was not a priest himself, they were forbidden to eat from the sacred donations the priests received.

Chapter 2: Conclusions

The meager evidence from ancient Near Eastern law concerning gender differentiation in the sphere of the division of labor is inconclusive. The scattered specifications of salaries and wages show that at times the prestige of the task prevailed over masculine gender superiority, while at other times women were discriminated against compared to men. Biblical law, however, shows an unambiguous picture, according to which women had a lesser economic value than men.

In LH a debtor could sell any of his family members – wife and children – in order to clear his debt, while in biblical law only daughters could be sold for this purpose. In both corpora the slavery period was fixed, but in biblical law the duration was twice longer.

Another set of regulations that was unique to LH was a group of statutes that enforced rules of adoption for two types of palace personnel: the male *girseqû* and the female *sekretu*, who could not – or were not allowed to – have biological progeny. The *girseqû* may have been a eunuch, and so was the *ša rēši*/lú-sag, another palace attendant attested in the Assyrian and Hittite legal sources (MAL, MAPD, HL).

Ancient Near Eastern law regulated some of the activities of several female cult personnel, mostly within the economic sphere. No parallel statutes were issued for male cult attendants, which emphasizes the need to legally control and regulate women's economic activities, but not men's. This situation stemmed from the fact that these women had a special role in Mesopotamian society, unlike most other women, who were utterly dependent on men, so that their lack of independence denied them accessibility to any significant economic matters in which the law might intervene. Biblical law does not mention female cult attendants, other than one laconic prohibition on women from becoming *qĕdēšā* (as well as the prohibition on men from becoming *qadēš*).

Chapter 3: The familial perspective: regulation of family life

The family, as the basic social unit, stood at the center of numerous legal rules. These were meant to regulate social interaction within the nuclear and the extended family, define acceptable and unacceptable behavior patterns between kin and delineate the economic and moral framework within which the family existed and operated.

Slaves and family life

ANE law

Most ancient Near Eastern law collections included statutes that pertained to slaves and their family life. The main topics these statutes covered are the following: rules of marriage and divorce between free persons and slaves; inheritance rights; seduction of female slaves; legal status of slaves' children; and giving slaves' children in adoption.

Biblical law

The CC specified several rules for handling slaves, some of which referred to their family life. Since according to this collection female slaves were not to be released like male ones after six years of servitude, questions arose as to what happened with married couples. The CC determined that if the marriage took place prior to the beginning of the enslavement period, the wife would be released together with her husband. However, if the wife was given to the husband by her master, she and her children remained in the master's possession when their husband/father was released. If, consequently, the slave preferred to remain enslaved together with his wife and children, his servitude was to become permanent.

Several scenarios existed of slave-women whose husbands – intended or actual ones – changed their minds about the marriage. The law protected these women: a man who changed his mind after purchasing a slave-woman in order to marry her was to let her be redeemed; a man who took a second wife and did not take care of the slave-woman to whom he was already married was to release her free of charge; the same rule applied to a man who wished to marry a woman that was captured during war but then changed his mind.

Parental legal authority

ANE law

Both father and mother appear to have had similar authority in the following cases, all deriving from the Old Babylonian and Hittite periods: consent for marriage of their daughter; participation in the marriage process (contract, ceremonies); ownership of an infant whose death his wet-nurse tries to conceal (only Old Babylonian).

Biblical law

Legal provisions that reflect paternal authority appear in the CC and in Num. According to the CC, a girl's father had the prerogative to prevent her marriage, while according to the rules of vows in Num., a woman's male governing figure – father or husband – could overrule her vows. Joint paternal and maternal authority is attested in the DC rules for a disobedient and disrespectful son.

Betrothal and its infringement

ANE law

Statutes from all ancient Near Eastern law collections regulated and secured the procedure of betrothal. Others specified financial sanctions in case the procedure was infringed. The head of the household or, in his absence, other male members of the family, were responsible for making sure that daughters were betrothed. Canceled betrothal required the payment of compensation; the active agents in such a cancellation – the perceived perpetrators and victims – were usually male. The victim was usually the groom's or the bride's father, whose economic interests were harmed.

Biblical law

The biblical sanctions for breaching an agreed betrothal are found in HC. These result from sexual misbehavior, and as such were sanctioned with potential execution and sacrificial atonement. This implies that the biblical view of infringing on betrothal was concerned with moral implications rather than with financial ones, which is a major difference from the ancient Near Eastern legal attitude in this respect.

Economic dynamics in marriage life

ANE law

The pertinent evidence that sheds light on economic matters within marriage life derives almost exclusively from LH and MAL. The evidence demonstrates that the head of the household was always male, and as such he had absolute control over the family financial dealings. Married couples, however, could be mutually responsible for each other's debts.

In case the head of the household was taken captive, the law financially assisted his lone wife, regulated her entitlement to marry again and set the status of their children. The necessity of these rules stemmed from the fact that women were not independent and relied on their husbands for sustenance.

Sexual misbehavior frequently bore financial implications for the family. Thus, adultery, fornication and even rape could be sanctioned with fines. The victim was almost always the offended male figure, whether the father or husband of the woman involved. The perpetrator could be the woman, the man or both – depending on the nature of the crime.

Biblical law

Two sets of rulings in biblical law pertain to the economic aspects of marriage: daughters' inheritance and levirate marriage. In the absence of male heirs, a deceased person's inheritance belonged to his daughters. They could then only marry husbands from within their tribe, which might imply that their assets became their husbands' upon marriage. In DC we encounter the institution of the levirate marriage, which had clear financial implications.

Termination of marriage: divorce

ANE law

Almost all ancient Near Eastern law collections referred to divorce. The law distinguished between various cases of divorce, according to several factors: the gender of the initiator, the reason for the divorce, the moral behavior of both husband and wife prior to the divorce, whether it was the first or second marriage and whether the couple had children. All these factors could be considered when settling the divorce conditions. The law usually favored men, but women still had certain rights, especially if the divorce resulted from their husbands' improper behavior.

Biblical law

A divorced woman was considered unsuitable for the priestly circles: priests could not marry divorcées, and divorcée priest daughters could not eat from their father's food. The DC forbade a divorcée to return to her first husband after she was married to another man and her second marriage terminated.

Termination of marriage: widowing

ANE law

Almost all ancient Near Eastern law collections addressed widowing. Most statutes pertained to the economic implications of the death of one of the spouses. The laws referred much more frequently to widows than to widowers, which emphasizes the legislators' will to regulate and determine women's social and economic situation once their status as subject to their husbands has changed. Often, the laws decided what should be done with dowries, marriage gifts, brideprice and other payments that formed part of the marriage procedures. Some statutes determined whether and how widows could remarry and the financial implications involved.

Biblical law

Biblical law only referred to widows and never to widowers. In contrast with most of the pertinent ancient Near Eastern statutes, biblical law was not concerned with widows' socioeconomic status as much as with protecting them and securing the continuation of their family. This reflects the social gender inequality that made widows – as women without a male governing figure – vulnerable and in need of legal protection. One of the legal methods applied in such cases was the levirate marriage, which provided a widow who had no son with a husband from within her extended family. This institution has clear ancient Near Eastern parallels in MAL and HL.

Inheritance

ANE law

Almost all ancient Near Eastern law collections addressed issues of inheritance. According to some, the widow inherited from her husband, but according to others, male – or occasionally female – children were to inherit from their father, and then support their mother in case she outlived her husband. Specific issues regulated by law were inheritance of marriage gifts, inheritance by female cult personnel, inheritance by slaves and their children, disinheritance and the distribution of inheritance between brothers/sisters. These rules frequently emphasize women's inferiority or dependency compared to men's superiority and independency.

Biblical law

The rules of inheritance, as specified in Num., emphasize the right of the firstborn (primogeniture): the eldest son was the primary heir of his father. In the absence of sons, however, daughters were the legal heirs. In the absence of daughters, the order of alternative heirs was as follows: the deceased's brothers, the brothers of his father or his closest relative. There was a clear preference for male heirs, but other than sons, daughters were preferred over any other heir. In contrast with ancient Near Eastern law, widows are not attested in biblical law as possible heirs.

Adoption

ANE law

The pertinent evidence concerning adoption derives entirely from the Old Babylonian period and almost exclusively from LH. A child given for adoption is once regarded as his mother's (LLI) and once as his father's (LE). In LH children given for adoption were regarded as belonging to both parents. Biological parents of children given for adoption were labeled as the children's "father's house". This, together with the fact that the adopter was almost always a man, highlights the fact that adoption existed for economic reasons and was part of the socioeconomic system of the Old Babylonian period.

Polygamy

ANE law

A man could marry a second wife if the first one became ill, but he was still required to take care of his first wife. Polygyny was further allowed if someone's wife was immoral (squandering and disrespectful) or did not give birth. In the former case the first wife could be demoted to the status of a slave without being granted an official divorce. In the latter case, the husband could marry a second wife that will bear him children, but she was to remain secondary in status to the first wife. The MAL allowed a form of levirate marriage to take place if the levir was already engaged before marrying his deceased brother's widow.

Biblical law

Biblical law is not explicit as regards polygamy, whether in permitting or prohibiting it. One statute in DC refers indirectly to a polygynous situation. Levirate marriage could lead to polygyny in case the levir was already married.

Prostitution

ANE law

Since prostitution contradicted some of the basic elements upon which the institution of the family was based, several statutes were meant to limit its influence – but never to ban it altogether. Some statutes in MAL and HL imply that prostitutes belonged to a relatively low social class.

Biblical law

Biblical law considered prostitution negatively when it was somehow connected with the priestly circles. Otherwise, the law ignored prostitution altogether. Thus, priests were forbidden to marry prostitutes, and their daughters were forbidden to become ones. Further, the earnings of prostitution were not to be accepted as donations by the temple officials.

Chapter 3: Conclusions

The opening section of this chapter examined slaves' family life. In ancient Near Eastern mixed marriages, social status usually prevailed over gender hierarchy. The status of children was determined by the fact that at least one parent was a free person, even if that parent was their mother. Biblical law set certain rules in protecting the rights of female slaves who were married to free husbands, when they lost their favor with their husbands.

The head of the household was male, and he decided on all economic matters. In his absence, his wife needed the support of law in order to sustain herself and her family. But did this mean that the father had higher legal authority within the family than the mother? According to some Old Babylonian and Hittite Laws, this was not necessarily so, and the mother had an equal right in deciding on daughters' marriage. Biblical law is not unanimous in this respect. On the one hand, fathers could prevent their daughters' marriage and overrule their vows. However, in the cases of a disobedient son and of a daughter blamed for not being virgin upon her marriage, both parents had equal authority. Pressler claimed that the three statutes found in Deut. 21:10–21 highlight the importance of hierarchical and paternal authority within the family of both father and mother, but especially of the male head of the household. Additionally, according to her, these statutes concern the status and rights of less privileged members of the hierarchically structured family: women and children.[2] She also suggested that the difference between the higher status of the father (as reflected in, *inter alia*, Deut. 21:20), compared to that of the mother (as reflected in, *inter alia*, Deut. 22:16), derived from the difference between the social settings of inter- and intra-family associations. The mother enjoyed a relatively high status as long as matters remained within the household, so that children were required to obey and respect their mothers no less than their fathers. However, when it came to interaction with people from outside the nuclear family, the male head of the household had clear superiority over his wife.[3]

As to gender differentiation in intra-familial inter-generational relations, male and female offspring were not regarded similarly. The main obligation of a son to his parents involved obedience and respect, while the main obligation of a daughter to her parents involved obedience and chastity. The son's obligations were meant to preserve the intra-familial hierarchy, while the daughter's obligations were meant to make her a proper wife-to-be, for the economic sake of the family.

Betrothal was economic in nature, and hence its infringement was regarded in the ancient Near East as equivalent to the breaching of an economic transaction. In contrast, in the Hebrew Bible the implications of infringing on an agreed betrothal seem to have had moral implications rather than economic ones.

Marriage could terminate for two main reasons: divorce and widowing. Divorce could be initiated by both husband and wife, and the financial settlements involved depended on several factors. Men were usually favored over women, but only as long as they did not exhibit immoral behavior towards their wives, in which case the law sided with the latter. Widowing, like divorce, had many economic implications. Ancient Near Eastern law rarely referred to widowers, and biblical law utterly ignored them. The reason why laws of widowing were mainly issued for widows derives from women's general inferiority and economic dependence on men. When they lost their male provider, they required the assistance of official law to handle their new situation.

And what about inheritance? As we have seen, gender differentiation was apparent in this sphere as well. Different collections exhibit different relevant stipulations. Some allowed the widow to inherit from her husband, while others determined that the children – frequently male, but occasionally also female – were to inherit from the father and take care of their mother. In many legal rules of inheritance men seemed to have been more privileged than women. A similar picture emerges from the biblical rules of inheritance. Widows are never documented as possible heirs, and other than daughters, all legal heirs were males. However, daughters were still preferred over any other heir other than sons.

Another financially oriented topic that involved the familial structure was adoption. The evidence for adoption derives exclusively from the Old Babylonian period, and there is no reference to it in biblical law. It served the economic needs of people during this time. In the few references to it, the biological parent of the adoptee was frequently the father, but rarely his mother. The adopter was always male.

The two main forms of deviation from the standard form of marriage as the acceptable framework of sexual intercourse were polygamy and prostitution. Polygamy – or more accurately, polygyny – was rare, but certain circumstances allowed it. Unless the first wife has acted immorally, her husband was required to care for her upon marrying a second wife. The institution of levirate marriage could in theory lead to polygyny, in case the levir was already married. As to prostitution, both ancient Near Eastern and biblical law scarcely refer to it. The attitude they reflect seems to be somewhat negative, though none of these corpora officially banned it.

Chapter 4: The individual perspective: morality and sex crimes

Sexual intercourse was only permitted between a man and a woman who were married to one another. Therefore, premarital sex, adultery and rape, incest and forbidden kin relations were deemed illicit. Other sexual felonies were homosexual intercourse and bestiality, but these were only rarely addressed by official law.

Virginity and premarital sex

ANE law

Almost all Mesopotamian law collections address female virginity and premarital sexual intercourse, although with very few statutes in each collection. Sanctions applied in the following cases: seducing a girl that was betrothed to another man (seducer executed); seducing a virgin slave-woman (seducer pays fine to her owner); betrothed girl initiates sexual intercourse with another man (girl executed); raping a virgin girl (rapist pays heavy fine to her father, might be compelled to marry her and his own wife be raped and given to the victim's father); consensual intercourse between a man and a virgin girl (man pays heavy fine to her father and is not allowed to marry her).

The perpetrator in all cases was the initiator: usually the man, rarely the girl. The victim in all cases was the girl's father, who was the head of her household (or her owner, in case she was a slave). This emphasizes the fact that the essence of the felony was economic: it infringed on the concept of the family and damaged the potential financial profit of the family from the future marriage of its daughters.

Biblical law

Sanctions applied in the following cases: seducing an unbetrothed virgin girl (seducer forced to pay the brideprice and marry her; if her father objects: seducer pays the cost of the brideprice without marrying her); seducing an unbetrothed slave-woman that was promised to another man (sacrificial atonement, hence the felony was moral rather than financial); husband falsely accusing his newly wedded wife of not being a virgin (slanderous husband pays heavy fine to her father); husband justifiably accusing his newly wedded wife of not being a virgin (girl executed).

The picture that emerges from these rulings is quite similar to what we see in the Mesopotamian law collections. The perpetrator was the seducer, the victim was the girl's father, as head of her household. As in Mesopotamia, the essence of the felonies was by and large financial.

Adultery and rape

ANE law

Most ancient Near Eastern law collections address the felonies of adultery and rape in an interrelated manner. Adultery was only applied to married women, while unfaithful husbands faced no legal punishment for adultery. For example, a statute that refers to a married man who has sexual intercourse with a prostitute, while being married to another woman, specifies no punishment for his adultery, while a married man who raped an unmarried girl was punished for rape, but not for adultery. Similarly, in case of consensual intercourse between a married man and an unmarried girl, both were to be punished, because her father's potential financial gain from her future marriage has been jeopardized by the act. The fact that the man committed adultery, however, constituted no legal issue, as is apparent from the fact that the perceived victim was the girl's father rather than the betrayed wife. An adulterous wife, on the other hand, was to be executed, together with her lover. A husband who wished his wife to be spared was forced to let her lover live as well. However, if a married man remained in captivity for several years, or had he fled his city, his lone wife was entitled to marry another man. The law, therefore, supplied women with certain protection in such cases and did not regard their acts as adultery.

A rapist of a married woman was to face execution. A rapist of a virgin girl was to pay a heavy fine to her father and marry her, and his own wife was to be raped and given to the girl's father. The father, however, could object to the marriage and only receive the fine.

Biblical law

According to HC and DC, consensual intercourse between a man and a woman who was married to another man was considered adultery, constituted a socially polluting offense and would lead to the execution of both paramours. Consensual intercourse between a man and a virgin who was betrothed to another man was regarded identically, and both perpetrators were to be executed. The rape of a girl betrothed to another man would lead to the rapist's execution.

Incest and forbidden kin relations

ANE law

The evidence concerning forbidden incestuous relations derives almost exclusively from LH and HL. The LH prohibited a man from having sexual intercourse with his daughter (banishment), daughter-in-law (execution), future daughter-in-law not yet married (payment of a heavy fine, cancellation of the marriage), mother, after the father's death (execution for both) and stepmother who had children (disinheriting). All these rules were inter-generational and thus reflect hierarchically vertical relations. However, the sanctions reveal that gender prevailed over age in these matters: the man was always perceived as the perpetrator, regardless of age. Only once is the older female considered as mutually liable as the younger male.

The HL prohibited a man from having sexual intercourse with his biological mother, daughter and son, stepmother while his father is alive, free sisters and their mother simultaneously, brother's wife while the brother is alive, stepdaughter, mother-in-law and sister-in-law. The sanction for these felonies was in all likelihood execution.

Biblical law

The HC specified a lengthy list of rules detailing sexual partners that were forbidden for a man, a few of which are repeated in DC. Most of them were his female kin relatives, but a few were women who were unrelated to him but related to one another, and hence simultaneous intercourse with them was prohibited. Sanctions were not always specified, but when they were, they included execution, banishment and the divine punishment of dying childless. The perpetrator was always the man, and the essence of the felonies was that they were perceived as immoral and polluting.

Same-sex intercourse

ANE law

Only two statutes from MAL address male same-sex intercourse. The first specifies sanctions for a man who spreads unfounded rumors that another man was regularly being sexually penetrated. The second can be understood in more than one way: it either banned consensual homosexual intercourse or homosexual rape.

Biblical law

The HC banned homosexual intercourse, decreeing execution for both men involved.

Bestiality

ANE law

Bestiality is only addressed by HL, where several animals are specified as prohibited (cow, sheep, pig and dog). The sanction was in all likelihood execution for both man and animal, even though it is not always explicitly mentioned. Intercourse with a horse or a mule was defined as "not an offense", but the act still defiled the individual, who was forbidden to approach the king or becoming a priest. Only men were regarded as possible perpetrators of this felony.

Biblical law

All three biblical law collections banned bestiality, stipulating four different statutes. The sanction for bestiality was execution, and it was applied to men, women and the animals involved. In contrast with ancient Near Eastern law, therefore, biblical law considered members of both genders to be possible perpetrators of this felony.

Chapter 4: Conclusions

The first felony discussed in this chapter was premarital sex. Since premarital sex jeopardized the household's future benefit from the marriage of its daughters, this act was viewed highly negatively. For this reason, only women's virginity was significant, and not men's – and therefore the law only addressed the former and utterly ignored the latter. The perpetrator in all felonies of premarital sex was the initiator; usually this was the man, but in rare cases it was the girl. The perceived victim was always the girl's father, who, as the head of her household, symbolized the financial loss of the family when a daughter's future marriage was jeopardized.

Adultery and rape were two felonies that resulted from essentially the same case: a man who had sexual intercourse with a woman to whom he was not married. From the point of view of law, the difference between these felonies was based on the question of consent: consensual intercourse with a woman married to another man was regarded as adultery; forcible intercourse was regarded as rape. In case of the latter, the act was regarded as a crime regardless of the marital status of the woman, but this status influenced the nature of the punishment. In adultery only the marital status of the woman was considered, while the law remained indifferent as to unfaithful husbands. The sanction on adultery was usually harsh: execution for both paramours. A similar sanction was decreed for a rapist of a married woman, but, had his victim been a virgin girl, his punishment was financial. The former crime was perceived as aimed at both the woman and her husband, while the latter crime was perceived as aimed against the girl's father. Biblical law considered adultery a polluting crime that resulted in execution. Rape was regarded similarly to in the ancient Near East.

Sexual relations between kin members were governed rather strictly by certain law collections – LH, HL and biblical law (mostly HC) – while all other collections utterly ignored this topic. LH supplied several basic inter-generational rules, while HL were very detailed on incestuous restrictions, decreeing execution for most felonies. Biblical law was far more elaborate than all ancient Near Eastern collections in this regard, viewing incest as immoral and polluting. In all legal sources the perpetrator was male.

Two further felonies that contradicted the customary framework of socially acceptable sexual relations were same-sex intercourse and bestiality. Same-sex relations were by and large ignored by ancient Near Eastern law. Two statutes in MAL addressed homosexual intercourse negatively, but it is unclear whether they actually proscribed it. Biblical law, in stark contrast, banned homosexual intercourse, decreeing execution for both men involved. Legal references to bestiality only appear in HL and biblical law. While the former specified several forbidden animals in this respect, biblical law only supplied the laconic rule that bestiality was to be punished by execution, both for male and female perpetrators. While HL exhibited the same sanction, they only considered men possible perpetrators. Both legal corpora decreed execution for the animal as well.

Gender differentiation is clearly apparent in the realm of sex crimes. The law usually considered males to be potential perpetrators of such felonies and only rarely viewed women as the perpetrators. The victim could be a woman or her male governing figure: her father, husband or owner.

2 First synthesis: regulating gender in ancient Near Eastern law

Comparing the different ancient Near Eastern law collections and royal decrees discussed in this book is a hazardous task, and any interpretation that derives from this synthesis must be taken with caution. In theory, the different sources may reflect a cultural – or even ethnic – diversity across the ancient Near East. We may ask ourselves in this regard, "who cared about what?" Can we compare different ethnic or social groups? Can we compare the Sumerians of the late third millennium, the Babylonians of the early second millennium, the Assyrians of the mid-late second millennium and the Hittites? We must bear in mind that many ideas flowed from one culture to another and from one generation to the next.

As the law collections evolved, their contents were many times built one upon the other, transmitting, borrowing, adopting and adapting contents. It is therefore hard to distinguish between "Sumerian notions" as reflected in LUN, "Babylonian notions" as reflected in LLI, LE and LH, and "Assyrian notions" as reflected in MAL. The Hittites were distinct in many respects from their Mesopotamian counterparts, but their laws still borrowed much from the earlier Mesopotamian collections. And what about NBL? How justified is it to compare it to Babylonian collections that were composed a millennium earlier?

Another major complication involves the incompleteness of most of the sources. Only one collection – LE – is known today in its full extent, while LUN, LH and HL are mostly complete. The other collections lack considerable portions, the extent of most of which cannot even be guessed. MAL A is almost complete, but all the other tablets of the collection – at least 13 – are extremely fragmentary. Similarly, NBL is mostly lost, and from LLI we are probably missing well over half of the collection. Understandably, had the sources been closer to complete, many of the interpretations presented in this book might have been entirely different. Nonetheless, this book is still based on well over 300 provisions from law collections and royal decrees, which cover most of the major periods in ancient Near Eastern history, especially the second millennium BCE.

For these and other reasons, I deem the comparative value of the current synthesis quite limited. I present the main finds and offer some possible interpretations, but these are not compelling and can easily be refuted, or perhaps even be dismissed altogether as the product of my own anachronistic assumptions. Avoiding altogether such interpretations, or even conjectures, however, is obviously impossible in a book that was meant exactly for this purpose. The synthesis between the different ancient Near Eastern legal sources that appears in what follows is largely in line with the topics discussed in the book.

General issues of gender inequality/asymmetry

One of the issues that stem from the discussion of gender inequality/asymmetry involves women's chastity, and the rules embedded in official law that were meant to enforce it. Many law collections, however, did not seem to include statutes that explicitly regulated women's chastity. We can mention in this regard the rules of veiling found in MAL A §40 and several stipulations of the MAPD concerning palace women; LH §133b also seems to be relevant to the topic. Other than these few sources, however, ancient Near Eastern law does not seem to has been particularly articulated with regard to women's chastity. Generally speaking, MAL A seems to have been rather harsh on women, but this is hardly a new observation.

An exclusive attitude to women is found, for example, in the way the law addresses the woman-innkeeper. This profession is attested almost exclusively in Old Babylonian sources: LE, LH and ESi/Ad/Aṣ, with one additional statute in LUN. The legal regulation of this female profession, therefore, seems to be an Old Babylonian phenomenon, even though the profession itself is attested in most other periods in ancient Near Eastern history. This may have to do with the fact that economic issues posed an increasing social problem in the Old Babylonian period, which required means such as official law to intervene and regulate the situation.

The same may be said concerning another legal issue that seems to have been typically Old Babylonian: debt-slavery and the legal regulation of selling family members (wives, sons and daughters) into servitude. This phenomenon is again only attested in Old Babylonian sources (LH, ESi/Ad/Aṣ) and may be explained in the same way.

Other issues that highlight the special attitude the law showed to women were more culturally and historically diverse. A recurring legal theme found in the laws involved a woman who was deprived of her husband, whether he was captured by an enemy or had fled. Unlike in cases of divorce or widowing, the woman was still formally married, and therefore special statutes regulated her situation. Such statutes are found in LE, LH and MAL, and they all exhibit a relatively coherent picture and similar regulations. Was this, therefore, a case of a diffusion of ideas between periods and cultures? Do these similarities reflect a certain common legal tradition, as suggested by scholars like Westbrook?

Another such recurring legal theme was that of a man beating a pregnant woman and causing her to miscarry. This could have hardly been a frequently occurring incident, but, nonetheless, it was addressed by statutes in LUN, LH, HL and MAL, making it a universal legal theme, attested in law collections from all over the ancient Near East: Sumerian, Babylonian, Assyrian and Hittite. Did the composers of all these collections deem it necessary to protect pregnant women, or was this a literary motif running throughout the ancient Near Eastern literary genre of legal corpora?

The administration of economy and cult

Another feature of the intersection of law and gender in the ancient Near East was the legal regulation of the economic affairs of female cult attendants, the implications of which are discussed previously. As to the comparative perspective discussed in the present synthesis, it must be noted that most of the pertinent evidence drives from LH, with a few scattered additional mentions in other sources. This limited phenomenon, therefore, seems to be mainly an Old Babylonian one. As before, it should probably be assessed against the background of the socioeconomic reality of this period and the use of official law for regulating this reality.

Laws concerning the family

The bulk of information in this book pertains to family life and its regulation by official law. Many of the pertinent statutes derive from Old Babylonian collections, especially LH. To begin with, as apparent in LE and LH, in determining the status of a child born in mixed marriages between free persons and slaves, social status prevailed over considerations of gender. Thus, the superior status of the parent – regardless of that parent's gende – determined the child's status. Another strictly Old Babylonian phenomenon (attested mostly in LH) was the existence of adoption as an economic institution governed by official law. Another feature unique to the Old Babylonian collections (LLI and LH) was the husband's obligation to take care of his wife if he married another woman without divorcing her. Polygamy, in the form of polygyny, is attested almost exclusively in LH.

The evidence concerning parental authority derives from Old Babylonian (LE and LH) and Hittites collections. All these sources exhibit a similar picture: equal parental authority was limited to the consent for marrying a daughter and involvement in the marriage procedures. Otherwise, the father's superiority over the mother was clear and apparent, for example, when financial matters were involved; this latter issue is indicated in all the law collections.

The evidence concerning economic dynamics in family life derives almost entirely from LH and MAL. It might seem a bit surprising that LLI and LE – the two closest collections to LH – do not include similar evidence. The fragmentary state of LLI might be a hypothetical reason for these differences, but LE is a complete collection. Be that as it may, a plausible explanation for the engagement of LH and MAL A with the economic dynamics within the family might involve some of the main aims of these two collections. LH, as we have seen, was greatly concerned with regulating matters of economy, while MAL A was much occupied with women and family matters. Therefore, LH aspired to regulate the economy, including the familial circles it contained, while MAL A aspired to regulate the family, including its economic aspects.

The issues that concerned all ancient Near Eastern law collections pertained to the regulation of the familial structure. Almost all the collections addressed matters of divorce, widowing and inheritance. In doing so, women were frequently discriminated against, and their subordinate status was maintained. Even when the law came to their aid, it merely perpetuated their subordinate and dependent status.

Sex crimes

The main felonies that were perceived as sex crimes involved seduction, adultery, fornication and rape. A homogeneous and consistent attitude prevailed in all the collections (LE, LH, MAL, HL) concerning adultery and rape. These two felonies differed on the basis of the female partner's consent, or lack of it. Only the female partner's marital status was taken into account, while an unfaithful married man committed no crime from the point of view of law. The usual punishment for adultery was execution for both paramours, but if the betrayed husband spared his wife, her lover was to be spared too. The rapist of a married woman was to be executed, while the rapist of a virgin girl, whether free or slave, was to pay a fine. The extremely different attitude to men and to women, as reflected in all these regulations, was overwhelmingly consistent throughout the history of ancient Near Eastern law and is apparent in the Babylonian, Assyrian and Hittite collections of the second millennium BCE.

The fact that these were considered to form the most notorious sex crimes in the law collections calls for special attention. What does it tell us about gender differentiation and about the need to regulate gender behavior using formal law in the ancient Near East? The emphasis in these regulations is on the woman's status as subordinate to her husband or her father. The perpetrator either damaged the exclusive rights of a married man to access his wife's sexuality, or the exclusive rights of a father to govern his daughter's sexuality, in monitoring her future marriage.

Further felonies bearing a sexual nature were far less frequently represented. Crimes of incest and forbidden kin relations are mostly ignored by the different collections. LH included a few basic inter-generational prohibitions, while HL is the sole collection to present a lengthy list of incestuous restrictions. Gender played a decisive role in these offences, since men were almost exclusively regarded as the perpetrators, and women only represented their legally forbidden partners. The frequent sanction in these cases was execution, even though in HL it is implicit.

Prohibitions on bestiality only appear in HL. As with the rules of incest, only men were considered possible perpetrators. The sanction for bestiality was the execution of both the man and animal involved. Since the sanction on incest- and bestiality-related offences was the harshest of all – execution – it seems obvious that these felonies were deemed very grave. This leaves open the question of how it happened that in Hatti these constituted severe offences, while in other ancient Near Eastern collections they were almost entirely ignored. Another question can be asked in this regard: if these offences were indeed ignored in non-Hittite collections, how did it happen that several prohibitions on incest were still included in LH? This cannot possibly be a case of a shared legal tradition or of diffusion of ideas. The answer may be a simple case of random local innovation.

3 Second synthesis: regulating gender in biblical law

Comparing the different law collections of the Hebrew Bible is no less problematic than comparing the ancient Near Eastern law collections, but for different reasons.[4] The different collections probably stemmed from separate sources of the Bible, the origins of which are still obscure. The "documentary hypothesis" and other theories attempt to elucidate how and under which circumstances the different biblical sources came to be, but a definitive answer is yet to be found. The following synthesis, therefore, should also be taken with caution.

General issues of gender inequality/asymmetry

The first gender-related point of comparison between the different biblical law collections we discuss is one of the most conspicuous: the different attitude shown in CC and in DC to female slaves. The fact that female slaves are denied their manumission in CC, but granted it in DC, has been discussed by numerous scholars. Some suggested that this difference reflects the overall positive attitude DC shows to women, in comparison to other collections. Others suggested that the later DC was meant to correct the problematic ruling in the earlier CC. Be the case as it may, female slaves were clearly discriminated against in CC but had an equal opportunity to males in DC. A more homogeneous attitude is reflected in the ruling that daughters could be sold into slavery, but no males are mentioned in this respect; both CC and DC have this ruling.

An interesting difference between the laws of Exodus and those of Leviticus involves the attitude to the performers of forbidden magic. CC refers specifically to women as such perpetrators, while HC explicitly notes both men and women in this regard. Both collections decree the death penalty for the practitioners. Here as well, therefore, CC appears to show gender differentiation and discrimination against women, while HC regards in this case both genders similarly.

The next points only involve CC. This collection includes certain rules that highlight women's vulnerability and their occasional need for legal intervention. The CC thus decrees punishment for a man who beats a pregnant woman and causes her to miscarry, and protects slave-women who were purchased for marriage but were then abandoned by their prospective husbands. On the other hand, some other statutes unique to this collection reflect gender equality. For example, CC includes rules that protect slaves – both male and female – against abuse by their owner, and the rules of a goring ox explicitly refer to both male and female victims, whether free persons or slaves. All these issues distinguish CC from the other biblical law collections.

Rules of purity in cult

The rules of purity for priests, as specified in HC, occasionally highlight women's role as somehow generating defilement, especially as regards their sexuality: prostitutes, divorcées and widows. Additionally, priests' daughters had certain restrictions concerning their sex life because of their fathers' holiness. Though these rules refer to very specific circumstances, and are by no means necessarily representative of the overall attitude to women, it must be stressed that no parallel rules refer to men in such defiling capacities. And, of course, the priestly circles included only men.

Laws concerning the family

Most of the biblical statutes that were meant to govern the family are found in DC, and only a few were included in CC. Thus, a son's obligation to respect his parents, and the rules of levirate marriage, are unique to DC. Inheritance rules for men and women are rare and only attested in Num.

Parental authority is alluded to in several legal provisions. It was by and large paternal, as seen by the father's exclusive decision concerning his daughter's marriage (CC) or his right to overrule his daughter's vows (Num.). At times, however, parental authority could be both paternal and maternal, as seen in the case of a disobedient son (DC) or when both parents defended their daughter's reputation against slanderous accusations by her new husband (DC).

Sex crimes

All the different law collections in the Hebrew Bible were preoccupied with sexual felonies, the most notable of which were premarital sex, adultery and rape.

The attitude to virginity and premarital intercourse is apparent in all three law collections, CC, HC and DC. The main issues addressed by the laws in this respect were seduction, betrothal and rape. A clearly financially oriented perspective is apparent in the attitude to these issues, as the male perpetrators were frequently required to pay financial compensation for their misbehavior.

Adultery and rape were mostly addressed by DC, with fewer references in HC and CC. If a married woman performed adultery, both paramours were to be executed (HC, DC); if the woman was betrothed to another man, she and her lover were both to be executed (DC); the rapist of a virgin betrothed girl was to be executed alone (DC). Biblical law does not address a case of rape of an unbetrothed girl: CC and DC only refer to the seduction of a virgin girl, following which the seducer was forced to pay a brideprice and marry her; her father could refuse the marriage, but the payment was still mandatory.

Incest and forbidden kin relations formed sinful illicit acts, but were almost exclusively addressed by HC. This collection supplied a lengthy list of prohibitions, a few of which were repeated in DC. The reasoning for these prohibitions was theological, as they were polluting crimes that offended God. This was entirely different than the financial perspective on premarital intercourse and in line with the attitude to the crimes of adultery and rape.

Homosexual intercourse was banned in HC alone, and sanctioned by death. Bestiality was banned in all three collections, CC, HC and DC: CC prescribed execution for the act, HC specified that the men, women and animals involved were to be executed and the list of curses that supplemented DC condemned bestiality.

4 Third synthesis: regulating gender in ancient Near Eastern and biblical law

The final synthesis compares ancient Near Eastern law with biblical law. As we have seen, generalizations concerning any of these two corpora are hazardous, and at times flawed. Taking these two sets of generalizations, and comparing them to one another, is understandably no less problematic. Having said that, and with due caution, the following synthesis can still be found useful, in illustrating an outline of general legal patterns and trends concerning gender-related issues that occupied law in the ancient world.

I wish to address several questions in this synthesis. How did the two corpora view similar gender-related legal issues? What were the main topics that were unique to each one of them? What were the notable similarities they shared?

General issues of gender inequality/asymmetry

As we have seen, debt-slavery, and the legal regulation of selling family members into it, was an Old Babylonian phenomenon. The Hebrew Bible also addresses this issue, but differently. According to LH and ESi/Ad/Aṣ, men could sell into slavery their wives, sons and daughters, while in CC and DC daughters are the only family members mentioned as being sold into slavery.

A recurring legal theme in ancient Near Eastern law, as attested in LE, LH and MAL, was that of a woman whose husband was missing, but still alive, whether he was captured or had fled. This theme is absent from biblical law altogether.

Another recurring legal theme in ancient Near Eastern law was that of a man beating a pregnant woman and causing her to miscarry (LUN, LH, HL, MAL). This theme is attested in CC in a very similar manner.

The attitude to the practice of magic is attested in both corpora, in very different ways. What is common, however, is that in some collections of each corpus (NBL, CC) only women are attested as such practitioners, while others (MAL, HC) mention both genders.

A notable difference between ancient Near Eastern and biblical law appears in the group of statutes of the goring ox: LE and LH only refer to men as victims, while CC explicitly refers to both men and women in this regard.

Several statutes were unique to biblical law. The rules protecting slaves – whether male or female – against abuse by their owner are only attested in CC, and so are the rules protecting slave-women who were purchased for marriage but then abandoned.

Cult: administration and rules of purity

The legal administration of economy and cult is unique to ancient Near Eastern law and was mainly an Old Babylonian phenomenon. The HC rules of purity for priests have no parallel in ancient Near Eastern law, but some parallels in Hittite instructions. Outside of the priestly rules of the Bible, it seems that the legal involvement with cult was very meager and had no impact on gender dynamics.

Laws concerning the family

The legal regulation of family affairs is notable in both ancient Near Eastern and biblical law. Statutes that governed the economic dynamics within the family are mostly found in LH and MAL, while biblical law usually ignored these issues.

When it comes to parental authority, both ancient Near Eastern and biblical law exhibit similar tendencies towards emphasized paternal superiority. Equal parental authority was limited to a few specific issues in each corpus. A case in point was a son's obligation to respect both his parents, an issue mentioned both in LH and in DC.

The legal regulation of the familial structure is apparent in both corpora, but noticeable differences sometimes occur. Infringement on betrothal was regarded very seriously in both corpora, but while in the ancient Near East it formed a financial matter, in biblical law it was also regarded as a moral issue. Many statutes in the ancient Near Eastern collections were dedicated to the financial aspects of divorce, while biblical law hardly addressed it. Widowing was also dealt with extensively in ancient Near Eastern law but only rarely in biblical law. The main similarity between both corpora in their attitude to widowing was their application of the levirate marriage in case a woman became widowed without having a male heir (HL, MAL, DC).

Inheritance, and its gender preferences, is attested in both corpora. The clear preference for male heirs was common to both, as well as the possibility of females to inherit under certain circumstances. One of the major differences was the wife's right to inherit: some ancient Near Eastern collections allowed it, but biblical law never mentioned a widow as a possible heir.

Sex crimes

When it comes to felonies of sexual nature, we notice many similarities between ancient Near Eastern and biblical law. The most conspicuous similarities regard the felonies of adultery and rape. Most collections in both corpora addressed these felonies, and the attitude they show was identical: only women were punished for adultery, while no statute punished a fornicating husband; both the adulteress and her lover were to face execution, but if the wife was spared, the lover was spared too. Rape was usually sanctioned with execution in both corpora, but several details differed between them: the ancient Near Eastern collections referred to the rape of a married woman (execution) or a virgin girl (payment of a fine), while biblical law referred to the rape of a virgin betrothed girl (execution).

The attitude to virginity and premarital intercourse was partially related to the issues of betrothal, seduction and rape, and was quite similar in both corpora. Virginity was valued and premarital intercourse prohibited, mainly because the economic value of marriage was undermined by such felonies.

Incest and forbidden kin relations were rarely addressed by ancient Near Eastern law: a few statutes were dedicated to it in LH, and several in HL. Biblical law, on the other hand, addressed this issue at length and viewed it as sinful acts against God that polluted the entire community. The ancient Near Eastern collections supplied no such reasoning for the punishment, though in HL incest felonies were regarded as an "abomination". All these sources with one exception in LH were identical in viewing men as the exclusive perpetrators.

Homosexual intercourse and bestiality distinguish biblical law from the ancient Near Eastern collections. The former was banned and sanctioned by execution in HC alone; the latter was banned in all three biblical collections and in HL, but while biblical law decreed execution for the men, women and animals involved, HL specified several forbidden animals, and only prescribed the death penalty for men and animals, not considering women to be possible perpetrators.

5 Concluding remarks

The aim of this book, as delineated in its introduction, was to describe how official law in Mesopotamia, Hatti and ancient Israel regulated gender dynamics in several different spheres: the societal, the institutional, the familial and the individual. I would like to make a few concluding remarks in this respect.

The research of formal legislation and gender dynamics in the ancient world offers numerous insights into the world of thought of past human societies. At the same time, the comparative analysis of various societies and structures of ideas, as this book exhibits, is relevant not only for the study of the ancient world but bears clear significance for the understanding of our modern society, its institutions, structures and gender relations, as they are all rooted in the human past. Law was not invented today, nor were the problems it attempts to solve – or those it actually creates.

The basic assumption of this book is that legislation was a tool used by social elites in the ancient Near East and ancient Israel in order to perpetuate certain norms and enforce social control. Mary Douglas suggested that the biblical rules of purity reflected society's wish to keep categories apart. Gender differentiation as embedded in official law can be viewed, similarly, as the reflection of society's will to keep social categories – in this case, those of gender – apart. But such explanations cannot clarify the picture of law and gender in full. The main questions this book attempts to answer pertain to who has the power to dictate official laws and decree statutes, and what are the motivations behind the nature of gender-oriented legislation. The answers are obvious: men were the legislators, and gender differentiation and inequality as embedded in official law reflected the broader androcentric or patriarchal tendencies of ancient societies. Theological reasoning might have occasionally been harnessed in order to justify such legislation – as shown at times in biblical law – but these were merely secondary justifications. Law was used as a social mechanism for separation, segregation and maintaining male superiority. There are, however, more aspects to consider: the law was applied not only in determining dynamics between the genders but also within the genders. We should not confine ourselves to examining associations between men and women but also between men and other men, and between women and other women; we will return to this point later on.

Some of the main issues highlighted by scholars of gender studies involve social superiority and power struggles between the genders. In the case of law and gender in the ancient Near East and the Hebrew Bible, however, there was no struggle. Women had lost the battle before it ever began – the male legislators made sure of that. This book demonstrates how official law was used in order to perpetuate gender inequality in these ancient societies. The examples are numerous, and I will only note a few of them: unlike men, women had strict legal restrictions on their sexuality: they were only allowed to have sexual intercourse with their husbands, and any deviation from this rule was met with harsh sanctions, at times even execution; thus, legal definitions of adultery only considered the marital status of the woman involved, and virginity was only significant in the case of females; alternatives to marriage as the legally acceptable frame of sexual intercourse – polygamy and prostitution – focused on women: the only polygamous form attested in the laws was polygyny, and never polyandry, while prostitutes were always women, and their male customers remained anonymous; the law decreed rules of chastity for women and regulated their behavior in the public and economic domains; financially, women were legally dependent on men, and therefore specific statutes were decreed for certain types of unmarried women: virgins, divorcées, widows, prostitutes and priestesses; in cases of divorce and inheritance, men were more privileged than women.

As noted previously, ancient Near Eastern and biblical law determined hierarchy not only between the genders but also within the genders. What about men, therefore? How were their roles and activities in society regulated by official law? Men were the ones who possessed social control – but, as we know, "with great power comes great responsibility", and this was true even before Spiderman. Men were the ones who were held in legal liability in almost all cases where sexual misconduct became a matter of criminal law: seduction, adultery, rape, incest and the more nuanced cases of homosexuality and bestiality. There were a few exceptions, such as women who initiated illicit sexual intercourse with men, or women who performed bestiality in biblical law – but these were merely the exceptions that prove the rule. As we have seen, numerous statutes governed the internal hierarchy within the family, between fathers and sons, between grooms and their future fathers-in-law, between married and unmarried men, young and old, and at times between men of different social statuses, such as free and slaves, or higher- and lower-ranking men in society. The purpose of most of these statutes was to stabilize society by strengthening the familial circles and protecting the institution of marriage from external interferences, whether moral or economic.

Hierarchy within the feminine gender is harder to trace in official law. The most obvious categorizations in this respect are between mistresses and female slaves, and between mothers and daughters. Both sets of categorizations were based on nuanced, albeit clear, notions of subordination. As it appears, women were not only legally subordinate to men but at times also to other women. The notable scarcity of references to female hierarchy reflects, yet again, the fact that men were the dominant gender in society and as such the active one, who required more regulation and attention on the part of official law. Being the dominant gender, men could do more harm than women – and the law was there to restrain them. Law was issued by men in order to prevent men from depriving other men of their rights; subordinating women may have only been secondary to this.

The question of the enforcement of social norms of gender roles is a complicated one. As explained in the introduction of this book, I do not address here the issue of law enforcement, but that of official law as a means of regulating gender dynamics. Social norms concerning chastity and sexual behavior were already discussed. As to gender roles, the main division apparent in the laws is between the man as associated with the public domain, and the woman as associated with the private/domestic domain. Rules of chastity and restrictions on sexual behavior are only one dimension of this topic. Another dimension involves the socialization process that shapes gender identities and roles and eventually generates functional differences between sons and daughters.[5] We can observe an end-product of this socialization process embedded in certain statutes that exhibit two different forms of parental obedience: a differentiation was apparent between sons' obligation to respect their parents and daughters' obligation to remain chaste under their parents' auspices. The gender roles were already firmly established by this early stage of someone's life, compelling the child to function properly in society according to his or her gender. Differentiation in the division of gender roles is later on apparent in every aspect of someone's adulthood, as shown by the unique statutes stipulated for specific types of women – priestesses, women-innkeepers and wet-nurses – let alone in the differentiation between husbands and wives, fathers and mothers, divorcés and divorcées, widowers and widows.

Another question involves social stratification: how does law reflect the interests of the elite, given the fact that members of the elite are the legislators in every ancient society? This is another complicated question, because the different law collections reflect different social elites. I can therefore only offer several general comments in this regard. A notable case in point is the visibility of crime and punishment. One of the main functionalities of law is preventive: law does not only provide sanctions in reaction to a vice that has been committed, but aspires to prevent the occurrence of such vices by means of deterrence. The mere knowledge of the existence of sanctions is usually enough to deter potential perpetrators. The visibility of punishment is therefore crucial: public denunciation lingers long after the legal sanction has already been implemented. Criminals may pay their legal dues, but in many cases their public humiliation is perpetuated. This is one of the reasons why on numerous occasions ancient Near Eastern and biblical law involve the community in the legal or punitive procedure. Social elites cannot govern the entire population in a direct manner, and therefore many control mechanisms operate by proxy. Public penalty is one such example: the retaliation it generates ensures that most people keep their social conduct and interaction within the acceptable norms, even without the need to actually resort to penal means. We may term it "control by fear": fear of retaliation but also of public humiliation.

Many lessons can be learned from our ancient past. Some are surely relevant to us, right here, right now. Ancient Near Eastern and biblical law functioned as a means of generating social conformity. Law was supposedly good and constructive: obey the law, and no harm will happen. But law was abusive no less than constructive. If it protected the weak, it was usually only in serving someone else's need: a slave's owner, a daughter's father or a wife's husband. Law was used by men in order to oblige other men to behave in specific manners. When the law was used for perpetuating certain norms, these were the norms of the elite and not necessarily those of the wider population. All this does not mean, of course, that society can – or even should – live lawlessly. But it does highlight the fact that law should not always be taken at face value and be blindly and thoughtlessly obeyed. We should always ask ourselves what the source of law is, who dictates it and why. Raising such questions can sometimes be the final barrier to oppression, discrimination, fascism and racism. In the ancient past people usually lacked the power to raise these questions or protest against oppressive or unjust law – this is not the case anymore, nor should it ever be in a healthy, functioning society.

Notes

1 Westbrook 1998: 237.
2 Pressler 1993: 20.
3 Pressler 1993: 85, 113.
4 For a comparison between the different biblical law collections, see Patrick 1985.
5 For a theoretical discussion of gender socialization in the ancient Near East, see Peled 2016: 34–38.

Bibliography

Patrick, Dale. 1985. *Old Testament Law*. Atlanta, GA: John Knox Press.
Peled, Ilan. 2016. *Masculinities and Third Gender: The Origins and Nature of an Institutionalized Gender Otherness in the Ancient Near East*. Münster: Ugarit-Verlag.
Pressler, Carolyn. 1993. *The View of Women Found in the Deuteronomic Family Laws*. Berlin: De Gruyter.
Westbrook, Raymond. 1998. "The Female Slave". In *Gender and Law in the Hebrew Bible and the Ancient Near East*, edited by Victor H. Matthews, Bernard M. Levinson and Tikva S. Frymer-Kensky. Sheffield: Sheffield Academic Press. Pp. 214–238.

Part II

Texts: The primary sources mentioned and discussed in the book

The second part of the book includes all the legal provisions and statutes discussed in the first part. The texts are given in their original languages – Sumerian, Akkadian (Babylonian and Assyrian), Hittite and biblical Hebrew – and in English translation. It must be stressed that these are by no means new critical text editions, since I did not personally collate any of the texts. That being said, I did my best to corroborate the transliterations and transcriptions based on photos of the original texts, where available, whether online or in print. In translating the texts, I have obviously consulted previous publications, even though on numerous occasions I differ from them, whether for the sake of clarity and simplicity, or for the sake of philological or terminological accuracy. I take full responsibility for the translations and any error they might exhibit.

This part is meant to allow the reader an easier understanding and orientation throughout the book, without the constant need to resort to other works where the pertinent texts are published, whether these are more or less accessible to the non-professional audience. The reader can thus independently assess the accuracy of the translations given in the book, follow and critically judge the argumentations and interpretations presented throughout and, in case of need, examine specific terms and passages in the original texts.

The texts of this part are organized chronologically, from the earliest Mesopotamian law collection – LUN – to the latest – NBL, followed by the Hittite and finally biblical provisions. The biblical texts follow the Masoretic version; their English translations mostly follow the NIV, but since I find this translation unsatisfactory at times, I frequently deviate from it and offer my own translations. The verse numbering always agrees with the Masoretic text, which is not necessarily the case in the NIV.

Editions and translations of the pertinent ancient Near Eastern sources are abundant. The most recent and relevant ones are found in Civil 2011 (LUN), Kraus 1958, 1984 (ESi/Ad/Aṣ), Hoffner 1997 (HL), Miller (2013 (Hittite instructions), Pfeiffer and Speiser 1936 (AASOR 16.51), Roth 1997 (LUN, LLI, LE, LH, MAL, MAPD, NBL) and Wilcke 2014 (LUN, LLI), almost all with previous literature. Statute and provision numbers in this book follow these editions, except for Roth's (1997) tentative "LLI §§a–g", which are actually LUN §§B1–3, 33–36, as in Civil 2011 and Wilcke 2014.

Statutes from law collections are cited in full, while from most royal decrees (ESi/Ad/Aṣ, MAPD, Hittite instructions) only the pertinent excerpts are presented; only AASOR 16.51 (=SMN 553) is presented in its entirety.

In the Sumerian transliterations, no distinction is made between /g/ and /ĝ/. The reader will thus encounter writings such as sag rather than saĝ, dingir rather than diĝir and so on.

All the Akkadian texts are given in normalized/bound script, to stylistically conform to Roth's example in her authoritative editions, a method also employed by Richardson in his edition of LH. They are thus easier to read than transliterated editions, but inevitably entail a certain compromise, in terms of philological accuracy and indecisive choices such as the use of macron or circumflex for marking vowel lengths.

Several other complications involve the translation of specific terms. Throughout the book, "slave" refers to males, while "slave-woman" refers to females, thus reflecting the fact that in the original languages each one of these terms was designated by a specific word: arad/*wardu*(*m*)/*urdu* or géme/*amtu*(*m*). The Akkadian term *ḫīṭu* was variably translated as "punishment" or "punishable-offense", depending on context. The use of hyphen in these cases was meant to reflect the fact that the original term consisted of only one word. The verb *niāku*/*nâku*, that conveys in the MAL the notion of illicit sexual intercourse, was translated as "fornicate" or "sodomize", depending on the object of the act: a woman or a man, respectively.

At times, the same phrase had slightly different meanings in different periods, and hence its translation is context-related and varies according to the varying circumstances. For example, I have translated *e'iltum* (LH), *i'iltum* (ESi/Ad/Aṣ) and *u'iltu* (NBL) as "debt", "obligation" and "transaction", respectively.

The debate whether the term *awīlu*(*m*)/*a'īlu* in the law collections should be understood as designating a male person or a social class cannot be easily resolved.[1] I follow the view already expressed by Yaron,[2] translating the term by default as "man", unless clearly opposed with a member of a different social class – most commonly the Old Babylonian *muškēnum* – in which case I render it "an *awīlu*(*m*)/*a'īlu*(-class) man". The same applies to *mārat awīlim*/*a'īle*, "a man's daughter" or "an *awīlu*(*m*)/*a'īlu*(-class) woman", literally "daughter of the *awīlu*(*m*)/*a'īlu*(-class)". I have left untranslated most terms pertaining to the financial arrangements of marriage (some of the common translations of which are "dowry", "marriage gifts", "marriage prestations", "bridewealth", "bridal gift" and the like). Though there is usually a general consensus concerning most modern translations of these terms, they still convey at times modern judgmental views and ambiguities, and the differences between these terms are not always clear. The reader can nonetheless find the acceptable translations of these terms in Part I of this book, under "Technical Terms" (p. 16).

Some of the previously mentioned considerations can definitely be questioned, but for the very least, I did my best to remain consistent.

The Sumerian and Hittite texts are given in transliteration, as is still the usual scholarly custom when presenting text editions. In Sumerian transliterations, logograms which reading is uncertain are given in cups (e.g., SU). In Hittite transliterations, Sumerograms/logograms are given in cups, separated by dots in case of need (e.g., LÚ; SAG.DU), while Akkadograms are given in italicized cups (e.g., *ME*), and transliterated Akkadian terms – as well as phonetic complements – are given in italicized cups separated by hyphens (e.g., *EL-LAM*; *-ŠU*).

The Hittite statutes presented here are those of the earlier versions of the collection, rather than the so-called late/parallel version, which slightly modified some of the penalties. The latter is only used for restorations when none of the older manuscripts preserved the pertinent text. Since the different manuscripts of the HL show on numerous occasions orthographic and formulaic variations for the same provision, the transliterations presented hereby (and hence, inevitably, the translations that follow) combine all the pertinent sources, using the best-preserved – and usually earlier – manuscripts, while significant variations are mentioned in footnotes.

The following sigla are employed:

[ ] restored text

⸢ ⸣ partially restored text

‹ › emendation to original text: addition of a sign erroneously omitted by scribe

! collation/correction within published edition

? uncertain reading or restoration

x traces of illegible sign

It is my hope that these brief notes clarify what might otherwise seem a mixture of sources, languages, presentation methods and translation preferences.

1 LUN (Laws of Ur-Namma)

LUN §4

tukum-bi arad-dè géme á-áš-a-ni in-tuku arad-bi ama-ar-gi$_4$-ni ì-gá-gá é-ta nu-ub-ta-è

If a slave marries a slave-woman of his choice, (and) that slave is given his freedom: she shall not leave the household.

LUN §5

tukum-bi arad-dè dumu-gir$_{15}$ in-tuku ibila 1-àm lugal-a-ni-ir in-na-gub-bu dumu lugal-a-ni-ir in-na-ab[?]-gub-bu-da níg-gur$_{11}$ é ad-da-na [...] ½-bi é-gar$_8$ é ad-da-na [ì-ba-e] dumu dumu-gir$_{15}$ lugal-da nu-me-a nam-arad-d[a-ni-šè] la-ba-an-ku$_4$-re

If a slave marries a freed-woman,[3] and presents his master with one heir: the son who had to be presented to his master [will share] one-half of the goods of his father's household, (and) his father's house;[4] a son of a freed-woman shall not become a slave without the consent of the master.

LUN §6

tukum-bi dam guruš-a é[!15] nu-gi$_4$-a níg-á-gar-šè lú in-ak é[!16] bí-in-gi$_4$ nita-bi ì-gaz-e

If a man seduces by deception a betrothed unmarried woman[7] and takes her into (his) household: they shall kill that male.

LUN §7

tukum-bi dam guruš-a me-te-a-ni-ta lú ba-an-ús úr-ra-na ba-an-ná munus-bi lú ì-gaz-e nita-bi ama-ar-gi$_4$-ni ì-gar

If a betrothed woman, on her own initiative, pursues a man (and) has sex with him: (if) the man (=her prospective husband) kills that woman, that man shall be set free.[8]

LUN §8

tukum-bi géme lú é nu-gi$_4$-a níg-á-gar-šè lú ì-ak é bí-gi$_4$ lú-bi 5 gín kù ì-lá-e

If a man seduces by deception an unmarried slave-woman[9] and takes her into (his) household: that man shall pay five shekels of silver.

LUN §9

tukum-bi lú dam-nitadam-ni ì-tak$_4$-tak$_4$ 1 ma-na kù-àm ì-lá-e

If a man divorces his first-ranking wife: he shall pay 1 mina (=60 shekels) of silver.

LUN §10

tukum-bi nu-mu-SU ì-tak$_4$-tak$_4$ ½ ma-na kù ì-lá-e

If (a man) divorces a widow:[10] he shall pay half a mina (=30 shekels) of silver.

LUN §11

tukum-bi nu-mu-SU dub ka-kéš-a-da nu-me-a lú úr-ra-na ba-an-ná kù nu-na-lá-e

If a man has sex with a widow, without a written document: he shall not pay her silver (when they divorce).

LUN §12

tukum-bi ereš-dingir [. . .]-ba lú úr-na ba-ná ⌜ereš-dingir ù⌝[11] nita-bi ì-bíl-i-dè-eš

If [someone] has sex with a high priestess: the high priestess and that male shall be burned.

LUN §14

tukum-bi dam guruš-a-da úr-ra ná-a lú ì-da-lá íd-dè ù-um-zalag-zal[ag] lú ì-da-l[á-a] ⅓ ŠA [ma-na kù] ì-[lá-e]

If a man accuses about having sex with a betrothed woman: after the River Ordeal clears him/her, the man who made the accusation shall [pay] one-third [of a mina (=20 shekels) of silver].

LUN §15

tuku[m-bi] mu$_{10}$-ús-[sa-tur] é ú-[úr-ra-na-ka] ì-[in-ku$_4$] ú-ú[r-ra-ni dumu-munus-a-ni] egir$_5$-[bi-ta] lú [kúr-ra][12] ba-a[n-na-šúm] níg-[mu$_{10}$-ús-sá] a-rá-[2-àm] ì-n[a-šúm$^{?}$]

I[f] a son-i[n-law enter]s the household [of his] fa[ther-in-law], and afterwards [his] fathe[r-in-law give]s [his daughter to another] man: he (=the father-in-law) shall [give back] to him (=the prospective son-in-law) tw[ice] (the worth of) the wedding-[gifts].

LUN §16

tu[kum-bi] ⌜x⌝ [. . .]-⌜a?⌝ géme ba-[zà]ḫ ki-sur-ra ⌜ere⌝-na-ka íb-te-bal lú ⌜im⌝-mi-gur [lu]gal sag-gá-ke$_4$ lú im-mi-in-gur-ra 2 gín kù-babbar ì-n[a]-lá-e

I[f a slave or?] a slave-woman [esca]pes and crosses the township limits, and someone brings him/her back: the [ow]ner of the person shall pay two shekels of silver to the man who brought him/her back.

LUN §27

tukum-bi lú ba-úš dam-ni úr-a-na-šè ì-na-ni-⌜tuš?⌝ ⌜sag⌝ a-⌜ga⌝-na ne-dé-a ḫa-ba-an-túm-mu

If a man dies (and) his wife goes to reside with her father-in-law: she may take with her the slaves of her inheritance and the marriage-gifts.

LUN §28

tukum-bi géme nu-tuku 10 gín kù-babbar ḫé-na-lá-e

If she has no slave-women: she may pay him ten shekels of silver.

LUN §29

tukum-bi kù nu-tuku níg-na-me nu-na-ab-šúm-mu

If she has no silver: she does not need to give him anything.

LUN §30

tukum-bi géme lú nin-a-ni-gin$_7$ dím-ma-ar áš ì-ni-dug$_4$ 1 sìla mun-àm ka-ka-ni ì-sub$_6$-é

If a slave-woman insults someone who is acting as/on behalf her mistress: they shall rub her mouth with one sila of salt.

LUN §31

tukum-bi géme lú nin-a-ni-gin$_7$ dím-ma-ar ì-ni-ra [. . .]

If a slave-woman strikes someone acting as/on behalf her mistress [. . .]

LUN §33

tuk[um-bi á-su]ḫ[13] dumu-munus l[ú-ka ì-ni-in]-ra níg šà-[ga-na] šu mu-u[n-da-an-lá] ½ ma-na [kù-babbar ì-lá]-e

I[f] (someone) beat[s] (with his) [elbo]w a ma[n's] daughter and causes [her] to mis[carry her] fetus: [he shall pay] half a mina (=30 shekels) [of silver].

LUN §34

tukum-b[i b]a-úš nitá-bi ì-[gaz]-⌜e⌝

If she dies: they shall [kill] that male.

LUN §35

tukum-bi ˹á-suḫ[14] géme˺ lú-ka i-ni-in-ra níg-šà-ga-na šu mu-un-da-an-lá 5 gín-àm ì-lá-e

If (someone) beats (with his) elbow a man's slave-woman and causes her to miscarry her fetus: he shall pay five[15] shekels.

LUN §36

tukum-bi géme ba-úš sag sag-šè ì-gub-bé

If the slave-woman dies: he shall give slave for slave.

LUN §B2

tukum-bi lú ba-úš dumu-nita n[u]-un-tuku dumu-munus dam nu-un-tuku-a ibila-a-ni ˹ḫé-a˺[16]

If a man dies and has no son: an unmarried daughter shall be his heir.

LUN §B3

tukum-[bi dumu-nita nu-tuku[17]] dumu-munus-a-n[i . . .] níg-gur$_{11}$ é ad-da-na [. . .] nin$_{9}$-bàn-da egir$_{5}$ é-˹a˺ [. . .] šuku ad-da erín-e [ì]-ba-e

I[f he has no son] (and) hi[s] daughter [is married$^{?}$] the goods of her father's household [shall be inherited by$^{?}$] a younger sister, after [. . .] the household [. . .] the working teams will share the father's allowances.

LUN §B7

tukum-bi [l]ú dam ì-tuku-àm dam-ni in-tak$_{4}$ itu 6 ù-na-tuš-àm munus-dam šà-ga-na-ke$_{4}$ ḫa-ba-an-tuku-tuku

If [a m]an takes a wife and his wife divorces him: after waiting six months the woman may marry a spouse of her choice.

LUN §B8

tukum-bi lú dam ì-tuku-àm dam-ni ba-úš nita en-na ba-an-tuku-tuku sag-rig$_{7}$ dam-na ḫé-na-túm u$_{4}$ ba-an-tuku-tuku-a sag-rig$_{7}$ é lú-na-ka ḫé-eb-gi$_{4}$

If a man takes a wife, and his wife dies: until the male (re-)marries, his wife's sag-rig$_{7}$[18] shall remain by him, (but) when he (re-)marries, he shall return the sag-rig$_{7}$ to the household of her man (=father?).

LUN §D8

géme uš-bar tan$_{4}$-tan$_{4}$-na á u$_{4}^{?}$ 1-a-ka-n[i . . .]

The daily$^{?}$ wages of a female weaver, when washing (fibers), shall be [x sila].

géme u[š-bar] ama-tuk$_{5}$-ka ˹á u$_{4}^{?}$˺ 1-ni 0.0.2

The daily$^?$ wages of a female we[aver] of skilled$^?$ weaving shall be 20 sila.
géme uš-[bar] ˹šu$^?$˺-dur$^?$-ka á u$_4$ 1-[ni] 0.0.2
The daily wages of a female wea[ver] of *šutur*$^?$-garments shall be 20 sila.
[ì-du$_8$$^?$ . . .]-˹x˺ á-bi 6 sìla š[e-àm]
[The doormen$^?$. . .] their wages shall be six sila of ba[rley].
˹a-ga˺-[am o]-˹(x) x˺ á-bi 0.0.1 sìla še-àm
The doorman's helpers [. . .] their wages shall be one sila of barley.

LUN §D9[19]

tukum-bi [^{munus}lú-]kurun-ke$_4$ u$_4$ bur[u$_{14}$-ka] 1 pihu$_4$ lú-[ra] šu-lá-a-šè in-[na-šúm] níg-diri-bi [. . .] en-te-[n]a-[ka . . .]
If a woman-innkeeper [give]s [at] harve[st] time one beer-jar [to] someone on credit: its níg-diri(-tax shall be) [. . . in] wint[e]r [. . .]
tuk[um-b]i ^{munus}lú-geštin-na-àm 1 ˹pihu˺-ka-ni lú-ra in-na-an-šúm [u$_4$] ˹buru$_{14}$-ke$_4$˺ 0.0.5 še [. . .]-˹x˺
If a woman-innkeeper gives to someone one beer-jar of hers: at harvest [time she shall receive] 50 sila of barley.

LUN §E2

tukum-bi dumu lú-ra lú ga ì-ni-gu$_7$ mu 3-a še-ni 6 gur sík-ni 30 ma-na ì-ni 30 sìla níg nam-nu-gig-kam um-[me]-da hun-gá mu ˹á˺-ni 1 gín-àm
If someone nurses a man's child: for three years her barley (shall be) 6 gur, her wool 30 minas, her oil 30 sila; it is (part of) the nugig-functions.[20] A hired wet-[nu]rse, her yearly wages shall be 1 shekel.

LUN §E4

tukum-bi lú ˹ba˺-úš dam-nitadam-ni ibila 1-gin$_7$ é-a hè-dím
If a man dies: his first-ranking wife shall act as a single heir in the house.

LUN §E5

˹tukum˺-bi lú dam šeš-gal-na ba-an-tuku-tuku ì-gaz
If a man marries the (widowed) wife of his older brother: he shall be killed.

LUN §E6

tukum-bi arad-[d]è nin-a-ni ba-an-tuku-tuku ì-gaz
If a slave marries his female-owner: he shall be killed.

2 LLI (Laws of Lipit-Ištar)

LLI §12

tukum-bi géme arad lú-ù šà-uru-ka ba-záḫ é lú-ka 1 itu-àm ì-tuš-a ba-an-ge-en sag sag-gin$_7$ ba-ab-sum-mu

If a man's slave-woman or (male) slave flees within the city, and it is confirmed that the slave dwelt in a man's house for one month: he (who harbored the slave) shall give slave for slave.

LLI §18

tukum-bi lugal é-a ù nin é-a-ke$_4$ gú-un é-a in-šub-bu-uš lú kúr-e in-íl mu 3-kám-ma-ka nu-ub-ta-è-e lú gú-un é-a in-íl-la é-bi ba-an-tùm lugal é-a-ke$_4$ inim nu-um-gá-gá-a

If the master of the household or the mistress of the household has defaulted on the taxes of the household, (and) an outsider bears them: for three years (the head of the household) shall not be evicted, (but after this period) the person who bore the household tax shall take that household; the master of the household shall not make any claims.

LLI §20b[21]

tukum-bi lú-ù dumu á-è-[a] á-kala-ni-gin$_7$ nu-bùlug-[e-dè] igi di-kud-dè-šè un-ge-en ama tu-du-na ba-an-ši-gur-ru

If a man does not raise a son whom he contracted to raise in an apprenticeship, (and) it is confirmed before the judges: he shall be returned to his birth mother.

LLI §20c[22]

[tukum-bi lú]-ù dumu-munus á-è-[a . . .]-x-na-a-e-na [. . .]

[If a ma]n [does not raise] the daughter whom he contracted to raise [. . .]

LLI §21[23]

[tukum-bi . . .] in-tuku níg-ba é ad-da-na-ka ba-an-na-ba-a ibila-ni-im ba-an-tùmu [. . . tukum-bi . . .] dam-e ba-an-sum níg-ba é ad-da-na-ka ba-an-na-ba-a šeš-a-ne-ne nu-um-da-ba-e-ne ù [. . .]

[If . . .] marries, the (marriage-)gift which is given by? her/his father's household shall be taken for her/his heir. [. . . If . . .] is given to a wife, the (marriage-)gift which had been given by? her/his father's household, her/his brothers shall not divide, but [. . .]

LLI §22

tukum-bi ad-da ti-la dumu-munus-a-ni-ir ereš-dingir lukur ù nu-gíg ḫé-a ibila-gin_7-nam é ì-ba-e-ne

If, while a father is alive, his daughter becomes an *ugbabtu*, a *nadītu*, or a *qadištu*: they (=her brothers) shall divide the household (considering her) as an (equal) heir.

LLI §23

tukum-bi dumu-munus é ad-da-ka ti-la dam-ra la-ba-[an-sum] šeš-a-ne-ne dam-ra in-na-an-sum-mu

If a daughter is not [give]n to a spouse while her father is alive:[24] her brothers shall give her to a spouse.

LLI §24

[tuku]m-bi [dam eg]ir-ra [ba-a]n-tuku-a [du]mu in-ši-in-tu-ud sag-rig_7 é ad-da-na-ta mu-un-túm-ma dumu-na-ka dumu dam-nitadam ù dumu dam-egir-ra níg-gur_{11} ad-da-ne-ne téš-a sì-ga-bi ì-ba-e-ne

[I]f [the sec]ond [wife] whom he marries bears him [a ch]ild: the sag-rig_7 which she brought from her father's household shall belong only to her children; the children of the first-ranking wife and the children of the second wife shall divide the property of their father equally.

LLI §25

tukum-bi lú-ù dam in-tuku dumu in-ši-in-tu-ud dumu-bi i-ti ù géme lugal-a-ni-ir dumu in-ši-in-tu-ud ad-da-a géme ù dumu-ne-ne ama-ar-gi_4-bi in-gar dumu géme-ke_4 dumu lugal-a-na-ra é nu-un-da-ba-e

If a man marries a wife, she bears him a child, the child lives, and a slave-woman also bears a child to her master: the father shall free the slave-woman and her children; the children of the slave-woman shall not divide the household with the children of the master.

LLI §26

[t]ukum-bi [da]m-nitadam-a-ni [ba]-úš [eg]ir dam-a-na-ta [géme]-ni nam-dam-šè [ba-a]n-tuku-tuku [dumu] dam-nit[adam-a-na] ibi[la-a-ni ì-me-en] dumu géme lugal-a-ni-[ir] in-ši-in-tu-ud dumu dumu-gir$_{15}$-gin$_{7}$-nam é-a-ni íb-dùg-g[e]

[I]f his first-ranking [wif]e [di]es, and [aft]er his wife's death he marries his [slave-woman]: the [child of his] first-[ranking wife shall be his] he[ir]; the child that the slave-woman bore [to] her master is considered equal to a native freeborn son, and they shall make good his household.

LLI §27

tukum-bi lú-ù dam-a-ni dumu nu-un-ši-in-tu-ud kar-kid-da tílla-a dumu in-ši-in-tu-ud kar-kid-ba še-ba ì-ba síg-ba-ni in-na-ab-sum-mu dumu kar-kid-dè in-ši-in-tu-ud-da ibila-ni ì-me-en ud dam-a-ni a-na-ti-la-aš kar-kid dam-nitadam-ra é-a nu-mu-un-da-an-tuš

If a man's wife does not bear him a child, but a prostitute from the street does bear him a child: he shall provide grain-rations, oil-rations and clothing-rations for the prostitute; the child whom the prostitute bore him shall be his heir; as long as his wife is alive, the prostitute will not reside in the house with his first-ranking wife.

LLI §28

tukum-bi lú-ù dam-nitadam-a-ni igi-ni ba-ab-gi$_{4}$ ù šu ba-an-lá-lá é-ta nu-ub-ta-è dam-a-ni dam galam-na ba-an-tuku-tuku dam-egir-ra dam-nitadam in-íl-il

If a man's first-ranking wife loses her sight/attractiveness or becomes a paralyzed: she shall not be evicted from the house; her husband may marry a healthy wife;[25] the second wife shall support the first-ranking wife.[26]

LLI §29

tukum-bi mu$_{10}$-ús-sá-tur é ur$_{7}$-ra ì-in-ku$_{4}$ níg-mu$_{10}$-ús-sá in-ak egir-bi-ta im-ta-an-è-eš dam-a-ni ku-li-ni-ir ba-na-an-sum-mu-uš níg-mu$_{10}$-ús-sá in-túm-a-ni in-na-ab-tab-e-ne dam-bi ku-li-ni nu-un-tuku-tuku

If a son-in-law enters the household of a father-in-law (and) performs the marriage-gift, but later they evict him and give his wife to his comrade: the marriage-gift which he brought they shall restore to him twofold, and his comrade shall not marry that wife.

LLI §30

tukum-bi guruš dam-tuku kar-kid-dè tílla-a in-tuku-àm kar-kid-bi-ir nu-un-ši-gur-ru-da di-kud-e-ne in-na-an-eš egir-bi-ta dam-nitadam dam-a-ni ba-an-tag$_{4}$ kù dam-tag$_{4}$-a-ni ù-na-an-sum kar-kid-bi nu-un-tuku-tuku

If a young married man has a prostitute from the street, the judges order him not to go back to that prostitute, afterwards he divorces his first-ranking wife (and) gives her the silver of her divorce settlement: he shall not marry that prostitute.

LLI §33

[tuk]um-bi dumu-munus lú é nu-gi$_4$-a gìš ì-zu lú ba-ab-dug$_4$ gìš nu-un-zu-a un-ge-en 10 gín kù-babbar ì-lá-e

[I]f a man claims that another man's virgin daughter[27] has had sex, but it is proven that she has not had sex: he shall pay ten shekels of silver.

3 LE (Laws of Ešnunna)

<u>LE §15</u>

ina qāti wardim u amtim tamkārum u sābītum kaspam še'am šipātim šamnam adi mādim ul imaḫḫar

A merchant or a woman-innkeeper shall not receive from a slave or slave-woman silver, grain, wool, oil or anything else.

<u>LE §17</u>

mār awīlim ana bīt emim terḫatam lībilma šumma ina kilallīn ištēn ana šīmtim ittalak kaspum ana bēlišuma itâr

Should a man's son bring the *terḫatum* to the house of his father-in-law, if one of the two[28] goes to his/her fate: the silver shall return to its owner.[29]

<u>LE §18</u>

šumma īḫussima ana bītišu īrub lu āḫizānu lu kallatum ana šīmtim ittalak mala ublu ul ušeṣṣi wataršuma ileqqe

If he marries[30] her, she enters to his house, (and later) either the groom or the bride goes to his/her fate: he shall not take out everything he brought, but shall only take its excess.

<u>LE §22</u>

šumma awīlum eli awīlim mimma la išūma amat awīlim ittepe bēl amtim nīš ilim i[zakkar] mimma eliya la tīšû kaspam mala ⌜šīm?⌝ amtim išaqqal

If a man has no claim against (another) man, but he takes the man's slave-woman: the owner of the slave-woman shall [swear] an oath by the god, "You have no claim against me!"; he (=the defendant) shall pay silver as much as is the value? of the slave-woman.

<u>LE §23</u>

šumma awīlum eli awīlim mimma la išūma amat awīlim ittepe nipûtam ina bītišu iklāma uštamīt 2 amātim ana bēl amtim iriab

If a man has no claim against (another) man, but he takes the man's slave-woman, imprisons the detainee in his house and causes her death: he shall restore two slave-women to the slave-woman's owner.

LE §24

šumma mimma elišu la išūma aššat muškēnim mār muškēnim ittepe nipûtam ina bītišu iklāma uštamīt dīn napištim nēpû ša ippû imât

If he has no claim against him, but he takes a commoner's wife or a commoner's child, imprisons the detainee in his house and causes her/his death: it is a capital offense, the detainer that detained shall die.

LE §25

šumma awīlum ana bīt emi issīma emušu ikšīšuma mārassu ana [*šanîm it*]*tadin abi mārtim terḫat imḫuru tašna utâr*

If a man lays a claim against the house of his father-in-law,[31] because his father-in-law mistreats[?] him (and) [g]ives his daughter to [another]: the daughter's father shall return twofold the *terḫatum* which he received.

LE §26

šumma awīlum ana mārat awīlim terḫatam ubilma šanû balum šâl abiša u ummiša imšu'šima ittaqabši dīn napištimma imât

If a man brings the *terḫatum* for a man's daughter, but another, without asking her father and her mother, abducts her and deflowers her: it is indeed a capital offense, and he shall die.

LE §27

šumma awīlum mārat awīlim balum šâl abiša u ummiša īḫussima u kirram u rik‹sā›tim ana abiša u ummiša la i[*škun*] *ūmī šattim ištiat ina bītišu līšimma ul aššat*

If a man marries a man's daughter without asking her father and her mother, and does not [submit] a (ceremonial) jar[32] and a contract to her father and her mother: (even) should she reside in his house for a whole year, a wife (she is) not.

LE §28

šumma ‹awīlum›[33] *riksātim u kirram ana abiša u ummiša iškunma īḫussi aššat ūm ina sūn awīlim iṣṣabbatu imât ul iballuṭ*

If (a man) submits to her father and her mother a contract and a (ceremonial) jar and marries her: a wife (she is); the day she is seized in the lap of a(nother) man, she shall die; she shall not live.

LE §29

šumma awīlum ina ḫarrān šeḫṭim u sakpim it[tašlal] ulu naḫbutum ittaḫbat ūmī [arkūtim] ina mātim šanītimma itta[šab] aššassu šanûmma ītaḫaz u māram ittalad inūma ittūram aššassu ita[bbal]

If a man is [captured] during a raiding expedition or patrol?, or plundered by plunderers, re[side]s for a [long] time in another land, then another marries his wife and she bears a child: when he returns he shall [take back] his wife.

LE §30

šumma awīlum ālšu u bēlšu izērma ittaḫbit aššassu šanûmma ītaḫaz inūma ittūram ana aššatišu ul iraggam

If a man hates his city and his master and flees, and another marries his wife: when he returns he shall not claim for his wife.

LE §31

šumma awīlum amat awīlim ittaqab ⅓ mana kaspam išaqqal u amtum ša bēlišama

If a man deflowers a(nother) man's slave-woman: he shall pay one-third of a mina (=20 shekels) of silver, and the slave-woman (shall remain) of her master.

LE §32

šumma awīlum mārašu ana šūnuqim ana tarbītim iddinma epram piššatam lubuštam šalaš šanātim la iddin 10 *šiqil kaspam tarbīt mārišu išaqqalma mārašu itarru*

If a man gives his child for nourishing and for upbringing, but does not give (the caregiver) grain, oil and clothing for three years: he shall pay ten shekels of silver for upbringing his child, and he shall take back his child.

LE §33

šumma amtum usarrirma māraša ana mārat awīlim ittadin inūma irtabū bēlšu immaršu iṣabbassuma itarrūšu

If a slave-woman is deceiving and gives her child to a (free) man's daughter, (and) when he grows up his master identifies him: he shall seize him and take him back.

LE §34

šumma amat ekallim māraša lu mārassa ana muškēnim ana tarbītim ittadin māram lu mārtam ša iddinu ekallum itabbal

If a palace slave-woman gives her son or her daughter to a commoner for upbringing: the palace shall take back the son or daughter that she gave.

LE §35

u lēqû ša mār amat ekallim ilqū meḫeršu ana ekallim iriab

However?,[34] an adopter who adopts a palace slave-woman's child shall restore his equal to the palace.

LE §40

šumma awīlum wardam amtam alpam u šīmam mala ibaššû išāmma nādinānam la ukīn šûma šarrāq

If a man buys a slave, a slave-woman, an ox, or a commodity – all that there is – but does not identify the seller: a thief he is.

LE §41

šumma ubarum napṭarum u mudû šikaršu inaddin sābītum maḫīrat illaku šikaram inaddinšum

If a foreigner, a *napṭaru*, or a *mudû* wishes to sell his beer: the woman-innkeeper shall sell the beer for him at the current rate.

LE §49

šumma awīlum ina wardim šarqim amtim šariqtim ittaṣbat wardum wardam amtum amtam iredde

If a man is caught with a stolen slave (or) a stolen slave-woman: a slave shall lead a slave, a slave-woman shall lead a slave-woman.

LE §50

šumma šakkanakkum šāpir nārim bēl tērtim mala ibaššû wardam ḫalqam amtam ḫaliqtam alpam ḫalqam imēram ḫalqam ša ekallim u muškēnim iṣbatma ana Ešnunna la irdiamma ina bītišu iktala ūmī eli warḫim ištēn ušētiqma ekallum šurqam ittišu ītawwu

If a military governor, a canal controller, (or) any commissioner there may be, seizes an escaped slave, escaped slave-woman, escaped ox, (or) escaped donkey of the palace or a commoner, and does not lead it to Ešnunna but confines it in his house and lets more than one month's time to elapse: the palace shall litigate with him for the theft.

LE §51

wardum u amtum ša Ešnunna ša kannam maškanam u abbuttam šaknu abul Ešnunna balum bēlišu ul uṣṣi

A slave or slave-woman of (a resident of) Ešnunna, who bears fetters, shackles or a slave-hairstyle shall not leave Ešnunna's gate without his master.

LE §52

wardum u amtum ša itti mār šiprim naṣruma abul Ešnunna īterbam kannam maškanam u abbuttam iššakkanma ana bēlišu naṣir

A slave or slave-woman who has entered Ešnunna's gate by the keeping of an envoy shall be imposed fetters, shackles or a slave-hairstyle, and shall be kept for his master.

LE §59

šumma awīlum mārī wulludma aššassu īzimma šanītam ītaḫaz ina bītim u mal[*a ib*]*aššû innassaḫma warki ša i*[. . .]*ma ittallak* [. . .] *bīt* [. . .]

If a man that sired sons divorces his wife and marries another: he shall be expelled from the house *and whatever there is,*[35] and after the one who [. . .] he shall depart. [. . .] the house [. . .]

4 LH (Laws of Hammurabi)

LH §7

šumma awīlum lu kaspam lu ḫurāṣam lu wardam lu amtam lu alpam lu immeram lu imēram ulu mimma šumšu ina qāt mār awīlim ulu warad awīlim balum šībī u riksātim ištām ulu ana maṣṣarūtim imḫur awīlum šû šarrāq iddâk

If a man receives silver, gold, a slave, a slave-woman, an ox, a sheep, a donkey – or anything whatsoever – from a man's son or a man's slave without witnesses or a contract or for safekeeping: that man is a thief, he shall be killed.

LH §15

šumma awīlum lu warad ekallim lu amat ekallim lu warad muškēnim lu amat muškēnim abullam uštēṣi iddâk

If a man lets a palace slave, a palace slave-woman, a commoner's slave, or a commoner's slave-woman to leave through the (city-)gate: he shall be killed.

LH §16

šumma awīlum lu wardam lu amtam ḫalqam ša ekallim ulu muškēnim ina bītišu irtaqīma ana šisīt nāgirim la uštēṣiam bēl bītim šû iddâk

If a man harbors in his house an escaped slave or slave-woman of the palace or (of) a commoner, and does not bring him out to the herald's proclamation: that house master shall be killed.

LH §17

šumma awīlum lu wardam lu amtam ḫalqam ina ṣērim iṣbatma ana bēlišu irtediaššu 2 šiqil kaspam bēl wardim inaddiššum

If a man seizes an escaped slave or slave-woman in the steppe, and leads him back to his owner: the slave owner shall give him two shekels of silver.

LH §29

šumma mārušu ṣeḫerma ilik abišu alākam la ile'i šalušti eqlim u kirîm ana ummišu innaddinma ummašu urabbāšu

If his son is young and is unable to perform his father's service-obligation: one-third of the field and orchard shall be given to his mother, and his mother shall raise him.

LH §38

rēdûm bā'irum u nāši biltim ina eqlim kirîm u bītim ša ilkišu ana aššatišu u mārtišu ul išaṭṭar u ana e'iltišu ul inaddin

A soldier, fisherman or a state tenant shall not write (=assign) to his wife or his daughter any part within a field, orchard or house of his service-obligation, and he shall not give it for his debt.

LH §39

ina eqlim kirîm u bītim ša išammuma iraššû ana aššatišu u mārtišu išaṭṭar u ana e'iltišu inaddin

A part within a field, orchard or house that he acquires and purchases he can write (=assign) to his wife or his daughter, or give for his debt.

LH §40

nadītum tamkārum u ilkum aḫûm eqelšu kirāšu u bīssu ana kaspim inaddin šāyimānum ilik eqlim kirîm u bītim ša išammu illak

A *nadītu*, a merchant or a holder of a field with service-obligation[36] may sell his field, his orchard or his house; the buyer shall perform the service-obligation of the field, orchard or house that he bought.

LH §108

šumma sābītum ana šīm šikarim še'am la imtaḫar ina abnim rabītim kaspam imtaḫar u maḫīr šikarim ana maḫīr še'im umtaṭṭi sābītam šuāti ukannušima ana mê inaddûši

If a woman-innkeeper does not accept grain for the price of beer, (but) accepts silver (measured) by large weight, thus reducing beer value comparing to grain value: that woman-innkeeper, they shall convict[37] her, and they shall cast her into the water.

LH §109

šumma sābītum sarrūtum ina bītiša ittarkasuma sarrūtim šunūti la iṣṣabtamma ana ekallim la irdiam sābītum šî iddâk

If a woman-innkeeper, criminals gather in her house, and she does not seize those criminals and lead them to the palace: that woman-innkeeper shall be killed.

LH §110

šumma nadītum ugbabtum ša ina gagîm la wašbat bīt sībim iptete ulu ana šikarim ana bīt sībim īterub awīltam šuāti iqallûši

If a *nadītu* (or) an *ugbabtu* who does not reside in the cloister opens a tavern (door?) or enters to a tavern for beer: they shall burn that woman.

LH §111

šumma sābītum ištēn pīḫam ana qīptim iddin ina ebūrim 5 sūt še'am ileqqe

If a woman-innkeeper gives 1 vat of beer as a loan: she shall take 50 sila of grain at the harvest.

LH §117

šumma awīlam e'iltum iṣbassuma aššassu mārašu u mārassu ana kaspim iddin ulu ana kiššātim ittandin šalaš šanātim bīt šāyimānišunu u kāšišišunu ippešu ina rebûtim šattim andurāršunu iššakkan

If a man, a debt befalls him and he sells his wife, his son or his daughter, or gives (them) into debt-service: for three years they shall work in the house of their buyer or their creditor; in the fourth year their release shall be granted.

LH §118

šumma wardam ulu amtam ana kiššātim ittandin tamkārum ušetteq ana kaspim inaddin ul ibbaqqar

If a slave or a slave-woman is given into debt-service: the merchant may exceed (the three-year period), he may sell him; he shall not be claimed.

LH §119

šumma awīlam e'iltum iṣbassuma amassu ša mārī uldušum ana kaspim ittadin kasap tamkārum išqulu bēl amtim išaqqalma amassu ipaṭṭar

If a man, a debt befalls him and he sells his slave-woman who bore him children: the owner of the slave-woman shall pay the silver which the merchant has paid, and redeem his slave-woman.

LH §127

šumma awīlum eli ugbabtim u aššat awīlim ubānam ušatriṣma la uktīn awīlam šuāti maḫar dayānī inaṭṭûšu u muttassu ugallabu

If a man causes a finger to be pointed against an *ugbabtu* or a man's wife, but it is unsubstantiated: they shall hit that man before the judges, and they shall shave half his (hair?).

LH §128

šumma awīlum aššatam īḫuzma riksātiša la iškun sinništum šî ul aššat

If a man takes a wife, but does not grant her contract: that woman is not a wife.

LH §129

šumma aššat awīlim itti zikarim šanîm ina itūlim ittaṣbat ikassûšunūtima ana mê inaddûšunūti šumma bēl aššatim aššassu uballaṭ u šarrum warassu uballaṭ

If a man's wife is caught lying with another male: they shall bind them and cast them into the water; if the wife's master lets his wife live, then the king shall let his slave live.

LH §130

šumma awīlum aššat awīlim ša zikaram la idûma ina bīt abiša wašbat ukabbilšima ina sūniša ittatīlma iṣṣabtušu awīlum šû iddâk sinništum šî ūtaššar

If a man pins down a(nother) man's virgin wife who is residing in her father's house, and they catch him lying in her lap: that man shall be killed; that woman shall be released.

LH §131

šumma aššat awīlim mussa ubbiršima itti zikarim šanîm ina utūlim la iṣṣabit nīš ilim izakkarma ana bītiša itâr

If a man's wife, her husband accuses her, but she has not been caught lying with another male: she shall swear an oath by the god and return to her house.

LH §132

šumma aššat awīlim aššum zikarim šanîm ubānum eliša ittariṣma itti zikarim šanîm ina utūlim la ittaṣbat ana mutiša Id išalli

If a man's wife has a finger pointed against her concerning another male, but she is not caught lying with another male: for her husband, she shall undergo the divine-River-Ordeal.

LH §133a

šumma awīlum iššalilma ina bītišu ša akālim ibašši [ašš]assu [. . .]ša [. . . ana bīt šanîm ul ir]rub

If a man is captured and there are sufficient provisions in his house: his [wif]e [. . . she shall not en]ter [another's house].

LH §133b

šu[*mma*] *sinništum šî* [*pa*]*garša la iṣṣurma ana bīt šanîm īterub sinništam šuāti ukannušima ana mê inaddûši*

I[f] that woman does not keep her [b]ody (chaste), and enters to another's house: that woman, they shall convict her, and they shall cast her into the water.

LH §134

šumma awīlum iššalilma ina bītišu ša akālim la ibašši aššassu ana bīt šanîm irrub sinništum šî arnam ul išu

If a man is captured and there are not sufficient provisions in his house: his wife may enter another's house; that woman shall not bear penalty.

LH §135

šumma awīlum iššalilma ina bītišu ša akālim la ibašši ana panīšu ašassu ana bīt šanîm īterubma mārī ittalad ina warka mussa ittūramma ālšu iktašdam sinništum šî ana ḫāwiriša itâr mārū warki abišunu illaku

If a man is captured and there are not sufficient provisions in his house, before him his wife enters to another's house and bears children, (and) afterwards her husband returns and reaches his city: that woman shall return to her first-husband; the children shall go after their father.

LH §136

šumma awīlum ālšu iddīma ittābit warkišu aššassu ana bīt šanîm īterub šumma awīlum šû ittūramma aššassu iṣṣabat aššum ālšu izēruma innabitu aššat munnabtim ana mutiša ul itâr

If a man deserts his city and flees, after his (departure) his wife enters to another's house, if that man returns and seizes his wife: because he hated his city and fled, the fugitive's wife shall not return to her husband.

LH §137

šumma awīlum ana šugītim ša mārī uldušum ulu nadītim ša mārī ušaršûšu ezēbim panīšu ištakan ana sinništim šuāti šeriktaša utarrušim u muttat eqlim kirîm u bīšim inaddinušimma mārīša urabba ištu mārīša urtabbû ina mimma ša ana mārīša innadnu zittam kīma aplim ištēn inaddinušimma mutu libbiša iḫḫassi

If a man decides to divorce a *šugītu* who bore him children or a *nadītu* who provided him with children: they shall return to that woman her *šeriktum* and they shall give her one-half of a field, orchard and possessions, and she shall raise her children; after she has raised her children, from whatever that is given to her children they shall give her a share as one heir, and a husband of her choice may marry her.

LH §138

šumma awīlum ḫīrtašu ša mārī la uldušum izzib kaspam mala terḫatiša inaddiššim u šeriktam ša ištu bīt abiša ublam ušallamšimma izzibši

If a man divorces his first-ranking-wife who did not bear him children: he shall give her silver as much as her *terḫatum* and restore to her the *šeriktum* that she brought from her father's house, and he shall divorce her.

LH §139

šumma terḫatum la ibašši 1 *mana kaspam ana uzubbêm inaddiššim*

If there is no *terḫatum*: he shall give her 1 mina (=60 shekels) of silver for the divorce-settlement.

LH §140

šumma muškēnum ⅓ *mana kaspam inaddiššim*

If (he is) a commoner: he shall give her one-third of a mina (=20 shekels) of silver.

LH §141

šumma aššat awīlim ša ina bīt awīlim wašbat ana waṣêm panīša ištakanma sikiltam isakkil bīssa usappaḫ mussa ušamṭa ukannušima šumma mussa ezēbša iqtabi izzibši ḫarrānša uzubbûša mimma ul innaddiššim šumma mussa la ezēbša iqtabi mussa sinništam šanītam iḫḫaz sinništum šî kīma amtim ina bīt mutiša uššab

If a man's wife who is residing in the man's house decides to depart, and she appropriates properties, disperses her household, mistreats her husband: they shall convict her; and if her husband declares her divorce, he shall divorce her; her travel(-expenses), her divorce-settlement, nothing shall be given to her; if her husband declares not her divorce:[38] her husband may marry another woman, that woman[39] shall reside in her husband's house as a slave-woman.

LH §142

šumma sinništum mussa izērma ul taḫḫazanni iqtabi warkassa ina bābtiša ipparrasma šumma naṣratma ḫiṭītam la išu u mussa waṣīma magal ušamṭāši sinništum šî arnam ul išu šeriktaša ileqqēma ana bīt abiša ittallak

If a woman hates her husband and declares, "You shall not remain married to me!": her background shall be investigated in her district, and if she is kept (=prudent) and has no fault, but her husband is wayward and greatly mistreats her, that woman shall not bear penalty; she shall take her *šeriktum* and shall go to her father's house.

LH §143

šumma la naṣratma waṣiat bīssa usappaḫ mussa ušamṭa sinništam šuāti ana mê inaddûši

If she is not kept (=prudent) but is wayward, disperses her household, mistreats her husband: that woman, they shall cast her into the water.

LH §144

šumma awīlum nadītam īḫuzma nadītum šî amtam ana mutiša iddinma mārī uštabši awīlum šû ana šugītim aḫāzim panīšu ištakan awīlam šuāti ul imaggarušu šugītam ul iḫḫaz

If a man marries a *nadītu*, and that *nadītu* gives to her husband a slave-woman and (thus) provides children, (and) that man decides to marry a *šugītu*: that man, they shall not allow him, he shall not marry the *šugītu*.

LH §145

šumma awīlum nadītam īḫuzma mārī la ušaršīšuma ana šugītim aḫāzim panīšu ištakan awīlum šû šugîtam iḫḫaz ana bîtišu ušerrebši šugîtum šî itti nadītim ul uštamaḫḫar

If a man marries a *nadītu*, and she does not supply him with children, and he decides to marry a *šugītu*: that man may marry the *šugītu*, he may bring her into his house; that *šugītu* shall not make herself equal with the *nadītu*.

LH §146

šumma awīlum nadītam īḫuzma amtam ana mutiša iddinma mārī ittalad warkānum amtum šî itti bēltiša uštatamḫir aššum mārī uldu bēlessa ana kaspim ul inaddišši abbuttam išakkanšimma itti amātim imannūši

If a man marries a *nadītu*, and she gives to her husband a slave-woman, and she[40] bears children, afterwards that slave-woman makes herself equal with her mistress: because she bore children, her mistress shall not sell her; she shall impose upon her the slave-hairstyle, and shall count her among the slave-women.

LH §147

šumma mārī la ūlid bēlessa ana kaspim inaddišši

If she does not bear children: her mistress may sell her.

LH §148

šumma awīlum aššatam īḫuzma la'bum iṣṣabassi ana šanītim aḫāzim panīšu ištakkan iḫḫaz aššassu ša la'bum iṣbatu ul izzibši ina bīt īpušu uššamma adi balṭat ittanaššīši

If a man marries a woman, and a *la'bum*-disease seizes her, he decides to marry another: he may marry; his wife whom *la'bum*-disease seized, he shall not divorce her; she shall reside in a house he constructs, and while she lives he shall continue to support her.

LH §149

šumma sinništum šî ina bīt mutiša wašābam la imtagar šeriktaša ša ištu bīt abiša ublam ušallamšimma ittallak

If that woman does not agree to reside in her husband's house: he shall restore to her her *šeriktum* that she brought from her father's house, and she shall go.

LH §150

šumma awīlum ana aššatišu eqlam kirâm bītam u bīšam išrukšim kunukkam īzibšim warki mutiša mārūša ul ipaqqaruši ummum warkassa ana māriša ša irammu inaddin ana aḫîm ul inaddin

If a man awards to his wife a field, orchard, house or possessions and leaves her a sealed-document: after her husband (dies) her children shall not claim against her; the mother shall give her remaining-estate[41] to her child which she loves, she shall not give to an outsider.

LH §151

šumma sinništum ša ina bīt awīlim wašbat aššum bēl ḫubullim ša mutiša la ṣabātiša mussa urtakkis ṭuppam uštēzib šumma awīlum šû lāma sinništam šuāti iḫḫazu ḫubullum elišu ibašši bēl ḫubullīšu aššassu ul iṣabbatu u šumma sinništum šî lāma ana bīt awīlim irrubu ḫubullum eliša ibašši bēl ḫubullīša mussa ul iṣabbatu

If a woman who is residing in a man's house makes her husband leave her a document, that a creditor of her husband may not seize her: if that man has a debt from before he has married that woman, his creditors shall not seize his wife; and if that woman has a debt from before she has entered the man's house, her creditors shall not seize her husband.

LH §152

šumma ištu sinništum šî ana bīt awīlim īrubu elišunu ḫubullum ittabši kilallāšunu tamkāram ippalu

If after that woman enters to the man's house a debt is incurred over them: both of them shall satisfy the merchant.

LH §153

šumma aššat awīlim aššum zikarim šanîm mussa ušdîk sinništam šuāti ina gašīšim išakkanuši

If a man's wife has her husband killed because of another male: they shall impale that woman.

LH §154

šumma awīlum mārassu iltamad awīlam šuāti ālam ušeṣṣûšu

If a man knows his daughter: they shall banish that man from the city.

LH §155

šumma awīlum ana mārišu kallatam iḫīrma mārušu ilmassi šû warkānumma ina sūniša ittatīlma iṣṣabtušu awīlam šuāti ikassûšuma ana mê inaddûšu

If a man chooses a bride for his son, and his son knows her, (and) he, afterwards, they catch him lying in her lap: that man, they shall bind him and cast him into the water.

LH §156

šumma awīlum ana mārišu kallatam iḫīirma mārušu la ilmassima šû ina sūniša ittatīl ½ mana kaspam išaqqalšimma u mimma ša ištu bīt abiša ublam ušallamšimma mutu libbiša iḫḫassi

If a man chooses a bride for his son, and his son does not know her, and he lies in her lap: he shall pay her half a mina (=30 shekels) of silver; furthermore, he shall restore to her whatever that she brought from her father's house, and a husband of her choice may marry her.

LH §157

šumma awīlum warki abišu ina sūn ummišu ittatīl kilallīšunu iqallûšunūti

If a man, after his father('s death), is lying in his mother's lap: the both of them, they shall burn them.

LH §158

šumma awīlum warki abišu ina sūn rabītišu ša mārī waldat ittaṣbat awīlum šû ina bīt abim innassaḫ

If a man, after his father('s death), is seized in the lap of his (=the father's) principal wife who bore children: that man shall be disinherited from the father's household.

LH §159

šumma awīlum ša ana bīt emišu biblam ušābilu terḫatam iddinu ana sinništim šanītim uptallisma ana emišu māratka ul aḫḫaz iqtabi abi mārtim mimma ša ibbablušum itabbal

If a man who has the *biblum* brought to his father-in-law's house (and) gives the *terḫatum* has his attention diverted to another woman, and declares to his father-in-law, "I shall not marry your daughter!": the daughter's father shall take hold of whatever that was brought to him.

LH §160

šumma awīlum ana bīt emim biblam ušābil terḫatam iddinma abi mārtim mārtī ul anaddikkum iqtabi mimma mala ibbablušum uštašannāma utâr

If a man has the *biblum* brought the father-in-law's house (and) gives the *terḫatum*, but the daughter's father then declares, "I shall not give to you my daughter!": he shall return twofold everything that had been brought to him.

LH §161

šumma awīlum ana bīt emišu biblam ušābil terḫatam iddinma ibiršu uktarrissu emušu ana bēl aššatim mārtī ul taḫḫaz iqtabi mimma mala ibbablušum uštašannāma utâr u aššassu ibiršu ul iḫḫaz

If a man has the *biblum* brought to his father-in-law's house (and) gives the *terḫatum*, but (since) his comrade slanders him, his father-in-law declares to the wife owner, "You shall not marry my daughter!": he shall return twofold everything that had been brought to him, and his comrade shall not marry his wife.

LH §162

šumma awīlum aššatam īḫuz mārī ūlissumma sinništum šî ana šīmtim ittalak ana šeriktiša abuša ul iraggum šeriktaša ša mārīšama

If a man marries a wife, she bears him children, and that woman goes to (her) fate: her father shall not claim for her *šeriktum*; her *šeriktum* is only of her children.

LH §163

šumma awīlum aššatam īḫuzma mārī la ušaršīšu sinništum šî ana šīmtim ittalak šumma terḫatam ša awīlum šû ana bīt emišu ublu emušu uttēršum ana šerikti sinništim šuāti mussa ul iraggum šeriktaša ša bīt abišama

If a man marries a wife but she does not provide him with children, (and) that woman goes to (her) fate: if the *terḫatum* that that man brought to his father-in-law's house, his father-in-law returns to him, her husband shall not claim for that woman's *šeriktum*; her *šeriktum* is only of her father's household.

LH §164

šumma emušu terḫatam la uttēršum ina šeriktiša mala terḫatiša iḫarraṣma šeriktaša ana bīt abiša utâr

If his father-in-law does not return to him the *terḫatum*: he shall deduct the whole of her *terḫatum* from her *šeriktum*, and shall restore her *šeriktum* to her father's household.

LH §166

šumma awīlum ana mārīšu ša iršû[42] *aššātim īḫuz ana mārišu ṣiḫrim aššatam lā īḫuz warka abum ana šīmtim ittalku inūma aḫḫū izuzzū ina makkūr bīt abim ana aḫišunu ṣiḫrim ša aššatam lā aḫzu eliāt zittišu kasap terḫatim išakkanūšumma aššatam ušaḫḫazūšu*

If a man takes wives for his sons that he had, but does not take a wife for his young son: after the father goes to (his) fate, when the brothers divide (the inheritance), they shall grant from the father's household assets for their young brother who did not take a wife the *terḫatum* silver on top of his (inheritance) share, and they shall enable him to take a wife.

LH §167

šumma awīlum aššatam īḫuzma mārī ūlissum sinništum šī ana šīmtim ittalak warkiša sinništam šanītam ītaḫazma mārī ittalad warkānum abum ana šīmtim ittalku mārū ana ummātim ul izuzzu šerikti ummātišunu ileqqûma makkūr bīt abim mitḫāriš izuzzū

If a man marries a wife and she bears him children, that woman goes to (her) fate, after her (death) he marries another woman and she bears children, afterwards the father goes to (his) fate: the children shall not divide (the inheritance) according to the mothers; they shall take the dowries of their (respective) mothers, and they shall divide equally the father's household assets.

LH §170

šumma awīlum ḫīrtašu mārī ūlissum u amassu mārī ūlissum abum ina bulṭišu ana mārī ša amtum uldušum mārūa iqtabi itti mārī ḫīrtim imtanūšunūti warka abum ana šīmtim ittalku ina makkūr bīt abim mārū ḫīrtim u mārū amtim mitḫāriš izuzzū aplum mār ḫīrtim ina zittim inassaqma ileqqe

If a man, his first-ranking-wife bears him children and his slave-woman bears him children, the father in his lifetime declares to the children whom the slave-woman bore to him, "My children!": he counts them among the first-ranking-wife's children; after the father goes to (his) fate, the first-ranking-wife's children and the slave-woman's children shall divide equally in the father's household assets; an heir, a first-ranking-wife's son, shall choose and take in the (first inheritance) share.

LH §171

u šumma abum ina bulṭišu ana mārī ša amtum uldušum mārūya lā iqtabi warka abum ana šīmtim ittalku ina makkūr bīt abim mārū amtim itti mārī ḫīrtim ul izuzzū andurār amtim u mārīša iššakkan mārū ḫīrtim ana mārī amtim ana wardūtim ul iraggumu ḫīrtum šeriktaša u nudunnâm ša mussa iddinušim ina ṭuppim išṭurušim ileqqēma ina šubat mutiša uššab adi balṭat ikkal ana kaspim ul inaddin warkassa ša mārīšama

And if the father in his lifetime does not declare to the children whom the slave-woman bore to him, "My children!": after the father goes to (his) fate, the slave-woman's children shall not divide equally with the first-ranking-wife's children in the father's household assets; the release of the slave-woman and of her children shall be granted; the first-ranking-wife's children shall not claim the slave-woman's children for slavery; the first-ranking-wife shall take her *šeriktum* and the *nudunnûm* which her husband gave her (and) wrote her on a tablet, and she shall reside in her husband's residence; as long as she is alive she shall consume (it, but) she shall not sell it; her remaining-estate[43] is only of her children.

LH §172

šumma mussa nudunnâm lā iddiššim šeriktaša ušallamūšimma ina makkūr bīt mutiša zittam kīma aplim ištēn ileqqe šumma mārūša aššum ina bītim šūṣîm usaḫḫamuši dayyānū warkassa iparrasuma mārī arnam immidu sinništum šī ina bīt mutiša ul uṣṣi šumma sinništum šī ana waṣêm pānīša ištakan nudunnâm ša mussa iddinušim ana mārīša izzib šeriktam ša bīt abiša ileqqēma mut libbiša iḫḫassi

If her husband does not give her a *nudunnûm*: they shall restore to her her *šeriktum*, and she shall take a share as one heir from her husband's household assets; if her children oppress her concerning her forced departure from the house, the judges shall investigate her case, and shall impose a penalty on the children; that woman shall not depart from her husband's house; if that woman decides to depart, she shall leave for her children the *nudunnûm* that her husband gave her; she shall take the *šeriktum* of her father's household, and a husband of her choice may marry her.

LH §173

šumma sinništum šī ašar īrubu ana mutiša warkîm mārī ittalad warka sinništum šī imtūt šeriktaša mārū maḫrûtum u warkûtum izuzzu

If that woman entered a (man's) place,[44] bears children to her latter husband: after that woman dies, (her) former and latter children shall divide her *šeriktum* (equally).

LH §174

šumma ana mutiša warkîm mārī lā ittalad šeriktaša mārū ḫāwirišama ileqqû

If she does not bear children to her latter husband: only her first-husband's children shall take her *šeriktum*.

LH §175

šumma lu warad ekallim u lū warad muškēnim mārat awīlim īḫuzma mārī ittalad bēl wardim ana mārī mārat awīlim ana wardūtim ul iraggum

If either a palace slave or a commoner's slave marries an *awīlum*(-class) woman, and she bears children: the slave owner shall not claim the *awīlum*(-class) woman's children for slavery.

LH §176a

u šumma warad ekallim u lū warad muškēnim mārat awīlim īḫuzma inūma īḫuzuši qadum šeriktim ša bīt abiša ana bīt warad ekallim u lū warad muškēnim īrubma ištu innemdū bītam īpušū bīšam iršû warkānumma lu warad ekallim u lū warad muškēnim ana šīmtim ittalak mārat awīlim šeriktaša ileqqe u mimma ša mussa u šī ištu innemdū iršû ana šinīšu izuzzūma mišlam bēl wardim ileqqe mišlam mārat awīlim ana mārīša ileqqe

And if a palace slave or a commoner's slave marries an *awīlum*(-class) woman, and when he marries her she enters together with the *šeriktum* of her father's household to the palace slave's or the commoner's slave's house, and after they move in together they establish a household (and) accumulate possessions, afterwards either the palace slave or the commoner's slave goes to (his) fate: the *awīlum*(-class) woman shall take her *šeriktum*, and they shall divide in two whatever that her husband and she accumulated after they moved in together; and the slave owner shall take half, (and) the *awīlum* (-class) woman shall take half for her children.

LH §176b

šumma mārat awīlim šeriktam la išu mimma ša mussa u šī ištu innemdū iršû ana šinīšu izuzzūma mišlam bēl wardim ileqqe mišlam mārat awīlim ana mārīša leqqe

If the *awīlum*(-class) woman has no *šeriktum*: they shall divide in two whatever that her husband and she accumulated after they moved in together; and the slave owner shall take half, (and) the *awīlum*(-class) woman shall take half for her children.

LH §177

šumma almattum ša mārūša ṣeḫḫerū ana bīt šanîm erēbim pānīša ištakan balum dayyānī ul irrub inūma ana bīt šanîm irrubu dayyānū warkat bīt mutiša panîm iparrasūma bītam ša mutiša panîm ana mutiša warkîm u sinništim šuāti ipaqqidūma ṭuppam ušezzebūšunūti bītam inaṣṣarū u ṣeḫḫerūtim urabbû uniātim ana kaspim ul inaddinū šāyyāmānum ša unūt mārī almattim išammu ina kaspišu ītelli makkūrum ana bēlišu itâr

If a widow that her children are young decides to enter another's house: she shall not enter without (permission by) the judges; when she enters to another's house, the judges shall investigate her previous husband's remaining-estate,[45] and they shall entrust the household of her previous husband to her latter husband and to that woman, and they shall make them leave a document; they shall keep the household and they shall raise the young-children; they shall not sell the belongings; a buyer that buys the widow's children's belongings shall forfeit his silver; the asset shall return to its owner.

LH §178

šumma ugbabtum nadītum u lū sekretum ša abuša šeriktam išrukušim ṭuppam išṭurušim ina ṭuppim ša išṭurušim warkassa ēma eliša ṭābu nadānamma lā išṭuršimma mala libbiša lā ušamṣīši warka abum ana šīmtim ittalku eqelša u kirāša aḫḫūša ileqqûma kīma emūq zittiša ipram piššatam u lubūšam inaddinūšimma libbaša uṭabbū šumma aḫḫūša kīma emūq zittiša ipram piššatam u lubūšam lā ittadnušimma libbaša lā uṭṭibbū eqelša u kirāša ana errēšim ša eliša ṭābu inaddinma errēssa ittanaššīši eqlam kirâm u mimma ša abuša iddinušim adi balṭat ikkal ana kaspim ul inaddin šaniām ul uppal aplūssa ša aḫḫīšama

If an *ugbabtu*, a *nadītu*, or a *sekretu* that her father awarded to her a *šeriktum*, wrote to her a tablet, (but) in the tablet that he wrote to her he did not write her and did not concede her full discretion to give her remaining-estate[46] however she pleases: after the father goes to (his) fate, her brothers shall take her field and her orchard, and they shall give to her rations, oil and clothing commensurately with her share, and they shall (thus) satisfy her; if her brothers shall not give to her rations, oil and clothing commensurately with her share, and they (thus) do not satisfy her: she shall give her field and her orchard to a cultivator as she pleases, and her cultivator shall support her; as long as she is alive she shall consume the field, orchard and whatever that her father gave to her, (but) she shall not sell (it, and) she shall not satisfy another person (with it); her inheritance is only of her brothers.

LH §179

šumma ugbabtum nadītum u lū sekretum ša abuša šeriktam išrukušim kunukkam išṭurušim ina ṭuppim ša išṭurušim warkassa ēma eliša ṭābu nadānam išṭuršimma mala libbiša uštamṣīši warka abum ana šīmtim ittalku warkassa ēma eliša ṭābu inaddin aḫḫūša ul ipaqqaruši

If an *ugbabtu*, a *nadītu*, or a *sekretu* that her father awarded to her a *šeriktum*, wrote to her a sealed-document, (and) in the tablet that he wrote to her he wrote her and conceded her full discretion to give her remaining-estate[47] however she pleases: after the father goes to (his) fate, she shall give her remaining-estate[48] however she pleases; her brothers shall not claim against her.

LH §180

šumma abum ana mārtišu nadīt gagîm ulu sekretim šeriktam la iš‹r›ukšim warka abum ana šīmtim ittalku ina makkūr bīt abim zittam kīma aplim ištēn izâzma adi balṭat ikkal warkassa ša aḫḫīšama

If a father, to his daughter who is a *gagûm nadītu* or a *sekretu*, he did not award to her a *šeriktum*: after the father goes to (his) fate, she shall divide a share as one heir from the father's household assets; as long as she is alive she shall consume (it); her remaining-estate[49] is only of her brothers.

LH §181

šumma abum nadītam qadištam u lū kulmašītam ana ilim iššīma šeriktam la išrukšim warka abum ana šīmtim ittalku ina makkūr bīt abim šalušti aplūtiša izâzma adi balṭat ikkal warkassa ša aḫḫīšama

If a father dedicates a *nadītu*, a *qadištu*, or a *kulmašītu* to a god, but did not award to her a *šeriktum*: after the father goes to (his) fate, she shall divide as her inheritance one-third from the father's household assets; as long as she is alive she shall consume (it); her remaining-estate[50] is only of her brothers.

LH §182

šumma abum ana mārtišu nadīt Marduk ša bābilim šeriktam lā išrukšim kunukkam lā išṭuršim warka abum ana šīmtim ittalku ina makkūr bīt abim šalušti aplūtiša itti aḫḫīša izâzma ilkam ul illak nadīt Marduk warkassa ēma eliša ṭābu inaddin

If a father, to his daughter (who is) the Marduk-of-Babylon's *nadītu*, he did not award to her a *šeriktum*, did not write to her a sealed-document: after the father goes to (his) fate, she shall divide with her brothers as her inheritance one-third from the father's household assets, and she shall not serve at the service-obligation; the Marduk's *nadītu* shall give her remaining-estate[51] however she pleases.

LH §183

šumma abum ana mārtišu šugītim šeriktam išrukšim ana mutim iddišši kunukkam išṭuršim warka abum ana šīmtim ittalku ina makkūr bīt abim ul izâz

If a father, to his daughter (who is) a *šugītu*, he awarded to her a *šeriktum*, gives her to a husband, wrote to her a sealed-document: after the father goes to (his) fate, she shall not divide from the father's household assets.

LH §184

šumma awīlum ana mārtišu šugītim šeriktam lā išrukšim ana mutim lā iddišši warka abum ana šīmtim ittalku aḫḫūša kīma emūq bīt abim šeriktam išarrakūšimma ana mutim inaddinūši

If a man, to his daughter (who is) a *šugītu*, he did not award to her a *šeriktum*, does not give her to a husband: after the father goes to (his) fate, her brothers shall award to her a *šeriktum* commensurately with the father's household, and they shall give her to a husband.

LH §185

šumma awīlum ṣiḫram ina mêšu ana mārūtim ilqēma urtabbīšu tarbītum šī ul ibbaqqar

If a man takes in adoption a newborn[52] and rears him: that rearling shall not be reclaimed.

LH §186

šumma awīlum ṣiḫram ana mārūtim ilqe inūma ilqûšu abašu u ummašu iḫiaṭ tarbītum šī ana bīt abišu itâr

If a man takes in adoption a youth, and when he takes him, he (=the child) is seeking his father and his mother: that rearling shall return to his father's house.

LH §187

mār girseqîm muzzaz ekallim u mār sekretim ul ibbaqqar

A(n adopted) child of a *girseqû* who is a palace attendant, and a(n adopted) child of a *sekretu* shall not be reclaimed.

LH §188

šumma mār ummânim ṣiḫram ana tarbītim ilqēma šipir qātišu uštāḫissu ul ibbaqqar

If a craftsman takes a youth for rearing, and teaches him his handiwork: he shall not be reclaimed.

LH §189

šumma šipir qātišu lā uštāḫissu tarbītum šī ana bīt abišu itâr

If he does not teach him his handiwork: that rearling shall return to his father's house.

LH §190

šumma awīlum ṣiḫram ša ana mārūtišu ilqûšuma urabbûšu itti mārīšu lā imtanūšu tarbītum šī ana bīt abišu itâr

If a man does not count among his children a youth that he took in adoption and reared him: that rearling shall return to his father's house.

LH §191

šumma awīlum ṣiḫram ša ana mārūtišu ilqûšuma urabbûšu bīssu īpuš warka mārī irtašīma ana tarbītim nasāḫim panam ištakan ṣiḫrum šū rēqūssu ul ittallak abum murabbīšu ina makkūrišu šalušti aplūtišu inaddiššumma ittallak ina eqlim kirîm u bītim ul inaddiššum

If a man establishes his household with a youth that he took in adoption and reared him, afterwards he gets (biological) children, and decides to disinherit the rearling: that youth shall not go empty-handed; the father who reared him shall give to him as his inheritance one-third from his household assets, and he shall go; he shall not give to him from a field, an orchard or a house.

LH §192

šumma mār girseqîm u lū mār sekretim ana abim murabbīšu u ummim murabbītišu ul abī atta ul ummī atti iqtabi lišānšu inakkisū

If a *girseqû*'s (adopted) child or a *sekretu*'s (adopted) child says to the father who raised him and the mother who raised him, "You are not my father!", "You are not my mother!": they shall cut out his tongue.

LH §193

šumma mār girseqîm u lū mār sekretim bīt abišu uweddīma abam murabbīšu u ummam murabbīssu izērma ana bīt abišu ittalak īnšu inassaḫū

If a *girseqû*'s (adopted) child or a *sekretu*'s (adopted) child recognizes his father's house, and becomes estranged with the father who raised him and the mother who raised him, and goes to his father's house: they shall pluck out his eye.

LH §194

šumma awīlum mārašu ana mušēniqtim iddinma ṣiḫrum šū ina qāt mušēniqtim imtūt mušēniqtum balum abišu u ummišu ṣiḫram šaniamma irtakas ukannūšima aššum balum abišu u ummišu ṣiḫram šaniam irkusu tulāša inakkisū

If a man gives his son to a wet-nurse, and that youth dies at the wet-nurse, the wet-nurse contracts for another child without (asking) his father and his mother: they shall convict her, and because she contracted for another child without (asking) his father and his mother, they shall cut off her breast.

LH §209

šumma awīlum mārat awīlim imḫaṣma ša libbiša uštaddīši ešeret šiqil kaspam ana ša libbiša išaqqal

If a man strikes an *awīlum*(-class) woman and causes her to miscarry her fetus: he shall pay ten shekels of silver for her fetus.

LH §210

šumma sinništum šī imtūt mārassu idukkū

If that woman dies: they shall kill his daughter.

LH §211

šumma mārat muškēnim ina maḫāṣim ša libbiša uštaddīši ḫamšat šiqil kaspam išaqqal

If he causes a commoner(-class) woman to miscarry her fetus by beating: he shall pay five shekels of silver.

LH §212

šumma sinništum šī imtūt mišil mina kaspam išaqqal

If that woman dies: he shall pay half a mina (=30 shekels) of silver.

LH §213

šumma amat awīlim imḫaṣma ša libbiša uštaddīši šina šiqil kaspam išaqqal

If he strikes a man's slave-woman and causes her to miscarry her fetus: he shall pay two shekels of silver.

LH §214

šumma amtum šī imtūt šaluš mina kaspam išaqqal

If that slave-woman dies: he shall pay one-third of a mina (=20 shekels) of silver.

LH §273

šumma awīlum agram īgur ištu rēš šattim adi ḫamšim warḫim 6 *uṭṭet kaspam ina ūmim ištēn inaddin ištu šiššim warḫim adi taqtīt šattim* 5 *uṭṭet kaspam ina ūmim ištēn inaddin*

If a man hires a hired-worker: from the beginning of the year until the fifth month he shall give six grains of silver for one day, from the sixth month until the end of the year he shall give five grains of silver for one day.

LH §274

šumma awīlum mār ummânim iggar idī [. . .] 5 *uṭṭet kaspam idī kāmidim* 5 *uṭṭet kaspam* [*idī*] *ša kitîm*$^{?}$ [x *uṭṭet*] *kaspam* [*idī*] *purkullim* [x *uṭṭet ka*]*spam* [*idī*] *sasinnim*$^{?}$ [x *uṭṭet*] *kaspam* [*idī nap*]*pāḫim* [x *uṭṭet kas*]*pam* [*idī*] *naggārim* 4$^{?}$ *uṭṭet kaspam idī aškāpim* [x] *uṭṭet kaspam idī atkuppim* [x *uṭ*]*ṭet kaspam* [*idī*] *itinnim* [x *uṭṭet kas*]*pam* [*ina ūmim*] *ištēn* [*inadd*]*in*

If a man would hire a craftsman, [he shall gi]ve [for] one [day]: a [. . .]'s wage: five grains of silver; a weaver's wage: five grains of silver; [the wage] of a flax-worker$^{?}$: [x grains] of silver; a stone-cutter's [wage]: [x grains of si] lver; a bow-maker$^{?}$'s [wage]: [x grains] of silver; [a sm]ith's [wage: x grains of sil]ver; a carpenter's [wage]: 4$^{?}$ grains of silver; a leather-worker's wage: [x] grains of silver; a reed-worker's wage: [x gr]ains of silver; a builder's [wage]: [x grains of sil]ver.

LH §278

šumma awīlum wardam amtam išāmma waraḫšu la imlāma benni elišu imtaqut ana nādinānišu utârma šāyimānum kasap išqulu ileqqe

If a man buys a slave (or) slave-woman, and while his month is not complete epilepsy befalls him: he shall return him to his seller, and the buyer shall take the silver that he paid.

LH §279

šumma awīlum wardam amtam išāmma baqrī irtaši nādinānšu baqrī ippal

If a man buys a slave (or) slave-woman, and claims arise: his seller shall satisfy the claims.

LH §280

šumma awīlum ina māt nukurtim wardam amtam ša awīlim ištām inūma ina libbū mātim ittalkamma bēl wardim ulu amtim lu warassu ulu amassu ūteddi šumma wardum u amtum šunu mārū mātim balum kaspimma andurāršunu iššakkan

If a man buys in a foreign land the slave (or) slave-woman of a(nother) man, and when he is walking around within the land the slave or slave-woman's owner recognizes either his slave or his slave-woman: if the slave (or) slave-woman, they are the land's sons (=natives), their release shall be granted without any silver (=payment).

LH §281

šumma mārū mātim šanītim šāyimānum ina maḫar ilim kasap išqulu iqabbīma bēl wardim ulu amtim kasap išqulu ana tamkārim inaddinma lu warassu lu amassu ipaṭṭar

If (they are) another land's sons (=natives): the buyer shall declare before the god the (amount) of silver that he paid, and the slave or slave-woman's owner shall give to the merchant the (amount) of silver that he paid; he shall redeem his slave or his slave-woman.

5 ESi/Ad/Aṣ (Edicts of Samsu-iluna/Ammi-ditana/ Ammi-ṣaduka)

ESi/Ad/Aṣ §16

sābīt nawê ša še'am u kaspam sābî ana ekallim išaqqalu aššum šarrum mîšaram ana mâtim iškunu ana ribbâtišunu mušaddinu ul išassi

A rural woman-innkeeper who pays the palace for the barley and silver of the brewer, because the king has decreed justice for the land, the tax-collector shall not claim their arrears.

ESi/Ad/Aṣ §17

sābītum ša šikaram u še'am iqīpu mimma ša iqīpu ul ušaddan

A woman-innkeeper who has sold beer or barley on credit shall not collect for whatever she has sold on credit.

ESi/Ad/Aṣ §18

sābītum u tamkārum [*š*]*a ina* [*k*]*unu*[*kki l*]*a kittim* [. . .] *imâ*[*t*]

A woman-innkeeper or a merchant [w]ho, by an [u]ntrue [s]ea[l . . .] shall die.

ESi/Ad/Aṣ §20

[*šumma m*]*ār Numḫia mār Emutbalu*[*m mār Ida*]*maras mār Uruk* [*mār Isi*]*n mār Kisurra* [*mār Malgium*] *i'iltum i'ilšuma* [*paga*]*ršu aššassu* [*ulu mārī*?] *šu ana kaspim ana k*[*išš*]*ātim* [*ulu ana manz*]*azāni* [. . . *aššum šarrum m*] *īšaram* [*ana mātim išk*]*unu* [*ušš*]*ur and*[*urā*]*ršu* [*ša*]*kin*

[If a res]ident of Numḫia, resident of Emutbal, [resident of Ida]maras, resident of Uruk, [resident of Isi]n, resident of Kisurra, (or) [resident of Malgium], an obligation obliges him [to give] [hi]mself, his wife, [or] his [children?] for silver, to work off the d[e]bt, [or as a ple]dge, [because the king has dec] reed [j]ustice [for the land, it is remitt]ed; his rel[eas]e [is gr]anted.

ESi/Ad/Aṣ §21

šumma aštapiru wilid bīt [*mār Nu*]*mḫia mār Emutbalum* [*mār Id*]*amaras mār Uruk* [*mār I*]*sin mār Kisurra mār Malgium* [. . .] *š*[*a*] *šī*[*m* . . . *ana k*]*aspim inn*[*adin ul*]*u a*[*n*]*a* [*k*]*iššātim* [*i*]*kk*[*a*]*šiš* [*ul*]*u ana m*[*an*]*zazāni* [*i*]*nne*[*z*]*ib* [*an*]*durār*[*š*]*u* [*u*]*l iššа*[*kk*]*an*

If (one among) the slaves who was born in the house of [a resident of Nu]mḫia, resident of Emutbal, [resident of Id]amaras, resident of Uruk, [resident of I] sin, resident of Kisurra, resident of Malgium [. . .] fo[r] the pri[ce . . . is s] old [for m]oney, [o]r is [m]a[d]e to work off a [d]ebt, [o]r [ha]s been l[e]ft as a p[l]edge: [h]is [re]lease [shall n]ot be gra[n]ted.

6 AASOR 16.51 (=SMN 553)

šūdūtu annû ša amīlūti warad ekallim u ša [n]īš bīti ša ekallim labēr[u]ma umma [šarru]ma mamma warad ekallim u nīš bīti ša ekallim mārassu ana ekûti u ana ḫarīmūti balu šarri la ušallak mannummê warad ekallim mārassu ana e[kû]ti u ana ḫarīmūti balu šarri uštēl[i]kšu mārassu ana ekûti u ana ḫarīmūti iqīšaše ana ekallim ileqqû u mārassu šanû ana liqti ana ekallim kīma ileqqû u ileqqû u šû kazzaurna ištu muḫḫišu ippušaššu u ṭuppu annû ina 3 šanāti u ina 4 šanāti ana panīšunu išasû ana la mašê

This edict concerning the personnel – the palace slaves and the palace retainers – is an old one. Thus says [the king]: no one – a palace slave or a palace retainer – shall force his daughter into homelessness or into prostitution without (the permission of) the king. Whomever, a palace slave who has forced his daughter into homelessness or into prostitution without (the permission of) the king, or has given his daughter into homelessness or into prostitution: they shall take him to the palace and they shall also take to the palace a second daughter of his as a gift, on account of (the daughter he has deprived the palace of). And as for him, they shall impose upon him a compensation (to pay). They shall proclaim this document before them (=the palace personnel) every three or four years, so it is not forgotten.

7 MAL (Middle Assyrian Laws)

MAL A §1

šumma sinniltu lu aššat a'īle u lu mār[at] a'īle [ana] bēt ile tētarab ina bēt ile mimma [ša eš]rēte t[alti]riq [ina qātēša] iṣṣabi[t] u lu ubta'eruši lu ukta'inu[ši] bārûta [. . .] ilaqqima ila iša'[ulu] u kî ša ilu [ana epāše iq] ab[biuni] eppušuši

If a woman,[53] whether a man's wife or a man's daught[er], enters [to] a temple, s[te]als anything [of the san]ctuary[54] from the temple, it is discovere[d by her] or they prove her (guilty) and convict [her]: [they shall perform?] a divination, they shall cons[ult] the deity and they shall treat her according to what the deity [in]stru[cts them to do].

MAL A §2

šumma sinniltu lu aššat a'īle u lu mārat a'īle šillata taqṭibi lu miqit pê tartiši sinniltu šīt aranša tanašši ana mutiša mārēša mārāteša la iqarribu

If a woman,[55] either a man's wife or a man's daughter, says a disgraceful thing, or utters blasphemy: that woman shall bear her penalty; they shall not lay a claim against her husband, her sons (or) her daughters.

MAL A §3

šumma a'īlu lu mariṣ lu mēt aššassu ina bētišu mimma taltiriq lu ana a'īle lu ana sinnilte u lu ana mamma šanêmma tattidin aššat a'īle u māḫirānūtema idukkušunu u šumma aššat a'īle ša mussa balṭuni ina bēt mutiša taltiriq lu ana a'īle lu ana sinnilte u lu ana mamma šanêmma tattidin a'īlu aššassu uba'ar u ḫīṭa emmed u māḫirānu ša ina qāt aššat a'īle imḫuruni šurqa iddan u ḫīṭa kî ša a'īlu aššassu ēmiduni māḫirāna emmidu

If a man, either ill or dead, his wife steals anything from his house, gives it either to a man, or to a woman, or to anyone else: they shall kill the man's wife and the receivers; and if a man's wife, that her husband is healthy, steals from her husband's house, gives it either to a man, or to a woman, or to anyone else: the man shall prove his wife (guilty) and impose a punishment;

and the receiver that received from the man's wife shall give (back) the theft; and they shall impose a punishment on the receiver according to that (which) the man imposed on his wife.

MAL A §4

šumma lu urdu lu amtu ina qāt aššat a'īle mimma imtaḫru ša urde u amte appēšunu uznēšunu unakkusu šurqa umallû a'īlu ša aššiti[*šu*] *uznēša unakkas u šumma aššassu uššer* [*uz*]*nēša la unakkis ša urde u amte la unakkusuma šurqa la umallû*

If either a slave or a slave-woman receives anything from a man's wife: they shall cut off their nose (and) their ears, of the slave or slave-woman; they shall restore in full the theft; the man shall cut off her ears, of [his] wife; but if he releases his wife (and) does not cut off her [e]ars: they shall not cut off (the nose and ears) of the slave or slave-woman, and they shall not restore in full the theft.

MAL A §5

šumma aššat a'īle ina bēt a'īle šanêmma mimma taltiriq ana qāt 5 *mana anneke tūtatter bēl šurqe itamma mā šumma ušāḫizušini mā ina bētiya širqī šumma mussa magir šurqa iddan u ipaṭṭarši uznēša unakkas šumma mussa ana paṭāriša la imaggur bēl šurqe ilaqqēši u appaša inakkis*

If a man's wife steals from another man's house anything that exceeds 5 minas (=300 shekels) of lead: the theft owner shall vow thus, "If I incited her thus, 'Steal in my house!'"; if her husband is willing, he shall give (back) the theft and he shall ransom her; he shall cut off her ears; if her husband does not agree to her ransom: the theft owner shall take her and he shall cut off her nose.

MAL A §6

šumma aššat a'īle maškatta ina kīde taltakan māḫirānu šurqa inašši

If a man's wife places goods outside: the receiver shall bear the theft.

MAL A §7

šumma sinniltu qāta ana a'īle tattabal ubta'eruši 30 *mana annaka taddan* 20 *ina ḫaṭṭāte imaḫḫuṣuši*

If a woman lays a hand upon a man, they prove her (guilty): she shall give 30 minas (=1,800 shekels) of lead, they shall strike her 20 (times) with rods.

MAL A §8

šumma sinniltu ina ṣalte iška ša a'īle taḫtepi 1 *ubānša inakkisu u šumma asū urtakkisma išku šanītu iltešama tattalpat* [. . .]*rīma tartiši* [*u*] *lu ina ṣalte* [*iš*]*ka šanīta taḫtepi* [. . .]*ša kilallūn inappulu*

If a woman crushes the testicle of a man during a quarrel: they shall cut off one of her fingers; and if a physician bandages it, but the second testicle is affected by it and becomes [. . .], or she crushes the second [test]icle during the quarrel: they shall gouge out both her [eye]s?/[breast]s?[56]

MAL A §9

[šumma] a'īlu qāta ana aššat a'īle [u]bil kî būre ēpussi [ub]ta'eruš [uk]ta'inuš [1] ubānšu inakkisu [šumm]a ittišiqši [ša]passu šaplīta [ana p]an erimte ša pāse [iša]ddudu inakkisu

[If] a man [l]ays a hand upon a man's wife, treats her in the manner of a bull, [they p]rove him (guilty, and) [co]nvict him: they shall cut off [one] of his fingers; [i]f he kisses her: [they shall [d]raw his lower [l]ip [ov]er the blade?[57] of an ax and cut it off.

MAL A §10

[šumma l]u a'īlu lu sinniltu [ana bēt a'īle] ērubuma [lu a'īla l]u sinnilta idūku [ana bēl bēte] dā'ikānūte [iddunu] panūšuma [idukk]ušunu [panūšuma imma]ggar [mimmâšunu] ilaqqe [u šumma ina bē]t dā'i[kānūte] mimm[a ša tadāne laššu] lu mā[ra lu mārta . . .] im[. . .]

[If eit]her a man or a woman enters [to (another) man's house] and kills [either a man o]r a woman: [they shall give] the killers [to the head of the household]; if he so chooses, [he shall kill] them; [if he so chooses, he shall reach an agree]ment, he shall take [their property; and if in the] ki[llers' hou]se [there is no]thin[g to give:] he shall [take?] either a so[n or a daughter . . .]

MAL A §12

šumma aššat a'īle ina rebēte tētetiq a'īlu iṣṣabassu lanīkkime iqṭibiašše la tamaggur tattanaṣṣar emūqamma iṣṣabassi ittiakši lu ina muḫḫi aššat a'īle ikšuduš u lu kî sinnilta inīkuni šēbūtu ubta'eruš a'īla idukku ša sinnilte ḫīṭu laššu

If a man's wife passes through the main-street, a man seizes her, tells her, "May I fornicate[58] with you!", she shall not agree, she shall protect herself; but (if) he seizes her by force (and) fornicates with her, whether they find him upon the man's wife or whether witnesses prove him (guilty) as he fornicated with the woman: they shall kill the man; there is no punishment for the woman.

MAL A §13

šumma aššat a'īle ištu bētiša tattiṣīma ana muḫḫi a'īle ašar usbuni tattalak ittiakši kî aššat a'īlenni īde a'īla u aššata idukku

If a man's wife goes out from her house and goes to a man, (to) the place where he resides, he fornicates with her knowing that she is a man's wife: they shall kill the man and the wife.

MAL A §14

šumma aššat a'īle a'īlu lu ina bēt altamme lu ina rebēte kî aššat a'īlenni īde ittiakši kî a'īlu ša aššassu ana epāše iqabbiuni nā'ikāna eppušu šumma kî aššat a'īlenni la īde ittiakši nā'ikānu zaku a'īlu aššassu ubâr kî libbišu eppassi

If a man's wife, a man – whether in an inn or in the main-street – fornicates with her knowing that she is a man's wife: they shall treat the fornicator as the man declares that his wife is to be treated; if he fornicates with her without knowing that she is a man's wife: the fornicator is clear; the man shall prove his wife (guilty), he shall treat her as he wishes.

MAL A §15

šumma a'īlu ištu aššitišu a'īla iṣṣabat ubta'eruš ukta'inuš kilallēšunuma idukkušunu aranšu laššu šumma iṣṣabta lu ana muḫḫi šarre lu ana muḫḫi dayānī ittabla ubta'eruš ukta'inuš šumma mut sinnilte aššassu iduak u a'īla iduakma šumma appa ša aššitišu inakkis a'īla ana ša rēšēn utâr u panīšu gabba inaqquru u šumma aššass[u uššar] a'īla u[ššar]

If a man seizes a man upon his wife, they prove him (guilty), they convict him: they shall kill both of them; there is no penalty for him; if he seizes him (and) brings him either before the king or before judges, they prove him (guilty), they convict him: if the woman's husband kills his wife, then he shall kill the man; if he cuts off the nose of his wife, he shall turn the man into a eunuch, and they shall mutilate his entire face; and if [he releases] hi[s] wife, he shall [release] the man.

MAL A §16

šumma a'īlu aššat [a'īle . . .] pīša [. . .] ḫīṭu ša a'īle laššu a'īlu aššassu ḫīṭa kî libbišu emmid šumma emūqamma ittiakši ubta'eruš ukta'inuš ḫīṭašu kî ša aššat a'īlemma

If a man [fornicates with a man]'s wife [. . . by] her initiative: there is no punishment for the man; the man shall impose upon his wife punishment as he wishes; if he fornicates with her by force, they prove him (guilty), they convict him: his punishment shall be as that of the man's wife.

MAL A §17

šumma a'īlu ana a'īle iqṭibi mā aššatka ittinikku šēbūtu laššu riksāte išakkunu ana Id illuku

If a man says to a man thus, "They are (all) fornicating with your wife!", (but) there are no witnesses: they shall submit an agreement, they shall undergo the divine-River-Ordeal.

MAL A §18

šumma a'īlu ana tappā'išu lu ina puzre lu ina ṣalte iqbi mā aššatka ittinikku mā anāku ubâr ba'ura la ila'e la uba'er a'īla šuātu 40 *ina ḫaṭṭāte imaḫḫuṣuš iltēn uraḫ ūmāte šipar šarre eppaš igaddimuš u* 1 *bilat annaka iddan*

If a man says to his fellow – whether in secret or in a quarrel – thus, "They are (all) fornicating with your wife!", (and) thus, "I shall prove (it)!", (but) he is unable to prove, (and) does not prove: they shall strike that man 40 (times) with rods; he shall perform the king's service for one full month; they shall cut him off;[59] and he shall give 1 talent (=3,600 shekels) of lead.

MAL A §19

šumma a'īlu ina puzre ina muḫḫi tappā'išu abata iškun mā ittinikkuš lu ina ṣalte ana pani ṣābē iqbiaššu mā ittinikkuka mā ubârka ba'ura la ila'e la uba'er a'īla šuātu 50 *ina ḫaṭṭāte imaḫḫuṣuš iltēn uraḫ ūmāte šipar šarre eppaš igaddimuš u* 1 *bilat annaka iddan*

If a man has spread rumors[60] in secret over his fellow thus, "They are (all) sodomizing him!", or in a quarrel before the public says to him thus, "They are (all) sodomizing you!" (and further) thus, "I shall prove you!", (but) he is unable to prove, (and) does not prove: they shall strike that man 50 (times) with rods; he shall perform the king's service for one full month; they shall cut him off;[61] and he shall give 1 talent (=3,600 shekels) of lead.

MAL A §20

šumma a'īlu tappāšu inīk ubta'erus ukta'inuš inikkuš ana ša rēšēn utarruš

If a man sodomizes his fellow, they prove him (guilty), they convict him: they shall sodomize him, they shall turn him into a eunuch.

MAL A §21

šumma a'īlu mārat a'īle imḫaṣma ša libbiša ultaṣlēš ubta'eruš ukta'inuš 2 *bilat* 30 *mana annaka iddan* 50 *ina ḫaṭṭāte imaḫḫuṣuš iltēn uraḫ ūmāte šipar šarre eppaš*

If a man strikes a man's daughter, and causes her to abort her fetus, they prove him (guilty), they convict him: he shall give 2 talents and 30 minas (=9,000 shekels) of lead; they shall strike him 50 (times) with rods; he shall perform the king's service for one full month.

MAL A §22

šumma aššat a'īle la abuša la aḫuša la māruša a'īlu šaniumma ḫarrāna ultaṣbissi u kî aššat a'īlenni la īde itamma u 2 *bilat annaka ana mut sinnilte iddan* [*šu*]*mma kî* [*aššat a'īlenni īde b*]*itqāte idd*[*anma itamma m*]*ā šumma anī[kušini] u šumma aššat [a'īle taqṭibi m]ā ittīkanni [kî a']īlu bitqāte [ana] a'īle iddinuni [ana] Id illak [rik]sātušu laššu šumma ina Id ittūra kî mut sinnilte aššassu eppušuni ana šuâšu eppušuš*

If a man's wife – not her father, not her brother, not her son, (but) another man – makes her travel with him: then he shall swear he did not know that she is a man's wife, and he shall give 2 talents (=7,200 shekels) of lead to the woman's husband; [i]f [he knew that she is a man's wife:] he shall gi[ve d]amages, [and swear th]us, "If I forni[cated with her!";] but if the [man]'s wife [says th]us, "He fornicated with me!": [since the m]an gave damages [to] the man, he shall undergo the divine-River-Ordeal; he has no [ag]reement; if he refuses the divine-River-Ordeal: they shall treat him as the woman's husband treats his wife.

MAL A §23

šumma aššat a'īle aššat a'īlimma ana bētiša talteqe ana a'īle ana niāke tattidinši u a'īlu kī aššat a'īlenni īde kî ša aššat a'īle inīkuni eppušuš u kī ša mut sinnilte aššassu nīkta eppušuni mummerta eppušu u šumma mut sinnilte aššassu nīkta mimma la eppaš nā'ikāna u mummerta mimma la eppušu uššurušunu u šumma aššat a'īle la tīde u sinniltu ša ana bētiša talqeušini kî pīge a'īla ana muḫḫiša tultērib u ittiakši šumma ištu bēte ina uṣāiša kî nīkutuni taqṭibi sinnilta uššuru zakuat nā'ikāna u mummerta idukku u šumma sinniltu la taqṭibi a'īlu aššassu ḫīṭa kî libbišu emmid nā'ikāna u mummerta idukku

If a man's wife takes a man's wife to her house, gives her to a man for fornication, and the man knows that she is a man's wife: they shall treat him as one who fornicated with a man's wife, and they shall treat the procuress as the woman's husband treats his fornicating wife; and if the woman's husband does nothing to his fornicating wife: they shall do nothing to the fornicator and to the procuress, they shall release them; but if the man's wife does not know, and the woman that takes her to her house brings the man in to her by deception, and he fornicates with her, if upon her leaving from the house she declares, "I have been fornicated!": they shall release the woman, she is clear; they shall kill the fornicator and the procuress; but if the woman does not declare: the man shall impose upon his wife punishment as he wishes; they shall kill the fornicator and the procuress.

MAL A §24

šumma aššat a'īle ina pani mutiša ramanša taltadad lu ina libbi āle ammiemma lu ina ālāni qurbūte ašar bēta uddûšenni ana bēt Aššuraye tētarab ištu bēlet bēte usbat 3-šu 4-šu bēdat bēl bēte kî aššat a'īle ina bētišu usbutuni la īde ina urkette sinniltu šī‹t› tattaṣbat bēl bēte ša aššassu [ina pa]nīšu ramanša [tald]uduni aššassu [unakkasma la][62] ilaqqe [ašša]t a'īle ša aššassu ilteša usbutuni uznēša unakkusu ḫadīma mussa 3 bilat 30 mana annaka šīmša iddan u ḫadīma aššassu ilaqqeu u šumma bēl bēte kî aššat a'īle ina bētišu ištu aššī[tišu] usbutuni ī[de] šalšāte iddan u šumma itteker la īdema iqabbi ana Id illuku u šumma a'īlu ša aššat a'īle ina bētišu usbutuni ina Id ittūra šalšāte iddan šumma a'īlu ša aššassu ina panīšu ramanša talduduni ina Id ittūra zaku gimrī ša Id umalla u šumma a'īlu ša aššassu ina panīšu ramanša talduduni aššassu la unakkis aššassu ilaqqe emittu mimma laššu

If a man's wife draws herself from her husband, enters to the house of an Assyrian – whether in that city or in (one of the) closeby cities – a house where he assigns her, is residing with the house mistress, staying overnight three or four times, (while) the house owner does not know that a man's wife resided in his house, (and) afterwards tha[t] woman is caught: the house owner that his wife [dr]ew herself [from h]im shall [mutilate and not?][63] take back his wife; the man's [wif]e that his wife resided with her, they shall cut off her ears; if he wishes, her husband shall give as her worth 3 talents and 30 minas (=12,600 shekels) of lead, and if he wishes he shall take back his wife; and if the house owner k[nows] that a man's wife resided in his house with [his] wif[e]: he shall give threefold; and if he denies: he shall declare, "I did not know!", they shall undergo the divine-River-Ordeal; and if the man that the man's wife resided in his house refuses the divine-River-Ordeal: he shall give threefold; if the man that his wife drew herself from him refuses the divine-River-Ordeal: he[64] is clear, he shall pay in full the costs of the divine-River-Ordeal; and if the man that his wife drew herself from him does not mutilate his wife: he shall take back his wife, there is no imposed punishment.

MAL A §25

šumma sinniltu ina bēt abišama usbat u mussa mēt aḫḫū mutiša la zēzu u māruša laššu mimma dumāqē ša mussa ina muḫḫiša iškununi la ḫalquni aḫḫū mutiša la zīzūtu ilaqqeu ana rīḫāte ilāni ušettuqu ubarru ilaqqeu ana Id u māmīte la iṣṣabbutu

If a woman is residing in her own father's house, and her husband is dead, her husband's brothers have not divided (their inheritance), and she has no son: any assets[65] that her husband granted her (and) are not lost, her husband's brothers (that) have not divided (their inheritance) shall take; as for the rest, they shall resort to the gods; they shall prove, (and) they shall take; they shall not be seized for the divine-River-Ordeal or an oath.

MAL A §26

šumma sinniltu ina bēt abišama usbat u mussa mēt mimma dumāqē ša mussa iškunušini šumma mārū mutiša ibašši ilaqqeu šumma mārū mutiša laššu šītma talaqqe

If a woman is residing in her own father's house, and her husband is dead, any assets[66] that her husband granted her: if there are sons of her husband, they shall take; if there are no sons of her husband, she herself shall take.

MAL A §27

šumma sinniltu ina bēt abišama usbat mussa ētanarrab mimma nudunnâ ša mussa iddinaššenni šuamma ilaqqe ana ša bēt abiša la iqarrib

If a woman is residing in her own father's house, (and) her husband frequents her: any *nudunnû* that her husband gave to her he himself shall take back; he shall not lay a claim to anything of her father's house.

MAL A §28

šumma almattu ana bēt a'īle tētarab u mārasa ḫurda ilteša naṣṣat ina bēt āḫizāniša irtibi u ṭuppu ša mārūtišu la šaṭrat zitta ina bēt murabbiānišu la ilaqqe ḫubullē la inašši ina bēt ālidānišu zitta kî qātišu ilaqqe

If a widow enters to a man's house, and she is carrying her surviving son with her, he grows up in her husband's[67] house, and a document of his son-ship was not written: he shall not take a share from the household of he who raised him, he shall not bear (its) debts; he shall take a share from the household of he who begot him, according to his portion.

MAL A §29

šumma sinniltu ana bēt mutiša tētarab širkīša u mimma ša ištu bēt abiša naṣṣutuni u lu ša emuša ina erābiša iddinaššenni ana mārēša zaku mārū emeša la iqarribu u šumma mussa ipūagsi ana mārēšu ša libbišu iddan

If a woman enters to her husband's house: her *širkū* and anything that she carries with her from her father's house, and whatever that her father-in-law gave her upon her entering, are clear for her sons; her father-in-law's sons shall not lay a claim; but if her husband deprives her, he shall give to his sons as he wishes.

MAL A §30

šumma abu ana bēt eme ša mārišu bibla ittabal ‹zubullâ› izzibil sinniltu ana mārišu la tadnat u mārušu šaniu ša aššassu ina bēt abiša usbutuni mēt aššat mārišu mēte ana mārišu šanā'iye ša ana bēt emešu izbiluni ana aḫuzzete iddanši šumma bēl mārte ša zubullâ imtaḫḫuruni mārassu ana tadāne la imaggur ḫadīma abu ša zubullâ izbiluni kallassu ilaqqea ana mārišu iddan u ḫadīma ammar izbiluni annaka ṣarpa ḫurāṣa ša la akāle qaqqadamma ilaqqe ana ša akāle la iqarrib

If a father brings the *biblu* and delivers the ‹*zubullû*› to the house of the father-in-law of his son, the woman is not given to his son, and his other son – that his wife resided in her father's house – is dead: he shall give her in marriage – his dead son's wife – to his other son, that to his father-in-law's house he delivered (the *zubullû*); if the daughter's master, that receives the *zubullû*, does not agree to give his daughter: if he wishes, the father that delivered the *zubullû* shall take his daughter-in-law (and) give to his son; or, if he wishes, as much as he delivered – lead, silver, gold – that is not edible, he shall take (back) in the original amount; he shall not lay a claim to what is edible.

MAL A §31

šumma a'īlu ana bēt emišu zubullâ izbil u aššassu mētat mārāt emišu ibašši ḫadīma "emu" mārat emišu kî aššitišu mette iḫḫaz u ḫadīma kaspa ša iddinuni ilaqqe lu še'am lu immerē lu mimma ša akāle la iddununeššu kaspamma imaḫḫar

If a man delivers the *zubullû* to his father-in-law's house, and though his wife is dead, there are daughters of his father-in-law: if he[68] wishes, he shall marry his father-in-law's daughter instead of his dead wife; or, if he wishes, he shall take (back) the silver that he gave; they shall not give (back) to him any grain, or sheep, or anything that is edible; he shall receive only silver.

MAL A §32

šumma sinniltu ina bēt abišama usbat [. . .]*ša tadnat lu ana bēt emiša laqiat lu la laqiat ḫubullē arna u ḫīṭa ša mutiša tanašši*

If a woman is residing in her own father's house, and her [. . .] is given, whether she is taken to her father-in-law's house, or she is not taken: she shall bear the debts, penalty, and punishment of her husband.

MAL A §33

[*šumma*] *sinniltu ina bēt abišama usbat mussa mēt u mārū ibašši* [. . .] *u* [*ḫadīma*] *ana emiša ana aḫuzzete iddanši šumma mussa u emuša mētuma u māruša laššu almattu šīt ašar ḫadi*[*ut*]*uni tallak*

[If] a woman is residing in her own father's house, her husband is dead, and she has sons: [. . .] or, [if he wishes], he shall give her to her father-in-law for marriage; if her husband and her father-in-law are both dead, and she has no son: she is a widow; she shall go where she wish[e]s.

MAL A §34

šumma a'īlu almattu ētaḫaz rikassa la rakis 2 šanāte ina bētišu usbat aššutu šīt la tuṣṣa

If a man marries a widow, her contract is not contracted, (and) she is residing in his house for two years: she is a wife; she shall not leave.

MAL A §35

šumma almattu ana bēt a'īle tētarab mimma ammar naṣṣatuni gabbu ša mutiša u šumma a'īlu ana muḫḫi sinnilte ētarab mimma ammar naṣṣatuni gabbu ša sinnilte

If a widow enters to a man's house: anything, as much as she is carrying with her, all belongs to her husband; and if a man enters to a woman('s house): anything, as much as he is carrying with him, all belongs to the woman.

MAL A §36

šumma sinniltu ina bēt abiša usbat lu mussa bēta ana batte ušēšibši u mussa ana eqle ittalak la šamna la šapāte la lubulta la ukullâ la mimma ēzibašše la mimma šūbulta ištu eqle ušēbilašše sinniltu šīt 5 *šanāte pani mutiša tadaggal ana mute la tuššab šumma mārūša ibašši innagguru u ekkulu sinniltu mussa tuqa'a ana mute la tuššab šumma mārūša laššu* 5 *šanāte mussa tuqa'a* 6 *šanāte ina kabāse ana mut libbiša tuššab mussa ina alāke la iqarribašše ana mutiša urkie zakuat šumma ana qāt* 5 *šanāte uḫḫeranni ina raminišu la ikkaluni lu qāli iṣbassuma innabi*[*t*] *lu kî sar*[*te*] *ṣabitma ūtaḫ*[*ḫer*] *ina alāke ubâr sinnilta ša kî aššitišu iddan u aššassu ilaqqe u šumma šarru ana māte šanītemma iltaparšu ana qāt* 5 *šanāte ūtaḫḫera aššassu tuqa'ašu ana mute la tuššab u šumma ina pani* 5 *šanāte ana mute tattašab u tattalad mussa ina alāke aššum riksa la tuqa'iuni u tannaḫizuni ana šuāša u līdānišama ilaqqēšunu*

If a woman is residing in her father's house, or her husband settles her in a house elsewhere, and her husband travels abroad but leaves her no oil, no wool, no clothing, no provisions, no anything, sends her no provisions[69] from abroad: that woman shall await her husband for five years, she shall not reside with (another) husband; if she has her sons: they shall be hired out and sustain themselves; the woman shall wait (for) her husband, she shall not reside with (another) husband; if she has no sons: she shall wait (for) her husband for five years, *in the sixth year*[70] she shall reside with a husband of her choice; her (first) husband, upon returning, shall not lay a claim to her – she is clear for her latter husband; if he delays beyond five years, (but) is not detained of his own (will), whether (because) a *qāli*[71] seized him and he fle[d], or (because) he was fals[ely] seized and was detai[ned]: upon returning he shall prove (it); he shall give a woman similar to his wife and he shall take his wife; and if the king sends him to another country (and) he is delayed beyond five years: his wife shall wait for him, she shall not reside with (another) husband; and if she resides with (another) husband before five years (have passed), and bears (children): because she did not wait according to the agreement, and was taken in marriage, her (former) husband, upon returning, shall take them, her and her offspring.

MAL A §37

šumma a'īlu aššassu ezzib libbušuma mimma iddanašše la libbušuma mimma la iddanašše rāqūteša tuṣṣa

If a man divorces his wife: if it is his wish, he shall give her something; if it is not his wish, he shall not give her anything, she shall leave empty-handed.

MAL A §38

šumma sinniltu ina bēt abišama usbat u mussa ētezibši dumāqēša šūtma iškunušenni ilaqqe ana terḫete ša ubluni la iqarrib ana sinnilte zaku

If a woman is residing in her own father's house, and her husband divorces her: he shall take her assets[72] that he himself granted her; he shall not lay a claim to the *terḫetu* that he brought, it is clear for the woman.

MAL A §39

šumma a'īlu la mārassu ana mute ittidin šumma panīma abuša ḫabbul kî šaparte šēšubat ummiānu paniu ittalka ina muḫḫi tādināne ša sinnilte šīm sinnilte išallim šumma ana tadāne laššu tādināna ilaqqe u šumma ina lumne balluṭat ana muballiṭāniša zakuat u šumma āḫizā[nu š]a sinnilte lu ṭuppa ulta[ṭar]ušu[73] *u lu rugu[mmān]ā irtišiuneššu šīm sinnilte u[šallam] u tādinānu [zaku]*[74]

If a man gives (a girl who is) not his daughter to a husband, if previously her father was in debt and she was made to reside as pledge: (if) a prior creditor comes forward, he shall receive in full the woman's worth from the giver of the woman; if he has nothing to give: he shall take the giver; but if she was saved from a catastrophe: she is clear for her savior; and if the take[r o]f the woman either causes a document to be wri[tte]n for him, or they (lay) a cl[ai]m against him: he shall [pay in full] the woman's worth, and the giver [is clear.]

MAL A §40

lu aššāt a'īle lu [almanātu] u lu sinnišātu [Aššurayātu] ša ana rebēte u[ṣṣâni] qaqqassina [la pattu] mārāt a'īle [. . .] lu ša ri[. . .] lu ṣubāti lu [. . .] paṣ[ṣuna] qaqqassina [. . .] lu [. . .] lu [. . .]aṣṣa[. . .] ina ūme ina rebēte e[. . .] illakāni uptaṣṣ[namma] esirtu ša ištu bēlti[ša] ina rebēte tallukuni paṣṣunat qadiltu ša mutu aḫzušini ina rebēte paṣṣunatma ša mutu la aḫzušini ina rebēte qaqqassa pattu la tuptaṣṣan ḫarīmtu la tuptaṣṣan qaqqassa pattu ša ḫarīmta paṣṣunta ētamruni i‹ṣa›bbassi šēbūte išakkan ana pī ekalle ubbalašši šukuttaša la ilaqqeu lubultaša ṣābitānša ilaqqe 50 *ina ḫaṭṭāte imaḫ‹ḫu›ṣuši qīra ana qaqqidiša itabbuku u šumma a'īlu ḫarīmta paṣṣunta ētamarma ūtaššer ana pī ekalle la ublašši a'īlu šuātu* 50 *ina ḫaṭṭāte imaḫḫuṣuš bātiqānšu lubultušu ilaqqe uznēšu upallušu ina eble išakkuku ina kutallišu irakkusu iltēn uraḫ ūmāte šipar šarre eppaš amātu la uptaṣṣanama ša amta paṣṣunta ētamruni iṣabbatašši ana pī ekalle ubbalašši uznēša unakkusu ṣābitānša lubultaša ilaqqe šumma a'īlu amta paṣṣunta ētamaršima ūtaššer la iṣṣabtašši ana pī ekalle la ublašši ubta'eruš ukta'inuš* 50 *ina ḫaṭṭāte imaḫḫuṣuš uznēšu upallušu ina eble išakkuku [ina kut]allišu irakkusu [bāti]qānšu lubultušu ilaqqe iltēn uraḫ ūmāte šipar [šarre] eppaš*

A man's wife, or [widows], or [Assyrian] women that g[o out] to the main-street, their heads [shall not be bear]; a man's daughters [. . .] either/or of *ri*[. . .], or garment or [. . . shall be] vei[led . . .] their heads [. . .] or [. . .] or [. . . v]eile[d . . .]; on the day they go about [. . .] in the main-street they shall be veil[ed]; a concubine that goes about in the main-street with [her] mistress is to be veiled; a married[75] *qadiltu* is to be veiled in the main-street; but an unmarried,[76] her head shall be bare in the main-street, she shall not be veiled; a prostitute shall not be veiled, her head shall be bare; he who sees a veiled prostitute shall seize her, establish witnesses (and) bring her to the palace entrance; they shall not take her jewelry; her seizer shall take her clothing; they shall strike her 50 (times) with rods; they shall pour pitch over her head; but if a man sees and releases a veiled prostitute, (and) does not bring her to the palace entrance: they shall strike that man 50 (times) with rods; his informer shall take his clothing; they shall pierce his ears, thread on a cord, (and) tie on his back; he shall perform the king's service for one full month; slave-women shall not be veiled; and he who sees a veiled slave-woman shall seize her, (and) bring her to the palace entrance; they shall cut off her ears; her seizer shall take her clothing; if a man sees and releases a veiled slave-woman, does not seize her, (and) does not bring her to the palace entrance, they prove him (guilty), they convict him: they shall strike that man 50 (times) with rods; they shall pierce his ears, thread on a cord (and) tie [on] his [ba]ck; his informer shall take his clothing; he shall perform the [king's] service for one full month.

MAL A §41

šumma a'īlu esirtušu upaṣṣan 5 6 *tappa'ēšu ušeššab ana panīšunu upaṣṣanši mā aššitī šīt iqabbi aššassu šīt esirtu ša ana pani ṣābē la paṣṣunutuni mussa la iqbiuni mā aššitī šīt la aššat esirtumma šīt šumma a'īlu mēt mārū aššitišu paṣṣunte laššu mārū esrāte mārū šunu zitta ilaqqeu*

If a man veils his concubine: he shall gather five, six of his comrades, he shall veil her in front of them; he shall declare thus, "She is my wife!"; she is his wife; a concubine that is not veiled before the public (and) her husband did not declare thus, "She is my wife!": she is not a wife, she is merely a concubine; if a man is dead (and) there are no sons of his veiled wife: the sons of concubines, they are (legally) sons; they shall take a(n inheritance) share.

MAL A §42

šumma a'īlu ina ūme rāqe šamna ana qaqqad mārat a'īle itbuk lu ina šākulte ḫuruppate ubil tūrta la utarru

If a man pours oil on the head of a man's daughter on a holiday,[77] or brings dishes on a banquet: a restitution shall not be made.

MAL A §43

šumma a'īlu lu šamna ana qaqqade itbuk lu ḫuruppāte ubil māru ša aššata uddiuneššunni lu mēt lu innabit ina mārēšu rīḫāte ištu muḫḫi māre rabê adi muḫḫi māre ṣeḫre ša 10 *šanātušuni ana ša ḫadiuni iddan šumma abu mēt u māru ša aššata uddiuniššunni mētma mār māre mēte ša* 10 *šanātušuni ibašši eḫḫazma šumma ana qāt* 10 *šanāte mārū māre ṣeḫḫeru abu ša mārte ḫadīma mārassu iddan u ḫadīma tūrta ana mitḫār utâr šumma māru laššu ammar imḫuruni abna u mimma ša la akāle qaqqadamma utâr u ša akāle la utâr*

If a man either pours oil on the head or brings dishes, (and) the son that he assigned the wife for him either dies or flees: he shall give (her) to whomever he wishes among his remaining sons, from the oldest son to the youngest son of (at least) ten years (of age); if the father is dead and the son that he assigned the wife for him is also dead, (but) there is a son of the dead son, of (at least) ten years (of age): he shall marry her; if the (dead) son's sons are young under ten years (of age): the father of the daughter, if he wishes, shall give his daughter (to one of them); or, if he wishes, he shall make an equal restitution;[78] if there is no son: as much as he received – precious stones, or anything that is not edible – he shall return in the original amount; but he shall not return what is edible.

MAL A §44

šumma Aššurayau u šumma Aššurayītu ša kî šaparte ammar šīmišu ina bēt a'īle usbuni ana šīm gamer laqeuni inaṭṭu ibaqqan uznēšu uḫappa upallaš

If an Assyrian-man or if an Assyrian-woman that resides in a man's house as a pledge for as much as his worth is taken for the full worth: he shall hit (the pledge), pluck out (his hair? and) mutilate (or) pierce his ears.

MAL A §45

[*šumm*]*a sinniltu tadnat* [*u*] *mussa nakru ilteqe emuša u māruša laššu* 2 *šanāte pani mutеša tadaggal ina* 2 *šanāte annâte šumma ša akāle laššu tallakamma taqabbi* [*šumma*] *ālāyītu ša ekalle šīt* [*ab*]*uša*? *ušakkalši* [*u šip*]*aršu teppaš* [*šumma aššutu š*]*a ḫupše šīt* [. . . *ušakk*]*alši* [*šiparšu teppaš*] *u* [*šumma aššat a'īle*? *šīt ša*] *eqla u* [*bēta* . . .] *tallaka*[*mma ana dayānē taqabbi*] *mā ana akā*[*le laššu*] *dayānū ḫaziāna rabiūte ša āle iša'ulu kî eqla ina āle šuātu illukuni eqla u bēta ana ukullāiša ša* 2 *šanāte uppušu iddununešše usbat u ṭuppaša išaṭṭuru* 2 *šanāte tumalla ana mut libbiša tuššab ṭuppaša kî almattemma išaṭṭuru šumma ina arkât ūmē mussa ḫalqu ana māte ittūra aššassu ša ana kīde aḫzutuni ilaqqeašši ana mārē ša ana mutiša urkie uldutuni la iqarrib mussama urkiu ilaqqe eqlu u bētu ša kî ukullāiša ana šīm gamer ana kīde taddinuni šumma ana dannat šarre la ērub kî tadnunima iddan u ilaqqe u šumma la ittūra ina māte šanītemma mēt eqelšu u bēssu ašar šarru iddununi iddan*

[I]f a woman is given (in marriage) [and] the enemy takes her husband, she has no father-in-law or son: she shall await her husband for two years; during these two years, if she has no sustenance she shall come forward and declare (it); [if] she is a citizen of (=dependent on) the palace: her [fathe]r? shall sustain her, [and] she shall perform his [wo]rk; [if] she is [the wife o]f a *ḫupšu*(-soldier): [. . . shall sust]ain her, [and she shall perform his work?]; and [if she is a man's wife, that] a field and [a house . . .]: she shall come forward [and declare to the judges] thus, "[I have nothing] to ea[t]!"; the judges shall question the mayor (and) noblemen of the city; according to (how much) a field is going (=valued?) in that city,[79] they shall give her to utilize a field and a house for her sustenance for two years; she will be residing (there), and they shall write her a document; she shall let two years to be complete, (after which) she shall reside with a husband of her choice; they shall write her a document as a widow; if later on her lost husband returns to the country: he shall take her, his wife that was married outside; he shall not lay a claim to the sons that she bore to her latter husband, but her latter husband shall take (them); the field and the house, that she gave outside for the full worth as her sustenance, if it is not entered into the *royal holdings*:[80] he shall give as (much as) was given, and he shall take (it); and if he does not return, but dies in another country: the king shall give his field and his house where he (decides) to give.

MAL A §46

šumma sinniltu ša mussa mētuni mussa ina muāte ištu bētiša la tuṣṣâ šumma mussa mimma la ilṭurašše ina bēt mārēša ašar panūšani tuššab mārū mutiša ušakkuluši ukullâša u maltīssa kî kallete ša ira'umûšini irakkusunešše šumma urkittu šīt mārūša laššu ištu iltēn tuššab ana puḫrišunu ušakkuluši šumma mārūša ibašši mārū panîte ana šâkuliša la imagguru ina bēt mārē raminiša ašar panūšani tuššab mārū raminišama ušakkuluši u šiparšunu teppaš u šumma ina mārē mutišama ša eḫḫuzušini i[baš]ši [. . . mārūšama l]a ušakkuluši

If a woman that her husband is dead does not leave her house upon the death of her husband, if her husband did not award-in-writing anything to her: she shall reside in a house of (one of) her sons, where she so chooses; her husband's sons shall sustain her; they shall contract for her (=guaranty) her food and her drink, as a daughter-in-law that they love; if she is a second (wife and) has no sons: she shall reside with one (of her dead husband's sons), they shall sustain her collectively; if she has sons, (and) the sons of the first (wife) do not agree to sustain her: she shall reside in (one of) her own sons' house, where she so chooses; her own sons shall sustain her, and she shall perform their work; and if among her husband's sons t[here i]s one who will marry her: [. . . her own sons shall n]ot sustain her.

MAL A §47

šumma lu a'īlu lu sinniltu kišpī uppišuma ina qātēšunu iṣṣabtu ubta'erušunu ukta'inušunu muppišāna ša kišpē idukku a'īlu ša kišpē epāša ēmuruni ina pī āmerāne ša kišpē išme'uni mā anāku ātamar iqbiaššunni šāme'ānu illaka ana šarre iqabbi šumma āmerānu ša ana šarre iqbiuni itteker ana pani ᵈGUD. DUMU.ᵈUTU *iqabbi mā šumma la iqbianni zaku āmerānu ša iqbiuni u ikkeruni šarru kī ila'uni iltana'alšu u kutallušu emmar āšipu ina ūme ullulūni a'īla ušaqba u šūt iqabbi mā māmīta ša ana šarre u mārišu tam'ātani la ipaššarakkunu kî pī ṭuppimma ša ana šarre u mārišu tam'ātani tam'āta*

If either a man or a woman perform witchcraft, and (the paraphernalia) are discovered by them, they prove them (guilty), they convict them: they shall kill the performer of the witchcraft; a man that heard from an eyewitness of the witchcraft that saw the witchcraft performance, (and) told him thus, "I myself have seen (it)!": the hearer shall go, he shall report to the king; if the eyewitness denies what (the hearer) reports to the king: he shall declare in front of the divine Bull-Son-of-the-Sun-god thus, "If he did not tell me!", (and) he is clear; the eyewitness that spoke and denied: the king shall interrogate him as necessary, and investigate his case; an exorcist shall make the man speak on a day he is purified, and (the exorcist) shall declare thus, "No one shall release you (pl.) from the oath that you swore by the king and his son! You are obliged-by-oath according to the document that you swore by the king and his son!"

MAL A §48

šumma a'īlu mārat ḫabbulišu ša kî ḫubulle ina bētišu usbutuni abuša iša'al ana mute iddanši šumma abuša la mager la iddan šumma abuša mēt iltēn ina aḫḫēša iša'al u šūt ana aḫḫēša iqabbi šumma aḫu iqabbi mā aḫātī adi iltēn uraḫ ūmāte apaṭṭar šumma adi iltēn uraḫ ūmāte la iptaṭar bēl kaspe ḫadīma uzakkašši ana mute iddanši [. . . *kī*?] *pī* [. . . *id*]*danši* [. . .]*šunu* [. . .] *šunu* [. . .]*šu*

If a man, his debtor's daughter that resides in his house because of the debt:[81] he shall ask her father!,[82] he shall give her to a husband; if her father does not agree: he shall not give (her); if her father is dead: he shall ask one of her brothers, and he shall tell her (other) brothers; if a brother declares thus, "I will redeem my sister within one full month!", if within one full month he has not redeemed (her): the creditor,[83] if he wishes, shall clear her (and) he shall give her to a husband; [. . .] according to [. . . he shall g]ive her [. . .] their [. . .] their [. . .] his [. . .]

MAL A §49

[. . .] *kî aḫe* [. . .] *u šumma ḫarīmtu mētat* [*aš*]*šum aḫḫūša iqabbiūni* [. . .] *ša kî* [. . .] *aḫe zitte* [. . .] *aḫḫē* [*um*]*mišunu* [*izu*]*zzu*

[. . .] as a brother [. . .] and if the prostitute is dead: [be]cause her brothers declare [. . .] that as [. . .] a brother, the share [. . .] [they shall div]ide [with?] their [mot]her's brothers.

MAL A §50

[*šumma a'īlu aššat a'īli i*]*mḫaṣma* [*ša libbiša ušaṣlī*]*ši* [. . . *ašša*]*t a'īle š*[*a* . . .] *ni u* [*kî ša ēpuš*]*ušini eppu*[*šušu kīmū š*]*a libbiša napšāte umalla u šumma sinniltu šīt mētat a'īla idukku kīmū ša libbiša napšāte umalla u šumma ša mut sinnilte šiāte mārušu laššu aššassu imḫuṣuma ša libbiša taṣli kīmū ša libbiša māḫiṣāna idukku šumma ša libbiša ṣuḫārtu napšātemma umalla*

[If a man s]trikes [a(nother) man's wife and causes] her [to miscarry her fetus . . .] a man's [wif]e th[at . . .] and [as he treat]ed her, they shall tre[at him; in return for] her fetus he shall pay in full for a life; and if that woman dies: they shall kill the man; in return for her fetus he shall pay in full for a life; and if there is no son of that woman's husband, (and) his wife (that) he struck miscarried her fetus: in return for her fetus they shall kill the striker; if her fetus was a female: he shall pay in full for a life only.

MAL A §51

šumma a'īlu aššat a'īle la murabbīta imḫaṣma ša libbiša ušaṣlīši ḫīṭu anniu 2 *bilat annaka iddan*

If a man strikes a(nother) man's wife, who does not raise (her children), and causes her to miscarry her fetus: it is a punishable-offense, he shall give 2 talents (=7,200 shekels) of lead.

MAL A §52

šumma a'īlu ḫarīmta imḫaṣma ša libbiša ušaṣlīši miḫṣī kî miḫṣī išakkunuš napšāte umalla

If a man strikes a prostitute and causes her to miscarry her fetus: they shall inflict upon him blow for blow, he shall pay in full for a life.

MAL A §53

šumma sinniltu ina raminiša ša libbiša taṣṣili ubta'eruši ukta'inuši ina iṣṣē izaqqupuši la iqabberuši šumma ša libbiša ina ṣalê mētat ina iṣṣē izaqqupuši la iqabberuši šumma sinnilta šīt kî ša libbiša taṣliuni [*uptazz*]*eruši* [. . .] *iqbiu* [. . .]*me* [. . .]*te* [. . .]

If a woman miscarries her fetus on her own, they prove her (guilty), they convict her: they shall impale her, they shall not bury her; if she dies because of miscarrying her fetus:[84] they shall impale her, they shall not bury her; if that woman, because she miscarried her fetus, (anyone) [conc]eals her [. . .] spoke [. . .]

MAL A §55

[*šumma a'ī*]*lu batulta* [*ša ina bēt a*]*biša* [*usbu*]*tuni* [. . .] *ša la ūtarrišuni* [*puš*] *qa*? *la patteatuni la aḫzatuni u rugummānâ ana bēt abiša la iršiuni a'īlu lu ina libbi āle lu ina ṣēre lu ina mūše ina rebēte lu ina bēt qarīte lu ina isinni āle a'īlu kî da'āne batulta iṣbatma umanzi'ši abu ša batulte aššat nā'ikāna ša batulte ilaqqe ana manzu'e iddanši ana mutiša la utâršši ilaqqēši abu mārassu nīkta ana nā'ikāniša kî aḫuzzete iddanši šumma aššassu laššu šalšāte kaspe šīm batulte nā'ikānu ana abiša iddan nā'ikānša iḫḫassi la isammakši šumma abu la ḫadi kaspa šalšāte ša batulte imaḫḫar mārassu ana ša ḫadiuni iddan*

[If a ma]n, an adolescent-girl [that resid]es [in] her [fa]ther['s house . . .] that is not . . .[85] (that her) [wo]mb?[86] is not opened, not married and no claim is laid against her father's house; a man (that) whether in the city or in the countryside, whether in the night, in the main-street or in a granary, or during the city festival, a man (that) seizes an adolescent-girl by force and rapes her: the father of the adolescent-girl shall take the wife of the fornicator of the adolescent-girl, he shall give her to be raped; he shall not return her to her husband, he shall take her; the father shall give his daughter that has been fornicated in marriage to her fornicator; if (the fornicator) has no wife: the fornicator shall give silver threefold the worth of the adolescent-girl to her father; her fornicator shall marry her, he shall not reject her; if the father does not wish (it): he shall receive silver threefold for the adolescent-girl; he shall give his daughter to whomever he wishes.

MAL A §56

šumma batultu ramanša ana a'īle tattidin a'īlu itamma ana aššitišu la iqarribu šalšāte kaspe šīm batulte nā'ikānu iddan abu māras[*su*] *kî ḫadiuni epp*[*aš*]

If an adolescent-girl gives herself to a man on her own initiative: the man shall swear (so); they shall not lay a claim against his wife; the fornicator shall give silver threefold the worth of the adolescent-girl; the father shall tre[at] [his] daughter as he wishes.

MAL A §59

uššer ḫīṭāni ša [*aššat a'īle*] *ša ina ṭuppe* [*šaṭruni*] *a'īlu aššassu* [*inaṭṭu*] *ibaqqan u*[*znēša*] *uḫappa ul*[*appat*] *aranšu laššu*

Additionally to the punishments of [a man's wife] that are [written] in the document, a man (may) [hit] his wife, pluck out (her hair?), mutilate [her] e[ars] (and) b[eat] (her); there is no penalty for him.

MAL C §1

[. . .] *bēlšunu* [. . .]*nu u šumma lāqiānu* [*iqabbi mā* . . .] *ša apṭuranni mi*[. . . *urda ana* x] *bilat anneke amta ana* 4 *bilat anneke* [. . .] *u šumma māḫirānu iqabbi mā* [. . .] *ana pani ile itamma u ammar ina* [. . .] *ilaqqe* [. . .]

[. . .] their owner [. . .] and if the buyer [declares thus, ". . .] that I redeemed [. . "., a slave for x] talents of lead and a slave-woman for 4 talents (=14,400 shekels) of lead [. . .] and if the receiver declares thus, [". . ".], he shall swear before the god, and as much as [. . .] he shall take [. . .]

MAL C §2

[*šumma a'īlu lu mār a'īle*] *u lu mārat a'īle ša kî kaspe u kî* [*šaparte ina bētišu us*]*buni ana kaspe ana a'īle šanîmma* [*iddin u mamma šaniam*]*ma ša ina bētišu usbuni id*[*din ubta'erušu*] *ina kaspišu qāssu el*[*li . . .*]*šu ana bēl mimmû idd*[*an* x *ina ḫaṭṭāte im*]*aḫuṣušu* 20 *ūmāte šipar šarre eppaš*

[If a man] sel[ls] to another man [either a man's son] or a man's daughter that [re]sides [in his house], whether for silver or as [a pledge], or gi[ves anyone els]e that resides in his house, [they prove him (guilty)]: he shall forfei[t] his silver; [. . .] he shall give his/its [. . .] to the property owner; [they shall s]trike him [x (times) with rods]; he shall perform the king's service for 20 days.

MAL C §3

[*šumma a'īlu lu mār a'īle*] *u lu mārat a'īle ša kî kaspe u kî šaparte* [*ina bētišu usbuni*] *ana māte šanīte ana kaspe iddin* [*ubta'erušu ukt*]*a'inušu ina kaspišu qāssu elli* [x-*šu ana bē*]*l mimmû iddan* [x *ina ḫaṭṭāte i*]*maḫḫuṣušu* 40 *ūmāte šipar šarre eppaš* [*u šumma a'īlu ša iddinu*]*ni ina māte šanīte mēt* [*napšāte umal*]*la Aššurayau u Aššurayītu* [*ša ana šīm gam*]*er laqeuni ana māt šanīte* [*inad*]*din*

[If a man] sells to a foreign land [either a man's son] or a man's daughter that [resides in his house], whether for silver or as a pledge, [they prove him (guilty), they co]nvict him: he shall forfeit his silver; he shall give [his/its . . . to the] property [own]er; [they shall s]trike him [x (times) with rods]; he shall perform the king's service for 40 days; and if the man that he sold dies in the foreign land: [he shall pay in ful]l [for a life]; he (may) [se]ll to a foreign land an Assyrian-man or an Assyrian-woman [that] is taken [for the ful]l [worth].

8 MAPD (Middle Assyrian Palace Decrees)

MAPD §1

[. . .] *sabsūtu u qadiltu* [. . .] *la irraba la uṣṣâ*

[. . .] A midwife and a *qadiltu* [. . .] shall not go in or go out (the palace).

MAPD §3

[*sinnišātu . . . ša*] *kīdânu aḫḫuzāni ina bēt mutēšina us*[*bāni . . .*] *lu* [*ina*] *ūme rāqe balut šarre ša'ā*[*le la . . . šumma . . . ša ina libbi-āl*]*e usbuni la iš'aluni* [*. . . us*]*buni atû* [*. . . l*]*u ša rēš šarre lu mazz*[*iz pane . . .*]

[Women . . . (working in the palace) who are] married to men from outside of it and who are residing in their husbands' houses [shall not . . . either during . . .] or on the day of a holiday, without asking permission of the king; [if . . . who] resides within the inner-city does not ask permission [. . . who] resides, the doorkeepers [. . .], or a royal eunuch, or a cour[tier . . .]

MAPD §5

sinniltu ša ek[*alle*] *lu ḫurāṣa lu ṣarpa u lu abna ana urad ekalle la* [*taddan . . . ēpiš*] *šipre la ute*[*. . . šumma . . .*] *u rab ekalle ultēṣi sinnilta ša ekalle la uššuru*

A woman of the pa[lace] shall not [give] either gold, silver, or (precious) stones to a palace slave; [. . .] a craftsman shall not [. . . if . . .] and the palace commander should allow (him/her) to leave, they shall not release the woman of the palace.

MAPD §6

sinniltu ša ekal[*le*] *la tašapparamma ištu muḫḫi ṣubāte ša qable lēdē paṣiūte ṣubāte ša ḫarrā*[*ne . . .*] *šuḫuppāte u mim*[*ma šumšu*] *balut šarre u rab ekalle ša'āle la tašapparamma ištu ek*[*all*]*e la ušēṣû ina ūme a*[*na . . .*] *tuṣṣûni lubultaša rab ekalle u atû emmuru la ikallû*[*ši*]

A woman of the pala[ce] shall not send for anything; she shall not send for a skirt, white wraps, a travel cloak [. . .], leather boots or anyth[ing else], without asking the king or of the palace commander, and they shall remove nothing from the pa[lac]e. On the day she leaves t[o . . .], the palace commander and the doorkeepers shall inspect her wardrobe but they shall not detain [her].[87]

MAPD §7

ištu niqiāte kašāde sinniltu ša ekalle ša la qarābšani ana pan šarre la terrab

When the time arrives for making sacrifices, a woman of the palace who is menstruating[88] shall not come before the king.

MAPD §8

ina ūm il ḫarrāne kî ana ekalle errabuni ša muḫḫi ekalle nāgir ekalle rab zāriqē asû ša bētānu kî mazziz panūte iḫirrūni lu ša rēš šarre lu mazziz pane ša la marruruni iqabbiu ša šanuttešu ana mazziz panutte iddunuš šumma qēpūtu annûtu la iqṭibiu ḫīṭa inaššiu

On the day of the God-of-the-Journey, when he enters to the palace, and when the palace administrator, the palace herald, the chief of the water-sprinklers and the physician of the inner-quarters inspect the courtiers, they shall report whether a royal eunuch or a courtier who is not *checked*.[89] For a second time, they shall give him for becoming a courtier. If these officials should not report, they will bear a punishable-offense.

MAPD §9

šumma šarru ša rēš šarre ina kal ūme ana muḫḫi [sinnišāte ša ekalle] išappar šumma ina āle balut rab ekalle ša āle ana ekall[e ad]i[?] *maškan-itḫuru šaknuni [la errab ana rab] ekalle iqabbi adi errabuni uṣṣâni rab ekalle ina pī [. . .]sate izzaz šumma ina ḫūle [balut rab ek]alle u rab zāriqē la errab šumma ša rēš šarre balut qēp[ūte] annûte ētarab ḫīṭa inašši*

If the king sends a royal eunuch during daytime to [the women of the palace], if (the women are) in the city, [he shall not enter] into the palac[e] without the palace commander of the city, [as long a]s[?] the tent of the *itḫuru*-standard is placed. He shall report [to the] palace [commander]. As long as he enters, (the women) shall leave and the palace commander shall stand at the entrance of the [. . .] If (the women are) in the processional residence, he shall not enter [without the pa]lace [commander] and the chief of the water-sprinklers. If the royal eunuch enters without these offi[cials], he bears a punishable-offense.

MAPD §10

lu aššāt šarre lu sinnišātu mādātu [ša ekalle ša . . .] aḫā'iš idūkāni ina ṣaltišina šu[m il]e ana masikte tazzakrūni [. . . e]rrab napšāte ša Aššur it[. . .] inakkisu ina ṣaltišina [. . .]ki ana pi[. . .] la tappal

Either the king's wives or other women [of the palace, who . . .] fight among themselves, and in their quarrel blasphemously swear by the nam[e of the go]d [. . . he shall e]nter; they shall cut the throat of the one who has c[ursed?] the god Aššur; in their quarrel [. . .] . . . [. . .] she shall not satisfy the claim.

MAPD §11

[. . .] *šum ile ana la kitte* [. . .] . . . [. . .] *la uballuṭuši*

[. . . They shall kill a woman of the palace who swears] by the name of the god for improper purposes [. . .], they shall not spare her life.

MAPD §12

[. . .] *aššat šarre* [. . .]*šu* [. . .]*šina* [. . .] *izzakar* [. . . *(la)*? *tap*]*pal*

[. . .] a wife of the king, his [. . .], their (fem.) [. . .], he has sworn. [. . . she? shall (not)? sati]sfy the claim.

MAPD §13

šumma [. . .]*tat* [. . .] *sinniltu ša ekal*[*le* . . .]*ni* [. . .] . . . [. . .]*ru*

If [. . .] a woman of the pala[ce . . .]

MAPD §14

šumma [*sinniltu ša ekalle*? *ma*]*šikta* [. . .]*ma taqṭibi kinat*[*tu* . . .] . . . [. . .]*runi tašmeuni la* [. . .]

If [a woman of the palace?, ev]il [. . .] or she utters [. . .], (a woman) of equa[l status . . . sa]w (or) heard, [she shall] not [. . .]

MAPD §15

[. . .] *ḫaliqta* [. . .] *adi šarru iqabbiašš*[*enni* . . .] *šarru* [. . .] *la iqbiaššenni* [. . .]

[. . .] a fugitive woman [. . .] until the king tells [her . . .] the king [. . .] did not tell her [. . .]

MAPD §17

[*šumma sinniltu ša*] *ekalle* [. . .] *tātarar lu mār Tukultī-Ninurta* [*lu* . . . *lu ša bē*]*te ša šarre ša mayā*[*le* . . . *lu*] *ša litte* [. . . *tātarar lu sinnilta*] *ša šaplānuša tātarar lemniš* [. . .]*na našā'enni sinniltu ša* [*ekalle a*]*ppaša ipallušu* [x *ina ḫaṭṭāte*] *imaḫḫuṣuši*

[If a woman of] the palace should curse [. . .], or [should she curse] either a descendant of Tukulti-Ninurta, [or another member of the] royal [house] hold, or (an official) of the royal bedro[om . . . or] (an official) of the stool;? or if she should spitefully curse [a woman] who is inferior to her [. . .]

carrying (a child?): (that) woman of [the palace], they shall pierce her [n]ose; they shall strike her [x (times) with rods].

MAPD §18

[l]u aššat šarre [lu sinniltu ša ekalle šumma amassa lu ḫīṭa ana bēltiša taḫṭia lu . . .] lu sarta mimma tētapaš lu [aššat šarre lu] sinniltu ša [ekalle ša am] assa ḫīṭa taḫṭiaššini 30 *ina ḫaṭṭāte tamaḫḫassi* [. . . *šumma amtu*] *naṭītu tur*[. . . *lu ḫī*]*ṭa ana bēltiša taḫṭi*[*a lu* . . . *lu s*]*arta tētapaš bēltuša ana* [*muḫḫi šarre tušerr*]*ab pan šarre ḫīṭa š*[*a libb*]*išu emmid*[*uši* . . .] *šanītamma ana bēltiša iddan šumma sinniltu* [*ša ekall*]*e ša pī ri*[*kse ša šarre* . . . *ša amassa*] *tattuṭu ina ḫaṭṭāte mētat lu ana muḫ*[*ḫi* . . . *sinniltu ša ekal*]*le ša amassa taddūkuni ana šilliteša* [. . .] *ḫīṭa ša šarre ta*[*našši*]

[Eit]her a wife of the king, [or a woman of the palace, if her slave-woman] commits [a punishable-offense against her mistress, or . . .], or should commit any misdeed, either [the wife of the king or] the woman of [the palace whose slave]-woman committed the punishable-offense against her shall strike her 30 (times) with rods. [. . . If the slave-woman] who was beaten [. . .] commit[s] an(other) [punishable-off]ense against her mistress, [or . . . or] commits [another mi]sdeed, her mistress [shall brin]g [her before the king]; in front of the king, they shall impose [upon her] the punishment th[at he deci]des; [. . .] a second time he shall give her to her mistress. If the woman [of the palac]e [whose slave-woman] she beat in accordance with [the royal] de[cree . . . is excessive and her slave-woman] dies from the blows, or to [. . . the woman of the pala]ce who has killed her slave-woman [shall be punished] for her impudence; she b[ears] a punishable-offense of the king.

MAPD §19

šumma sinniltu ša ekall[*e* . . .]*si udīšunu izzazzu šaššu iltešunu laššu lu namutta* [. . .] *idukkušunu šumma lu mazziz pane lu sinnišat kinattēša ša tāmurušini* [. . .]*a ana bēliša katmat lu sinnilta lu a'īla āmerāna ana libbi utūne ikarrurušunu*

If a woman of the palac[e and a . . . (man)] are standing by themselves, no third person with them, whether [they are behaving] in a flirtatious manner [or in a serious manner?], they shall kill them. If a courtier or a woman of her equal status who sees her [does not report it? . . .]; she is veiled for her master; whether woman or man eyewitness, they shall throw them into the kiln.

MAPD §20

lu mazziz panūte ša šarre u lu širkū ša ṣābē ekalle ša ana ekalle errabūni balut ḫiāre [*an*]*a ekalle la errab šumma la marrur ša šanuttešu ana mazziz panutte utarrušu šumma lu rab ekalle ša libbi-āle lu nāgir ekalle lu rab zāriqē ša ḫūle lu asû ša bētānu u lu ša muḫḫi ekallāte ša šiddi māte gabbu mazziz pane la marrura ana ekalle ultēribu urkis ētamru ša qēpūte annûte iltēnâ*[90] *šēpēšunu ubattuqu*

Royal courtiers or dedicatees of the palace personnel who have access to the palace shall not enter the palace without an inspection; if he is not (properly) *checked*,[91] for a second time they shall turn him for becoming a courtier. If either the palace commander of the inner-city, or the palace herald, or the chief of the water-sprinklers of the processional residence, or the physician of the inner-quarters, or the administrator of all the palaces of the entire expanse of the country allows an *unchecked* courtier to enter into the palace, and he is later discovered, they shall amputate one foot of each of these officials.

MAPD §21

lu ša rēš šarranu lu mazziz panūte u lu širkū šumma sinniltu ša ekalle lu tazammur u lu ṣalta ištu meḫertiša gar'at u šūt izzaz iltanamme 100 *immaḫḫaṣ uzanšu inakkisu* [*šumm*]*a sinnišat ekalle naglabāša pattua kindabašše la kattumat ana ma*[*zziz*] *pane tartugum* [*mā . . . al*]*ka lašpurka u šūt iltuḫur ilteša idabbub* 100 [*immaḫḫ*]*aṣ āmerānšu* [*kuz*]*ippēšu ilaqqe u šua sāga qablīšu irakkusu šumma mazzi*[*z pane*] *ištu sinnišat ekalle* [*i*]*dabbub* 7 *ebrāte ana muḫḫiša la iqarrib . . . šumma zāriqū ina qabal ekalle šipra ana epāše u sinnišātu ša ekalle ina pī ḫūlišunu ana r*[*ab ekalle*] *iqabbiu ištu pī ḫūle upaṭ*[*ṭarši*]*na*

Either royal eunuchs or courtiers or dedicatees, if a woman of the palace either sings, or quarrels with her colleague, and he stands by and eavesdrops, he shall be struck 100 blows, they shall cut off one of his ears. [I]f a palace woman has bared her shoulders and is not covered with a *kindabašše*-garment, and she summons a courtier, [saying: ". . . come] here, may I give you an order!", and he delays speaking with her: [he shall be str]uck 100 blows. His eyewitness shall take his [clot]hing; and as for him, they shall tie a sackcloth around his waist. If a cou[rtier] wishes to speak with a palace woman, he shall not come near to her (more than) seven paces. . . . If the water-sprinklers have a task to perform within the palace and the women of the palace are at the entrance to their (masc.) processional residence, they shall report it to the [palace] co[mmander]; he shall cl[ear th]em (fem.) from the entrance to the processional residence.

MAPD §22

[. . .] *lu širku lu nuāru mā ṣābē ekalle* [. . .] *šumma ṣābē ekalle ištu ekal šarre ana* [. . .] *š*[*a rēš*] *šarrane mazziz panūte u širkē* [. . .] *ša akelē u šikerē ana ekalle* [. . .] *ša* [. . .]*ni la iptete* [. . .] *lu ummi* [*šarre l*]*u aššat šarre* [. . .] *upaṭṭar* [. . .] *lu ekurr*[*e . . .*] *usbat* [. . .] *ša rēš šarre* [. . .]

[. . .] either a dedicatee or a musician, saying, "The palace personnel [. . ".] If the palace personnel, from the royal palace to [. . .] the royal e[unuch]s, courtiers and dedicatees [. . .] who [bring?] food and beer to the palace [. . .] . . . he has not opened [. . .] either the king's mother or the king's wife [. . .] he shall clear [. . .] either the templ[e . . .] she is residing [. . .] the royal eunuch [. . .]

9 NBL (Neo-Babylonian Laws)

NBL §6

amēlu ša amēlutti ana kaspi iddinuma paqāru ina muḫḫi ibšûma abkati nādinānu kaspa kî pī u'ilti ina qaqqadišu ana māḫirānu inandin kî mārē tuldu ina ištēn ½ šiqil kaspa inandin

A man that sells a slave-woman, and a claim arises against (her), so she is taken away: the seller shall give to the buyer silver according to the transaction, in its capital (-amount); in case she bears children, for (each) one he shall give half a shekel of silver.

NBL §7

amēltu ša nēpešu lu takpirtu ina eqel amēli[92] *lu ina [elip]pi lu ina utūni lu ina mimma šumšu*[!93] *tukappiru iṣṣī ša [ina lib]bi tukappiru bilassu ištēn adi 3 ana bēl eqli tanandin šumma ina elippi ina utūni u mimma šumšu tukappiru miṭīti ša ina eqli taššakkanu ištēn adi 3 tanandin kî ina bāb [bīt] amēli [. . .] ṣabtatu taddâ[ku] dīnšu ul qati u ul šaṭir*

A woman that *performs*[94] a magical procedure or a purification rite upon a man's field, or upon [a boa]t, or upon a kiln, or upon anything whatsoever: the trees [amon]g which she performs (the ritual), she shall give to the field owner threefold its yield; if she performs (the ritual) upon a boat, upon a kiln or anything whatsoever: for the losses that she has imposed upon the field she shall give threefold; in case she is caught [performing the ritual] upon a man's [house] door: she shall be killed; its case is not complete and is not written (here).

NBL §8

amēlu ša mārassu ana mār amēli iddinuma abu mimma ina ṭuppišu ušēdûma ana mārišu iddinu u emu nudunnû ša mārtišu ušēdûma ṭuppī itti aḫāmeš išṭuru ṭuppašunu ul innû abi nušurrû ina mimma ša ana mārišu ina ṭuppi išṭuruma ana emišu ukallimu ul išakkan kīma abu aššassu šīmti ublu[?] *aššati arkīti ītaḫzuma mārē ittaldušu šalšu ina rēḫet nikkassīšu mārū arkīti ileqqû*

A man that gives his daughter to a(nother) man's son, and the (groom's) father assigns anything in his document and gives to his son; and the father-in-law assigns the *nudunnû* of his daughter, and they mutually write documents: they shall not alter their documents; the father shall not lay a reduction on anything that he wrote to his son in the document and showed to his father-in-law; as the father – his wife is carried by fate – marries a second[95] wife, and she bears him sons, the sons of the second (wife) shall take one-third of his property's remainder.

NBL §9

amēlu ša nudunnû ana mārtišu iqbūma lu ṭuppi isṭurušu u arki nikkassīšu imṭū akī nikkassīšu ša rēḫi nudunnû ana mārtišu inandin emu u ḫatanu aḫâmeš ul innû

A man that declares a *nudunnû* to his daughter, or writes it on a document, and afterwards his property decreases: he shall give to his daughter the *nudunnû* according to his property that remained; the father-in-law and the groom shall not mutually alter (the agreement).

NBL §10

amēlu ša nudunnû ana mārtišu iddinuma māra u mārta la tišû u šīmti ubluš nudunnāšu ana bīt abišu itâri

A man that gives a *nudunnû* to his daughter, and she has no son or daughter, and she is carried by fate: her *nudunnû* shall return to her father's house.

NBL §11

[*aššatu ša . . .*] *ana* [. . .] *šī*[*mti ubluš . . .*] *ana muḫḫi māri* [. . .] *nudunnāšu ana mutišu u ana mamma ša panīšu maḫru tanandin*

[A wife that . . .] to [. . .] [carried by] fa[te . . .] to a son [. . .] she shall give her *nudunnû* to her husband or to whomever she wishes.

NBL §12

aššatu ša nudunnāšu mussu ilqû māra u mārta la tišû u mussu šīmti ublu ina nikkassī ša mutišu nudunnû mala nudunnû innandinšu šumma mussu širiktu ištarakšu širikti ša mutišu itti nudunnêšu taleqqēma aplat šumma nudunnū la tiši dayānu nikkassī ša mutišu imma[*r*]*ma kî nikkassī ša mutišu mimma inandinšu*

A wife that her husband takes her *nudunnû*, has no son or daughter, and her husband is carried by fate: from the property of her husband a *nudunnû* – the whole *nudunnû* – shall be given to her; if her husband awards her a *širiktu*: she shall take the *širiktu* of her husband together with her *nudunnû*, and she shall be satisfied; if she has no *nudunnû*: a judge shall review the property of her husband, and shall give her anything according to the property of her husband.

NBL §13

amēlu aššata īḫuzma mārē ulissu arki amēlu šuāti šīmti ubilšuma amēltu šuāti ana bīt šanî erēbi panīšu iltakan nudunnā ša ultu bīt abišu tublu u mimma ša mussu išrukušu ileqqēma muti libbišu iḫḫassi adi ūmē balṭatu akalu itti aḫ[*āmeš*] *ina libbi ikk*[*alu*] *šumma ana mu*[*tišu*] *mārē it*[*taldu*] *arkišu mārū* [*arkî*] *u mārū maḫ*[*rî*] *nudun*[*nāšu*] *aḫāti* [. . .]

A man marries a wife, and she bears him sons, afterwards that man is carried by fate, and that woman decides to enter another's house: she shall take the *nudunnû* that she brought from her father's house, and anything that her husband awarded her, and a husband of her choice may marry her; as long as she is alive they shall jointly consume (it); if she b[ears] sons to [her] (second) hus[band], after her (death) the [latter] sons and form[er] sons shall have equal shares [in her] *nudun*[*nû*] [. . .]

NBL §15

amēlu ša aššata īḫuzuma mārē uldušuma aššassu šīmti ublu aššati šanīti īḫuzuma mārē uldušu arki abu ana šīmtu ittalku ina nikkassī ša bīt abi 2.TA *qātāti mārē maḫrīti u šalšu mārē arkīti ileqqû aḫḫātišunu ša ina bīt abi ašbāma* [. . .]

A man that marries a wife, and she bears him sons, and his wife is carried by fate; he marries a second wife, and she bears him sons; afterwards the father goes to (his) fate: of the property of the father's household the former sons shall take two-thirds, and the latter sons one-third; their sisters that reside in the father's house [. . .]

10 HL (Hittite Laws)

HL §1

[*ták-ku* LÚ-*an n*]*a-aš-ma* MUNUS-*an š*[*u-ul-la-a*]*n-na-*[*a*]*z ku-iš-ki ku-en-zi* [*a-pu-u-un ar-nu-z*]*i Ù* 4 SAG.DU *pa-a-i* LÚ-*na-ku* MUNUS-*na-ku* [*pár-na-aš-še-e-a*] *šu-wa-a-ez-zi*

[If] anyone kills [a man] or a woman in a [quarr]el: he shall [bring him] (for burial$^{?}$) and shall pay[96] four persons, whether male or female; he shall look [to his house for it.]

HL §2

[*ták-ku* ARAD-*an na-a*]*š-ma* GÉME-*an šu-ul-la-an-na-az ku-iš-ki ku-en-zi* ⸢*a-pu-u-un*⸣ *ar-nu-zi* [*Ù* 2 SAG.D]U *pa-a-*⸢*i*⸣ LÚ-*na-ku* MUNUS-*na-ku pár-na-aš-še-e-a šu-wa-a-ez-zi*

[If] anyone kills [a slave o]r slave-woman in a quarrel: he shall bring him (for burial$^{?}$) [and] shall pay [two perso]ns, whether male or female; he shall look to his house for it.

HL §3

[*ták-ku* LÚ-*a*]*n na-aš-ma* MUNUS-*an EL-LAM wa-al-aḫ-zi ku-iš-*[*k*]*i na-aš a-ki ke-eš-šar-ši-iš* [*wa-aš-t*]*a-i a-pu-u-un ar-nu-zi Ù* 2 SAG.DU *pa-a-i* [*pá*]*r-na-aš-še-e-a šu-wa-a-ez-zi*

[If] anyo[n]e strikes a free [man] or woman, and (s)he dies, (but) his hand [si]ns:[97] he shall bring him (for burial$^{?}$) and pay two persons; he shall look to his [ho]use for it.

HL §4

[*ták*]-*ku* ARAD-*an na-aš-ma* GÉME-*an ku-iš-ki wa-al-aḫ-zi na-aš a-ki QA-AS-SÚ wa-aš-ta-i* [*a*]-*pu-u-un ar-nu-zi Ù* 1 SAG.DU *pa-a-i pár-na-aš-še-e-a šu-wa-a-ez-zi*

[I]f anyone strikes a slave or slave-woman, and (s)he dies, (but) his hand sins:[98] he shall bring [h]im (for burial$^{?}$) and pay one person; he shall look to his house for it.

HL §5

⸢*ták*⸣-*ku* ^{LÚ}DAM.GÀR *ku-iš-ki ku-e-en-zi* 1 *ME* MA.NA KÙ.BABBAR *pa-a-i pár-na-aš-še-e-a šu-wa-i-ez-zi ták-ku I-NA* KUR ^{URU}*Lu-ú-i-ia na-aš-ma I-NA* KUR ^{URU}*Pa-la-a* 1 *ME* ⸢MA⸣.NA KÙ.BABBAR *pa-a-i a-aš-šu-uš-še-et-ta šar-ni-ik-zi na-aš-ma*[99] *I-NA* KUR ^{URU}*Ḫa-at-ti nu-uz-za ú-na-at-ta-al-la-an-pát ar-nu-uz-zi*

If anyone kills a merchant:[100] he shall pay 100 minas (=4,000 shekels)[101] of silver; he shall look to his [ho]use for it; if (it happens) in the land of Luwiya or in the land of Pala: he shall pay 100 minas (=4,000 shekels)[102] of silver, and he shall compensate (for) his goods; or (if it happens) in the land of Hatti: he himself shall (also) bring (for burial) that very merchant.

HL §6

ták-ku LU.U$_{19}$.LU-*aš* LÚ-*aš na-aš-ma* MUNUS-*za ta-ki-ia* URU-*ri a-ki ku-e-la-aš ar-ḫi a-ki* 1 *ME gi-pé-eš-šar* A.ŠÀ *kar-aš-ši-i-e-ez-zi na-an-za da-a-i*

If a person, man or woman is killed in another city: (the victim's heir) shall deduct 100 *gipeššar* from the field(-plot) of the person on whose property the person was killed, and take it for himself.

HL §8

⸢*ták*⸣-*ku* ARAD-*na-na na-aš-ma* GÉME-*an ku-iš-ki da-šu-wa-aḫ-ḫi na-aš-ma* ZU$_9$-*ŠU la-a-ki* 10 GÍN KÙ.BABBAR *pa-a-i pár-na-aš-še-e-a šu-wa-a-ez-zi*

If anyone blinds a slave or slave-woman, or knocks out his/her tooth: he shall pay ten shekels of silver; he shall look to his house for it.

HL §12

ták-ku ARAD-*na-an na-aš-ma* GÉME-*an QA-AS-SÚ na-aš-ma* GÌR-*ŠU ku-iš-ki tu-wa-ar-na-zi* 10 GÍN KÙ.BABBAR *pa-a-i pár-na-aš-še-e-a šu-wa-a-i-ez-zi*

If anyone breaks the arm or leg of a slave or slave-woman: he shall pay ten[103] shekels of silver; he shall look to his house for it.

HL §14

ták-ku ARAD-*an na-aš-ma* GÉME-*an* KIR$_{14}$-*še-et ku-iš-ki wa-a-ki* 3 GÍN KÙ.BABBAR *pa-a-i pár-na-aš-še-e-a šu-wa-a-i-ez-zi*

If anyone bites off the nose of a slave or slave-woman: he shall pay three shekels of silver; he shall look to his house for it.

HL §16

ták-ku ARAD-*an na-aš-ma* GÉME-*an* GEŠTU-*aš-ša-an ku-iš-ki iš-kal-la-a-ri* 3 GÍN KÙ.BABBAR *pa-a-i*

If anyone tears off the ear of a slave or slave-woman: he shall pay three shekels of silver.

HL §17

ták-ku MUNUS-*aš EL-LI šar-ḫu-wa-an-du-uš-šu-uš ku-iš-ki pé-eš-ši-ia-zi* [*ták-ku*] ⌜ITU.10.KAM 10⌝ GÍN KÙ.BABBAR *pa-a-i ták-ku* "-*uš*" ITU.5.KAM 5 GÍN K[Ù.BABBAR] ⌜*pa-a-i pár-na-aš-še-e*⌝*-a šu-wa-a-i-*[*ez*]*-zi*

If anyone causes a free woman to miscarry: [if] it is her tenth month, he shall pay ten shekels of silver; if it is her fifth month, he shall pay five shekels of s[ilver];[104] he shall look to his house for it.

HL §18

ták-ku GÉME-*aš šar-ḫu-wa-an-d*[*u-u*]*š-šu-uš ku-iš-ki pé-eš*[*-ši-i*]*a-zi* ⌜*ták-ku* ITU.10.KAM 5 GÍN⌝ KÙ.BABBAR *pa-a-i*

If anyone causes a slave-woman to miscarry: if it is her tenth month, he shall pay five shekels of silver.[105]

HL §19a

⌜*ták-ku* LÚ.U$_{19}$.LU-*an*⌝ LÚ-*na-ku* MUNUS-*na-ku* URU*Ḫa-at-tu-ša-az ku-iš*[*-ki*] LÚ URU*Lu-ú-i-ia-aš*![106] ⌜*ta-a-i*⌝*-ez-zi na-an A-NA* KUR URU*Ar-za-u-wa pé-e-ḫu-te-ez-zi* [*i*]*š-*⌜*ḫa-aš-ši*⌝*-ša-an ga-ne-eš-zi nu* ⌜É⌝*-er-še-et-pát ar-nu-zi*

If any Luwian man abducts a person, whether man or woman, from the land of Hatti, and leads him/her away to the land of Arzawa,[107] and (subsequently) his/her master recognizes him/her: he (=the abductor) shall bring his own house (as compensation?).

HL §24

⌜*ták-ku*⌝ ARAD-*aš na-aš-ma* GÉME-*aš ḫu-wa-a-i iš-ḫa-aš-ši-ša-*⌜*an ku-e*⌝*-el ḫa-aš-ši-i ú-e-mi-*⌜*ia*⌝*-zi* LÚ-*na-aš ku-uš-ša-an* ITU.1.KAM 12 GÍN KÙ.BABBAR *pa-a-i* MUNUS-*ša-*⌜*ma*⌝ *ku-ša-an* ITU.1.KAM 6 GÍN K[Ù.BABBAR] *pa-a-i*

If a slave or slave-woman runs away: the one by whose hearth his/her owner finds him/her shall pay 12 shekels of silver (as) a man's wage for one month, (or) he shall pay 6 shekels of s[ilver] (as) a woman's wage for one month.

HL §26a

ták-ku-za MUNUS-*za* LÚ-*an m*[*i-im-ma-i nu-uš-ši* LÚ-*aš* . . .] *pa-a-i Ù ŠA* NUMUNḪI.A-*aš ku-uš-ša-an* [MUNUS-*za da-a-i* A.ŠÀḪI.A] *Ù* DUMUMEŠ LÚ-*pát* [*da-a-i* . . .]

If a woman r[efuses][108] a man: [the man] shall give [to her . . .], and [the woman shall take] a wage for his/her seeds;[109] but the man [shall take the fields] and the children [. . .]

HL §26b

ták-ku-za LÚ-*ša* MUNUS-*an šu-ú-*[*iz-zi* . . .] *na-an ḫa-ap-ra-iz-zi w*[*a-a-ši-an ku-iš nu-uš-ši* 12 GÍN KÙ.BABBAR *pa-a-i*]

If a man divorc[es] a woman [. . .] he shall sell her; [he who] b[uys her shall pay him 12 shekels of silver].

HL §26c

ták-ku[*-za* LÚ-*ša* MUNUS-*an*] *šu-wa-a*[*-iz-zi na-an ḫa-ap-ra-iz-zi wa-a-ši-an*] *ku-iš* [*nu-uš-ši*] 12 GÍN KÙ.BABBAR *pa*[*-a-i*]

If [a man] divorc[es a woman: he shall sell her;] he who [buys her shall] p[ay him] 12 shekels of silver.

HL §27

ták-ku LÚ-*aš* DAM-*SÚ da-a-i* ˹*na-an*˺ *pár-na-aš-š*[*a*] *pé-e-ḫu-te-ez-zi i-wa-ru-uš-še-ta-az an-da pé-e-da-i ták-ku* MUNUS-*za a-*[*pí-ia a-ki*] LÚ-*na-aš a-aš-šu-še-et wa-ar-nu-an-zi i-wa-ru-še-ta-az* LÚ-*aš da-a-i ták-ku-aš at-ta-aš-ša-ša* É-*ri a-ki* ˹*Ú*˺ DUMU.NITA-*ši i-wa-ru-uš-še-et* LÚ-*aš na-at-ta* [*da-a-i*]

If a man takes his wife and leads her away to his house: he shall carry her *iwaru*[110] in (to his house); if the woman [dies] t[here], they shall burn the personal possessions of the man, and the man shall take her *iwaru*; if she dies in her father's house, and (has) her children, the man shall not [take] her *iwaru*.

HL §28a

ták-ku DUMU.MUNUS LÚ-*ni ta-ra-an-za ta-ma-i-ša-an pít-te-nu-uz-zi ku-uš-ša-*[*a*]*n pít-te-nu-uz-zi-ma nu ḫa-an-te-ez-zi-ia-aš* LÚ-*aš ku-it ku-*˹*it*˺ *p*[*é-eš-ta*] *ta-aš-še šar-ni-ik-zi at-ta-aš-ša an-na-aš Ú-UL šar-ni-in-ká*[*n-zi*]

If a daughter has been promised to a man, but another (man) runs off with her: as soon as he runs off with her, he shall compensate[111] the first man for whatever he g[ave]; the father and mother (of the woman) shall not compensate.[112]

HL §28b

ták-ku-wa-an at-ta-aš an-na-aš-ša ta-me-e-da-ni LÚ-*ni pí-an-z*[*i*] *nu at-ta-aš an-na-aš-ša šar-ni-in-kán-zi*

If her father and mother give her to another man: the father and mother shall compensate (the first man).

HL §28c

ták-ku at-ta-aš-ša an-na-aš mi-im-ma-i na-an-ši-kán tu-uḫ-ša-an-˹*ta*˺

If the father and mother refuse (to compensate the first man): they shall separate her from him.

HL §29

ták-ku DUMU.MUNUS-*aš* LÚ-*ni ḫa-me-in-kán-za nu-uš-ši ku-ú-ša-ta píd-da-iz-zi ap-pé-ez-zi-na-at at-ta-aš an-na-aš ḫu-ul-la-an-zi na-an-kán* LÚ-*ni túḫ-ša-an-zi ku-ú-ša-ta-ma* 2-*ŠU* ⸢*šar-ni-in*⸣*-kán-zi*

If a daughter has been betrothed to a man, and he brings the brideprice for her, but afterwards the father and mother quash it (=the agreement): they may separate her from the man, but they shall compensate (for) the brideprice double.

HL §30

ták-ku LÚ-*ša* DUMU.MUNUS *na-ú-i da-a-i na-an-za mi-im-ma-i ku-ú-ša-ta-ma ku-it píd-da-a-it na-aš-kán ša-me-en-zi*

But if the man has not yet taken the daughter (sexually), and he refuses her: he shall forfeit the brideprice which he has brought.

HL §31

ták-ku LÚ-*aš EL-LUM* GÉME-*aš-ša* ⸢*ši*⸣*-e-le-eš na-at an-da a-ra-an-zi na-an-za A-NA* DAM-*ŠU da-a-i nu-za* É-*er Ù* DUMU^{MEŠ} ⸢*i*⸣*-en-zi ap-pé-ez-zi-an-na-at-kánna-aš-šui-da-a-la-u-e-eš-ša-an-zina-aš-ma-at-kánḫar-pa-an-ta-ri nu-za* É-⸢*er*⸣ *ták-ša-an šar-ra-an-zi* DUMU^{MEŠ}-*az* LÚ-*aš da-a-i* 1 ⸢DUMU-*AM*⸣ MUNUS-*za da-a-i*

If a free man and a slave-woman are unmarried and come together, and he takes her as his wife, and they establish a household and children, but afterwards either they become estranged or are associated (with other spouses): they shall divide the household equally; the man shall take the children, (and) the woman shall take one child.

HL §32

ták-ku ARAD-*aš* MUNUS-*n*[*a-an da-a-i nu-uz-za* DUMU^{MEŠ} *i-en-zi ma-a-an* É-*ŠU-NU šar-ra-*

an-zi] *a-aš-šu-uš-še-me-*[*et ḫa-an-ti ḫa-an-ti š*]*ar-ra-an-zi m*[*e-e*]*k-*[*ku-uš* DUMU^{MEŠ} MUNUS-*za da-a-i*] *Ù* 1 DUMU-*AM* [ARAD-*aš*] *d*[*a-a-i*]

If a slave [takes (=marries)] a (free) woman, [and they have[113] children: when they divide their household], they shall [d]ivide the[ir] goods [equally; the free woman shall take] m[o]s[t] of [the children], and [the slave shall] t[ake] one child.

HL §33

ták-ku ARAD-*aš* GÉME-*an da-a-i nu-uz-za* [DUMU^{MEŠ} *i-en-z*]*i ma-a-an* É-*ŠU-NU šar*[*-ra-an-zi*] *a-aš-šu-uš-še-me-et ḫa-an-ti ḫ*[*a-an-ti*] *šar-r*[*a-a*]*n-zi me-ek-ku-uš* [DUMU^{MEŠ} GÉME-*aš da-a-i*] *Ù* 1 DUMU-*AM* ARAD-*aš da-a-i*

If a slave takes (=marries) a slave-woman, and [they have children]: when [they] divide their household, they shall divide their goods equ[al]ly; [the slave-woman shall take] most of [the children], and the slave shall take one child.

HL §34

ták-ku ARAD-*iš* ⸢*A-NA*⸣ MUNUS-*TIM* *ku*-⸢*ú*⸣-*ša-ta* ⸢*píd-da-a-iz-zi*⸣ *na-an-za A-NA* DAM-*ŠU* ⸢*da-a-i*⸣ *na-an-kán pa-ra-a Ú-UL ku*-⸢*iš-ki tar*⸣-*na-i*

If a slave brings a brideprice for a (free) woman and takes her as his wife: no one shall change her social status.[114]

HL §35

ták-ku MUNUS-*na-an EL-LE*-⸢*TAM* LÚSIPA⸣ [*da-a-i n*]*a-aš I-NA* MU.3.KAM GÉME-*re-e*[*z-zi*]

If a herdsman[115] [takes (=marries)] a free woman:[116] she will be enslaved for three years.

HL §36

ták-ku ARAD-*iš A-NA* DUMU.NITA *EL-LIM ku-ú-ša-ta píd-d*[*a-a-iz*]-⸢*zi*⸣ *na-an* LÚ*an*-⸢*ti-ia-an-ta*⸣-*an e-ep-zi na-an-kán pa-ra-a* [*Ú-U*]*L* ⸢*ku-iš-ki*⸣ *tar-na-i*

If a slave bri[ng]s brideprice for a free young man and acquires him as a live-in son-in-law: [n]o one shall change his social status.[117]

HL §37

ták-ku MUNUS-*na-an ku-iš-ki pít-ti-nu-uz-zi n*[*u-kán ša*]*r*-⸢*di*⸣-*i-eš a-ap-pa-an-an-da pa-a-a*[*n*]-*z*[*i*] *ták-ku* 3 LÚMEŠ *na-aš-ma* 2 LÚMEŠ *ak-kán-zi šar-ni-ik-zi-il* NU.GÁL *zi-ik-wa* UR.BAR.RA-*aš ki-iš-ta-at*

If anyone runs off with a woman, and a [group of su]pporters goes after them, if three men or two men are killed: there shall be no compensation, "You (sg.) have become a wolf!"

HL §38

ták-ku LÚ.U$_{19}$.LUMEŠ *ḫa-an-ne-eš-ni ap-pa-an-te-eš nu šar-ti/di-ia-aš ku-iš-ki pa-iz-zi ták-ku ḫa-an-ne-eš-na-aš iš-ḫa-a-aš le*-⸢*e*⸣-[*la*]-*ni-at-ta* [o]-x *šar-ti/di-an-n*[*a*] *wa-al-aḫ-z*[*i*] *na-aš a-ki šar-ni-ik-zi-il* [N]U.GÁL

If persons are engaged in a lawsuit, and any supporter goes to h[im],[118] if a litigant becomes en[r]aged [and he?] strike[s] the supporter, and he dies: there shall be [n]o compensation.

HL §43

ták-ku LÚ-*aš* GU_4-*ŠU* ÍD-*an zi-i-nu-uš-ki-iz-zi ta-ma-i-ša-an šu-wa-*[*a*]*-iz-zi nu* KUN GU_4 *e-ep-zi ta* ÍD-*an za-a-i nu BE-EL* GU_4 ÍD-*aš pé-e-da-i nu-za a-pu-un-pát da-an-zi*

If a man is crossing a river with his ox, another man pushes him and catches the tail of the ox, and crosses the river, but the river carries away the ox owner: they shall take that very person.[119]

HL §44a

ták-ku LÚ-*an pa-aḫ-ḫu-en-ni ku-iš-ki pé-eš-ši-ez-zi na-aš a-ki nu-uš-ši* EGIR-⸢*pa* DUMU.NITA⸣-*an pa-a-i*

If anyone makes a man fall into a fire, and he dies: (the killer) shall give a son in return for him.

HL §150

ták-ku LÚ-*eš ku-uš-ša-ni ti-i-e-ez-zi A-NA* ITU.1.KAM 1 GÍN.GÍN K[Ù.BABBAR *pa-a-i*] *ták-ku* MUNUS-*za ku-uš-ša-ni ti-i-e-ez-zi A-NA* ITU.1.KAM ½ GÍN.GÍN [KÙ.BABBAR *pa-a-i*]

If a man hires himself out for wages: (his employer) [shall pay] one shekel of s[ilver] for one month; if a woman hires herself out for wages: (her employer) [shall pay] half a shekel [of silver] for one month.

HL §158a

ták-ku LÚ-*aš* $BURU_{14}$-*i ku-uš-ša-ni-i ti-ia-zi še-e-pa-an iš-ḫi-an-za* ^{GIŠ}MAR.GÍD.DA${}^{ḪI.A}$ *e-ep-zi* É IN.NU.DA *iš-tap-pí* KISLAḪ-*an wa-ar-ši-ia-an-zi* ITU.3.KAM 30 *PA*.ŠE *ku-uš-ša-ni-iš-ši-it*

If a man hires himself out for wages in the harvest season, to bind sheaves, load on wagons, deposit in barns and clear the threshing floors: his wages for three months (shall be) 1,500 liters of barley.

HL §158b

ták-ku MUNUS-*za* $BURU_{14}$-*i ku-uš-ša-ni ti-ia-zi ŠA* ITU.3.KAM 12 *PA*.ŠE *ku-uš-ša-aš-še-et*

If a woman hires herself out for wages in the harvest season: her wages for three months (shall be) 600 liters of barley.

HL §171

ták-ku an-na-aš DUMU.NITA-*iš-ši* TUG-*SÚ e-di na-a-i nu-za-kán* DUMU-*ŠU pa-ra-a šu-wa-a-ez-zi ma-a-an* DUMU-*aš* EGIR-*pa an-da ú-iz-zi ta* ^{GIŠ}IG-*ŠU da-a-i ta e-di na-a-i* ^{GIŠ}*iš-ki-iš-ša-na-aš-ši-it* ^{GIŠ}*ḫu-u-up-pu-ul-li-iš-ši-it da-a-i ta e-di na-a-i tu-uš* EGIR-*pa da-a-i nu-za* DUMU-*ŠU* EGIR-*pa* DUMU-*ŠU i-ia-zi*

If a mother removes[120] her son's garment: she disinherits her son; when her son comes back in, (s)he takes her door(-bolt?) and removes it, (s)he takes her *iškiššana* and her *ḫūppulli* and removes them, and takes them back; she makes her son her son again.

HL §174

ták-ku LÚ.MEŠ *za-aḫ-ḫa-an-da ta* 1?-*aš a-ki* 1 SAG.DU *pa-a-i*

If men are hitting each other, and one of them dies: (the killer) shall give one slave.[121]

HL §175

ták-ku LÚSIPA.UDU *na-aš-ma* LÚAGRIG MUNUS-*an EL-LE-TAM da-a-i na-aš na-aš-šu I-NA* MU.2.KAM *na-aš-ma I-NA* MU.4.KAM GÉME-*e-eš-zi Ù* DUMUMEŠ-*ŠU iš-ḫu-na-a-an-zi iš-ḫu-uz-zi-ia-aš-ša Ú-UL ku-iš-ki e-ep-zi*

If a shepherd or a foreman takes (=marries) a free woman: she will be enslaved for either two or four years; and they shall degrade her children, but no one shall seize (their) belts.

HL §177

ták-ku LÚMUŠEN.DÙ-*an* [*a*]*n-na-nu-wa-an-ta-an ku-iš-ki wa-a-ši* 25 GÍN KÙ.BABBAR *pa-a-i ták-ku* LÚ-*an na-aš-ma* MUNUS-*an dam-pu-u-pí-in ku-iš-ki wa-a-ši* 20 GÍN KÙ.BABBAR *pa-a-i*

If anyone buys a [t]rained augur: he shall pay 25 shekels of silver; if anyone buys an unskilled man or woman: he shall pay 20 shekels of silver.

HL §187

ták-ku LÚ-*iš* GU_4-*aš kat-ta* [*wa-aš-t*]*a-i ḫu-u-ur-ki-il a-ki-aš* LUGAL-*an a-aš-ki ú-wa-da-an-zi ku-en-zi-ma-an* LUGAL-*uš ḫu-iš-n*[*u*]*-zi-i*[*a-an* LUGAL-*u*]*š* LUGAL-*i-ma-aš Ú-UL ti-ia-iz-zi*

If a man [si]ns with a cow: (it is) abomination; he shall be killed; they shall conduct (him) to the king's gate; the king may kill him, [the kin]g may spare [him], but he shall not approach the king.

HL §188

tá[*k-k*]*u* LÚ-*aš* UDU-*aš kat-ta w*[*a-aš-t*]*a-i ḫu-u-ur-ke-el a-ki-aš* [LUGAL-*aš a-aš-ki*] *ú-wa-da-an-zi ku-en-zi-ma-an* LUGAL-*uš ḫu-u-i*[*š-nu-zi-i*]*a-a*[*n* LUGAL-*u*]*š* LUGAL-*i-ma-aš Ú-UL ti-i-ez-zi*

If a man s[in]s with a sheep: (it is) abomination; he shall be killed; they shall conduct (him) [to the king's gate]; the king may kill him, [the kin]g may sp[are] h[im], but he shall not approach the king.

HL §189

ták-ku LÚ-*aš a-pé-e-el-pát an-na-ša-aš kat-ta wa-aš-ta-i ḫu-u-u[r-k]i-il ták-ku* LÚ-*aš* DUMU.MUNUS-*aš kat-ta wa-aš-ta-i* ˹*ḫu-*[*u*]*-ur-ki*˺*-il ták-ku* LÚ-[*aš*] DUMU.NITA-*aš kat-ta wa-aš-ta-i ḫu-u-ur-ki-il*

If a man sins with his own mother: (it is) abomi[na]tion; if a man sins with (his) daughter: (it is) abomination; if a man sins with (his) son: (it is) abomination.

HL §190

ták-ku LÚ-*aš an-na-wa-an-na-aš-ša-aš kat-ta wa-as-ta-i Ú-UL ḫa-ra-tar ták-ku ad-da-aš-še-ša ḫu-iš-wa-an-za ḫu-u-ur-ki-il*

If a man sins with his stepmother: (it is) no offense; but if his father is alive: (it is) abomination.

HL §191

ták-ku LÚ *EL-LUM a-ra-u-wa-an-ni-uš an-na-ne-ku-uš an-na-aš-ma-an-na ú-en-zi ka-a-aš ta-ki-ia ut-ne-e ka-a-aš-ša ta-ki-ia ut-ne-e-ia Ú-UL ḫa-ra-a-tar ták-ku ša-ni-ia pé-di nu ša-ak-ki ḫu-ur-ki-il*

If a free man lies with free biological sisters and their mother, this one in one land, and that one in another land: (it is) no offense; (but) if both (women) are in the (same) place, and he knows (about it): (it is) abomination.

HL §192[122]

Version 1:

ták-ku LÚ-*aš* MUNUS-*ni a-ki* [L]ÚḪA.LA-*ŠU* DAM-*SÚ da-a-i*

If a man dies to his woman: his partner shall take his wife.

Version 2:

ták-ku LÚ-*aš* DAM-*SÚ a-ki* A ‹LÚ›ḪA[(.LA-*ŠU* DAM-*SÚ da-a-i*)] *Ú-UL ha-ra-a-*[*tar*]

If a man dies (to) his wife: the son of his partner shall take his wife; (it is) no offen[se.]

Or alternatively:

ták-ku LÚ-*aš* DAM-*SÚ a-ki A-ḪA*[(*-ŠU* DAM-*SÚ da-a-i*)] *Ú-UL ha-ra-a-*[*tar*]

If a man dies (to) his wife: his brother shall take his wife; (it is) no offen[se.]

HL §193

ták-ku LÚ-*aš* MUNUS-*an ḫar-zi ta* LÚ-*eš a-ki* DAM-*SÚ* ŠE[Š-*Š*]*U da-a-i ta-an A-BU-ŠU da-a-i ma-a-an da-a-an A-BU-ŠU-ia a-ki* MUNUS-*na-an-na ku-in ḫar-ta* DUMU ŠEŠ-*ŠU da-a-i Ú-UL ha-ra-tar*

If a man has a woman, and the man dies: [h]is broth[er] shall take his wife, or his father shall take her; if his father also dies, his brother's son shall take the woman that he had; (it is) no offense.

HL §194

ták-ku LÚ *EL-LUM* GÉME$^{\text{ḪI.A}}$-*uš an-na-né-ku-uš an-na-aš-ma-an-na ú-en-zi Ú-UL ḫa-ra-tar ták-ku a-ra-u-wa-an-ni-in AT-ḪU-U-TIM še-eš-kán-zi Ú-UL ḫa-ra-tar ták-ku* GÉME-*aš na-aš-ma* ^{MUNUS}KAR.KID-*aš kat-ta ad-da-aš Ù* DUMU-*ŠU še-eš-kán-zi Ú-UL ḫa-ra-tar*

If a free man lies with slave-women (who are) biological sisters and their mother: (it is) no offense; if brothers repeatedly sleep with (the same) free woman: (it is) no offense; if a father and his son repeatedly sleep with (the same) slave-woman or prostitute: (it is) no offense.

HL §195

ták-ku LÚ-*aš MA-ḪAR* DAM ŠEŠ-*ŠU še-eš-ki-iz-zi* ŠEŠ-*ŠU-ma ḫu-u-iš-wa-an-za ḫu-u-ur-ki-il ták-ku* LÚ-*aš* ^{MUNUS}*a-ra-u-wa-an-ni-in ḫar-zi ta* DUMU.MUNUS-*ši-ia ša-li-ga ḫu-u-ur-ki-il ták-ku* DUMU.MUNUS-*SÀ ḫar-zi ta an-ni-iš-ši na-aš-ma* NIN-*iš-ši ša-li-i-ga ḫu-u-ur-ke-el*

If a man repeatedly sleeps with the wife of his brother, while his brother is alive: (it is) abomination; if a man has a free woman, and he penetrates her daughter: (it is) abomination; if he has her daughter, and he penetrates her mother or her sister: (it is) abomination.

HL §196

ták-ku ARAD^{MEŠ}-*ŠU* GÉME^{MEŠ}-*ŠU ḫu-u-*[*ur-ki-i*]*l i-ia-an-zi tu-uš a-ar-nu-wa-an-z*[*i*] ⸢*ku-u-un-na ta*⸣*-ki-ia* URU-*ri ku-u-un-na ta-ki-ia* [U]RU-*ri a-še-ša-an-zi ke-e-el* 1 UDU *ke-*⸢*e*⸣-[*e*]*l-la* 1 UDU *ka-aš-ša-aš ḫu-u-it-ti-ia-an-ta*

If (anyone's) slaves (and) slave-women perform abom[inatio]n: they will be moved; they will settle one in one city, and one in another [c]ity; a sheep will be substituted (=sacrificed) for this one, and a(nother) sheep for the other one.

HL §197

ták-ku LÚ-*aš* MUNUS-*an* ḪUR.SAG-*i e-ep-zi* LÚ-*na-aš wa-aš-túl na-aš a-ki ták-ku* É-*ri-ma e-ep-zi* MUNUS-*na-aš wa-aš-ta-iš* MUNUS-*za a-ki ták-ku-uš* LÚ-*iš ú-e-mi-ia-zi tu-uš ku-en-zi ḫa-ra-a-tar-še-et* NU.GÁL

If a man seizes (=rapes) a woman in the mountain: (it is) the man's offense, he shall be killed; but if he seizes (her) in the house: (it is) the woman's offense, the woman shall be killed; if the man (=husband) finds them and kills them: it is not his offense.

HL §198

ták-ku-uš A-NA KÁ É.[G]AL *ú-wa-te-ez-zi nu te-ez-zi* ˹DAM˺-*TI le-e a-ki nu* DAM-*SÚ ḫu-iš-nu-zi* [LÚ]*pu-pu-un-na ḫu-iš-n*[*u*]*-zi ta* SAG.DU-*SÚ wa-aš-ši-e-ez-zi ták-ku te-ez-zi 2-pát ak-kán-du ta ḫu-ur-ki-in ḫa-l*[*i*]*-en-zi ku-en-zi-uš* LUGAL-*uš ḫu-u-iš-nu-zi-ia-aš* LUGAL-*uš*

If he brings them to the p[a]lace gate and says, "My wife is not to be killed!", and spares his wife: he will (also) spare the lover, (and) he will veil her; (however,) if he says, "May the two of them be killed!", and they roll the wheel: the king may kill them, the king may spare them.

HL §199

ták-ku ŠAḪ<-*aš*> UR.GI$_7$-*aš kat-ta ku-iš-ki wa-aš-ta-i a-ki-aš A-NA* KÁ É.GAL-*LIM ú-wa-te-ez-zi ku-en-zi-uš* LUGAL-*uš ḫu-iš-nu-zi-ia-aš* L[UG]AL-*uš* LUGAL-*i-ma-aš Ú-UL ti-i-ez-zi ták-ku* GU$_4$-*uš* L[Ú-*ni*] *wa-at-ku-zi* GU$_4$-*uš a-ki* LÚ-*aš-ša Ú-UL* ˹*a*˺[-*ki*] 1 UDU LÚ-*na-aš ka-a-aš-ša-aš ḫu-u-it-ti-ia-a*[*n-ta*] *na-an-kán ku-na-an-zi ták-ku* ŠAḪ-*aš* LÚ-*ni wa-at-ku-z*[*i*] *Ú-UL ḫa-ra-a-tar*

If someone sins with a pig (or) a dog: he shall be killed; he shall be conducted to the palace gate; the king may kill them, the k[in]g may spare them, but he shall not approach the king; if a bull leaps [on] a m[an]: the bull shall be killed, and the man shall not be k[illed]; they substitu[te] one sheep instead of the man, and they shall kill it; if a pig leap[s] on a man: (it is) no offense.

HL §200a

ták-ku LÚ-*aš* ANŠE.KUR.RA-*i na-aš-ma* ANŠE.GÌR.NUN.NA *kat-ta wa-aš-ta-i Ú-UL ḫa-ra-tar* LUGAL-*i-ma-aš*![123] *Ú-UL ti-ez-zi* [LÚ]SANGA-*ša Ú-UL ki-i-ša ták-ku ar-nu-wa-la-an ku-iš-ki kat-ta še-eš-ki-iz-zi an-na-aš-ša-an n*[*e-*]*k*[*a-aš*]*-š*[*a-an-n*]*a ú-en-zi Ú-UL ḫa-ra-tar*

If a man sins with a horse or a mule: (it is) no offense; but he shall not approach the king, and shall not become a priest; if someone repeatedly sleeps with a deportee-woman, (and also) lies with her mother and h[er] si[s]te[r]: (it is) no offense.

11 Hittite instructions

CTH 252 13–15

A-NA LÚ^{MEŠ} É.NA$_4$-*ia-kán AŠ-ŠUM* É.GI$_4$.A-*TÌ an-da-an pé-eš-kán-du pa-ra-a-ma-kán* DUMU.NITA DUMU.MUNUS *AŠ-ŠUM* É.GI$_4$.A-*TÌ* ^{LÚ}*an-da-i-ia-an-da-an-ni-ia le-e ku-iš-ki pa-a-i*

Let them give (young women) in as brides to the men of the royal mausoleum, but no one shall give out (from the royal mausoleum) a young man or girl as bride or a son-in-law.

CTH 258.1 §5’ 3–9

ma-a-an e-eš-ḫa-na-aš-ša ku-⸤iš⸥-ki šar-ni-ik-zi-il pí-ia-an ḫar-zi nu-za-ta SAG.DU-*ZU wa-aš-ta na-aš-šu* A.ŠÀ-*LA*$_{12}$ *na-aš-ma* LÚ.U$_{19}$.LU *na-aš-ta pa-ra-a Ú-UL ku-iš-ki tar-na-i ma-a-na-aš-za QA-DU* DAM^{MEŠ}-*ŠU* DUMU^{MEŠ}-*ŠU da-a-an ḫar-zi na-an-ši-iš-ta pa-ra-a ⸤tar⸥-na-i*

If someone has paid blood-compensation, and redeemed himself, whether (in the form of) a field or people, no one will turn him in. If he (=the victim’s representative) has taken them[124] together with his (=the killer’s) wives (and) his sons, then he will hand them over to him (=the killer).

CTH 261.I §37’ 9–14

nam-ma a-ú-ri-ia-aš EN-*aš* ^{LÚ}MAŠKIM.URU$^{\text{KI!}}$[125] $^{\text{LÚ.MEŠ}}$ŠU.GI *DI-NA-˹TÌ˺* SIG$_5$-*in ḫa-aš-ši-kán-du nu-⸤uš-ša⸥-an kat-ta ar-nu-uš-kán-du ka-ru-ú-li-ia-az-⸤ia ma⸥-aḫ-ḫa-an* KUR.KUR-*kán an-da ḫu-ur-ki-la-aš iš-ḫi-ú-ul i-ia-an ku-e-da-ni-aš-kán* URU-*ri ⸤ku⸥-aš-ke-er na-aš-kán ku-wa-aš-kán-du ku-e-da-ni-ma-aš-kán* URU-*ri ar-ḫa pár-ḫi-iš-ke-er na-aš-kán ar-ḫa pár-ḫi-iš-kán-du nam-ma-za* URU-*aš* EGIR-*an-da wa-ar-⸤ap-du⸥*

Further, the provincial post commander, the magistrate (and) the elders shall judge legal cases properly, and conclude them. And as was done before in the provinces concerning cases of (sexual) abomination, in a town where they used to execute, may they execute, and in a town where they used to banish, may they banish. Further, may the town(sfolk) bathe thereafter.

CTH 261.I §40’ 29–32

ku-e-da-ni-ma-aš-ša-an URU-*ri* EGIR-*pa a-ar-ti nu* LÚ^{MEŠ} URU-*LÌ ḫu-u-ma-an-du-uš pa-ra-a ḫal-za-a-i nu ku-e-da-ni di-na*$_{7}$ *e-eš-zi na-at-ši ḫa-an-ni na-an-kán aš-nu-ut* ARAD.LÚ GÉME.LÚ *wa-an-nu-mi-ia-aš* MUNUS-*ni ma-a-an* DI-*ŠU-NU e-eš-zi nu-uš-ma-ša-at ḫa-an-ni na-aš-kán aš-nu-ut*

In any town you return to, call out all the townsfolk, and any existing legal case, judge it for him and conclude it. If a legal case exists for a slave, slave-woman or a lone woman, judge it for them and conclude it.

CTH 264 §10’ ii 73”–iii 2

an-da-ma-za šu-me-eš ku-i-e-eš LÚ^{MEŠ} É DINGIR-*LÌ nu-za ḫa-li-i*[*a-aš*] *ud-da-ni-i me-ek-ki pa-aḫ-ḫa-aš-ša-nu-wa-an-te-eš e-eš-tén nu ne-ku-uz me-e-ḫu-u-ni ḫu-u-da-a-ak* GAM *pa-it-tén nu e-ez-za-tén e-ku-ut-tén ma-a-an-na* MUNUS-*aš ut-tar ku-e-da-ni-i*[*k-ki* . . .]x-⸤*zi*⸥ *na-aš-za* MUNUS-*ni-i* GAM-*an še-eš-du* [*na*]*m-ma-aš-ta ku-it-ma-an* x[. . . *wa-ar-ap*]-⸢*du*⸣ [*n*]*a-aš I-NA* É DINGIR-*LÌ še-e-šu-u-an-zi* ⸢*ḫu-u*⸣-[*da-a-ak š*]*a-ra-a ú-ed-du*

Additionally, you who are the personnel of the temple, be greatly attentive to the matter [of] the (night)watch. At nightfall, you shall promptly go down, and you shall eat and drink. And if anyo[ne . . .] the matter of a woman, may him sleep with the woman. [Th]en, while [. . .], [may he bath]e, and may he pro[mptly] come [u]p to sleep in the temple.

CTH 264 §14’ iii 68–83

ma-a-an-na-za MUNUS-*i ku-iš* GAM-*an še-eš-zi nu-kán ma-aḫ-ḫa-an* DINGIR^{MEŠ}-*aš* ⸤*ša-ak*⸥*-la-in aš-ša-nu-zi* DINGIR-*LÌ-ni a-da-an-na a-ku-wa-an-na pa-a-i na-aš* ⸤*IT*⸥-*TI* MUNUS-*TI QA-TAM-MA pa-id-du* ⸤*nam-ma*⸥ [. . .]-⸤*pát*⸥ *na-aš-ta ku-it-ma-‹an›* ^{d}UTU-*uš ša-ra-a nu-za* ⸤*ḫu-u-da*⸥-*a-*⸤*ak wa-ar*⸥-[*ap*]-⸤*du*⸥ *na-aš-kán lu-uk-kat-ti* DINGIR^{MEŠ}-*aš a-da-an-na-aš me-e-ḫu-u-ni ḫu-u-da-a-ak a-ru ma-a-an-ma-aš kar-aš-ta-ri-ma na-at-ši wa-aš-túl ma-a-an-ma-za IT-TI* MUNUS-*TI ku-iš še-eš-zi* [*na-a*]*n-kán* ⸢*MAḪ*⸣-*RI-ŠU* ^{LÚ}GAL-*šu* EGIR-*an ta-ma-aš-zi nu me-ma-ú-pát* [*m*]*a-a-*[*a*]*n a-pa-a-aš-ma me-mi-ia-u-an-zi UL ma-az-za-az-zi* ⸢*nu*⸣ ^{LÚ}*a-ri-iš-ši me-ma-a-ú nu-za wa-ar-ap-tu*$_{4}$*-pát* “*ma-a-an*” *ma-a-an še-ek-kán-ti-it-ma* ZI-*it pa-ra-a da-a-i wa-ar-ap-zi-ma-za na-a-ú-i na-aš* DINGIR^{MEŠ}-*aš* ^{NINDA}*ḫarši* ⸤^{DUG}*iš*⸥*-pa-an-tu-uz-zi ma-ni-in-ku-wa-an ša-ak-nu-an-za ša-a-li-ka*$_{4}$ *na-aš-ma-an* ^{LÚ}*a-ra-aš-ši-iš ša-ak-ki na-aš-ták-kán u-wa-it-ta na-an ša-an-na-a-i* EGIR-*zi-an-ma-at iš-du-wa-a-ri nu-uš-ma-ša-at* SAG.DU-*aš* ÚŠ-*tar 2-uš-ša-at ak-kán-d*[*u*]

When someone (intends) to sleep with a woman, once he conducts the rite of the gods, gives the deity to eat (and) to drink, (then) may he thus go with the woman. Further [. . .] and while the sun rises, may he promptly bath[e], and in the morning, by the god’s eating-time, may he promptly arrive. But if he fails, then he commits an offense. But if someone sleeps with a woman, but his superior, his supervisor, presses[126] [h]im, he must tell. But [i]f he dare not tell (his superiors), then he should tell his comrade, and he should definitely bathe. But if he knowingly postpones/omits (it), does not yet bathe, and he, while unclean, approaches the bread-loaf (and) libation vessel of the gods, or his comrade knows, and you feel sorry for him,[127] and he conceals him, but it later becomes known, it (demands) capital punishment for them: may they both be killed!

CTH 265 §7” 17’–19’

ku-iš pa-ap-ri-iš-zi-ma na-an-za-an LUGAL-*uš Ú-UL* ⌞*i*⌟*-la-a-li-ia-mi QA-DU*$_4$ DAM-*ŠU-ši* DUMU^{MEŠ}-*ŠU* Ḫ[U]L-*lu ḫi-in-kán pé-e-an-*⌞*zi*⌟

he who is found guilty, I, the king, will not want him. To him, together with his wife (and) his sons, (the gods) will assign an e[v]il death.

CTH 265 §10” 9’–13’, §12” 18’–20’

an-da-ma-za šu-me-eš ku-i-e-eš $^{\text{LÚ.MEŠ}}$AŠGAB *ŠA* É ^{LÚ}*tar-ši-pa-a-li-ia-aš ŠA* É ^{LÚ}*tup-pa-a-aš Ù* ^{LÚ}UGULA 10 ^{LÚ}*tar-ši-pa-a-la-aš* LUGAL-*wa-aš* ^{GIŠ}GIGIR$^{\text{ḪI.A}}$ *ti-ia-u-wa-aš ku-i-e-eš an-ni-eš-kat-te-e-ni nu* KUŠ.GU$_4$ KUŠ.MÁŠ *ŠA* É ^{LÚ}MUḪALDIM *ta-aš-kat-tén ta-ma-a-i-ma le-e da-at-te-ni . . . ták-ku ša-a-na-at-te-e-ni-ma ap-pé-ez-zi-ia-an-ma-at iš-tu-wa-a-ri nu-uš-ma-aš QA-DU*$_4$ DAM^{MEŠ}-*KU-NU* DUMU^{MEŠ}-*KU-NU i-da-a-lu ḫi-in-kán pí-ia-an-zi*

Additionally, you who are the leather workers of the coachmen-institution, of the warehouse and the overseer of ten coachmen, (you) who prepare the king’s standing-chariot: you shall always take from the kitchen cow-hide (and) ram-hide; but you shall not take a different (hide). . . . But if you conceal (it), and it later becomes known, to you, together with your wives (and) your sons, (the gods) will assign an evil death.

CTH 265 §§16”–17” 1’–7’

[. . .]x-⸢*ša*⸣ *ma-a-an* ^{LÚ}MUḪALDIM [. . . *ḫu-u-m*]*a-an-du-uš* [. . . *šu*]*-me-e-ša* EGIR-*pa* [. . .] [. . . *pa-a*]*p-re-eš-zi-ma* [. . . *nu-uš-š*]*i QA-DU* DAM-*ŠÚ* DUMU^{MEŠ}-*ŠÚ* [ḪUL-*lu* ÚŠ-*an pí-ia-an-zi*]

[. . .] If the chef [. . . a]ll [. . .] and [y]ou again/back [. . .] but he will be [im] pure/[gu]ilty [. . . To h]im, together with his wife (and) his sons, [(the gods) will assign an evil death.]

12 Biblical provisions

Exod. 21:1–11, 15, 17, 20–32

שמות פרק כא

א וְאֵלֶּה, הַמִּשְׁפָּטִים, אֲשֶׁר תָּשִׂים, לִפְנֵיהֶם. ב כִּי תִקְנֶה עֶבֶד עִבְרִי, שֵׁשׁ שָׁנִים יַעֲבֹד; וּבַשְּׁבִעִת--
יֵצֵא לַחָפְשִׁי, חִנָּם ג אִם-בְּגַפּוֹ יָבֹא, בְּגַפּוֹ יֵצֵא; אִם-בַּעַל אִשָּׁה הוּא, וְיָצְאָה אִשְׁתּוֹ עִמּוֹ. ד אִם-אֲדֹנָיו
יִתֶּן-לוֹ אִשָּׁה, וְיָלְדָה-לוֹ בָנִים אוֹ בָנוֹת--הָאִשָּׁה וִילָדֶיהָ, תִּהְיֶה לַאדֹנֶיהָ, וְהוּא, יֵצֵא בְגַפּוֹ. ה וְאִם-
אָמֹר יֹאמַר, הָעֶבֶד, אָהַבְתִּי אֶת-אֲדֹנִי, אֶת-אִשְׁתִּי וְאֶת-בָּנָי; לֹא אֵצֵא, חָפְשִׁי. ו וְהִגִּישׁוֹ אֲדֹנָיו,
אֶל-הָאֱלֹהִים, וְהִגִּישׁוֹ אֶל-הַדֶּלֶת, אוֹ אֶל-הַמְּזוּזָה; וְרָצַע אֲדֹנָיו אֶת-אָזְנוֹ בַּמַּרְצֵעַ, וַעֲבָדוֹ לְעֹלָם. ז
וְכִי-יִמְכֹּר אִישׁ אֶת-בִּתּוֹ, לְאָמָה--לֹא תֵצֵא, כְּצֵאת הָעֲבָדִים. ח אִם-רָעָה בְּעֵינֵי אֲדֹנֶיהָ, אֲשֶׁר-לא
(לוֹ) יְעָדָהּ--וְהֶפְדָּהּ: לְעַם נָכְרִי לֹא-יִמְשֹׁל לְמָכְרָהּ, בְּבִגְדוֹ-בָהּ. ט וְאִם-לִבְנוֹ, יִיעָדֶנָּה--כְּמִשְׁפַּט
הַבָּנוֹת, יַעֲשֶׂה-לָּהּ. י אִם-אַחֶרֶת, יִקַּח-לוֹ--שְׁאֵרָהּ כְּסוּתָהּ וְעֹנָתָהּ, לֹא יִגְרָע. יא וְאִם-שְׁלָשׁ-אֵלֶּה--
לֹא יַעֲשֶׂה, לָהּ: וְיָצְאָה חִנָּם, אֵין כָּסֶף.

טו וּמַכֵּה אָבִיו וְאִמּוֹ, מוֹת יוּמָת.

יז וּמְקַלֵּל אָבִיו וְאִמּוֹ, מוֹת יוּמָת.

כ וְכִי-יַכֶּה אִישׁ אֶת-עַבְדּוֹ אוֹ אֶת-אֲמָתוֹ, בַּשֵּׁבֶט, וּמֵת, תַּחַת יָדוֹ--נָקֹם, יִנָּקֵם. כא אַךְ אִם-יוֹם אוֹ יוֹמַיִם,
יַעֲמֹד--לֹא יֻקַּם, כִּי כַסְפּוֹ הוּא.

כב וְכִי-יִנָּצוּ אֲנָשִׁים, וְנָגְפוּ אִשָּׁה הָרָה וְיָצְאוּ יְלָדֶיהָ, וְלֹא יִהְיֶה, אָסוֹן--עָנוֹשׁ יֵעָנֵשׁ, כַּאֲשֶׁר יָשִׁית עָלָיו
בַּעַל הָאִשָּׁה, וְנָתַן, בִּפְלִלִים. כג וְאִם-אָסוֹן, יִהְיֶה--וְנָתַתָּה נֶפֶשׁ, תַּחַת נָפֶשׁ. כד עַיִן תַּחַת עַיִן, שֵׁן תַּחַת שֵׁן,
יָד תַּחַת יָד, רֶגֶל תַּחַת רָגֶל. כה כְּוִיָּה תַּחַת כְּוִיָּה, פֶּצַע תַּחַת פָּצַע, חַבּוּרָה, תַּחַת חַבּוּרָה.

כו וְכִי-יַכֶּה אִישׁ אֶת-עֵין עַבְדּוֹ, אוֹ-אֶת-עֵין אֲמָתוֹ--וְשִׁחֲתָהּ: לַחָפְשִׁי יְשַׁלְּחֶנּוּ, תַּחַת עֵינוֹ. כז וְאִם-שֵׁן
עַבְדּוֹ אוֹ-שֵׁן אֲמָתוֹ, יַפִּיל--לַחָפְשִׁי יְשַׁלְּחֶנּוּ, תַּחַת שִׁנּוֹ.

כח וְכִי-יִגַּח שׁוֹר אֶת-אִישׁ אוֹ אֶת-אִשָּׁה, וָמֵת--סָקוֹל יִסָּקֵל הַשּׁוֹר, וְלֹא יֵאָכֵל אֶת-בְּשָׂרוֹ, וּבַעַל הַשּׁוֹר,
נָקִי. כט וְאִם שׁוֹר נַגָּח הוּא מִתְּמֹל שִׁלְשֹׁם, וְהוּעַד בִּבְעָלָיו וְלֹא יִשְׁמְרֶנּוּ, וְהֵמִית אִישׁ, אוֹ אִשָּׁה--הַשּׁוֹר,
יִסָּקֵל, וְגַם-בְּעָלָיו, יוּמָת. ל אִם-כֹּפֶר, יוּשַׁת עָלָיו--וְנָתַן פִּדְיֹן נַפְשׁוֹ, כְּכֹל אֲשֶׁר-יוּשַׁת עָלָיו. לא אוֹ-בֵן
יִגָּח, אוֹ-בַת יִגָּח--כַּמִּשְׁפָּט הַזֶּה, יֵעָשֶׂה לּוֹ. לב אִם-עֶבֶד יִגַּח הַשּׁוֹר, אוֹ אָמָה--כֶּסֶף שְׁלֹשִׁים שְׁקָלִים, יִתֵּן
לַאדֹנָיו, וְהַשּׁוֹר, יִסָּקֵל.

1 These are the laws you are to set before them:
2 If you buy a Hebrew slave, he is to serve you for six years. But in the seventh year, he shall go free, without paying anything. 3 If he comes alone, he is to go free alone; but if he has a wife when he comes, she is to go with him. 4 If his master gives him a wife and she bears him sons or daughters, the woman and her children shall belong to her master, and only the man shall go free.

[5] But if the slave declares, "I love my master and my wife and children and do not want to go free", [6] then his master must take him before God. He shall take him to the door or the doorpost and pierce his ear with an awl. Then he will be his slave for life.

[7] If a man sells his daughter as a slave, she is not to go free as male slaves do. [8] If she does not please the master who has selected her for himself, he must let her be redeemed. He has no right to sell her to foreigners, because he has broken faith with her. [9] If he selects her for his son, he must grant her the rights of a daughter. [10] If he marries another woman, he must not deprive the first one of her food, clothing and marital rights. [11] If he does not provide her with these three things, she is to go free, without any payment of money.

[15] Anyone who beats their father or mother is to be put to death.

[17] Anyone who curses their father or mother is to be put to death.

[20] Anyone who beats their male or female slave with a rod must be punished if the slave dies as a direct result, [21] but they are not to be punished if the slave recovers after a day or two, since the slave is their property.

[22] If people are fighting and hit a pregnant woman so that her offspring are delivered prematurely but there is no disaster, the offender must be fined whatever the woman's husband demands and an assessment (of the judges?). [23] But if there is a disaster, you are to take life for life, [24] eye for eye, tooth for tooth, hand for hand, foot for foot, [25] burn for burn, wound for wound, bruise for bruise.

[26] An owner who beats a male or female slave in the eye and destroys it must let the slave go free to compensate for the eye. [27] And an owner who knocks out the tooth of a male or female slave must let the slave go free to compensate for the tooth.

[28] If a bull gores a man or woman to death, the bull is to be stoned to death, and its meat must not be eaten. But the owner of the bull will not be held responsible. [29] If, however, the bull is a known gorer and the owner has been warned but has not kept it penned up and it kills a man or woman, the bull is to be stoned and its owner also is to be put to death. [30] However, if payment is demanded, the owner may redeem his life by the payment of whatever is demanded. [31] This law also applies if the bull gores a son or daughter. [32] If the bull gores a male or female slave, the owner must pay 30 shekels of silver to the master of the slave, and the bull is to be stoned to death.

Exod. 22:15–18, 21–23

שמות פרק כב

טו וְכִי-יְפַתֶּה אִישׁ, בְּתוּלָה אֲשֶׁר לֹא-אֹרָשָׂה--וְשָׁכַב עִמָּהּ: מָהֹר יִמְהָרֶנָּה לּוֹ, לְאִשָּׁה. טז אִם-מָאֵן יְמָאֵן
אָבִיהָ, לְתִתָּהּ לוֹ--כֶּסֶף יִשְׁקֹל, כְּמֹהַר הַבְּתוּלֹת.
יז מְכַשֵּׁפָה, לֹא תְחַיֶּה. יח כָּל-שֹׁכֵב עִם-בְּהֵמָה, מוֹת יוּמָת.
כא כָּל-אַלְמָנָה וְיָתוֹם, לֹא תְעַנּוּן. כב אִם-עַנֵּה תְעַנֶּה, אֹתוֹ--כִּי אִם-צָעֹק יִצְעַק אֵלַי, שָׁמֹעַ אֶשְׁמַע צַעֲקָתוֹ.
כג וְחָרָה אַפִּי, וְהָרַגְתִּי אֶתְכֶם בֶּחָרֶב; וְהָיוּ נְשֵׁיכֶם אַלְמָנוֹת, וּבְנֵיכֶם יְתֹמִים.

[15] If a man seduces a virgin who is not betrothed and lies with her, he must pay the
brideprice, and she shall be his wife. [16] If her father utterly refuses to give her to
him, he must still pay the brideprice for virgins.
[17] Do not allow a sorceress to live.
[18] Anyone who has sexual relations with an animal is to be put to death.
[21] Do not take advantage of the widow or the orphan. [22] If you do and they cry out
to me, I will certainly hear their cry. [23] My anger will be aroused, and I will kill
you with the sword; your wives will become widows and your children orphans.

Lev. 18:6–20, 22–23

ויקרא פרק יח

ו אִישׁ אִישׁ אֶל-כָּל-שְׁאֵר בְּשָׂרוֹ, לֹא תִקְרְבוּ לְגַלּוֹת עֶרְוָה: אֲנִי, יְהוָה.
ז עֶרְוַת אָבִיךָ וְעֶרְוַת אִמְּךָ, לֹא תְגַלֵּה: אִמְּךָ הִוא, לֹא תְגַלֶּה עֶרְוָתָהּ.
ח עֶרְוַת אֵשֶׁת-אָבִיךָ, לֹא תְגַלֵּה: עֶרְוַת אָבִיךָ, הִוא.
ט עֶרְוַת אֲחוֹתְךָ בַת-אָבִיךָ, אוֹ בַת-אִמֶּךָ, מוֹלֶדֶת בַּיִת, אוֹ מוֹלֶדֶת חוּץ--לֹא תְגַלֶּה, עֶרְוָתָן.
י עֶרְוַת בַּת-בִּנְךָ אוֹ בַת-בִּתְּךָ, לֹא תְגַלֶּה עֶרְוָתָן: כִּי עֶרְוָתְךָ, הֵנָּה.
יא עֶרְוַת בַּת-אֵשֶׁת אָבִיךָ מוֹלֶדֶת אָבִיךָ, אֲחוֹתְךָ הִוא--לֹא תְגַלֶּה, עֶרְוָתָהּ.
יב עֶרְוַת אֲחוֹת-אָבִיךָ, לֹא תְגַלֵּה: שְׁאֵר אָבִיךָ, הִוא.
יג עֶרְוַת אֲחוֹת-אִמְּךָ, לֹא תְגַלֵּה: כִּי-שְׁאֵר אִמְּךָ, הִוא.
יד עֶרְוַת אֲחִי-אָבִיךָ, לֹא תְגַלֵּה: אֶל-אִשְׁתּוֹ לֹא תִקְרָב, דֹּדָתְךָ הִוא.
טו עֶרְוַת כַּלָּתְךָ, לֹא תְגַלֵּה: אֵשֶׁת בִּנְךָ הִוא, לֹא תְגַלֶּה עֶרְוָתָהּ.
טז עֶרְוַת אֵשֶׁת-אָחִיךָ, לֹא תְגַלֵּה: עֶרְוַת אָחִיךָ, הִוא.
יז עֶרְוַת אִשָּׁה וּבִתָּהּ, לֹא תְגַלֵּה: אֶת-בַּת-בְּנָהּ וְאֶת-בַּת-בִּתָּהּ, לֹא תִקַּח לְגַלּוֹת עֶרְוָתָהּ--שַׁאֲרָה הֵנָּה, זִמָּה
הִוא. יח וְאִשָּׁה אֶל-אֲחֹתָהּ, לֹא תִקָּח: לִצְרֹר, לְגַלּוֹת עֶרְוָתָהּ עָלֶיהָ—בְּחַיֶּיהָ. יט וְאֶל-אִשָּׁה, בְּנִדַּת טֻמְאָתָהּ-
-לֹא תִקְרַב, לְגַלּוֹת עֶרְוָתָהּ. כ וְאֶל-אֵשֶׁת, עֲמִיתְךָ--לֹא-תִתֵּן שְׁכָבְתְּךָ, לְזָרַע: לְטָמְאָה-בָהּ.
כב וְאֶת-זָכָר--לֹא תִשְׁכַּב, מִשְׁכְּבֵי אִשָּׁה: תּוֹעֵבָה, הִוא. כג וּבְכָל-בְּהֵמָה לֹא-תִתֵּן שְׁכָבְתְּךָ, לְטָמְאָה-בָהּ;
וְאִשָּׁה, לֹא-תַעֲמֹד לִפְנֵי בְהֵמָה לְרִבְעָהּ--תֶּבֶל הוּא.

[6] No one is to approach any close relative sexually. I am the Lord.
[7] Do not approach sexually your father or your mother. She is your mother; do not approach her sexually.
[8] Do not approach sexually your father's wife; that is your father's sexuality.
[9] Do not approach sexually your sister, either your father's daughter or your mother's daughter, whether she was born in the same home or elsewhere.
[10] Do not approach sexually your son's daughter or your daughter's daughter; for that is your sexuality.
[11] Do not approach sexually the daughter of your father's wife, born to your father; she is your sister.
[12] Do not approach sexually your father's sister; she is your father's close relative.
[13] Do not approach sexually your mother's sister; for she is your mother's close relative.
[14] Do not approach the sexuality of your father's brother by approaching sexually his wife; she is your aunt.

[15] Do not approach sexually your daughter-in-law. She is your son's wife; do not approach her sexually.
[16] Do not approach sexually your brother's wife; that is the sexuality of your brother.
[17] Do not approach sexually both a woman and her daughter. Do not approach sexually either her son's daughter or her daughter's daughter; they are her close relatives. That is abhorrence.
[18] Do not take your wife's sister as a rival wife and approach her sexually while your wife is living.
[19] Do not approach sexually a woman during the uncleanness of her monthly period.
[20] Do not lie with your neighbor's wife and defile yourself with her.
[22] Do not lie with a man as the lying of a woman; that is abomination.
[23] Do not lie with any animal and defile yourself with it. A woman must not present herself to an animal to have sexual relations with it; that is a perversion.

Lev. 19:20–22

ויקרא פרק יט

כ וְאִישׁ כִּי-יִשְׁכַּב אֶת-אִשָּׁה שִׁכְבַת-זֶרַע, וְהִוא שִׁפְחָה נֶחֱרֶפֶת לְאִישׁ, וְהָפְדֵּה לֹא נִפְדָּתָה, אוֹ חֻפְשָׁה לֹא
נִתַּן-לָהּ--בִּקֹּרֶת תִּהְיֶה לֹא יוּמְתוּ, כִּי-לֹא חֻפָּשָׁה. כא וְהֵבִיא אֶת-אֲשָׁמוֹ לַיהוָה, אֶל-פֶּתַח אֹהֶל מוֹעֵד--אֵיל,
אָשָׁם. כב וְכִפֶּר עָלָיו הַכֹּהֵן בְּאֵיל הָאָשָׁם, לִפְנֵי יְהוָה, עַל-חַטָּאתוֹ, אֲשֶׁר חָטָא; וְנִסְלַח לוֹ, מֵחַטָּאתוֹ אֲשֶׁר
חָטָא.

[20] If a man lies with a female slave who is promised to another man but who has not been redeemed or given her freedom, there must be an inquiry. Yet they are not to be put to death, because she had not been freed. [21] The man must bring his guilt to the Lord, to the entrance to the tent of meeting, a ram of guilt. [22] With the ram of guilt the priest is to make atonement for him before the Lord for the sin he has committed, and his sin will be forgiven.

Lev. 20:9–21, 27

ויקרא פרק כ

ט כִּי-אִישׁ אִישׁ, אֲשֶׁר יְקַלֵּל אֶת-אָבִיו וְאֶת-אִמּוֹ--מוֹת יוּמָת: אָבִיו וְאִמּוֹ קִלֵּל, דָּמָיו בּוֹ. י וְאִישׁ, אֲשֶׁר
יִנְאַף אֶת-אֵשֶׁת אִישׁ, אֲשֶׁר יִנְאַף, אֶת-אֵשֶׁת רֵעֵהוּ--מוֹת-יוּמַת הַנֹּאֵף, וְהַנֹּאָפֶת. יא וְאִישׁ, אֲשֶׁר יִשְׁכַּב
אֶת-אֵשֶׁת אָבִיו--עֶרְוַת אָבִיו, גִּלָּה; מוֹת-יוּמְתוּ שְׁנֵיהֶם, דְּמֵיהֶם בָּם. יב וְאִישׁ, אֲשֶׁר יִשְׁכַּב אֶת-כַּלָּתוֹ--
מוֹת יוּמְתוּ, שְׁנֵיהֶם: תֶּבֶל עָשׂוּ, דְּמֵיהֶם בָּם. יג וְאִישׁ, אֲשֶׁר יִשְׁכַּב אֶת-זָכָר מִשְׁכְּבֵי אִשָּׁה--תּוֹעֵבָה עָשׂוּ,
שְׁנֵיהֶם; מוֹת יוּמָתוּ, דְּמֵיהֶם בָּם. יד וְאִישׁ, אֲשֶׁר יִקַּח אֶת-אִשָּׁה וְאֶת-אִמָּהּ--זִמָּה הִוא; בָּאֵשׁ יִשְׂרְפוּ
אֹתוֹ, וְאֶתְהֶן, וְלֹא-תִהְיֶה זִמָּה, בְּתוֹכְכֶם. טו וְאִישׁ, אֲשֶׁר יִתֵּן שְׁכָבְתּוֹ בִּבְהֵמָה--מוֹת יוּמָת; וְאֶת-הַבְּהֵמָה,
תַּהֲרֹגוּ. טז וְאִשָּׁה, אֲשֶׁר תִּקְרַב אֶל-כָּל-בְּהֵמָה לְרִבְעָה אֹתָהּ--וְהָרַגְתָּ אֶת-הָאִשָּׁה, וְאֶת-הַבְּהֵמָה; מוֹת
יוּמָתוּ, דְּמֵיהֶם בָּם. יז וְאִישׁ אֲשֶׁר-יִקַּח אֶת-אֲחֹתוֹ בַּת-אָבִיו אוֹ בַת-אִמּוֹ וְרָאָה אֶת-עֶרְוָתָהּ וְהִיא-תִרְאֶה
אֶת-עֶרְוָתוֹ, חֶסֶד הוּא--וְנִכְרְתוּ, לְעֵינֵי בְּנֵי עַמָּם; עֶרְוַת אֲחֹתוֹ גִּלָּה, עֲוֹנוֹ יִשָּׂא. יח וְאִישׁ אֲשֶׁר-יִשְׁכַּב

אֶת-אִשָּׁה דָּוָה, וְגִלָּה אֶת-עֶרְוָתָהּ אֶת-מְקֹרָהּ הֶעֱרָה, וְהִוא, גִּלְּתָה אֶת-מְקוֹר דָּמֶיהָ--וְנִכְרְתוּ שְׁנֵיהֶם, מִקֶּרֶב
עַמָּם. יט וְעֶרְוַת אֲחוֹת אִמְּךָ וַאֲחוֹת אָבִיךָ, לֹא תְגַלֵּה: כִּי אֶת-שְׁאֵרוֹ הֶעֱרָה, עֲוֹנָם יִשָּׂאוּ. כ וְאִישׁ, אֲשֶׁר
יִשְׁכַּב אֶת-דֹּדָתוֹ--עֶרְוַת דֹּדוֹ, גִּלָּה; חֶטְאָם יִשָּׂאוּ, עֲרִירִים יָמֻתוּ. כא וְאִישׁ, אֲשֶׁר יִקַּח אֶת-אֵשֶׁת אָחִיו--
נִדָּה הִוא; עֶרְוַת אָחִיו גִּלָּה, עֲרִירִים יִהְיוּ.
כז וְאִישׁ אוֹ-אִשָּׁה, כִּי-יִהְיֶה בָהֶם אוֹב אוֹ יִדְּעֹנִי--מוֹת יוּמָתוּ; בָּאֶבֶן יִרְגְּמוּ אֹתָם, דְּמֵיהֶם בָּם.

9 Anyone who curses their father or mother is to be put to death. Because they have cursed their father or mother, their blood will be on their own head.
10 If a man commits adultery with another man's wife – with the wife of his neighbor – both the adulterer and the adulteress are to be put to death.
11 If a man lies with his father's wife, he has approached his father's sexuality. Both the man and the woman are to be put to death; their blood will be on their own heads.
12 If a man lies with his daughter-in-law, both of them are to be put to death. What they have done is a perversion; their blood will be on their own heads.
13 If a man lies with a man the lying of a woman, both of them have done abomination. They are to be put to death; their blood will be on their own heads.
14 If a man takes both a woman and her mother, it is abhorrence. Both he and they must be burned in the fire, so that no abhorrence will be among you.
15 If a man lies with an animal, he is to be put to death, and you must kill the animal.
16 If a woman approaches an animal to lie with it, kill both the woman and the animal. They are to be put to death; their blood will be on their own heads.
17 If a man takes his sister, the daughter of either his father or his mother, and they approach each other sexually, it is a disgrace. They are to be publicly removed from their people. He has approached sexually his sister and will be held responsible.
18 If a man lies with a woman during her monthly period, he has exposed the source of her flow, and she has also uncovered it. Both of them are to be cut off from their people.
19 Do not approached sexually the sister of either your mother or your father, for that is approaching the sexuality of a close relative; both of you would be held responsible.
20 If a man approaches sexually his aunt, he has approached the sexuality of his uncle. They will be held responsible; they will die childless.
21 If a man takes his brother's wife, it is an act of impurity; he has approached his brother's sexuality. They will be childless.
27 A man or woman who is a medium or spiritist among you must be put to death. You are to stone them; their blood will be on their own heads.

Lev. 21:7, 9, 13–15

ויקרא פרק כא

ז אִשָּׁה זֹנָה וַחֲלָלָה לֹא יִקָּחוּ, וְאִשָּׁה גְּרוּשָׁה מֵאִישָׁהּ לֹא יִקָּחוּ: כִּי-קָדֹשׁ הוּא, לֵאלֹהָיו.
ט וּבַת אִישׁ כֹּהֵן, כִּי תֵחֵל לִזְנוֹת--אֶת-אָבִיהָ הִיא מְחַלֶּלֶת, בָּאֵשׁ תִּשָּׂרֵף.
יג וְהוּא, אִשָּׁה בִבְתוּלֶיהָ יִקָּח. יד אַלְמָנָה וּגְרוּשָׁה וַחֲלָלָה זֹנָה, אֶת-אֵלֶּה לֹא יִקָּח: כִּי אִם-בְּתוּלָה מֵעַמָּיו,
יִקַּח אִשָּׁה. טו וְלֹא-יְחַלֵּל זַרְעוֹ, בְּעַמָּיו: כִּי אֲנִי יְהוָה, מְקַדְּשׁוֹ.

[7] They must not marry women defiled by prostitution or divorced from their husbands, because holy he is to his God.
[9] If a priest's daughter begins prostituting, she disgraces her father; she must be burned in fire.
[13] The woman he marries must be a virgin. [14] He must not marry a widow, a divorced woman or a woman defiled by prostitution, but only a virgin from his own people, [15] so that he will not defile his offspring among his people. For I the Lord sanctifies him.

Lev. 22:12–13

ויקרא פרק כב

יב וּבַת-כֹּהֵן--כִּי תִהְיֶה, לְאִישׁ זָר: הִוא, בִּתְרוּמַת הַקֳּדָשִׁים לֹא תֹאכֵל. יג וּבַת-כֹּהֵן כִּי תִהְיֶה אַלְמָנָה
וּגְרוּשָׁה, וְזֶרַע אֵין לָהּ--וְשָׁבָה אֶל-בֵּית אָבִיהָ כִּנְעוּרֶיהָ, מִלֶּחֶם אָבִיהָ תֹּאכֵל; וְכָל-זָר, לֹא-יֹאכַל בּוֹ.

[12] If a priest's daughter marries anyone other than a priest, she may not eat any of the sacred contributions. [13] But if a priest's daughter becomes a widow or is divorced, yet has no children, and she returns to live in her father's household as in her youth, she may eat her father's food. No unauthorized person, however, may eat it.

Lev. 27:3–7

ויקרא פרק כז

ג וְהָיָה עֶרְכְּךָ, הַזָּכָר, מִבֶּן עֶשְׂרִים שָׁנָה, וְעַד בֶּן-שִׁשִּׁים שָׁנָה: וְהָיָה עֶרְכְּךָ, חֲמִשִּׁים שֶׁקֶל כֶּסֶף--בְּשֶׁקֶל
הַקֹּדֶשׁ. ד וְאִם-נְקֵבָה, הִוא--וְהָיָה עֶרְכְּךָ, שְׁלֹשִׁים שָׁקֶל. ה וְאִם מִבֶּן-חָמֵשׁ שָׁנִים, וְעַד בֶּן-עֶשְׂרִים שָׁנָה--
וְהָיָה עֶרְכְּךָ הַזָּכָר, עֶשְׂרִים שְׁקָלִים; וְלַנְּקֵבָה, עֲשֶׂרֶת שְׁקָלִים. ו וְאִם מִבֶּן-חֹדֶשׁ, וְעַד בֶּן-חָמֵשׁ שָׁנִים--וְהָיָה
עֶרְכְּךָ הַזָּכָר, חֲמִשָּׁה שְׁקָלִים כָּסֶף; וְלַנְּקֵבָה עֶרְכְּךָ, שְׁלֹשֶׁת שְׁקָלִים כָּסֶף. ז וְאִם מִבֶּן-שִׁשִּׁים שָׁנָה וָמַעְלָה,
אִם-זָכָר--וְהָיָה עֶרְכְּךָ, חֲמִשָּׁה עָשָׂר שָׁקֶל; וְלַנְּקֵבָה, עֲשָׂרָה שְׁקָלִים.

[3] Set the value of a male between the ages of 20 and 60 at 50 shekels of silver, according to the sanctuary shekel; [4] for a female, set her value at 30 shekels; [5] for a person between the ages of 5 and 20, set the value of a male at 20 shekels and of a female at 10 shekels; [6] for a person between 1 month and 5 years, set the value of a male at 5 shekels of silver and that of a female at 3 shekels of silver; [7] for a person 60 years old or more, set the value of a male at 15 shekels and of a female at 10 shekels.

Num. 5:12–31

במדבר פרק ה

יב דַּבֵּר אֶל-בְּנֵי יִשְׂרָאֵל, וְאָמַרְתָּ אֲלֵהֶם: אִישׁ אִישׁ כִּי-תִשְׂטֶה אִשְׁתּוֹ, וּמָעֲלָה בוֹ מָעַל. יג וְשָׁכַב אִישׁ אֹתָהּ,
שִׁכְבַת-זֶרַע, וְנֶעְלַם מֵעֵינֵי אִישָׁהּ, וְנִסְתְּרָה וְהִיא נִטְמָאָה; וְעֵד אֵין בָּהּ, וְהִוא לֹא נִתְפָּשָׂה. יד וְעָבַר עָלָיו

רוּחַ-קִנְאָה וְקִנֵּא אֶת-אִשְׁתּוֹ, וְהִוא נִטְמָאָה; אוֹ-עָבַר עָלָיו רוּחַ-קִנְאָה וְקִנֵּא אֶת-אִשְׁתּוֹ, וְהִיא לֹא נִטְמָאָה. טו וְהֵבִיא הָאִישׁ אֶת-אִשְׁתּוֹ, אֶל-הַכֹּהֵן, וְהֵבִיא אֶת-קָרְבָּנָהּ עָלֶיהָ, עֲשִׂירִת הָאֵיפָה קֶמַח שְׂעֹרִים; לֹא-יִצֹק עָלָיו שֶׁמֶן, וְלֹא-יִתֵּן עָלָיו לְבֹנָה--כִּי-מִנְחַת קְנָאֹת הוּא, מִנְחַת זִכָּרוֹן מַזְכֶּרֶת עָוֺן. טז וְהִקְרִיב אֹתָהּ, הַכֹּהֵן; וְהֶעֱמִדָהּ, לִפְנֵי יְהוָה. יז וְלָקַח הַכֹּהֵן מַיִם קְדֹשִׁים, בִּכְלִי-חָרֶשׂ; וּמִן-הֶעָפָר, אֲשֶׁר יִהְיֶה בְּקַרְקַע הַמִּשְׁכָּן, יִקַּח הַכֹּהֵן, וְנָתַן אֶל-הַמָּיִם. יח וְהֶעֱמִיד הַכֹּהֵן אֶת-הָאִשָּׁה, לִפְנֵי יְהוָה, וּפָרַע אֶת-רֹאשׁ הָאִשָּׁה, וְנָתַן עַל-כַּפֶּיהָ אֵת מִנְחַת הַזִּכָּרוֹן מִנְחַת קְנָאֹת הִוא; וּבְיַד הַכֹּהֵן יִהְיוּ, מֵי הַמָּרִים הַמְאָרְרִים. יט וְהִשְׁבִּיעַ אֹתָהּ הַכֹּהֵן, וְאָמַר אֶל-הָאִשָּׁה אִם-לֹא שָׁכַב אִישׁ אֹתָךְ, וְאִם-לֹא שָׂטִית טֻמְאָה, תַּחַת אִישֵׁךְ--הִנָּקִי, מִמֵּי הַמָּרִים הַמְאָרְרִים הָאֵלֶּה. כ וְאַתְּ, כִּי שָׂטִית תַּחַת אִישֵׁךְ--וְכִי נִטְמֵאת; וַיִּתֵּן אִישׁ בָּךְ אֶת-שְׁכָבְתּוֹ, מִבַּלְעֲדֵי אִישֵׁךְ. כא וְהִשְׁבִּיעַ הַכֹּהֵן אֶת-הָאִשָּׁה, בִּשְׁבֻעַת הָאָלָה, וְאָמַר הַכֹּהֵן לָאִשָּׁה, יִתֵּן יְהוָה אוֹתָךְ לְאָלָה וְלִשְׁבֻעָה בְּתוֹךְ עַמֵּךְ--בְּתֵת יְהוָה אֶת-יְרֵכֵךְ נֹפֶלֶת, וְאֶת-בִּטְנֵךְ צָבָה. כב וּבָאוּ הַמַּיִם הַמְאָרְרִים הָאֵלֶּה, בְּמֵעַיִךְ, לַצְבּוֹת בֶּטֶן, וְלַנְפִּל יָרֵךְ; וְאָמְרָה הָאִשָּׁה, אָמֵן אָמֵן. כג וְכָתַב אֶת-הָאָלֹת הָאֵלֶּה, הַכֹּהֵן--בַּסֵּפֶר; וּמָחָה, אֶל-מֵי הַמָּרִים. כד וְהִשְׁקָה, אֶת-הָאִשָּׁה, אֶת-מֵי הַמָּרִים, הַמְאָרְרִים; וּבָאוּ בָהּ הַמַּיִם הַמְאָרְרִים, לְמָרִים. כה וְלָקַח הַכֹּהֵן מִיַּד הָאִשָּׁה, אֵת מִנְחַת הַקְּנָאֹת; וְהֵנִיף אֶת-הַמִּנְחָה לִפְנֵי יְהוָה, וְהִקְרִיב אֹתָהּ אֶל-הַמִּזְבֵּחַ. כו וְקָמַץ הַכֹּהֵן מִן-הַמִּנְחָה אֶת-אַזְכָּרָתָהּ, וְהִקְטִיר הַמִּזְבֵּחָה; וְאַחַר יַשְׁקֶה אֶת-הָאִשָּׁה, אֶת-הַמָּיִם. כז וְהִשְׁקָהּ אֶת-הַמַּיִם, וְהָיְתָה אִם-נִטְמְאָה וַתִּמְעֹל מַעַל בְּאִישָׁהּ--וּבָאוּ בָהּ הַמַּיִם הַמְאָרְרִים לְמָרִים, וְצָבְתָה בִטְנָהּ וְנָפְלָה יְרֵכָהּ; וְהָיְתָה הָאִשָּׁה לְאָלָה, בְּקֶרֶב עַמָּהּ. כח וְאִם-לֹא נִטְמְאָה הָאִשָּׁה, וּטְהֹרָה הִוא--וְנִקְּתָה, וְנִזְרְעָה זָרַע. כט זֹאת תּוֹרַת, הַקְּנָאֹת, אֲשֶׁר תִּשְׂטֶה אִשָּׁה תַּחַת אִישָׁהּ, וְנִטְמָאָה. ל אוֹ אִישׁ, אֲשֶׁר תַּעֲבֹר עָלָיו רוּחַ קִנְאָה--וְקִנֵּא אֶת-אִשְׁתּוֹ; וְהֶעֱמִיד אֶת-הָאִשָּׁה, לִפְנֵי יְהוָה, וְעָשָׂה לָהּ הַכֹּהֵן, אֵת כָּל-הַתּוֹרָה הַזֹּאת. לא וְנִקָּה הָאִישׁ, מֵעָוֺן; וְהָאִשָּׁה הַהִוא, תִּשָּׂא אֶת-עֲוֺנָהּ.

[12] Speak to the Israelites and say to them: If a man's wife goes astray and is unfaithful to him [13] so that another man has sexual relations with her, and this is hidden from her husband and her impurity is undetected, since there is no witness against her and she has not been caught in the act, [14] and if feelings of jealousy come over her husband and he suspects his wife and she is impure – or if he is jealous and suspects her even though she is not impure – [15] then he is to take his wife to the priest. He must also take an offering of a tenth of an ephah of barley flour on her behalf. He must not pour olive oil on it or put incense on it, because it is a grain offering for jealousy, a reminder-offering to draw attention to wrongdoing.

[16] The priest shall bring her and have her stand before the Lord. [17] Then he shall take some holy water in a clay jar and put some dust from the tabernacle floor into the water. [18] After the priest has had the woman stand before the Lord, he shall loosen her hair and place in her hands the reminder-offering, the grain offering for jealousy, while he himself holds the bitter water that brings a curse. [19] Then the priest shall put the woman under oath and say to her, "If no other man has had sexual relations with you and you have not gone astray and become impure while married to your husband, may this bitter water that brings a curse not harm you. [20] But if you have gone astray while married to your husband and you have made yourself impure by having sexual relations with a man other than your husband" – [21] here the priest is to put the woman under this curse – "may the Lord cause you to become a curse among your people when he makes your womb miscarry and your abdomen swell. [22] May this water that brings a curse enter your body so that your abdomen swells or your womb miscarries".

Then the woman is to say, "Amen. So be it".

[23] The priest is to write these curses on a scroll and then wash them off into the bitter water. [24] He shall make the woman drink the bitter water that brings a curse, and this water that brings a curse and causes bitter suffering will enter her. [25] The priest is to take from her hands the grain offering for jealousy, wave it before the Lord and bring it to the altar. [26] The priest is then to take a handful of the grain offering as a representative offering and burn it on the altar; after that, he is to have the woman drink the water. [27] If she has made herself impure and been unfaithful to her husband, this will be the result: When she is made to drink the water that brings a curse and causes bitter suffering, it will enter her, her abdomen will swell and her womb will miscarry and she will become a curse. [28] If, however, the woman has not made herself impure, but is clean, she will be cleared of guilt and will be able to have children.

[29] This, then, is the law of jealousy when a woman goes astray and makes herself impure while married to her husband, [30] or when feelings of jealousy come over a man because he suspects his wife. The priest is to have her stand before the Lord and is to apply this entire law to her. [31] The husband will be innocent of any wrongdoing, but the woman will bear the consequences of her sin.

Num. 27:8–11

במדבר פרק כז

ח וְאֶל-בְּנֵי יִשְׂרָאֵל, תְּדַבֵּר לֵאמֹר: אִישׁ כִּי-יָמוּת, וּבֵן אֵין לוֹ--וְהַעֲבַרְתֶּם אֶת-נַחֲלָתוֹ, לְבִתּוֹ. ט וְאִם-אֵין
לוֹ, בַּת--וּנְתַתֶּם אֶת-נַחֲלָתוֹ, לְאֶחָיו. י וְאִם-אֵין לוֹ, אַחִים--וּנְתַתֶּם אֶת-נַחֲלָתוֹ, לַאֲחֵי אָבִיו. יא וְאִם-אֵין
אַחִים, לְאָבִיו--וּנְתַתֶּם אֶת-נַחֲלָתוֹ לִשְׁאֵרוֹ הַקָּרֹב אֵלָיו מִמִּשְׁפַּחְתּוֹ, וְיָרַשׁ אֹתָהּ; וְהָיְתָה לִבְנֵי יִשְׂרָאֵל,
לְחֻקַּת מִשְׁפָּט, כַּאֲשֶׁר צִוָּה יְהוָה, אֶת-מֹשֶׁה.

[8] Say to the Israelites, If a man dies and leaves no son, give his inheritance to his daughter. [9] If he has no daughter, give his inheritance to his brothers. [10] If he has no brothers, give his inheritance to his father's brothers. [11] If his father had no brothers, give his inheritance to the nearest relative in his clan, that he may inherit it. This is to have the force of law for the Israelites, as the Lord commanded Moses.

Num. 30:3–17

במדבר פרק ל

ג אִישׁ כִּי-יִדֹּר נֶדֶר לַיהוָה, אוֹ-הִשָּׁבַע שְׁבֻעָה לֶאְסֹר אִסָּר עַל-נַפְשׁוֹ--לֹא יַחֵל, דְּבָרוֹ: כְּכָל-הַיֹּצֵא מִפִּיו,
יַעֲשֶׂה. ד וְאִשָּׁה, כִּי-תִדֹּר נֶדֶר לַיהוָה, וְאָסְרָה אִסָּר בְּבֵית אָבִיהָ, בִּנְעֻרֶיהָ. ה וְשָׁמַע אָבִיהָ אֶת-נִדְרָהּ,
וֶאֱסָרָהּ אֲשֶׁר אָסְרָה עַל-נַפְשָׁהּ, וְהֶחֱרִישׁ לָהּ, אָבִיהָ--וְקָמוּ, כָּל-נְדָרֶיהָ, וְכָל-אִסָּר אֲשֶׁר-אָסְרָה עַל-נַפְשָׁהּ,
יָקוּם. ו וְאִם-הֵנִיא אָבִיהָ אֹתָהּ, בְּיוֹם שָׁמְעוֹ--כָּל-נְדָרֶיהָ וֶאֱסָרֶיהָ אֲשֶׁר-אָסְרָה עַל-נַפְשָׁהּ, לֹא יָקוּם; וַיהוָה,
יִסְלַח-לָהּ, כִּי-הֵנִיא אָבִיהָ, אֹתָהּ. ז וְאִם-הָיוֹ תִהְיֶה לְאִישׁ, וּנְדָרֶיהָ עָלֶיהָ, אוֹ מִבְטָא שְׂפָתֶיהָ, אֲשֶׁר אָסְרָה
עַל-נַפְשָׁהּ. ח וְשָׁמַע אִישָׁהּ בְּיוֹם שָׁמְעוֹ, וְהֶחֱרִישׁ לָהּ: וְקָמוּ נְדָרֶיהָ, וֶאֱסָרֶהָ אֲשֶׁר-אָסְרָה עַל-נַפְשָׁהּ—
יָקֻמוּ. ט וְאִם בְּיוֹם שְׁמֹעַ אִישָׁהּ, יָנִיא אוֹתָהּ, וְהֵפֵר אֶת-נִדְרָהּ אֲשֶׁר עָלֶיהָ, וְאֵת מִבְטָא שְׂפָתֶיהָ אֲשֶׁר
אָסְרָה עַל-נַפְשָׁהּ--וַיהוָה, יִסְלַח-לָהּ. י וְנֵדֶר אַלְמָנָה, וּגְרוּשָׁה--כֹּל אֲשֶׁר-אָסְרָה עַל-נַפְשָׁהּ, יָקוּם עָלֶיהָ.

יא וְאִם-בֵּית אִישָׁהּ, נָדָרָה, אוֹ-אָסְרָה אִסָּר עַל-נַפְשָׁהּ, בִּשְׁבֻעָה. יב וְשָׁמַע אִישָׁהּ וְהֶחֱרִשׁ לָהּ, לֹא הֵנִיא
אֹתָהּ--וְקָמוּ, כָּל-נְדָרֶיהָ, וְכָל-אִסָּר אֲשֶׁר-אָסְרָה עַל-נַפְשָׁהּ, יָקוּם. יג וְאִם-הָפֵר יָפֵר אֹתָם אִישָׁהּ, בְּיוֹם
שָׁמְעוֹ--כָּל-מוֹצָא שְׂפָתֶיהָ לִנְדָרֶיהָ וּלְאִסַּר נַפְשָׁהּ, לֹא יָקוּם: אִישָׁהּ הֲפֵרָם, וַיהוָה יִסְלַח-לָהּ. יד כָּל-נֵדֶר
וְכָל-שְׁבֻעַת אִסָּר, לְעַנֹּת נָפֶשׁ--אִישָׁהּ יְקִימֶנּוּ, וְאִישָׁהּ יְפֵרֶנּוּ. טו וְאִם-הַחֲרֵשׁ יַחֲרִישׁ לָהּ אִישָׁהּ, מִיּוֹם אֶל-
יוֹם, וְהֵקִים אֶת-כָּל-נְדָרֶיהָ, אוֹ אֶת-כָּל-אֱסָרֶיהָ אֲשֶׁר עָלֶיהָ--הֵקִים אֹתָם, כִּי-הֶחֱרִשׁ לָהּ בְּיוֹם שָׁמְעוֹ. טז
וְאִם-הָפֵר יָפֵר אֹתָם, אַחֲרֵי שָׁמְעוֹ--וְנָשָׂא, אֶת-עֲוֺנָהּ. יז אֵלֶּה הַחֻקִּים, אֲשֶׁר צִוָּה יְהוָה אֶת-מֹשֶׁה, בֵּין אִישׁ,
לְאִשְׁתּוֹ--בֵּין-אָב לְבִתּוֹ, בִּנְעֻרֶיהָ בֵּית אָבִיהָ.

3 When a man makes a vow to the Lord or takes an oath to obligate himself by a pledge, he must not break his word but must do everything he said.
4 When a young woman still living in her father's household makes a vow to the Lord or obligates herself by a pledge 5 and her father hears about her vow or pledge but says nothing to her, then all her vows and every pledge by which she obligated herself will stand. 6 But if her father forbids her when he hears about it, none of her vows or the pledges by which she obligated herself will stand; the Lord will release her because her father has forbidden her.
7 If she marries after she makes a vow or after her lips utter a rash promise by which she obligates herself 8 and her husband hears about it but says nothing to her, then her vows or the pledges by which she obligated herself will stand.
9 But if her husband forbids her when he hears about it, he nullifies the vow that obligates her or the rash promise by which she obligates herself, and the Lord will release her.
10 Any vow or obligation taken by a widow or divorced woman will be binding on her.
11 If a woman living with her husband makes a vow or obligates herself by a pledge under oath 12 and her husband hears about it but says nothing to her and does not forbid her, then all her vows or the pledges by which she obligated herself will stand. 13 But if her husband nullifies them when he hears about them, then none of the vows or pledges that came from her lips will stand. Her husband has nullified them, and the Lord will release her. 14 Her husband may confirm or nullify any vow she makes or any sworn pledge to deny herself. 15 But if her husband says nothing to her about it from day to day, then he confirms all her vows or the pledges binding on her. He confirms them by saying nothing to her when he hears about them. 16 If, however, he nullifies them some time after he hears about them, then he must bear the consequences of her wrongdoing.
17 These are the rules the Lord gave Moses concerning relationships between a man and his wife, and between a father and his young daughter still living at home.

Num. 36:6–9

במדבר פרק לו

ו זֶה הַדָּבָר אֲשֶׁר-צִוָּה יְהוָה, לִבְנוֹת צְלָפְחָד לֵאמֹר, לַטּוֹב בְּעֵינֵיהֶם, תִּהְיֶינָה לְנָשִׁים: אַךְ, לְמִשְׁפַּחַת מַטֵּה
אֲבִיהֶם--תִּהְיֶינָה לְנָשִׁים. ז וְלֹא-תִסֹּב נַחֲלָה לִבְנֵי יִשְׂרָאֵל, מִמַּטֶּה אֶל-מַטֶּה: כִּי אִישׁ, בְּנַחֲלַת מַטֵּה אֲבֹתָיו,

יִדְבְּקוּ, בְּנֵי יִשְׂרָאֵל. ח וְכָל-בַּת יֹרֶשֶׁת נַחֲלָה, מִמַּטּוֹת בְּנֵי יִשְׂרָאֵל--לְאֶחָד מִמִּשְׁפַּחַת מַטֵּה אָבִיהָ, תִּהְיֶה
לְאִשָּׁה: לְמַעַן, יִירְשׁוּ בְּנֵי יִשְׂרָאֵל, אִישׁ, נַחֲלַת אֲבֹתָיו. ט וְלֹא-תִסֹּב נַחֲלָה מִמַּטֶּה, לְמַטֶּה אַחֵר: כִּי-אִישׁ,
בְּנַחֲלָתוֹ, יִדְבְּקוּ, מַטּוֹת בְּנֵי יִשְׂרָאֵל.

6 This is what the Lord commands for Zelophehad's daughters: They may marry
anyone they please as long as they marry within their father's tribal clan. 7 No
land-plot in Israel is to pass from one tribe to another, for every Israelite shall keep
the tribal land-plot of their ancestors. 8 Every daughter who inherits land-plot in
any Israelite tribe must marry someone in her father's tribal clan, so that every
Israelite will inherit the land-plot of their ancestors. 9 No land-plot may pass from
one tribe to another, for each Israelite tribe is to keep his land-plot.

Deut. 15:12–17

דברים פרק טו

יב כִּי-יִמָּכֵר לְךָ אָחִיךָ הָעִבְרִי, אוֹ הָעִבְרִיָּה--וַעֲבָדְךָ, שֵׁשׁ שָׁנִים; וּבַשָּׁנָה, הַשְּׁבִיעִת, תְּשַׁלְּחֶנּוּ חָפְשִׁי, מֵעִמָּךְ.
יג וְכִי-תְשַׁלְּחֶנּוּ חָפְשִׁי, מֵעִמָּךְ--לֹא תְשַׁלְּחֶנּוּ, רֵיקָם. יד הַעֲנֵיק תַּעֲנִיק, לוֹ, מִצֹּאנְךָ, וּמִגָּרְנְךָ וּמִיִּקְבֶךָ: אֲשֶׁר
בֵּרַכְךָ יְהוָה אֱלֹהֶיךָ, תִּתֶּן-לוֹ. טו וְזָכַרְתָּ, כִּי עֶבֶד הָיִיתָ בְּאֶרֶץ מִצְרַיִם, וַיִּפְדְּךָ, יְהוָה אֱלֹהֶיךָ; עַל-כֵּן אָנֹכִי
מְצַוְּךָ, אֶת-הַדָּבָר הַזֶּה——הַיּוֹם. טז וְהָיָה כִּי-יֹאמַר אֵלֶיךָ, לֹא אֵצֵא מֵעִמָּךְ: כִּי אֲהֵבְךָ וְאֶת-בֵּיתֶךָ, כִּי-טוֹב
לוֹ עִמָּךְ. יז וְלָקַחְתָּ אֶת-הַמַּרְצֵעַ, וְנָתַתָּה בְאָזְנוֹ וּבַדֶּלֶת, וְהָיָה לְךָ, עֶבֶד עוֹלָם; וְאַף לַאֲמָתְךָ, תַּעֲשֶׂה-כֵּן.

12 If your Hebrew brother or your Hebrew sister is sold to you and serve you six
years, in the seventh year you must let them go free. 13 And when you release
them, do not send them away empty-handed. 14 Award them indeed from your
flock, your threshing floor and your winepress. Give to them as the Lord your God
has blessed you. 15 Remember that you were slaves in Egypt and the Lord your
God redeemed you. That is why I give you this command today.
16 But if your slave says to you, "I do not want to leave you", because he loves you
and your family and is well off with you, 17 then take an awl and push it through
his earlobe into the door, and he will become your slave for life. Do the same for
your female slave.

Deut. 17:2–5

דברים פרק יז

ב כִּי-יִמָּצֵא בְקִרְבְּךָ בְּאַחַד שְׁעָרֶיךָ, אֲשֶׁר-יְהוָה אֱלֹהֶיךָ נֹתֵן לָךְ: אִישׁ אוֹ-אִשָּׁה, אֲשֶׁר יַעֲשֶׂה אֶת-הָרַע
בְּעֵינֵי יְהוָה-אֱלֹהֶיךָ--לַעֲבֹר בְּרִיתוֹ. ג וַיֵּלֶךְ, וַיַּעֲבֹד אֱלֹהִים אֲחֵרִים, וַיִּשְׁתַּחוּ, לָהֶם; וְלַשֶּׁמֶשׁ אוֹ לַיָּרֵחַ, אוֹ
לְכָל-צְבָא הַשָּׁמַיִם--אֲשֶׁר לֹא-צִוִּיתִי. ד וְהֻגַּד-לְךָ, וְשָׁמָעְתָּ; וְדָרַשְׁתָּ הֵיטֵב--וְהִנֵּה אֱמֶת נָכוֹן הַדָּבָר, נֶעֶשְׂתָה
הַתּוֹעֵבָה הַזֹּאת בְּיִשְׂרָאֵל. ה וְהוֹצֵאתָ אֶת-הָאִישׁ הַהוּא אוֹ אֶת-הָאִשָּׁה הַהִוא אֲשֶׁר עָשׂוּ אֶת-הַדָּבָר הָרַע
הַזֶּה, אֶל-שְׁעָרֶיךָ--אֶת-הָאִישׁ, אוֹ אֶת-הָאִשָּׁה; וּסְקַלְתָּם בָּאֲבָנִים, וָמֵתוּ.

2 If a man or woman living among you in one of the towns the Lord gives you is
found doing evil in the eyes of the Lord your God in violation of his covenant,

[3] and contrary to my command has worshipped other gods, bowing down to them or to the sun or the moon or the stars in the sky, [4] and this has been brought to your attention, then you must investigate it thoroughly. If it is true and it has been proved that this abomination has been done in Israel, [5] take the man or woman who has done this evil deed to your city gate and stone that person to death.

Deut. 20:10–14

דברים פרק כ

י כִּי-תִקְרַב אֶל-עִיר, לְהִלָּחֵם עָלֶיהָ--וְקָרָאתָ אֵלֶיהָ, לְשָׁלוֹם. יא וְהָיָה אִם-שָׁלוֹם תַּעַנְךָ, וּפָתְחָה לָךְ: וְהָיָה
כָּל-הָעָם הַנִּמְצָא-בָהּ, יִהְיוּ לְךָ לָמַס—וַעֲבָדוּךָ. יב וְאִם-לֹא תַשְׁלִים עִמָּךְ, וְעָשְׂתָה עִמְּךָ מִלְחָמָה--וְצַרְתָּ,
עָלֶיהָ. יג וּנְתָנָהּ יְהוָה אֱלֹהֶיךָ, בְּיָדֶךָ; וְהִכִּיתָ אֶת-כָּל-זְכוּרָהּ, לְפִי-חָרֶב. יד רַק הַנָּשִׁים וְהַטַּף וְהַבְּהֵמָה וְכֹל
אֲשֶׁר יִהְיֶה בָעִיר, כָּל-שְׁלָלָהּ--תָּבֹז לָךְ; וְאָכַלְתָּ אֶת-שְׁלַל אֹיְבֶיךָ, אֲשֶׁר נָתַן יְהוָה אֱלֹהֶיךָ לָךְ.

[10] When you march up to attack a city, make its people an offer of peace. [11] If they accept and open their gates, all the people in it shall be subject to forced labor and shall work for you. [12] If they refuse to make peace and they engage you in battle, lay siege to that city. [13] When the Lord your God delivers it into your hand, put to the sword all the men in it. [14] As for the women, the children, the livestock and everything else in the city, you may take these as plunder for yourselves. And you may use the plunder the Lord your God gives you from your enemies.

Deut. 21:10–21

דברים פרק כא

י כִּי-תֵצֵא לַמִּלְחָמָה, עַל-אֹיְבֶיךָ; וּנְתָנוֹ יְהוָה אֱלֹהֶיךָ, בְּיָדֶךָ--וְשָׁבִיתָ שִׁבְיוֹ. יא וְרָאִיתָ, בַּשִּׁבְיָה, אֵשֶׁת,
יְפַת-תֹּאַר; וְחָשַׁקְתָּ בָהּ, וְלָקַחְתָּ לְךָ לְאִשָּׁה. יב וַהֲבֵאתָהּ, אֶל-תּוֹךְ בֵּיתֶךָ; וְגִלְּחָה, אֶת-רֹאשָׁהּ, וְעָשְׂתָה,
אֶת-צִפָּרְנֶיהָ. יג וְהֵסִירָה אֶת-שִׂמְלַת שִׁבְיָהּ מֵעָלֶיהָ, וְיָשְׁבָה בְּבֵיתֶךָ, וּבָכְתָה אֶת-אָבִיהָ וְאֶת-אִמָּהּ, יֶרַח
יָמִים; וְאַחַר כֵּן תָּבוֹא אֵלֶיהָ, וּבְעַלְתָּהּ, וְהָיְתָה לְךָ, לְאִשָּׁה. יד וְהָיָה אִם-לֹא חָפַצְתָּ בָּהּ, וְשִׁלַּחְתָּהּ לְנַפְשָׁהּ,
וּמָכֹר לֹא-תִמְכְּרֶנָּה, בַּכָּסֶף; לֹא-תִתְעַמֵּר בָּהּ, תַּחַת אֲשֶׁר עִנִּיתָהּ.
טו כִּי-תִהְיֶיןָ לְאִישׁ שְׁתֵּי נָשִׁים, הָאַחַת אֲהוּבָה וְהָאַחַת שְׂנוּאָה, וְיָלְדוּ-לוֹ בָנִים, הָאֲהוּבָה וְהַשְּׂנוּאָה; וְהָיָה
הַבֵּן הַבְּכֹר, לַשְּׂנִיאָה. טז וְהָיָה, בְּיוֹם הַנְחִילוֹ אֶת-בָּנָיו, אֵת אֲשֶׁר-יִהְיֶה, לוֹ--לֹא יוּכַל, לְבַכֵּר אֶת-בֶּן-
הָאֲהוּבָה, עַל-פְּנֵי בֶן-הַשְּׂנוּאָה, הַבְּכֹר. יז כִּי אֶת-הַבְּכֹר בֶּן-הַשְּׂנוּאָה יַכִּיר, לָתֶת לוֹ פִּי שְׁנַיִם, בְּכֹל אֲשֶׁר-
יִמָּצֵא, לוֹ: כִּי-הוּא רֵאשִׁית אֹנוֹ, לוֹ מִשְׁפַּט הַבְּכֹרָה.
יח כִּי-יִהְיֶה לְאִישׁ, בֵּן סוֹרֵר וּמוֹרֶה--אֵינֶנּוּ שֹׁמֵעַ, בְּקוֹל אָבִיו וּבְקוֹל אִמּוֹ; וְיִסְּרוּ אֹתוֹ, וְלֹא יִשְׁמַע אֲלֵיהֶם.
יט וְתָפְשׂוּ בוֹ, אָבִיו וְאִמּוֹ; וְהוֹצִיאוּ אֹתוֹ אֶל-זִקְנֵי עִירוֹ, וְאֶל-שַׁעַר מְקֹמוֹ. כ וְאָמְרוּ אֶל-זִקְנֵי עִירוֹ, בְּנֵנוּ זֶה
סוֹרֵר וּמֹרֶה--אֵינֶנּוּ שֹׁמֵעַ, בְּקֹלֵנוּ; זוֹלֵל, וְסֹבֵא. כא וּרְגָמֻהוּ כָּל-אַנְשֵׁי עִירוֹ בָאֲבָנִים, וָמֵת, וּבִעַרְתָּ הָרָע,
מִקִּרְבֶּךָ; וְכָל-יִשְׂרָאֵל, יִשְׁמְעוּ וְיִרָאוּ.

[10] When you go to war against your enemies and the Lord your God delivers them into your hands and you take captives, [11] if you notice among the captives a beautiful woman and are attracted to her, you may take her as your wife. [12] Bring her into your home and have her shave her head, trim her nails [13] and put aside

the clothes she was wearing when captured. After she has lived in your house and mourned her father and mother for a full month, then you may go to her and be her husband and she shall be your wife. [14] If you are not pleased with her, let her go wherever she wishes. You must not sell her or treat her as a slave, since you have dishonored her.

[15] If a man has two wives, and he loves one but not the other, and both bear him sons but the firstborn is the son of the wife he does not love, [16] when he wills his property to his sons, he must not give the rights of the firstborn to the son of the wife he loves in preference to his actual firstborn, the son of the wife he does not love. [17] He must acknowledge the son of his unloved wife as the firstborn by giving him a double share of all he has. That son is the first sign of his father's strength. The right of the firstborn belongs to him.

[18] If someone has a stubborn and rebellious son who does not obey his father and mother and will not listen to them when they discipline him, [19] his father and mother shall take hold of him and bring him to the elders at the gate of his town. [20] They shall say to the elders, "This son of ours is stubborn and rebellious. He will not obey us. He is a glutton and a drunkard". [21] Then all the men of his town are to stone him to death. You must purge the evil from among you. All Israel will hear and be afraid.

Deut. 22:5, 13–29

דברים פרק כב

ה לֹא-יִהְיֶה כְלִי-גֶבֶר עַל-אִשָּׁה, וְלֹא-יִלְבַּשׁ גֶּבֶר שִׂמְלַת אִשָּׁה: כִּי תוֹעֲבַת יְהוָה אֱלֹהֶיךָ, כָּל-עֹשֵׂה אֵלֶּה.
יג כִּי-יִקַּח אִישׁ, אִשָּׁה; וּבָא אֵלֶיהָ, וּשְׂנֵאָהּ. יד וְשָׂם לָהּ עֲלִילֹת דְּבָרִים, וְהוֹצִא עָלֶיהָ שֵׁם רָע; וְאָמַר,
אֶת-הָאִשָּׁה הַזֹּאת לָקַחְתִּי, וָאֶקְרַב אֵלֶיהָ, וְלֹא-מָצָאתִי לָהּ בְּתוּלִים. טו וְלָקַח אֲבִי הַנַּעֲרָ, וְאִמָּהּ; וְהוֹצִיאוּ
אֶת-בְּתוּלֵי הַנַּעֲרָ, אֶל-זִקְנֵי הָעִיר—הַשָּׁעְרָה. טז וְאָמַר אֲבִי הַנַּעֲרָ, אֶל-הַזְּקֵנִים: אֶת-בִּתִּי, נָתַתִּי לָאִישׁ
הַזֶּה לְאִשָּׁה—וַיִּשְׂנָאֶהָ. יז וְהִנֵּה-הוּא שָׂם עֲלִילֹת דְּבָרִים לֵאמֹר, לֹא-מָצָאתִי לְבִתְּךָ בְּתוּלִים, וְאֵלֶּה, בְּתוּלֵי
בִתִּי; וּפָרְשׂוּ, הַשִּׂמְלָה, לִפְנֵי, זִקְנֵי הָעִיר. יח וְלָקְחוּ זִקְנֵי הָעִיר-הַהִוא, אֶת-הָאִישׁ; וְיִסְּרוּ, אֹתוֹ. יט וְעָנְשׁוּ
אֹתוֹ מֵאָה כֶסֶף, וְנָתְנוּ לַאֲבִי הַנַּעֲרָה--כִּי הוֹצִיא שֵׁם רָע, עַל בְּתוּלַת יִשְׂרָאֵל; וְלוֹ-תִהְיֶה לְאִשָּׁה, לֹא-יוּכַל
לְשַׁלְּחָהּ כָּל-יָמָיו.
כ וְאִם-אֱמֶת הָיָה, הַדָּבָר הַזֶּה: לֹא-נִמְצְאוּ בְתוּלִים, לַנַּעֲרָ. כא וְהוֹצִיאוּ אֶת-הַנַּעֲרָ אֶל-פֶּתַח בֵּית-אָבִיהָ,
וּסְקָלוּהָ אַנְשֵׁי עִירָהּ בָּאֲבָנִים וָמֵתָה--כִּי-עָשְׂתָה נְבָלָה בְּיִשְׂרָאֵל, לִזְנוֹת בֵּית אָבִיהָ; וּבִעַרְתָּ הָרָע, מִקִּרְבֶּךָ.
כב כִּי-יִמָּצֵא אִישׁ שֹׁכֵב עִם-אִשָּׁה בְעֻלַת-בַּעַל, וּמֵתוּ גַּם-שְׁנֵיהֶם--הָאִישׁ הַשֹּׁכֵב עִם-הָאִשָּׁה, וְהָאִשָּׁה;
וּבִעַרְתָּ הָרָע, מִיִּשְׂרָאֵל.
כג כִּי יִהְיֶה נַעֲרָ בְתוּלָה, מְאֹרָשָׂה לְאִישׁ; וּמְצָאָהּ אִישׁ בָּעִיר, וְשָׁכַב עִמָּהּ. כד וְהוֹצֵאתֶם אֶת-שְׁנֵיהֶם אֶל-
שַׁעַר הָעִיר הַהִוא, וּסְקַלְתֶּם אֹתָם בָּאֲבָנִים וָמֵתוּ--אֶת-הַנַּעֲרָ עַל-דְּבַר אֲשֶׁר לֹא-צָעֲקָה בָעִיר, וְאֶת-הָאִישׁ
עַל-דְּבַר אֲשֶׁר-עִנָּה אֶת-אֵשֶׁת רֵעֵהוּ; וּבִעַרְתָּ הָרָע, מִקִּרְבֶּךָ.
כה וְאִם-בַּשָּׂדֶה יִמְצָא הָאִישׁ, אֶת-הַנַּעֲרָ הַמְאֹרָשָׂה, וְהֶחֱזִיק-בָּהּ הָאִישׁ, וְשָׁכַב עִמָּהּ: וּמֵת, הָאִישׁ אֲשֶׁר-
שָׁכַב עִמָּהּ—לְבַדּוֹ. כו וְלַנַּעֲרָ לֹא-תַעֲשֶׂה דָבָר, אֵין לַנַּעֲרָ חֵטְא מָוֶת: כִּי כַּאֲשֶׁר יָקוּם אִישׁ עַל-רֵעֵהוּ,
וּרְצָחוֹ נֶפֶשׁ—כֵּן, הַדָּבָר הַזֶּה. כז כִּי בַשָּׂדֶה, מְצָאָהּ; צָעֲקָה, הַנַּעֲרָ הַמְאֹרָשָׂה, וְאֵין מוֹשִׁיעַ, לָהּ.
כח כִּי-יִמְצָא אִישׁ, נַעֲרָ בְתוּלָה אֲשֶׁר לֹא-אֹרָשָׂה, וּתְפָשָׂהּ, וְשָׁכַב עִמָּהּ; וְנִמְצָאוּ. כט וְנָתַן הָאִישׁ הַשֹּׁכֵב
עִמָּהּ, לַאֲבִי הַנַּעֲרָ--חֲמִשִּׁים כָּסֶף; וְלוֹ-תִהְיֶה לְאִשָּׁה, תַּחַת אֲשֶׁר עִנָּהּ--לֹא-יוּכַל שַׁלְּחָהּ, כָּל-יָמָיו.

[5] A woman must not put on men's apparel, nor a man wear women's clothing, for anyone who does this is the abomination of the Lord your God.
[13] If a man takes a wife and, after sleeping with her, dislikes her [14] and slanders her and gives her a bad name, saying, "I married this woman, but when I approached her, I did not find proof of her virginity", [15] then the young woman's father and mother shall bring to the town elders at the gate proof that she was a virgin. [16] Her father will say to the elders, "I gave my daughter in marriage to this man, but he dislikes her. [17] Now he has slandered her and said, 'I did not find your daughter to be a virgin'. But here is the proof of my daughter's virginity". Then her parents shall display the cloth before the elders of the town, [18] and the elders shall take the man and punish him. [19] They shall fine him 100 shekels of silver and give them to the young woman's father, because this man has given an Israelite virgin a bad name. She shall continue to be his wife; he must not divorce her as long as he lives.
[20] If, however, the charge is true and no proof of the young woman's virginity can be found, [21] she shall be brought to the door of her father's house and there the men of her town shall stone her to death. She has done an outrageous thing in Israel by being promiscuous while still in her father's house. You must purge the evil from among you.
[22] If a man is found lying with another man's wife, both the man who lies with the woman and the woman must die. You must purge the evil from Israel.
[23] If a man finds in a town a betrothed virgin girl and he lies with her, [24] you shall take both of them to the gate of that town and stone them to death – the young woman because she was in a town and did not scream for help, and the man because he violated another man's wife. You must purge the evil from among you.
[25] But if the man finds the betrothed girl in the countryside and holds her and lies with her, only the man who has done this shall die. [26] Do nothing to the woman; she has committed no sin deserving death. This case is like that of someone who attacks and murders a neighbor, [27] for the man found the girl in the countryside, and though the betrothed girl screamed, there was no one to rescue her.
[28] If a man finds a virgin girl who is not betrothed and seizes her and lies with her and they are discovered, [29] he shall pay her father 50 silver. He must marry her, for he has violated her. He can never divorce her as long as he lives.

Deut. 23:1–2, 18–19

דברים פרק כג

א לֹא-יִקַּח אִישׁ, אֶת-אֵשֶׁת אָבִיו; וְלֹא יְגַלֶּה, כְּנַף אָבִיו.
ב לֹא-יָבֹא פְצוּעַ-דַּכָּא וּכְרוּת שָׁפְכָה, בִּקְהַל יְהוָה.
יח לֹא-תִהְיֶה קְדֵשָׁה, מִבְּנוֹת יִשְׂרָאֵל; וְלֹא-יִהְיֶה קָדֵשׁ, מִבְּנֵי יִשְׂרָאֵל. יט לֹא-תָבִיא אֶתְנַן זוֹנָה וּמְחִיר כֶּלֶב,
בֵּית יְהוָה אֱלֹהֶיךָ--לְכָל-נֶדֶר: כִּי תוֹעֲבַת יְהוָה אֱלֹהֶיךָ, גַּם-שְׁנֵיהֶם.

[1] A man is not to marry his father's wife; he must not reveal his father's garment.
[2] No one who has been emasculated by crushing or cutting may enter the assembly of the Lord.

[18] There shall be no cult prostitute among the daughters or the sons of Israel. [19] You must not bring the earnings of a female prostitute or of a male prostitute[128] into the house of the Lord your God to pay any vow, for both of these are the abomination of the Lord your God.

Deut. 24:1–5

דברים פרק כד

א כִּי-יִקַּח אִישׁ אִשָּׁה, וּבְעָלָהּ; וְהָיָה אִם-לֹא תִמְצָא-חֵן בְּעֵינָיו, כִּי-מָצָא בָהּ עֶרְוַת דָּבָר--וְכָתַב לָהּ סֵפֶר
כְּרִיתֻת וְנָתַן בְּיָדָהּ, וְשִׁלְּחָהּ מִבֵּיתוֹ. ב וְיָצְאָה, מִבֵּיתוֹ; וְהָלְכָה, וְהָיְתָה לְאִישׁ-אַחֵר. ג וּשְׂנֵאָהּ, הָאִישׁ
הָאַחֲרוֹן, וְכָתַב לָהּ סֵפֶר כְּרִיתֻת וְנָתַן בְּיָדָהּ, וְשִׁלְּחָהּ מִבֵּיתוֹ; אוֹ כִי יָמוּת הָאִישׁ הָאַחֲרוֹן, אֲשֶׁר-לְקָחָהּ לוֹ
לְאִשָּׁה. ד לֹא-יוּכַל בַּעְלָהּ הָרִאשׁוֹן אֲשֶׁר-שִׁלְּחָהּ לָשׁוּב לְקַחְתָּהּ לִהְיוֹת לוֹ לְאִשָּׁה, אַחֲרֵי אֲשֶׁר הֻטַּמָּאָה--
כִּי-תוֹעֵבָה הִוא, לִפְנֵי יְהוָה; וְלֹא תַחֲטִיא, אֶת-הָאָרֶץ, אֲשֶׁר יְהוָה אֱלֹהֶיךָ, נֹתֵן לְךָ נַחֲלָה.
ה כִּי-יִקַּח אִישׁ, אִשָּׁה חֲדָשָׁה--לֹא יֵצֵא בַּצָּבָא, וְלֹא-יַעֲבֹר עָלָיו לְכָל-דָּבָר: נָקִי יִהְיֶה לְבֵיתוֹ, שָׁנָה אֶחָת,
וְשִׂמַּח, אֶת-אִשְׁתּוֹ אֲשֶׁר-לָקָח.

[1] If a man marries a woman who becomes displeasing to him because he finds something indecent about her, and he writes her a certificate of divorce, gives it to her and sends her from his house, [2] and if after she leaves his house she becomes the wife of another man, [3] and her second husband dislikes her and writes her a certificate of divorce, gives it to her and sends her from his house, or if he dies, [4] then her first husband, who divorced her, is not allowed to marry her again after she has been defiled. For this is an abomination before the Lord. Do not bring sin upon the land the Lord your God is giving you as an inheritance.
[5] If a man has recently married, he must not be sent to war or have any other duty laid on him. For one year he is to be free to stay at home and bring happiness to the wife he has married.

Deut. 25:5–12

דברים פרק כה

ה כִּי-יֵשְׁבוּ אַחִים יַחְדָּו, וּמֵת אַחַד מֵהֶם וּבֵן אֵין-לוֹ--לֹא-תִהְיֶה אֵשֶׁת-הַמֵּת הַחוּצָה, לְאִישׁ זָר: יְבָמָהּ יָבֹא
עָלֶיהָ, וּלְקָחָהּ לוֹ לְאִשָּׁה וְיִבְּמָהּ. ו וְהָיָה, הַבְּכוֹר אֲשֶׁר תֵּלֵד--יָקוּם, עַל-שֵׁם אָחִיו הַמֵּת; וְלֹא-יִמָּחֶה שְׁמוֹ,
מִיִּשְׂרָאֵל. ז וְאִם-לֹא יַחְפֹּץ הָאִישׁ, לָקַחַת אֶת-יְבִמְתּוֹ; וְעָלְתָה יְבִמְתּוֹ הַשַּׁעְרָה אֶל-הַזְּקֵנִים, וְאָמְרָה מֵאֵן
יְבָמִי לְהָקִים לְאָחִיו שֵׁם בְּיִשְׂרָאֵל--לֹא אָבָה, יַבְּמִי. ח וְקָרְאוּ-לוֹ זִקְנֵי-עִירוֹ, וְדִבְּרוּ אֵלָיו; וְעָמַד וְאָמַר,
לֹא חָפַצְתִּי לְקַחְתָּהּ. ט וְנִגְּשָׁה יְבִמְתּוֹ אֵלָיו, לְעֵינֵי הַזְּקֵנִים, וְחָלְצָה נַעֲלוֹ מֵעַל רַגְלוֹ, וְיָרְקָה בְּפָנָיו; וְעָנְתָה,
וְאָמְרָה, כָּכָה יֵעָשֶׂה לָאִישׁ, אֲשֶׁר לֹא-יִבְנֶה אֶת-בֵּית אָחִיו. י וְנִקְרָא שְׁמוֹ, בְּיִשְׂרָאֵל: בֵּית, חֲלוּץ הַנָּעַל.
יא כִּי-יִנָּצוּ אֲנָשִׁים יַחְדָּו, אִישׁ וְאָחִיו, וְקָרְבָה אֵשֶׁת הָאֶחָד, לְהַצִּיל אֶת-אִישָׁהּ מִיַּד מַכֵּהוּ; וְשָׁלְחָה יָדָהּ,
וְהֶחֱזִיקָה בִּמְבֻשָׁיו. יב וְקַצֹּתָה, אֶת-כַּפָּהּ: לֹא תָחוֹס, עֵינֶךָ.

[5] If brothers are living together and one of them dies without a son, his widow must not marry outside the family. Her husband's brother shall take her and marry her and fulfill the duty of a brother-in-law to her. [6] The first son she bears shall carry on the name of the dead brother so that his name will not be blotted out from Israel.

[7] However, if a man does not want to marry his brother's wife, she shall go to the
elders at the town gate and say, "My husband's brother refuses to carry on his
brother's name in Israel. He will not fulfill the duty of a brother-in-law to me".
[8] Then the elders of his town shall summon him and talk to him. If he persists in
saying, "I do not want to marry her", [9] his brother's widow shall go up to him
in the presence of the elders, take off one of his sandals, spit in his face and say,
"This is what is done to the man who will not build up his brother's family line".
[10] That man's line shall be known in Israel as "the family of the unsandaled one".
[11] If two men are fighting and the wife of one of them comes to rescue her husband
from his assailant, and she reaches out and seizes him by his private parts, [12] you
shall cut off her hand. Show her no pity.

Deut. 27:16, 20–23

דברים פרק כז

טז אָרוּר, מַקְלֶה אָבִיו וְאִמּוֹ; וְאָמַר כָּל-הָעָם, אָמֵן.
כ אָרוּר, שֹׁכֵב עִם-אֵשֶׁת אָבִיו--כִּי גִלָּה, כְּנַף אָבִיו; וְאָמַר כָּל-הָעָם, אָמֵן.
כא אָרוּר, שֹׁכֵב עִם-כָּל-בְּהֵמָה; וְאָמַר כָּל-הָעָם, אָמֵן.
כב אָרוּר, שֹׁכֵב עִם-אֲחֹתוֹ--בַּת-אָבִיו, אוֹ בַת-אִמּוֹ; וְאָמַר כָּל-הָעָם, אָמֵן.
כג אָרוּר, שֹׁכֵב עִם-חֹתַנְתּוֹ; וְאָמַר כָּל-הָעָם, אָמֵן.

[16] "Cursed is anyone who dishonors their father or mother". Then all the people shall say, "Amen!"
[20] "Cursed is anyone who lies with his father's wife, for he revealed his father's garment". Then all the people shall say, "Amen!"
[21] "Cursed is anyone who lies with any animal". Then all the people shall say, "Amen!"
[22] "Cursed is anyone who lies with his sister, the daughter of his father or the daughter of his mother". Then all the people shall say, "Amen!"
[23] "Cursed is anyone who lies with his mother-in-law". Then all the people shall say, "Amen!"

Notes

1 See most recently Roth 2013, 2014a, with previous literature.
2 Yaron 1998: 30.
3 Literally "native son/daughter".
4 Literally "walls of the house".
5 Text: a.
6 Text: a.
7 Literally "wife of a(n unmarried) man, not included in a household". Roth (1997: 17, 2014b: 148, 172 n. 6), however, translated: "deflowers the virgin wife / not-deflowered spouse", based on the relationship between the verb a/é–gi_4 and its object a nu-gi_4-a. Either translation conveys a similar legal notion.
8 The fact that Sumerian does not distinguish between grammatical genders, and at times between singular and plural forms, allows for a rather different translation of the apodosis, as suggested by Roth (1997: 18, 2014b: 148): "they shall kill that woman; that

male shall be released / given his freedom". Recently, Roth (2019) has offered a new interpretation of this statute, which differs from all previous ones (including her own). According to her new understanding of this statute, the active agent in the protasis was the man, and the woman was independent, probably non-virgin, who was executed in the apodosis for being promiscuous. Not ignoring these suggestions, I still view LUN §7 the same as it has always been understood, that is, that the offender is a betrothed woman who seduces another man to have sexual intercourse with her, a crime for which she is eventually executed.

9 Literally "slave-woman of a man, not included in a household". See p. 236 n. 7 concerning Roth's different translation of the verb and its object.

10 One manuscript adds lú in-tuku between nu-mu-SU and ì-tak$_4$-tak$_4$, and thus its apodosis reads "If a man marries a widow (and then) divorces (her)".

11 Partial restoration follows Wilcke 2014: 539.

12 Restoration follows Wilcke 2014: 541.

13 Restoration follows Wilcke 2014: 547.

14 Partial restoration follows Wilcke 2014: 548.

15 Variant: "ten".

16 Partial restoration follows Wilcke 2014: 552.

17 Restoration follows Wilcke 2014: 553.

18 Usually understood as "dowry".

19 This statute has two slightly different versions, which are both brought here.

20 Civil (2011: 281–283, 284) concluded that the term nu-gig designated midwives, and hence the present comment was meant to note that the hired wet-nurse was also to perform as a midwife.

21 Wilcke (2014: 603–605) claimed that LLI §20a–c do not belong to LLI at all but rather to another, hitherto unidentified, collection.

22 See previous note.

23 The two parts of this statute (separated by the break that contains the second [tukumbi]) may have actually formed two distinct statutes; see Roth 1997: 35 n. 6.

24 Literally "given to a spouse from the house of her live father".

25 Variant: "a second wife".

26 Variant: "he shall support the second wife and the first-ranking wife".

27 Literally "daughter of a man, not included in a household". For this phrase, and Roth's different interpretation of it, see p. 236 n. 7 previously.

28 The groom or bride.

29 The widower or his heir.

30 Here and throughout, I translate the Akkadian *aḫāzu(m)* – literally "to take/hold" – as "to marry", unless the context clearly points to a different meaning. Alternative translations, such as "take (in marriage)" and the like, while more philologically accurate, are needlessly cumbersome.

31 Concerning the wife that was promised to him.

32 Most commentators, beginning with Landsberger (1968: 76–82), translated *kirrum* here as "nuptial feast". This translation is contextual rather than literal, since *kirru(m)* means simply a vessel containing liquids, akin to a jar. That such vessel was used during a "nuptial feast" is certainly possible (see Landsberger's discussion) but not explicit in this specific text. I hence stick with the basic literal translation.

33 For this addition see Roth 1997: 69 n. 10.

34 This is how Roth (1997: 64) has interpreted the conjunction; see explanation of this and alternative possibilities in Roth 1997: 69 n. 13.

35 Thus Yaron 1998: 79, and similarly Roth (1997: 68): "*any possessions there may be*", based on the restoration *ma-l*[*a i-b*]*a-šu-ú*. For a different restoration (*ma-a*[*k-ku-r*]*i šu-ú*) and translation see Westbrook 1988: 72 n. 21.

36 For this translation of *ilkum aḫûm* see CAD I: 79, s.v. "*ilku* A 5a". Richardson (2000: 55) translated this term as "tenant with special duties".

37 Variant: "bind in fetters".

38 That is, if the husband declares that he shall not officially divorce his wife.
39 The previously mentioned wife.
40 The slave-woman.
41 Literally "rear, back" or "after", hence to be understood in the present context as "that which remains behind", that is, following the mother's death. In the law collections this term is always used in reference to inheritance.
42 Roth (1997: 112) emended to *irbû*, translating the phrase *mārīšu ša irbû* as "his eligible sons", but the original text can be understood as it is, without any emendation.
43 See n. 41.
44 That is, remarried.
45 See n. 41.
46 See n. 41.
47 See n. 41.
48 See n. 41.
49 See n. 41.
50 See n. 41.
51 See n. 41.
52 Literally, "a youth in his water (=amniotic fluid)".
53 Variant omits "woman".
54 Variant omits "of the sanctuary".
55 Variant omits "woman".
56 For these possible restorations see Paul 1990: 337–338.
57 Akkadian *erimtu* was usually understood as denoting "sheath" (CAD E: 302, s.v. "ermu 1b"), but the present context seems to favor an understanding such as "blade?" (see for example in CAD P: 267, s.v. "pāšu b").
58 Akkadian *nâku/niāku* should probably be understood as conveying the notion of illicit sexual intercourse; see Roth 1997: 192 n. 11 and Peled 2017b: 139 n. 52.
59 See p. 104 n. 35.
60 *abata iškun*; literally, "laid words".
61 See p. 104 n. 35.
62 Restoration follows Roth 1997: 161; see explanation in Roth 1997: 193 n. 18, with previous literature.
63 Restoration follows Roth 1997: 161; see explanation in Roth 1997: 193 n. 18, with previous literature.
64 It is unclear which one of the two men involved is being referred to here.
65 Literally, "jewelries".
66 Literally, "jewelries".
67 Literally, "he who married her".
68 The text has erroneously "the father-in-law".
69 Literally, "not any sending".
70 The phrase 6 *šanāte ina kabāse* should be understood as "once six years have passed", "in the passing of six years" and the like; the statute, however, clearly refers to the beginning of the sixth year.
71 The meaning of *qāli* is unknown; CAD (Q: 59, s.v. "*qāli*") suggests that it was possibly a foreign word.
72 Literally, "jewelries".
73 Restoration follows cdli (http://cdli.ucla.edu/P281779). Roth (1997: 193 n. 25) uncertain.
74 The restorations *ú-[šal-lam]* and *[za-a-ku]* follow cdli (http://cdli.ucla.edu/P281779). Roth (1997: 167) leaves these breaks unrestored.
75 Literally, "that a husband took her".
76 Literally, "that a husband did not take her".
77 Literally, "an idle (=work-free) day".

78 That is, any payments made will be returned.

79 The sentence *kî eqla ina āle šuātu illukuni* is complicated. Roth (1997: 171, 2014b: 167) has translated it as "in accordance with the going rate of a field in that city".

80 The phrase *dannat šarre* is not entirely clear, since *dannatu* has a rather wide semantic field, ranging between metaphors for hardship, strength or firmness to physical terms for buildings, especially fortified ones. The translation "royal holdings?" was suggested by Roth (1997: 171, 2014b: 167).

81 The sentence lacks an expected verbal element such as "wishes to give in marriage" or the like.

82 Text: "her father will ask".

83 Literally, "the silver owner".

84 Roth (1997: 193 n. 30) adds a possible alternative: "If the fetus dies as a result of the (attempted) abortion". This alternative reiterates the previous verdict of the statute, and hence seems less plausible.

85 The meaning of *ūtarrišuni* is unknown; any suggestion ever made to interpret it was contextual rather than etymological, and hence no suggestion is more compelling than any other.

86 Literally, "straits" or "narrow place".

87 Or: "withhold [it]".

88 Literally "unapproachable".

89 For the interpretation of *marrur*(*u*) see most recently Peled 2016: 215–216, with previous literature.

90 For this reading see Roth 1997: 209 n. 8.

91 See n. 89.

92 Following this word appears a sequence of illegible signs. Roth (1997: 148 n. 2) concluded that these "were incompletely erased by the scribe", and are hence to be ignored.

93 Text: *sùm-ma*.

94 This translation is not literal, but contextual; *kapāru* has a rather wide semantic field, see CAD K: 178–180, s.v. "kapāru" A and B.

95 Literally, "later".

96 Literally "give", here and throughout.

97 That is, the act was unintentional; the hand – rather than the head – has committed the sin.

98 See n. 97.

99 Variant: *ma-a-an*.

100 Variant adds "Hittite" to "merchant".

101 As noted by Hoffner (1997: 19 n. 12, 170–171) this sum is extremely high. Friedrich (1959: 17 n. 7) suggested that this was a scribal error, and should be emended to one and a half minas.

102 See previous note.

103 Variant: "six".

104 Later variants omit the passage distinguishing between the periods of ten or five months and establish the fine as 20 shekels of silver.

105 Later variants omit the passage about the tenth month and establish the fine as ten shekels of silver.

106 Text: *-az*.

107 Variant: "Luwiya".

108 Variant: "divorc[es]".

109 That is, be paid for the number of children she has borne? (suggestion by Hoffner 1997: 35 n. 71)

110 Usually understood as "dowry".

111 A different manuscript has "they (=her parents) shall make compensation".

112 A different manuscript has "but he (=the abductor) shall not compensate".
113 Literally "do/make".
114 *parā tarna-* is usually understood as denoting the meaning of "release, set free". Hoffner (1997: 185, following earlier suggestions by Hrozný and Goetze), however, convincingly offered the meaning of "change social status" in the present context.
115 A different manuscript adds "foreman".
116 A different manuscript has instead "elopes with a free woman and does not give a brideprice for her".
117 For this understanding of *parā tarna-* see n. 114.
118 A different manuscript has "to th[em]" instead.
119 That is, the deceased relatives will take his killer in servitude? See Hoffner 1997: 188.
120 For this understanding of *edi nai-* see CHD N: 362, s.v. "nai- 9c".
121 Literally, "head".
122 This statute has two different versions in two different manuscripts. My understanding of these versions differs from Hoffner's, and hence both my transliterations and translations – as presented here – differ from his; see Peled 2015: 290–291.
123 Text: LUGAL-*iš-aš*.
124 According to Miller (2013: 137), the items of compensation.
125 Text: DI.
126 Translation suggested by Miller (2013: 261); the meaning of *appan d/tamaš-* is unclear.
127 Translation suggested by Miller (2013: 261); see his explanation in p. 396 n. 570.
128 Literally, "dog".

Bibliography

Civil, Miguel. 2011. "The Law Collection of Ur-Namma". In *Cuneiform Royal Inscriptions and Related Texts in the Schøyen Collection*, edited by Andrew R. George. Bethesda, MD: CDL Press. Pp. 221–286.

Friedrich, Johannes. 1959. *Die hethitischen Gesetze: Transkription, Übersetzung, sprachliche Erläuterungen und vollständiges Wörterverzeichnis*. Leiden: Brill.

Hoffner, Harry A. Jr. 1997. *The Laws of the Hittites: A Critical Edition*. Leiden: Brill.

Kraus, Fritz R. 1958. *Ein Edikt des Königs Ammi-ṣaduqa von Babylon*. Leiden: Brill.

Kraus, Fritz R. 1984. *Königliche Verfügungen in altbabylonischer Zeit*. Leiden: Brill.

Landsberger, Benno. 1968. "Jungfräulichkeit: ein beitrag zum Thema 'beilager und eheschliessun'". In *Symbolae ivridicae et historicae Martino David dedicatae*, edited by J. A. Ankum, R. Feenstra and W. F. Leemans. Leiden: Brill. Pp. 41–105.

Miller, Jared L. 2013. *Royal Hittite Instructions and Related Administrative Texts*. Atlanta, GA: Society of Biblical Literature.

Paul, Shalom M. 1990. "Biblical Analogues to Middle Assyrian Law". In *Religion and Law: Biblical-Judaic and Islamic Perspectives*, edited by Edwin B. Firmage, Bernard G. Weiss and John W. Welch. Winona Lake, IN: Eisenbrauns. Pp. 333–350.

Peled, Ilan. 2015. "Crime and Sexual Offense in Hatti". *Near Eastern Archaeology* 78/4: 286–293.

Peled, Ilan. 2016. *Masculinities and Third Gender: The Origins and Nature of an Institutionalized Gender Otherness in the Ancient Near East*. Münster: Ugarit-Verlag.

Peled, Ilan. 2017. "Men in Question: Parallel Aspects of Ambiguous Masculinities in Mesopotamian and Biblical Sources". In *"And Inscribe the Name of Aaron": Studies in Bible, Epigraphy, Literacy and History Presented to Aaron Demsky* (*MAARAV, A*

Journal for the Study of the Northwest Semitic Languages and Literatures, vol. 21/1–2), edited by Yigal Levin and Ber Kotlerman. Rolling Hills Estates, CA: Western Academic Press. Pp. 127–148.

Pfeiffer, Robert H. and Speiser, Ephraim A. 1936. *One Hundred New Selected Nuzi Texts*. New Haven, CT: American Schools of Oriental Research.

Richardson, Mervyn E. J. 2000. *Hammurabi's Laws: Text, Translation and Glossary*. Sheffield: Sheffield Academic Press.

Roth, Martha T. 1997. *Law Collections from Mesopotamia and Asia Minor* (second edition). Atlanta, GA: Scholars Press.

Roth, Martha T. 2013. "On *mār awīlim* in the Old Babylonian Law Collections". *Journal of Near Eastern Studies* 72: 267–272.

Roth, Martha T. 2014a. "On Persons in the Old Babylonian Law Collections: The Case of *mār awīlim* in Bodily Injury Provisions". In *Extraction & Control: Studies in Honor of Matthew W. Stolper*, edited by Michael G. Kozuh, Wouter F. Henkelman, Charles E. Jones and Christopher Woods. Chicago, IL: The Oriental Institute of the University of Chicago. Pp. 219–227.

Roth, Martha T. 2014b. "Women and Law". In *Women in the Ancient Near East: A Sourcebook*, edited by Mark W. Chavalas. London; New York: Routledge. Pp. 144–174.

Roth, Martha T. 2019. "Seductress or Victim? Another Look at Laws of Ur-Namma §§6–8". In *De l'argile au numérique: Mélanges assyriologiques en l'honneur de Dominique Charpin*, edited by Grégory Chambon, Michaël Guichard and Anne-Isabelle Langlois. Leuven: Peeters. Pp. 879–892.

Westbrook, Raymond. 1988. *Old Babylonian Marriage Law*. Horn: Berger.

Wilcke, Claus. 2014. "Gesetze in sumerischer Sprache". In *Studies in Sumerian Language and Literature: Festschrift Joachim Krecher*, edited by Natalia V. Koslova, Ekaterina Vizirova and Gábor Zólyomi. Winona Lake, IN: Eisenbrauns. Pp. 455–616.

Yaron, Reuven. 1998. "A New Translation of Cuneiform Laws". *Journal of the American Oriental Society* 118/1: 29–35.

Indices

Note: Terms from Part II, whether from primary sources or from translations, only appear here in complete forms (including reconstructed ones). Unless otherwise stated, Akkadian substantives from Part II only appear here in nominative forms.

1. Ancient and Modern Terms

1.1. General Terms

abduct(ion) 33, 110, 154, 210
abominable/abomination 33, 37, 99, 101, 102, 104n29, 111, 135, 215–217, 219, 225, 226, 232, 234, 235
adoptee 50, 81, 123
adopter 50, 61, 81, 120, 123, 156
adoption 35, 46, 50, 55, 60, 61, 80, 81, 87n72, 113–117, 120, 123, 130, 173, 174
adultery/adulterous 1, 6, 7, 9, 33, 63, 67, 68, 72, 91, 94–98, 103n16, 103n17, 118, 123, 124–127, 130, 133, 135–137, 226

bestiality 91, 101–102, 104n38, 123, 126–127, 131, 133, 135, 137
betrothal/betrothed/betrothing 32, 60, 61, 63, 64, 65–67, 85n22, 85n29, 92–94, 97, 103n18, 110, 118, 122, 123–125, 133, 135, 144, 145, 212, 224, 234
Book of the Covenant 8, 15
bride 16, 32, 53, 65, 66, 79, 118, 153, 166, 219, 237n28
brideprice 16, 70, 85n5, 86n41, 93, 119, 124, 133, 212, 213, 224, 240n116
bridewealth 16, 142

castration 46, 50, 54–56, 57n2, 115
chastity 26, 29, 32, 33, 40n5, 109, 112, 122, 128, 137
commoner 154, 156, 158, 163, 170, 175
concubinage/concubine(s) 28, 29, 36, 42n63, 79, 84, 192
Covenant Code 8, 9, 15
creditor(s) 27, 49, 58n19, 68, 69, 109, 160, 165, 191, 15

daughter-in-law 98, 100, 125, 188, 194, 225, 226
debtor(s) 27, 69, 109, 113, 114, 116, 195
debt-slavery 40n9, 46, 49, 57n9, 57n10, 60, 69, 109, 113, 129, 134
defloration/deflower(ed)/deflowerer 65, 92–93, 95, 103n1, 103n18, 154, 155, 236n7
Deuteronomic Code 8, 9, 15
divine-River-Ordeal/River Ordeal 68, 69, 95, 96, 97, 145, 161, 184, 186, 187
divorcé(s)/divorcée(s) 30, 57, 62, 71, 72, 73, 74, 109, 116, 119, 132, 137, 138

eunuch(s) 14, 46, 47, 54–56, 57n2, 58n27, 113, 115, 116, 184, 185, 199, 200, 203, 204

father-in-law 65, 66, 69, 74, 75, 79, 146, 151, 153, 154, 167, 168, 188, 189, 194, 206, 238n68
fornication 68, 97, 103n16, 103n17, 118, 130, 186

groom 16, 66, 85n29, 93, 118, 137, 153, 206, 237n28

Holiness Code 8, 9, 15
homosexual(ity) 33, 55, 91, 101, 104n33, 104n36, 123, 126, 127, 135, 137

idolatry 34, 102, 110
incest(uous) 83, 91, 98–100, 104n27, 104n30, 123, 125, 127, 131, 133, 135, 137

1.2. Sumerian/Logographic Terms

1.3. Akkadian Terms

1.4. Hittite Terms

1.5. Biblical Terms

2. Names
2.1. Personal and Royal Names

2.2. Deity Names

2.3. Geographical Names

3. Texts Discussed

3.1. Cuneiform Texts

3.2. Biblical Texts

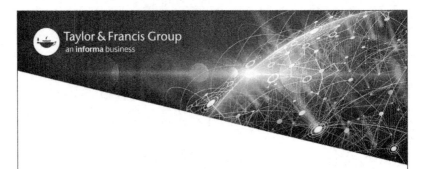

Printed in Great Britain
by Amazon

39168124R00145